# Real Time Systems

**Management and Design**

David Tebbs and
Garfield Collins

**McGRAW-HILL Book Company (UK) Limited**

**London** · New York · St Louis · San Francisco · Auckland · Bogotá · Düsseldorf
Johannesburg · Madrid · Mexico · Montreal · New Delhi · Panama · Paris · Sâo Paulo
Singapore · Sydney · Tokyo · Toronto

Published by
## McGRAW-HILL Book Company (UK) Limited
MAIDENHEAD · BERKSHIRE · ENGLAND

---

**Library of Congress Cataloging in Publication Data**

Tebbs, David.
   Real time systems.

   Includes index.
   1. Real-time data processing. 2. Real-time data processing—Management. I. Collins, Garfield,
joint author. II. Title.
HF 5548.3.T4     658'.05'4     77–23319
ISBN 0–07–084482–8

12345 PPL 807987

Text set in 11/12 pt Photon Imprint, printed by photolithography, and bound in Great Britain at The
Pitman Press, Bath

# Foreword

Some justification is needed for another book on real time systems, because there are already quite a number on the market. However, while some of these delve into the workings of the software or concentrate on communications aspects, others are typically either academic treatises or immerse the reader in abstruse technicalities within the first few pages.

The strength of this book is that it avoids these specialisms and pitfalls. It is above all a balanced book, giving an overview of virtually the whole real time field, and as such it fills an important gap in the existing literature. There is a laudable absence of jargon and plentiful evidence of practical experience. The book assumes nothing other than a general knowledge of conventional batch processing and should therefore be equally useful to the manager and to the computer professional who wishes to widen his experience in the real time area.

The book should also do much to correct what is still an insufficient realization of the scale of problem encountered in implementing real time systems as opposed to ordinary batch processing. Indeed, it could well become a standard basic primer for all those concerned with the management and design of real time systems.

P M R Hermon
Group Management Services Director
British Airways

21 June 1976

# Acknowledgements

The authors wish to express their appreciation to their colleagues for their support and assistance in the preparation of this book. We would also like to thank BIS Applied Systems Limited for permission to draw on material from its *Real Time Systems Design, Distributed Intelligence and Terminal Networks* courses and other related courses, the Company's project experience, and Technical Design Control procedures. Further thanks are due to Howard Beale, David Holtom and Geoff Penney for their contributions to material and to our other colleagues who helped edit chapters. Last but not least to Derek Potts for his contribution to the cross references.

# Contents

**Part 1**    **Introduction and management**                              **1**

1    Real Time Systems                                                  3
2    Systems Requirements                                               7
3    Justification of the Project                                      22
4    Project Structure, Skills and Staffing                            32
5    Monitoring Development                                            48

**Part 2**    **Stages of development**                                   **63**

6    Systems Analysis in Real Time                                     65
7    Computer Systems Design                                           79
8    Design to Live Running                                            90
9    Real Time and the User                                           114

**Part 3**    **Design technique**                                       **127**

10    Terminal Network Configuration                                  129
11    File Design                                                      172
12    Fail-Soft                                                        194
13    Security and Integrity                                           220
14    Program Organization                                             230
15    Timing                                                           253

**Part 4**    **Further references**                                     **281**

16    Queueing Theory and Practice                                    283
17    Data Transmission                                                304
18    Reliability Calculation                                          322
19    File Techniques                                                  331
20    Defining Real Time                                               344

**Index**                                                            **351**

# Part 1

## Introduction and management

# 1. Real Time Systems

We live in a world of change. In this world many observers will consider the advent of computers and their subsequent rapidly increasing use in business, government, aerospace and science to be one of the major examples of such change. Not only is the pace of change fast but it is also accelerating. Nowhere is this acceleration more apparent than in computing.

Data processing professionals are very sensitive to the extraordinary rate of development within the technology. From batch to real time to data bases to distributed intelligence to . . . ? Regrettably most readers will also be familiar with many intermediate 'steps of development' associated with manufacturers' hardware and software enhancements.

Add to this environment of change the dramatic growth in the number of analysts, designers, programmers and managers working with computers, and it is perhaps not surprising that the average DP professional faces a heavy drain on his time in keeping up to date technically and improving his methods as he and the industry learn from experience.

The development of real time (RT) systems is one area which, although relatively new, has passed through the pioneering stage to become well established. 'Established' in this context not only means that there is a reasonable supply of suitable hardware and software, but also that relevant techniques and procedures have been developed and proven.

These techniques and procedures can help to compensate for the problems that often arise from an ever increasing number of people being called upon to develop real time systems, and the very rapid pace of development in the nature of hardware and software. Unfortunately, the technical complexities of specific hardware and software tend to obscure the aspects which are common to most real time systems, and so it is difficult for staff concentrating on projects to know how to learn from the lessons of, and apply the methodology developed, elsewhere.

This book addresses the problem by setting down a broad range of ideas and techniques generally applicable in the areas of management and development of real time systems. The various aspects of development and management are discussed in enough depth to enable a meaningful approach to be presented, which can easily be adapted and applied to the specific environment.

This chapter develops the above theme a little further and provides a summary of the contents of the book and how to use it.

## 1.1 The Risks of Real Time

The study of techniques and methods pertinent to real time projects is clearly necessary for data processing staff about to undertake their first real time project. What of managers, analysts, designers and programmers with some prior experience or perhaps a less central or detailed role? Before devoting time and effort to such studies they may rightly ask:

- is there a need to study the topic beyond my earlier experience?
- does my role call for an understanding of real time techniques and procedures?

The history of real time projects suggests that the right answer to both of these questions is 'Yes', in the majority of cases.

Let us consider some of the reasons. First, in any well-loaded real time system the risk of late delivery or poor performance can be very much greater than in a batch project. Take two examples:

(1) One DP department seeking to upgrade their own skills for a major project, recruited staff with proven real time experience. Later, early system tests indicated potential performance problems and so consultants were called in to review the designs while logic testing proceeded.

Comparison between final detail designs and the original design projections identified a variance in device utilization of 2000 per cent. An accumulated error had built up from a series of detail variances and had not been detected by the project team before testing! Why did this occur? Probably the main cause was a weakness in real time development controls and procedures rather than in design. Once detected at that late stage the solution was a mixture of redesign, programming and hardware upgrade.

(2) In another case a system was developed to meet a three-second average response time criterion. The designs met this criterion. However on projected loadings that objective was only just met and at some risk. A 10 per cent adverse variance during implementation could create a 6-second average response time with frequent longer delays. Had the design been fully analysed at the outset a safer path could have been taken at minimal extra cost, by modifying the route that different transactions took through the system and using a different file design.

The second main reason why staff with only batch experience need to take care is that a number of the well-established, good practices for real time systems are completely different from what would be expected by applying common sense alone to the lessons of batch experience. There are new lessons on project organization, control and design techniques to be learned.

For both these reasons managers, analysts and designers (and designers titled 'programmers') will benefit from a thorough education in real time

4

covering both design techniques and good practice. While the case is clearest for designers, the need equally applies to analysts and project managers. The latter may not be involved in the details of the technology but they will take decisions, set plans, standards and controls, and established systems requirements, all of which can be best achieved from a basis of a good understanding of real time systems. Later chapters in this book examine this interdependence more fully.

Ideally real time education is gained from the right experience on earlier projects, but as in the first case history above, staff with prior real time experience often themselves need to study the topic further. There are several common reasons why earlier experience may have its limitations. An individual may have been limited by his role in the team, the restricted nature of the project, a lack of good practices set by the project manager, special emphasis enforced by earlier software, or training oriented to 'using the software'.

## 1.2  What is Real Time?

Nearly every author, lecturer and speaker who has discussed the subject has found it necessary to provide his own definition of real time, as there is no universal definition in common use. A pedantic definition is not attempted in this book since such precision has limited value when others choose a range of different interpretations.

However, we would describe this book as being relevant to those who have to develop (or evaluate the development of) a computer system, where data are being input and/or retrieved through terminals other than the computer room operators' console, whether main files are being updated or not.

Nevertheless, we require a more precise definition of real time. Such a definition can be achieved in the most practical way by identifying the range of types of terminal-based systems and determining which are covered by the book. Chapter 20 provides an analysis of the range of situations that are generally classified as real time and their relevance to the lessons of this book. In general terms, real time systems can be divided into two groups, namely, simple and complex. Simple systems, such as data capture, involve *no* real time file updating. Complex systems, such as order processing with running stock adjustment, update files in real time. Complex systems cover a wide spectrum and, as the name implies, are very much more difficult than simple systems. Updating files in real time has a big impact on the complexity of a system, primarily in the areas of recovery, security, and efficient use of resources, and hence on program organization.

Readers not in the mainstream of industrial, commercial, or governmental real time system development are advised to read chapter 20 next. Most will then find that the content of the book is relevant anyway, with some translation to their own special environments.

## 1.3  The Book and its Structure

This book has been written for all data processing staff who feel they need to understand more about on-line and real time systems—terminal-based systems. It presents both the design techniques and the steps that analysts, designers and managers can follow, and so is intended as a practical guide.

The book has been organized for reading cover-to-cover, with topics following a logical development of the subject. The chapters are grouped in four sets:

*Introduction and Management View*
Chapters 1–5.

*Main Stages of Project Development*
Chapters 6–9.

*Design Techniques*
Chapters 10–15.

*Details and Technical References*
Chapters 16–20.

It is recommended that anyone working on a real time project should read all the chapters initially. Further study or re-analysis of certain topics then depends on his individual role in the project and his prior experience. Data processing staff with real time experience can use several of the chapters for reference purposes, and the rest of the book can help them to formalize their own experience.

# 2. Systems Requirements

Before examining the design of real time systems, it is valuable first to consider those system requirements and features that make real time systems so different from batch processing systems. In examining a real time system externally, one can identify both the source of a number of the problems that have to be faced by the designer, as well as areas of choice open to the analyst when weighing business needs against potential technical problems and costs.

For the purpose of this chapter we are primarily considering the real time system in comparison with batch processing. It is assumed that the reader is reasonably familiar with batch systems, and for the moment we are considering the real time system in general terms as illustrated by Fig. 2.1, i.e., terminals connected via a network and communications controller to a central computer, which in turn is considered as a processing unit and a set of files.

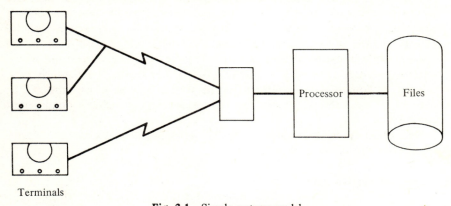

Terminals

**Fig. 2.1** Simple systems model

Let us now consider this system in operation, as viewed externally, and examine the more important differences from batch systems.

## 2.1 Message Arrival

In our simple model, messages will first be input to the system via the terminal.

They may originate from paper, conversation or observation. The first difference we detect is that, unlike the batch equivalent, there is no by-product computer-readable copy of transactions and possibly not even a paper copy. In batch mode some data preparation activity would have converted the input to cards, ocr, micr, tapes, or disks, etc., which will normally remain available after processing. The real time data arrive in the computer as digital signals ready for processing. If long-term storage of that data is required (say for analysis or recovery purposes) then extra steps need to be taken in the computer or externally or both to record the transaction.

As such a record of the transaction is not a by-product of normal processing, one must explicitly select what, how and when to record. While the selection of a method may be simple, choosing the best approach for a given situation can involve the evaluation of a wide range of approaches as are considered in chapter 12.

## 2.2  Work Load

It is important to determine the arrival pattern of transactions, both at the terminal and at the computer, with more detail than is typically the case in batch systems.

The manner in which the messages are originated may be little different in the business world, whether we have a batch or real time system. However, the effect on the computer in a real time system can be substantially different. In practice, there are three key patterns of variation: seasonal, hourly through the day, and random (second to second).

Apart from the fluctuations in the rate of message arrival, it is also necessary to consider the work content of the message; a simple enquiry may need one file access to one record which is then displayed; a complex order may require twenty records to be read and updated. The variation of work load on the system is a combination of message arrival rate (messages per hour) and arrival pattern (message type mix). To complicate matters further for the designers, 'work load' applies to each element of the system such as disks, tapes, CPU, network. Thus, different messages will place varying stresses on different elements.

The real time designer must consider the problem in detail and to summaries, the mix to be handled is:

Transaction arrival rate

> – by message type
> – by time

Transaction type work load (sometimes called transaction profile)

> – by message type
> – by element of the computer system
>   (e.g., disk, processor)

## 2.2.1 VARIATIONS IN LOAD

It is worth considering load variation further at the three levels mentioned above, i.e., seasonal, hourly within the day, and random.

### Seasonal Loading

The problem is not new, but a real time system by definition should process a message in a brief time after its arrival. Thus there is often a need to design the system to handle peak seasonal loading, with the result that there is excess capacity in the trough period. Batch systems can cope with such peaks and troughs by careful scheduling, delaying work that is not so critical, working extra shifts, or processing some work externally. With, say, a five-second response, this is not possible. There are ways of avoiding the full impact of this seasonal effect by scheduling other background work, but nevertheless a real time system does risk a severe cost penalty in peak season handling.

### The Daily Pattern

Weekly or daily batch systems have a limited need to consider the users' work-load pattern during the day and perhaps are concerned more with cut-off times. Real time systems must consider this level of detail. As well as providing yet another peak period problem (i.e., peak within the day) the pattern within the day becomes an extra area of statistics to be gathered by the analyst. Figure 2.2

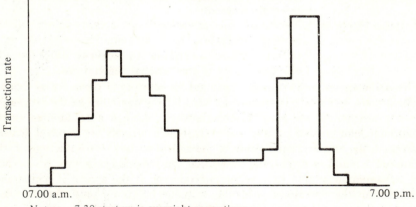

07.00 a.m.                                                      7.00 p.m.

*Notes*: — 7.30 start-up is overnight corrections
Morning and afternoon peaks are phone orders
Morning plateau is existing team working steadily on daily post.

**Fig. 2.2**   Daily work pattern

illustrates a common pattern for an order-processing system open from 8.00 a.m. to 6.00 p.m. Clearly any calculation based on an hourly message rate being one-tenth of the daily total of orders would have been in severe error at peak periods. In this case, analysis showed that while the typical order included 10 items during the mid-morning load, the afternoon phone orders were typically after-thoughts with one or two items per order. The result was that the peak

9

loading was in the morning and not the afternoon, which was only the period of peak arrival rate.

*Random Arrival*

Even within the peak period within the day there is a microscopic fluctuation of arrival rate which is 'random' in its nature (random may be mathematically defined, as in chapter 16, but here the word is used in its everyday sense, i.e., far from constant). The next section deals with how this random demand arises.

2.2.2 RANDOM DEMAND

Before examining in more detail the effect of random arrival, consider how and where arrivals occur, i.e., at the terminal, at the central computer or at individual hardware elements; disk, tape, CPU, etc.

*At the Terminal*—Three basic uses of the terminal exists, each with their own implications on arrival.

Pseudo Batch — The operator works through the pile of paper work in her in-tray, interacting with the computer to process each item, e.g., data capture via terminals from orders delivered by daily post.

External Demand — The operator reacts to external requests before initiating transaction, e.g., telephone orders or an airline seat reservation system.

Variable Operator — Terminals are considered as access points serving several operators, e.g., an enquiry terminal in a police station available to several officers. The effect is similar to the external demand case.

The implications on arrivals and demand for services of these are as follows. The pseudo batch case is straight forward for the operator like the processing of any in-tray. As will be seen later, however, there is a randomness in the computer load created by this use even though arrivals are batched at each terminal. By contrast, close study of the arrival pattern of transactions in the external demand case generally shows that the demand is not steady, i.e., there is a fluctuation around the average arrival rate. If the arrival is temporarily faster than the operator can handle, a queue builds up until she can cope. Equally there is a definite chance of periods of low demand when the operator will not be completely busy.

Generally the arrival pattern is referred to as random (see chapter 16;) the designers problem can now be illustrated by Fig. 2.3, where the peak hour is considered.

- Curve (1) represents the smoothed arrival rate of messages (orders) over the hour as perhaps recorded by an analyst.
- Curve (2) represents the random fluctuation that actually occurred if each arrival was recorded precisely. Often the fluctuations can be of a magnitude as large as the mean. (This must be expressed more precisely before mathematical treatment.)

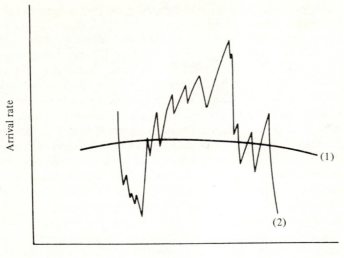

(1) Average rate
(2) Detail arrival

**Fig. 2.3**  Check for Loading

Now, while we can recognize the existence of the random effect, the analyst hardly wants to quantify the system with sufficient statistics at this level, and yet later the designer has to answer the question 'How powerful a system?' Figure 2.4 identifies three possible capacity levels for the load shown in Fig. 2.3. If the designer provides a system with capacity (A), then clearly he may be over-spending (too much capacity). On the other hand, (B) dips below the

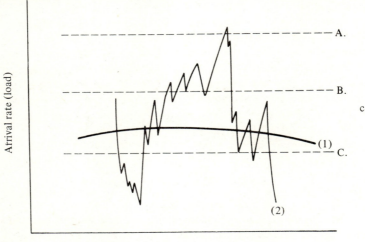

**Fig. 2.4**  Peak load and capacity

11

average and is in danger of being under capacity, so the answer lies somewhere in between, near (C), but where?

Fortunately, this type of random load has been well analysed for many years before the advent of real time systems. Much of the pioneering work arises from similar problems in the design of telephone exchanges. The resultant queueing theory can be used by the designer to carry out his first calculations and determine the probable effect of his design, yet he needs to know only the smoothed load. Queueing theory and its applications is explained further in chapter 15 on Timing and chapter 16 on Queueing Theory and Practice.

Queueing theory also provides a basis for handling different patterns of fluctuation, and variations in the computer service time, and projecting the delays in response for different loadings. In practice, the delay caused by queueing fluctuates (cf. waiting for traffic lights), and fortunately queueing theory helps to predict the range of fluctuation as well as average values.

Figure 2.5 illustrates a typical curve plotting queueing delays against systems loading. Such a curve may be generated through the use of queueing theory or practical tests or observation. The common characteristic is the increasing rate of increase of queueing time as the system under study approaches full load.

The importance of the behaviour of queues in systems timing can be illustrated by considering a system where the load increases from 70 per cent to 91 per cent of capacity (30 per cent increase). As Fig. 2.5 illustrates, the queueing delay may increase by + 200 per cent for this modest increase in load.

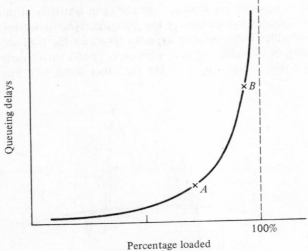

Fig. 2.5   Queueing with random arrival

## At the Processor

One can readily accept that a random arrival pattern at the terminals also results in a random arrival pattern at the computer. But it is important to consider the situation at the computer centre with pseudo batch arrival at terminals.

In a pseudo batch environment, each operator can work at a relatively steady rate (i.e., serving a full queue). However, consider the messages arriving at the computer. Each operator, in a simple order processing case, might work at a steady average rate of two minutes per order. In practice, performance varies between operators and for each operator performance varies during the day, e.g., the intervals in minutes for one operator may follow the pattern:

2·2, 2·1, 2·0, 2·4, 2·0, 2·3, 1·8.

This is a fluctuation of rate with a small deviation (range of values) compared with the average. With several operators the effect at the computer end is a random arrival with a much greater spread.

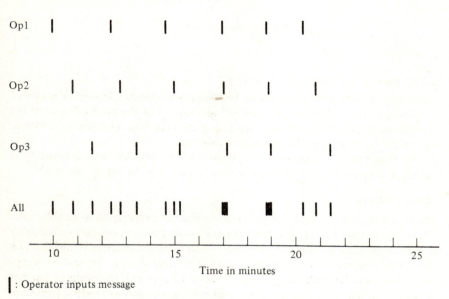

: Operator inputs message

**Fig. 2.6** Three unsynchronized operations

One can see the effect by the simple example in Fig. 2.6 of three operators. The individual variations are slight, but the rate at the computer varies from three messages in three minutes to three messages in two seconds. Such random fluctuations are the norm at the computer, unless arrival rates are affected by delays or bottlenecks in the network.

*Other System Elements*

Each element in the real time system has its own arrival rate of demand for work. The pattern is highly interdependent between each of the elements in the system and therefore is considered in more detail in chapter 15. However the general effect is to cause a random pattern of demand for each unit or set of units at the computer centre.

**13**

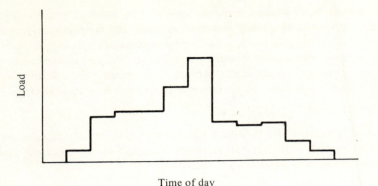

Time of day

**Fig. 2.7** The peak hour

### 2.2.3 HANDLING LOADING PROBLEMS

Loading problems arise from peaks, be they instantaneous, hourly or seasonal. However, lines of solutions are similar and several of the options open to the designer/analyst can be seen by considering the peak hour problem in isolation. Figure 2.7 (a) schematically represents this case.

The objective is to operate the system with a computer whose capacity is less than that required at the peak demand, i.e., 'how to lop off the peak'.

### *Planned Overload*

The first solution is simply 'to provide insufficient capacity to meet the peak.' This leads to queues and delays when peak loading occurs, but *controlled* delay at periods of peak loading may be better than wasted capacity. While this is a reasonable designer/analyst solution, it must be treated with care and be acceptable to the user. In practice, this approach is dangerous if the designer has not planned in detail what will occur on overload. Overloaded software systems are prone to break down (perhaps not enough queue space) or increase rather than just cause delays. Any solution based on deliberately allowing overloading to occur at peak loads needs very careful discussion between users, analysts and designers.

### *Removing the Peak*

Peaks arise both from business activity and from the amount of real time work included in the specification; both are worth challenging. In one case, peak monthly business loads were found to reflect the then existing batch systems. Billing one-quarter of the clients each week succeeded in partially smoothing the load. In other cases one should ask: is all the work scheduled in the peak period necessary in real time all the time?

There are two approaches to help answering that question: 'delay selected transactions' and 'delay elements of transactions'. These are illustrated in the

**14**

example below.

In this example, the peak work load is made up of a range of transaction types, e.g.,

- order entry,
- order cancellation,
- order amendment,
- stock update,
- stock correction,
- customer update,
- stock enquiry,

each with a range of work, e.g., for order entry,

- validate entry,
- check customer records,
- check stock records,
- process order,
- update order file,
- update stock file,
- acknowledge order,
- error procedure.

In the first approach, following the sequence of 'most active transaction first', the designer searches for the transactions that can be delayed until after the peak period. In the list above, a stock enquiry, which in this system is not part of the processing cycle, is a good potential for delay during peaks if the resultant capacity *is worth saving.*

Similarly, in the second approach, for each transaction the designer can ask 'Does all this processing need to be carried out straight away?' In the example, the stock update transaction could include ten 'record updates' in real time per order. (Ten items on average on each order in our simple model.) Recording them as one record for later processing could provide a substantial saving if the system could afford to accept orders against stock files which are not quite up to date. This could be valid, if in the existing manual system, order clerks do not even check stock! Again the transactions should be inspected in the sequence of busiest first.

Both of the above are but systematic approaches to searching for work to be delayed by 'selecting out' of the peak period. The alternative is to spend more money, be it on design or hardware, to do all the work in the peak. Selected delays may be more appropriate than ad hoc delays when overload occurs.

*How to Delay*

Having identified peak period elements that can stand delay, the question arises as to how the delayed processing will be handled. The range of choice covers such techniques as relegation to batch processing, handling at a separate level (i.e., priority on message type), and establishing a priority system that applies only when the queue builds up.

Priority systems are fine in principle, but suffer three major disadvantages in computer software terms, and therefore need to be considered in detail and agreed by designers as well as analysts.

- the searching of queues on a priority basis can be very expensive on computer time;
- messages can be held up at a bottle neck in the system that arises before the messages reach the priority handling mechanism (just observe the ambulance stuck at the back of a traffic jam, analogue of the high priority message delayed in a software chronological sequence queue);
- many computer operating systems allow background programs to interfere with higher priority foreground systems. This problem can apply, especially in claims on I/O activity, when the background systems are totally independent.

The division of responsibility between analyst and designer is outlined further in chapters 4, 6, and 7.

### 2.2.4  THE ANALYST AND WORK LOAD

This chapter has illustrated the importance of gathering quantitive data about the system during analysis. These data are particularly useful in deciding between alternative system designs, and in deciding if a system can be fitted into a given configuration. The degree of detail necessary depends on whether the required capacity for the system is near to exceeding some constraint, such as maximum main storage size or cost targets.

Analysis to the right level is difficult and frequently requires further work during design to obtain some important volumes. The better the analyst understands the techniques of real time design, the more likely he is to achieve the appropriate level of detail first time round as he can carry out quick design calculations to test the sensitivity of the data.

## 2.3  Units of Work

It has already been implied that the unit of work in a real time system is a transaction. Two immediate differences from batch arise from this factor.

The vast majority of batch systems have been designed both explicitly and by habit to optimize performance by taking account of the fact that all the transactions are available for that run. The common processing sequence of VET–SORT–UPDATE–SORT–PRINT reflects this form of optimization. Clearly, the designer of the real time system can only handle messages one at a time and loses some opportunity to optimize, thus facing greater design pressures in order to meet performance targets.

A transaction has been referred to as a set of data being transmitted from the terminal (and probably generating an associated response from the computer). In many applications, a set of such transactions is necessary to achieve one task for the operator, i.e., several interrogations may lead the operator to select the

16

required record for updating, or several line items may be independently transmitted to build up an order. Equally, one order could be transmitted as an entity or with certain terminal types, even a small batch of orders.

In any given situation, analysts and designers must be careful in their terminology, as confusion can lead to a misleading design. The recommended terminology is as follows.

Message — a set of data transmitted from terminal to computer or vice versa. At system level this includes the associated transmission control characters in each direction;

Message pair — a set of data being transmitted to the computer with its associated response;

Transaction — a set of logical and necessarily interrelated message pairs. In simple systems one message pair provides one transaction.

The transaction is the unit of user activity, and is often associated with one piece of paper, for example:

Order Entry Transaction: Input Messages

Message 1 — identify as an 'order entry' and request a display by customer code;

Message 2 — enter the customer variable data and the order identifier, implying a request for the order format;

Message 3 — Enter order details;

Message 4 — correct errors if notified.

Each input message has an associated computer response (a message pair). Thus the basic conversation involves 3 message pairs + 1 pair for each error.

Transactions can usually be identified by analysts. The precise messages are both user and designer dependent and therefore cannot be finally defined until design is near complete, although the pattern can be outlined during analysis.

## 2.4 Response

Many commentators have defined a real time system as one that reacts sufficiently quickly to affect the business activities of the 'operator'. Such response time can be measured in hours. In this book, as we discuss in chapter 20, we are handling a more limited definition where the computer response is probably measured in seconds for at least part of the system. In some circumstances the response time specified is dominated by the operational needs of the operator, e.g., airline reservation clerks with their customers at the counter. In other circumstances, the psychological needs of the operator, set the requirement. These are explained further in chapter 10.

Already we have implied that an input message is linked to its response. There are many valid exceptions but it is a good rule to start thinking of any real time system on the basis of 'input and response'. Figure 2.8 illustrates the simplest system.

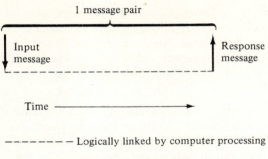

Fig. 2.8   A message pair

Response times fluctuate, but first let us consider the response in terms of average response time. Sooner or later every analyst needs to establish, for all transactions in the system, what response time is required, to what extent the response is complete, and how up to date the reference data need to be. Each of these aspects are considered below.

2.4.1   RESPONSE TIME

Every real time system needs a response time target to be set before design is undertaken (otherwise why not do it in batch monthly?).

Here the responsible analyst has to work carefully. Targets are important and a tight target may lead to unnecessary cost of design and implementation, while too slow a response may cause user problems. Equally, too vague a target may lead to unnecessary discussion during design.

If the loading is critical, the response time may need careful review between user and designer during development. Therefore it should not be *unnecessarily* frozen in the systems specification.

2.4.2   COMPLETE RESPONSE

In considering overloads, we identified the potential value of deliberately delaying the processing of complex transactions (i.e., out of 'immediate real time'). In these circumstances, rather than providing a long response, it is often useful to provide an intermediate but immediate response (see Fig. 2.9). In Fig. 2.9, the simple pair of Fig. 2.8 has been replaced by a more complex design and now consists of:

(1) The operator keys in the enquiry.
(2) Real time program—identifies it as a delayed class with immediate
　　　　　　　　　　　　　response;
　　　　　　　　　　—validates the enquiry;
　　　　　　　　　　—responds to the user with an enquiry reference
　　　　　　　　　　　number;
　　　　　　　　　　—initiates the background process to complete the
　　　　　　　　　　　enquiry

18

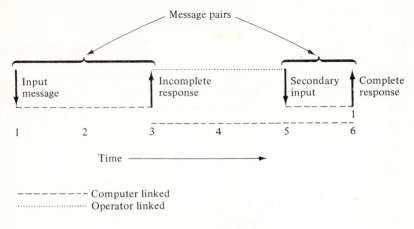

Fig. 2.9 Delayed response

(3) User satisfied by expected immediate but incomplete response. Notes the enquiry reference.
(4) Real time background program processes enquiry at low priority and records results in enquiry file under enquiry reference number.
(5) User enquiries again at a later time with enquiry reference number.
(6) Computer provides complete response from easy access enquiry file.

This is but one example of handling a delayed full response.

## 2.5 How up to Date?

While speed of response is important, the second prime question is how up to date the reference data need to be? A range of possible answers to the questions might include such targets as, month end position, overnight position, less than one hour out of date. Time conscious systems may demand data correct to the last minute or usually correct to the last transaction, but on heavy load can run up to one hour out of date, or correct to the last few minutes.

For the user, few systems really need reference files to be up to date to the last transaction, though logic may make this an easy approach to take inside the computer. The tighter the specification, the more real time need be the up-dating process, and usually the more costly the design. For this reason, experienced real time designers often choose to update files overnight in batch—it simplifies many technical aspects and can meet systems objectives.

Thus, the more flexibility the system specification can provide in the choice between real time and batch updating, the greater the chance of a successful and economic solution. When the designer has this flexibility, he can both handle recovery procedures more economically and delay time consuming updating from peak real time loads. The potential benefit is the use of less equipment or providing a better service at such periods of peak loading.

## 2.6 Overloads

Most batch processing installations have suffered the problem of overloads. Yet in most cases their advent has been forecast at least days, if not weeks, ahead and the problem has been solved by some combination of hard work, overtime, extra shifts, passing work out to bureau or 'friends down the road'.

Almost axiomatically, real time systems cannot meet overloads by overtime or going to another site. A limited scope may exist for re-scheduling some low priority batch work away from the real time configuration.

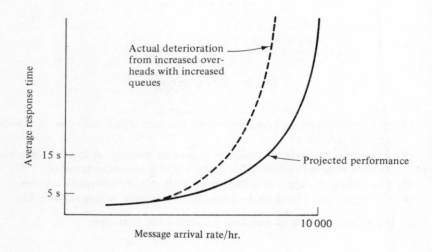

Fig. 2.10   Real time response

Figure 2.10 illustrates the change in response time to an input message with increasing work load for a typical real time system. In this case, the theoretical capacity is about 10 000 message pairs per hour. Queueing theory predicts the rapidly worsening performance as the load increases. However, the practical situation can be even worse. Long queues tend to find faults in software and add to the work load per message (software overheads rise with the size of the message queue). Thus real time overloads can arrive faster than expected.

The first lesson to be learned for system development is that much greater stress must be placed on design calculation and projection of performance, far beyond that practised in most batch situations. Second, it is important to test the system under various load conditions as well as logical variations. Third, many detailed internal usage statistics are important for any department with an operational real time system with a growing work load. Pending overloads can be detected from the growth of internal queues before becoming measurable at the terminal.

**20**

## 2.7 Customer Contact

Once terminals are made available to users, the performance of the DP function is exposed every minute of the production day. The user will be aware of most causes of failure, including such examples as hardware failures, operation error, software bugs, inaccurate data on files, overloads and line transmission errors.

Again, there is nothing substantially new here, but even careful control and supervision in operations and data control with blood, sweat and tears on re-runs will not mask the failures from the user as it often has in batch systems.

The lesson, greater stress on reliability of hardware, software, and the DP department's own programming and system testing.

## 2.8 Summary of Requirements

This chapter has examined a number of special system requirements of real time as opposed to batch. We have seen where some of the stresses arise and some lines of solution. Later chapters examine design techniques to achieve solutions. However, each area makes certain demands on the analyst. First, he must carry out numeric analysis to greater detail than he ever used in batch systems. Second, he must understand design implications, and finally be prepared for later trade-offs on design complexity (cost) against service provided.

Real time expertise needs to be injected in any real time project at both feasibility and analysis phases of development as well as in later stages. Thus, when considering project teams, chapter 4 covers the role of the real time (computer) designer in the analysis stage. However, for the analyst (who is not a designer) to be effective in his role in a real time project, he needs to obtain a reasonable understanding of the design process and its implications, even if he has a colleague who takes the design responsibility.

# 3. Justification of the Project

The question of how to justify computer projects has been much debated, with frequent arguments for and against cases basing justification on both 'direct benefits' and 'opportunity costs and information'. Experience in all forms of data processing has continually shown that careful analysis and quantification of both costs and benefits is the only way to ensure successful data processing development projects.

With real time and data base systems, the basic argument still applies. However, the greater costs and risks associated with real time, compared with batch, mean that *careful* justification is all the more important. This chapter therefore concentrates on the essential differences that apply when justifying a real time system solution as opposed to a batch solution. In some cases, 'batch' may not be practical, so the question is then: 'Is real time justified, as opposed to perhaps a manual approach?'

In chapter 2 we identified a number of options open to the analyst and their potential effect on system designs, together with the considerable range of choice that can arise. The choice involves a sometimes complex balance between service provided, design complexity, cost and risk. System justification can therefore be as much concerned with 'Which level of service for each element is justified?' as much as with the overall approach. The final cost and justification is determined by a form of an integration of each element of the system. Certain features may appear independent to the user but it is their combined effect that determines the cost of the system.

A particular example of a different level of service applying to different transaction types might be as follows. The main operational transactions may need a response of three seconds overall, from up-to-date files. Equally, the response for certain transactions, e.g., monthly file searches, may best be handled by overnight batch processing. Unless the justification for speed of response is carefully thought out for each of the transactions falling in between the two extremes, there is a danger that the system proposal is unnecessarily costly to implement or, in the opposite direction, results in a system perhaps too slow in certain aspects.

This chapter therefore concentrates on persuading the reader to ask continually: 'Is this application worth doing in real time?' 'How much of the application is worth doing in real time?' 'How tight a time specification is justified in each case?' These are important questions to ask in feasibility studies, but they must also be re-asked as development proceeds.

The general question to be answered is 'Why a real time system rather than a batch system?' In answering this question there can be a variety of replies. But it is important to establish for each project, and for each set of transactions in that project, the fundamental reason 'Why should this service be provided in real time?'

If the basic justifications are not clearly identified, then what too often occurs is that secondary criteria appear and take on too great an importance. For example, consider a simple real time system handling pseudo batch data capture in which speed of response is not an important issue:

- During the development process the analysts decided to set a target response time as a design criterion for later stages. A target of four seconds was considered reasonable and recorded.
- At a later stage in the project the designer found that his initial simple designs provided a response time outside the target; in fact five or six seconds. He then went to some lengths and incurred extra development and potential running costs to stay within the target level of service.
- Fortunately the problem was detected before the designs progressed too far. As the criterion of speed, i.e., four seconds, was not fundamental, the specification was reviewed and adopted without prejudice to the objectives.

Project teams working on large real time systems are particularly faced with this problem where several staff are involved in the development process and the criteria are set by one member/sub team and passed as targets to the next. Isolating the basic reason for real time often helps to avoid this pitfall.

However, looking at the subject more generally, some four primitive reasons can be identified, and most systems can be classified by an appropriate mix of the four: speed, communication, accuracy, and cost.

## Speed

'Speed' justified systems are those where it is important to the operational environment in which the terminal is used for the speed of response from the computer to be measured within a matter of seconds, i.e., the operators cannot carry out their jobs properly or effectively if the response time significantly rises above, say, five seconds.

## Communications

'Communications' justified systems are those where the need lies in solving a communication problem, either for input of data or extraction of information via the terminal, e.g., solving problems of geographic distribution or dealing with the difficulty of timely coordination between a number of staff in different departments. Therefore, one is concerned with reducing communication cycles, from weeks and days down to hours and minutes.

## Accuracy

Accuracy is reasonably self-defining. Many users have faced the problem of collecting accurate data and maintaining files with correct content in batch systems. Terminal interaction can be a method of improving both input accuracy and also the user's ability to check and correct file data.

## Cost

Here consideration is given to those few situations where through the use of a real time system, *as opposed to a batch system,* the organization can save more money. It is very important to note that the stress is on 'less cost' from real time as opposed to batch, and not talking about those general applications savings which, though gained in a real time situation, were equally attainable by a batch solution, e.g., the reduction in size of the old clerical section.

## 3.2  Speed—When Should It Apply?

The requirements for speed can be very clear in cases when the user organization is developing a system to serve customer sales or service situations; for example, the real time classic—airline reservations. Here, counter clerks are dealing with the general public and having taken an order for an airline reservation are not only concerned with accessing a flight inventory, which is relatively up to date, but doing so in a time cycle that does not irritate the customer standing at the counter to buy his airline ticket or to check in.

A similar situation exists in any industrial organization, with sales offices taking telephone or over the counter orders, and where plans are being considered for the operators to interact with the computer in order to accept orders. In this case, stocks may be rather more physical than airline inventory, but are just as liable to be fully sold. If the order clerk is to input orders through his terminal, then any reference records, such as a stock file, need to be sufficiently up to date for order acceptance checking. Equally, the customer certainly does not want to wait on the telephone or on the switchboard waiting to get through while the terminal operator is busy. In these circumstances, if the application is appropriate, the speed is a key aspect of real time.

However, let us consider the requirements that arose in one manufacturing company, in order to identify where speed might or might not be needed. This large engineering company sold a large range of standard products with a batch and jobbing approach to production. Sixty per cent of the production effort was for customer-tailored variants on standard products, and the market also forced a high development rate on most standard products. Twenty per cent of products were made for sale ex stock on a daily basis and these justify their own sales office, covering some eighty per cent of orders received. Feasibility studies were carried out, and the team considered the use of real time systems in the sales office, the production department and the forward planning department.

In the sales office, they identified a difficult order processing situation where telephone orders·are received against their high turnover stock items. The problems arose mainly in the existing situation due to stock-outs and a weak method of data capture of orders. Company policy demanded a continued low stock level, mainly due to the volatile market. A terminal based system was proposed with terminals in the sales office. The designers identified two choices.

In the first approach, the sales clerk would manually take orders against a 'nearest' hour stock status report and hand them across to a terminal operator. The operator would input orders in pseudo batch mode, for computer transfer to order processing and production of hourly status reports. In this approach, speed was not the essence, but rather, accuracy of data capture, and commitment to reducing the time cycle for stock status from 24 hours to 1 hour, and providing a rapid input into any order processing and production planning routines. This is a case where communications and accuracy were the fundamentals.

In the second approach, it was proposed that a sales clerk/operator would handle both telephone ordering and computer input. During the order conversation the clerk would key in the customer and order details. These would be immediately checked by the computer for customer credit rating, data accuracy and stock availability, so that queries/reports could be immediately taken up with the customer. At the same time the computer would search customer records, credit details and marketing files to suggest appropriate goods to promote. For these benefits to be meaningful, speed would be important, since the customer would be waiting on the phone. In these two cases the differences arose from the detailed use of the terminal to solve different aspects of the application.

More can be learned by examining the other two departments. In the production department the analysts had come to the conclusion that general production planning and scheduling was best done on a weekly cycle within the computer and that variations during the weeks could be handled most economically by the foreman. (The products that are the problem in the factory are not those that created the heavy numeric order taking load.) However, there was a considerable problem over the existing production paper work system. Production instructions were being continually updated after the order was placed in the factory. If production paperwork was produced once a month or once a week, there would be a trail of changes and corrections coming down from the engineering department. In practice, these arrive on separate pieces of paper that are continually chasing to catch up with the original 'make instructions' before work is set under way.

Following the feasibility study, the team arrived at a real time solution. They decided to load the weekly batch produced production plan on an on-line file with a full set of production information; to provide a terminal at each work centre and to feed all the changes to the computer to maintain up to date a central 'make file'.

Under the system proposed, the following procedure took place. On the shop floor the operator finished his production job, walked across to the terminal, keyed in his identity and job completion details. These were transmitted to the computer, which updated the progress records ready for real time interrogation and for overnight batch processing, and then printed at the shop floor operator's terminal the 'make instructions' for the next job.

Designs were carried out and it was found that an economic solution to this approach led to a heavily loaded system and with a risk of quite long computer delays, i.e., 10 seconds or more. The production staff were on a piecework bonus scheme and it was then drawn to the attention of the designers that such delays, although not significant in terms of the hours in a day, were unlikely to be acceptable to the work force. The designers were told to go back to find a solution more likely to meet their target of five seconds response. They therefore began to examine various alternatives, including the purchase of more equipment and more complex designs. Had this team sat down at the beginning of the project and recorded their prime justifications, they would have identified that this was not a basic speed requirement but a communications problem.

Once the designer hits response time problems and he knows he is in a communication environment, then rather than going flat out to meet the original response time criteria, he should first ask, 'Would a longer response time be acceptable?' In this case it was not, but again he could ask, 'Is there a different systems approach which still solves the problem?' In this particular case there are many; two of the various suggestions were (1) that paper work was still printed weekly and only the changes were printed out in real time, and (2) that each time jobs were reported the paper work was produced for the next job *but one*. As the jobs on average took a five hour run, this meant the paperwork was up to date to the nearest five hours.

### 3.3 Communications—a Justification

Usually communication is the basic justification when one is attempting to reduce the effects of 'distance', 'simultaneous access to the data by several staff' or 'long time lags'.

Once communication has been identified as the prime justification for a real time system, it is very important to challenge whether computer terminals are required at all. Communication justified systems can often be approached another way. For example, 'Can the data be communicated by conventional courier, telex, special van or top priority postal services?' 'Can communication be off line, tape to tape, disk to disk, etc?' 'Can communication be achieved by batch input from the terminal for later batch processing?'

Very often, where communication is the justification, on line terminal based systems are not a necessary solution, and if on line is selected, only the minimum of work needs to be done in real time. In such cases, there is a lot of scope for delayed processing, either of enquiries or by updating of files out of real time hours.

### 3.4 Accuracy

The use of the terminal based system can make substantial steps in the improvement of data accuracy, not only by capturing data at the earliest opportunity, and perhaps throwing error reports back to the operator straight away, but also by allowing users to browse through their own data files to check their accuracy and make early corrections.

A common example of the potential gain in accuracy can be seen in a production department. At the end of each job the operator fills in a job completion sheet, the foreman transcribes the job sheet on to a cleaner sheet of paper. The work summaries are transported daily to the computer centre, where it is punched on to cards and then repunched to verify, moved into job assembly, transported into the computer room, loaded on to the computer, converted to magnetic tape, validated, sorted and used to update the files. Print-outs are produced and at the end of the cycle, a number of error reports are ready to be sent back to the user.

Typically, in this situation, by the time the error reports have been recirculated to the user and his staff, they have forgotten what precisely happened for half the error reports, as by the time the cycle has been completed, there have already been several new sets of progress data. In this situation work-in-progress files, stock files, etc., are known to include a high number of errors yet continue to be used, as the information is the best available.

Compare this situation with a real time system, which several such organizations have turned to. At the end of the job the operator takes a job card, feeds it into a card reader on the terminal, takes his personal identity badge, feeds that into the same terminal, keys in the variable data and finally gets the computer response displayed back. He then corrects any error. The improvement in accuracy can be substantial, even if there is a risk of getting back to the timing problem seen under Speed. In practice, the batch systems are not all as bad as described and the on line solution may not justify such sophisticated terminals. Nevertheless, terminal systems used by line operators or the data input teams can significantly increase accuracy.

The change from the traditional card punch preparation centre to key to disk systems is an illustration of this development. Most key to disk systems are specialized real time systems in their own right and illustrate the scope for increased use of terminals in data capture. The very specialization of the system often makes them preferable to terminals on-line to the main computer, for pure data preparation applications. If access to main files as part of the validation process is required, then normally the main-frame approach is better.

However, with accuracy as a justification, care must still be taken. The question that certainly has to be answered is: 'Is accuracy the by-product of an approach to real time systems or is it the prime justification?' If accuracy is the end justification then considerations of productivity must be watched carefully so that speed does not build up as an *artificial* prime criterion or justification.

## 3.5  Costs—Cheaper or Greater Savings

There are two main ways in which costs can play their part in real time systems in comparison with the batch equivalent, especially when the real time solution is likely to start with a major cost disadvantage with line and communication costs. The two areas of potential cost advantage are:

- reduction in costs associated with the batch data capture and dissemination cycle;
- savings on scale.

### 3.5.1 DATA CAPTURE AND DISSEMINATION

A major area where real time systems differ from batch in costs, is that concerned with the physical transmission of data from its point of origination to the computer and again back to the final recipient. The real time network, although incurring cost in its own right, potentially replaces a large number of cost incurring steps associated with the equivalent batch system. The typical batch system may include:

- data recording,
- data coding,
- transcription,
- transport,
- data preparation punch,
- data preparation verify,
- control section,
- job control,
- transport,
- operator loading,
- media conversion,
- stationery handling,
- printing,
- bursting/decollating,
- job control,
- transport.

These activities, especially where complicated data coding is concerned, can be a substantial part of the cost of the running of a batch system. In some such cases, the costs of the terminal based system can be more than offset by the saving of the batch equivalent in these areas above.

A common example is the input of supplier invoices where each supplier item may need coding before data preparation and where typically the organization has no control on the format of invoices received. Many on-line systems involved in this activity start with the operator entering the supplier key and the computer responding with a display of supplier details enabling the operator to check name and address, etc. This is followed by the display of a formatted order form which simplifies the input and as a by-product probably automatically codes order items.

Where cost savings in data capture or in dissemination or in both in combination are seen as the prime justification, it is very important to prevent speed assuming too high a priority in design. As with communications, if cost saving is the essence, then technical problems can possibly be overcome by reviewing the question 'How much of this work really needs to be done in real time, and how quickly?'

### 3.5.2 ADVANTAGES OF SCALE

For many years, organizations with dispersed locations have argued the case for centralization versus decentralization of computers, with the arguments following the management cycles of the organization.

One of the arguments for centralization has been the cost advantage that can sometimes arise with scale. But such advantage brings with it the need for more data communication, that is communication between the computer centre and the operating sites, locations or separate subsidiary companies.

As terminal systems become more commonplace, they play a greater role in studies of the centre versus the periphery. Certainly, communications systems in this case may not be very sophisticated, being simple remote job entry systems or simple user batch input system, but they can include on-line and real time systems. However, if terminals are there to solve communications requirements and these communications requirements have arisen in order to reduce costs, it is important to recognize that the terminal system is there to save hardware costs through scale, i.e., the prime justification is cost saving, not communication nor speed.

In this case, the alternative to the terminal, must both solve communications by another form, and provide computer power by another form, i.e., relatively smaller local computers. Where the cost advantage of scale has been identified as the motivation for on-line systems, any design that will increase cost too far risks invalidating the original argument. This has not always been recognized.

If the centralized decision is already set, and is irreversible, then the justification for real time returns at that point to Communications.

## 3.6  Analysis of Prime Justifications

There was always a danger that trying to find a common framework for analysing different situations becomes an exercise in its own right independent of the main purpose, i.e., the development of effective systems. However, time and time again experience has shown that in the development of real time systems, secondary criteria have arisen which have deflected the designers into either wasting their time solving problems that need not be solved directly, or designing systems which are more sophisticated than the business requires. Therefore, in any particular case it is very important to go back to prime justifications, even if the project team choose slightly different definitions from those selected above. It is essential to be sure of the basic reasons, to record them and to remember them at all stages of development.

## 3.7  Elements of Justification

Response time, speed or communication, accuracy and cost objectives are but part of a real time system justification. In a practical case, justification has to be considered in more detail.

The evaluation process is one of matching the benefit against the cost for each element of the system, as well as looking at the overall cost benefit analysis. The elements identified in real time systems studies that need this separate justification include the following.

### 3.7.1 THE TRANSACTION

Response time criteria need to be established for each transaction in the system and within each transaction separate criteria may be justified for different parts, e.g., enquiry acknowledgements required in, say, five seconds enquiry reply required in, say, one minute. Response is specified in terms of response time to the operator and up-to-date status of the files.

### 3.7.2. SECURITY

Security is generally associated with files in the system. Each has a required level of protection to be individually determined, but every protection system carries its own overhead. Thus, security implies an extra cost and therefore requires justification as much as the application itself. Chapter 13 examines the range of choice open to the designer of the security system. It is important that just as the precise level of response time justification for each transaction in the system is challenged, so must the precise level of security. Given that security is not quantifiable, this is a difficult task in the early stages; however, it remains important.

### 3.7.3 RECOVERY

Ask any user how reliable the system needs to be and you have a high probability that the reply sounds like 100 per cent. In practice, the range provided is vast, as is explained in chapter 12. However, during feasibility studies it is crucial to set recovery targets for both transactions and files and to justify the level set.

Like security, failure and recovery are emotional subjects, and for that reason great care needs to be taken in discussing and presenting the subjects with senior user management.

One example illustrates the point. In the company in this case, orders are processed in the manual system as follows.

Telephone orders are written on slips with copies to the warehouse where goods are packed and despatched. The objective is to obtain daily clearance of morning orders. Typical operational statistics include the following: average delay in the warehouse is five hours, peak season average delay is one day; one major delay (sickness, strike, mechanical failures) of two–three days every other year.

On being asked to project reliability on the proposed real time system, the team leader reported to the sales manager as follows:

– three minor failures per day;

– full system stoppage once per week;

– CPU down for 24 hours or more once per year.

The sales manager, who thinks of the existing system as continuing at all times, is horrified, especially as he has been told a real time system provided a five second response. Had the analyst's statistics been presented in terms of current processes they would have been seen to have been a genuine improvement. This example has been simplified, but the real life effect was disastrous when badly handled. Two years later the same concept was accepted—by then properly presented.

The general solution is to present reliability performance to the user in terms of fluctuations of services related to what currently exists, as well as to the proposed new system's normal operation.

One hour off the air once per week on an order processing real time system may sound poor compared with the proposed five second response, but can be a lot better than a current situation that takes at least five hours to process an order.

## 3.8  Feasibility Study

The initial justification of a real time project is probably provided during some form of feasibility study or survey. In planning a real time feasibility study it is important to note:

– Technical as well as business feasibility must be thoroughly checked. This can only be achieved by carrying out a broad design task with detailed estimates for sensitive areas. A real time feasibility study should not be carried out without real time design skills in the team or at the very least a study of this book and at least one (non manufacturer oriented) training course in the subject.

– Good effective experience in batch systems is not sufficient alone to make independent judgements on potential real time systems.

Feasibility studies are considered further in chapters 4 and 6.

# 4. Project Structures, Skills, and Staffing

Every data processing department has its own organization and structure, and there exists a wide range of both satisfactory and unsatisfactory methods of organization. Many real time projects have been the trigger to a complete review of data processing organization, but the reader is asked to interpret the contents of this chapter in the context of the constraints of his own organization.

Project structure is one of the facets of real time system development which will be sensitive to the scale of the project. The numbers of staff involved in a simple two terminal enquiry system in an installation, where on-line systems already exist, is so small as to barely warrant 'special structures'. At the other end of the scale a government department entering into real time for the first time with some 1000 terminals and a 1000 Mega-character data base needs to consider project structure very carefully. However, it is our experience over a wide range of projects that good practices on project structure are reasonably situation independent. It is easy to argue for short cuts on small projects, but even with small projects lack of care on project structure has often led to poor projects. Small scale real time systems are usually best met by merging necessary roles in a few staff, rather than forgetting such roles.

Before considering real time project structures further, it is important to state that successful experience in the management of batch projects is not in itself sufficient for real time project management. The risks and pressures in both design, development and project management are different, and for that reason the most experienced batch systems project manager needs to review his techniques before tackling a real time project. For example, the first project in real time could include such changes as the use of new technology for the team, a strong interaction between user needs and potential computer system designs, and a new emphasis on the design stage of a project. Further, the environment may be such that a 10 per cent error in design, assumption, or implementation could lead to 200 per cent error in performance.

This chapter provides a general view of real time project management.

Chapters 6, 7 and 8 examine some of the staff duties in more detail and chapter 5 examines the elements of project planning and control, both managerial and technical.

## 4.1 Project Phases

To discuss project organization, it is first necessary to identify the stages or phases of project development. One possible approach is outlined below for reference.

### 4.1.1 FEASIBILITY STUDY

Project breakdown at this phase varies considerably from installation to installation, and often the statement of business requirements is separate from the examination of technical practicability. For consistency in this book, one practice has been assumed. That is, after an initial brief survey to establish that it is worth launching the project, as full feasibility study is carried out before system analysis, in detail, is attempted. Thus, the feasibility study is a systems overview study with the objective of determining the business needs and justification, together with establishing the technical feasibility of the project. The phase includes both analysis and design to a limited level.

Staff skills required during a real time feasibility study are probably the most demanding of any phase of development. Characteristics required by the team include:

- good business knowledge,
- systems analysis skills,
- real time experience,
- real time design skills,
- knowledge of available software, terminals, etc.,
- project management, planning and estimating.

In simple terms, the team needs to have the skills related to the later major phases of development with the ability to handle the study at an overview level without missing significant detail.

It is too easy to skip over design at the feasibility phase. A simple (but wrong) view on the performance of, say, disk message buffering in the communications software may cause the team to recommend an approach as being capable of meeting a five second response, when greater care could have identified a heavy overload on the projected hardware caused by this buffering technique, leading to excessive response times. The difference can remove the net benefits or be totally disruptive if discovered later.

All too often, initial studies set the user and technical direction of a real time project before the installation has obtained the necessary skills. But who wants to recruit real time expertise or undertake heavy real time training if the feasibility study is to end up recommending against real time? However, a compromise is possible.

- Hire in specialists with real time skills to work with your staff during the feasibility study. This probably means asking a consultancy if you want to avoid potential bias from a manufacturer or software house, or

– Keep the feasibility study as a two-stage affair. If real time looks viable after the first stage (a review), then invest in the necessary skills before completing the full feasibility study. Some delay for recruitment and in-depth training of existing staff is probable.

At both the feasibility and systems analysis phase it is difficult for a technically competent data processing leader, with, say, eight or more years' experience, to accept or recommend that he and his team have not got the experience for the job. One expects some five years' experience from him in data processing before allocating him to lead a significant batch project, therefore, if it is a real time project, should not several years (relevant) real time experience be a minimum for at least one member of the team?

### 4.1.2  SYSTEMS ANALYSIS

Systems analysis for real time systems is not only concerned with sufficient analysis and definition of user needs, but also with carrying out sufficient design to ensure a good balance between user and technical issues at this early phase.

One of the greatest difficulties of the real time analyst is to strike the right balance between too many and too few data. Too many data are time wasting in analysis. Too few can lead to wasted time during later stages of development when, say, design is held up while an extra data gathering and analysis task is initiated. Experience and a pre-knowledge of probable design calculations are the best path to getting the balance right.

The other difficulty in analysis is that of producing a business specification without unduly constraining the computer system design. The solution involves the development of a series of provisional designs during the analysis phase, closely linked to the development of the specification. It is necessary to include general real time design skills in the analysis team. An analyst can wrongly plant the desire in users for a systems feature which is expensive to provide. The result is an expensive system, difficult later phase, or an unhappy user when the feature is later rejected. For example, it is not a constructive approach to systems specification if the analysts set harsh targets for a specific transaction type and the file design needed to meet performance criteria makes hardware costs unacceptable.

Equally, if operator simplicity is a criterion implementing a user transaction in three message pairs with limited data per pair as opposed to in two message pairs may seem to be the obvious solution. However, the effect on the use of communication software and perhaps disk message buffering may cause crucial hardware resources to go from a stable load condition to a heavily loaded one with frequent long delays to messages.

The need to set a balance, during the specification stage, between too much definition and too little is crucial. Both users and analysts familiar with batch operations will initially have difficulty in understanding the problem before they have gained real time experience. The problem to the project manager is what to have specified in analysis as opposed to during design? If the balance is wrong, either the user is confused (too much detail in the system specification) or abused (too great a constraint set during analysis without proper care).

## The Solution

Firstly in all aspects of the system definition, define the logical need and minimize the physical definition in the systems specification. Nevertheless, consider the physical impact before setting that specification, so as to ensure that the required facilities are possible. For example,

— Define transactions and the pattern of messages where interactions will be necessary for the logic of the application. Avoid specifying message pairs determined by equipment limitations like screen sizes.
— Define message pair content but not layout.
— Define message layout characteristics rather than character positions on the screen.
— Do not quote precise figures just for the sake of being specific (i.e., do not say response in five seconds if the need is response without noticeable delay to operators. If qualification is needed set objective like 'average five seconds', '95 per cent not more than ten seconds').

When the system specification leaves options open as above, the options are closed at the design phase, when the cost of being specific can be discovered.

In this context the systems specification should be seen (and presented) as a definitive description of the system from a business view point, with as much operational detail as possible to allow users to check at both management and supervisory/operational level. Once accepted, the system specification should be frozen and only modified following a formal change procedure. It is also desirable to add to this formal specification, as an appendix, an outline design specification.

This appendix is included with the objective of providing a technical interpretation of some of the missing operational details in the system specification, an outline design as a guide for later phases of development and design work to validate the system specification in terms of cost and performance. While this outline design should not be changed lightly during the next phase (design), details may be changed without applying the formal change procedure needed with the systems specification.

### 4.1.3 COMPUTER SYSTEM DESIGN

Computer system design is the process of finally designing the computer system to implement the real time business system defined after analysis. Because of the close interaction between user and the machine, design includes specifying final details of the system as seen by the user (e.g., precise terminal input and output message conversation details; user recovery procedures after

**35**

hardware failure, etc.). For that reason analysis skills must be carried forward into design. Equally, much preliminary design will have been included in the earlier phases.

Any real time system will be made up of hardware, software, installation software and application code (for examples see chapter 14). Detailed definition of the use of supplier products for the first two (hardware, software), detailed design of the third (installation software), the interface to application code, and functions of modules of application code are all included under design.

Thus, apart from real time design experience, general skills sought include the following:

- broad design skills,
- detailed real time design skills,
- detailed knowledge of software,
- experience in timing of systems,
- ability to estimate and cost out alternative solutions.

Chapter 7 examines the design process in more detail and the subsequent chapters examine the design techniques.

### 4.1.4 PROGRAM SPECIFICATION

Program specification writing for real time should not call for different skills from the batch equivalent. If there is a special skill needed, it should have been applied in analysis and design. Program specification writing both for application code and user software should therefore be straightforward.

### 4.1.5 PROGRAMMING AND MODULE TESTING

If the right work has been carried out in the early phases, any competent programmer should be able to perform these tasks to the standards established for the project. Special programmer skills may be needed in such areas as high performance 'own' software (such as a user line interface, user control routines, etc.), detail interfaces with new software, validating design assumptions, writing test programs, and in those situations where design has *not* been carried out as fully as recommended.

Chapter 14 considers program structures and programming implications in more detail.

### 4.1.6 TESTING AND INTEGRATION

At this phase of any project, no new key staff are required for the development team, and real time is no exception. The phase is important but should be carried out by those who have worked in analysis, design and programming. However, the operations department will become more actively involved at this stage, so real time operations experience is very valuable.

Many projects have found this phase straightforward when the testing has been carefully planned for and reflected in the program designs during the earlier analysis and design phase. Real time programs can be designed in a manner that assists testing, and such benefits can be achieved with little detriment to operational performance or development effort.

Chapter 8 explores the testing process in more detail.

Testing for a real time project, because of the intimate interface to the user when live, is *very* important and can take a lot longer than the equivalent batch system. Not only must all program logic be tested, but so must time dependencies. This is impossible to plan precisely with test data. From an operational view point, system testing probably requires the testing of procedures not often included in batch system tests. This particularly applies to operators' reaction to a variety of failure conditions, and in larger systems rehearsing live operator control of the system (changes of priorities, assignments, etc.) and communication control section procedures for line monitoring and switching.

### 4.1.7 OPERATING THE SYSTEM

Real time systems bring special problems to the operations department as much as to the development team.

This book is primarily concerned with development aspects, and therefore does not consider real time operations in detail. However, it is important to stress that not only does the operations department need to prepare and train in advance, but the designers have to take operational problems into consideration at an earlier phase.

During the real time day, many of the scheduling decisions, taken by an operations department in batch mode, will be incorporated in the real time software and user programs. It is therefore essential that during the design process, time is taken in establishing those controls that will be needed (and efficient to handle) by operations.

Systems features to ease operator control can best be built in during early design. A sample set of such facilities is given below:

- Reconfigure—software, hardware, network.
- Change processing priorities.
- Change allocation of resources (e.g., core, disks, drives).
- Collect operational statistics.
- Initiate recovery and restart procedures.
- Modify files while still on-line.
- Change security routines—in a controlled manner.

The level of the new operations problems greatly depends on the scale of the real time project and the proportion of total CPU power expended by real time as opposed to batch and testing tasks. In large network systems, for example, complete new operations teams have been established as 'network controllers' separate from conventional computer room operations. In other cases operators have had too little to do, with eventual boredom except when things go wrong. Then the good operator is the one with the ability to react quickly and correctly and the management problem between failures is one of motivation. Other systems have justified a 24 hour operations control shift cover with systems and programming staff as part of each work shift.

Both design and operations personnel need to study and plan the operational implication to the same level of thoroughness advocated in each of the other areas discussed in the other chapters. As an example of what can happen if operations are not considered, a practical case is outlined below.

In this installation, there had been reasonable liaison within operations during systems development though primarily in terms of scheduling future machine resources. The real time system involving some 30 terminals was to be allocated to 'the real time machine' in a twin computer batch installation but multi programmed with other batch work. Design calculations had indicated that, given suitable CPU priority, the CPU loading from the real time system was light. The critical areas for performance were likely to be core space and disk utilization.

| File | Disk 1 | Disk Disk 2 | Disk 3 | Disk 4 |
|------|--------|------|--------|--------|
| A | A | A | A | A |
| B | B | B | | |
| C | | | C | C |
| D | D | | | |
| E | | E | | |

**Fig. 4.1**  File allocation—optimized

| File | Disk 1 | Disk 2 | Disk 3 | Disk 4 |
|------|--------|--------|--------|--------|
| A | A | | | |
| B | | B | | |
| C | | | C | |
| D | | | | D |
| E | | | | E |

**Fig. 4.2**  File allocation—file to disk

The design team soon identified that the main disk activity was associated with one of the general files used by the application. To optimize performance, files were assigned across disk packs, with several files allocated part of several disks; see Fig. 4.1. The performance improvement over an allocation of 1 file per disk, see Fig. 4.2, was substantial as the activity was spread more evenly across physical devices. However, once the team began system testing operators discovered their most difficult task was recovery from real (or suspected) disk failure. The spread file allocation was such that once a disk failed they found the need to reconstitute several files. Their reaction was to change the file allocation to that of Fig. 4.2 with the resultant deterioration of performance! A solution was eventually found but clearly system testing is too late to determine the impact of practical operational requirements and wishes on the design, and vice versa.

Structured programming and its associated techniques in design and documentation have been developed and installed to improve effective systems development. One of the key elements of structured programming is the application of formal disciplines to the development processes.

The authors' experience, both before and after the advent of structured programming on a wide scale, was that other formalized approaches to systems development were equally successful at achieving a high overall performance. Readers may find that the approaches outlined have some similarity to structured development. The fit really depends on what other environment is chosen for comparison.

Our experience with respect to projects structure, programming organization in real time and structured programming is as follows:

- *Well-organized, disciplined* real time project teams can develop real time systems along the lines set out in this book as effectively as with a more structured programming approach;
- those who have selected structured programming can adapt the approach set out in these chapters to fit their structured programming rules. If the adaptation is done well, the benefits of both should still apply, as the design philosophy is not significantly different. The book makes no comment on structure below the level of a functional application routine, but at a more detailed level, routines can be very effectively modularized and written as structured GO-TO-LESS code.

## 4.2 Developing Real Time Project Structures

The organization of the development side of the computer department tends to fall into either project oriented or functional oriented structure, with staff often labelled as analysts, programmers, analyst/programmers or other title prefixes to reflect seniority, e.g., senior programmer.

Already we have referred to real time design and the independent role of designer, as expanded in chapter 8, is often new to those who have worked in batch only installations, where design is done either by a programmer or by an analyst. In considering real time project structures, we have found it useful to identify four skills groups, namely analysis, design, programming and operations. Clearly many experienced real time staff are competent to varying degrees under several heads.

No matter what data processing structure has already existed in an installation, a project-oriented approach frequently has been found valuable for real time projects. On occasions such a structure has been applied alongside existing function-oriented departments. Therefore a project structure approach for real time projects has been taken as a base in this chapter.

### 4.2.1 BASIC STRUCTURES

Figure 4.3 represents a simple but useful starting point in planning the staff structure for a real time project. This chapter assumes the project is large

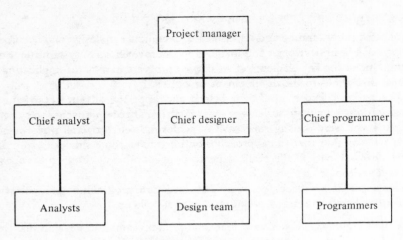

**Fig. 4.3**  A project structure

enough to justify the staff covered by the different titles. For small projects, several roles can be merged for one person to perform. Nevertheless the roles should remain.

### Project Manager

In the ideal world, the project manager is an experienced project manager who has worked on the design and control of real time projects. But at least he should not be a new or weak project manager without real time experience!

As project manager, the planning and control of the project falls on his shoulders in the normal way. If he has no personal real time experience, it is very important that he take steps to establish his personal education and training beyond a one or two day seminar, together with follow-up study.

### Chief Designer

The chief designer is shown in Fig. 4.3 as senior to the chief analyst and chief programmer but without line responsibility for them. Upon his shoulders falls the technical coordination of the project. Thus, he directly controls the design work and individually influences the analysts and programmers. After the project manager, this is a key role in a real time project, the person filling it should be the most experienced, competent member of the team. When the project team is thin on experience, what experience exists is best placed in this role. When outside help is sought to strengthen a team, the role of chief designer is often well allocated to the external consultant. A chief designer probably programmed at some phase in his career and has sufficient experience in analysis to hold his own as a senior analyst if not as chief business analyst. Conventional large team line management skills are not so important, but his ability to direct and lead by example are.

**40**

## Chief Analyst

Analysts working as individuals or as sub-project teams under a project leader, can report equally effectively to a chief analyst, the chief designer or the project manager. The need for a separate chief analyst role varies with the skills and commitments of the other senior members of the project team and the scale of the project. The larger the project and the greater the amount of discussion with senior user management, the more the need for an independent chief analyst.

## Chief Programmer

The chief programmer manages the programmers and should not be considered as a competitor with the chief designer in overall design responsibility. However, he and his staff may assist in design tasks, especially when it involves interpretation of software or lower level program design.

Where staff skills are such that the best chief designer is also the best chief programmer, the project manager should be wary of combining the roles in one man. The chief designer must guide the project at the analysis phase if he is to be successful. Therefore, make the candidate chief designer and, if a chief programmer is needed, compromise there. Then later support the chief designer in getting the programmers to follow his guidance.

## 4.2.2 EXTENDING THE STRUCTURE

The tasks in analysis and programming will be well known to the reader and are expanded further in later chapters, as is design. However, real time projects do call for other roles not often found in batch. These roles are often associated with the offices of the chief designer or the project manager.

## Project Control

Project control is a tool whereby the project manager (and staff) plan in detail the use of resources, then monitor, control and react if necessary to complete the project on cost, on time, or at least with advance projections of variances.

This is not new, but real time projects can call for considerable coordination and planning, such that the planning, the use of techniques like PERT, and the monitoring of progress can justify a section in their own right in support of the project manager. This is expanded in chapter 5.

## Design Control

Technical Design Control (TDC) was originally developed for real time systems but is now being used in other complex systems. It is a process by which the project manager, chief designer (and project staff) plan in detail the use of operational resources—disk, core, time, space, response times, etc., in the final operational real time system, and then monitor projections of performance as designs become more refined and data become more detailed and accurate as the development proceeds. Design control has been effective in the

41

advance detection of gross over-usage of resources as well as a useful tool during the design process.

The need for design control can be illustrated by a simple example. Consider a transaction that has an average profile:

1000 transactions per hour
10 records read per transaction
3 disk accesses needed to read record
50 ms needed to read the disks.

The disk usage arising from the transaction is:

$1000 \times 10 \times 3 \times 50$ mseconds per hour
$= 1\,500\,000$ mseconds per hour
$= 25$ minutes per hour.

If later analysis/design increases each figure by 10 per cent a simple check on individual items may not pick up the significance. However, the effect is a rise in disk usage by this transaction to

$25 \times 1 \cdot 1 \times 1 \cdot 1 \times 1 \cdot 1 \times 1 \cdot 1 = 37$ minutes per hour.

With the effects of other transactions this could lead to a system initially designed to meet five second response criteria moving to instability!

Section 5.2 examines the elements of technical design control, and how it can be applied to achieve the necessary control and pick up the combined effect of variances at the earliest opportunity.

### Quality Control

As data processing systems have become more complex the industry has learned from other technologies. Real time systems certainly constitute an area where an independent quality control group working for the project manager, or even outside the team, can make a valuable contribution to the project.

Quality control (or assurance) is concerned with validating all development work in the project with the object of a third party detecting errors missed by 'the man on the job', before these errors become costly to rectify. The design group can carry out a quality control role but cannot effectively monitor their own work that is crucial to the success of the project.

If a quality control role can be established as an independent unit in the project, not only will it review specifications, designs, documentation, plans and programming, to detect problems in advance, but also should make a major contribution to unit and systems testing.

Quality control will be seen, to users of structured programming techniques, as an extension of the 'structured walk through' within the team, to a form of structured walk through within the project.

### Library and Version Control

Chapter 8 on system testing and cut over identifies the problem of the controlled maintenance of the program library. With a dynamic real time system in its later phases of testing, a particular module of code could exist as:

(1) version handed over to system test;
(2) prior stable version to version (1) held for test fall back purposes;
(3) patched (1) in system test (yes, they do exist in some projects);
(4) (1) under rapid upgrade to clear bugs and replace (3);
(5) Later version of (1) modified by a programmer implementing a frozen system change for the next release of the whole system;
(6) New version of (5) under programmer control.

The list looks pedantic at first sight, but it is not an inaccurate reflection of many projects. Given that planning must cater for both difficult and smooth tests, version control should be established by the chief programmer before any testing starts. The detail control may be established in programming or operations. Do not forget that the library can also be allocated over several disk packs. Sub-sets that may be allocated their own packs include version for system test, fall back correction, and standard test data.

*Operation Liaison*

Not only will operations need close contact with development—the design team will make many decisions otherwise left to operations management and operators in batch systems—but will need to plan the operational impact of the change over to real time working, especially for the first major on-line system. This chapter does not cover the problems of new equipment, but for the moment assumes that the project manager and operations liaison handle all hardware contracting, line installation, telecommunication arrangements, etc.

Operation responsibilities are no trivial matter, but fall outside the direct scope of this book.

## 4.3  The Extended Structure

Figure 4.4 illustrates a possible structure for a large complex real time project whose scale has justified establishing many of the roles discussed as discrete jobs. In this particular project, the on-line and batch elements of the application were sufficiently independent to be set up as separate teams, with general systems and design coordination carried out by the project manager and the chief designer. Special support programs run in batch mode, but essential to the real time operation, were classified as part of the 'real time' element of the system and included a range of dump, reconstitution and set-up procedures.

## 4.4  The Project Cycle

This section considers the allocation of activities to the three main groups of staff (analysis, design, programming) during a project's progress. Adequate experience is assumed in the team, both for own staff and external support seconded to the project. The section relates the project phases of section 4.1 to the organization of staff as developed in section 4.2 and reflected in Fig. 4.4.

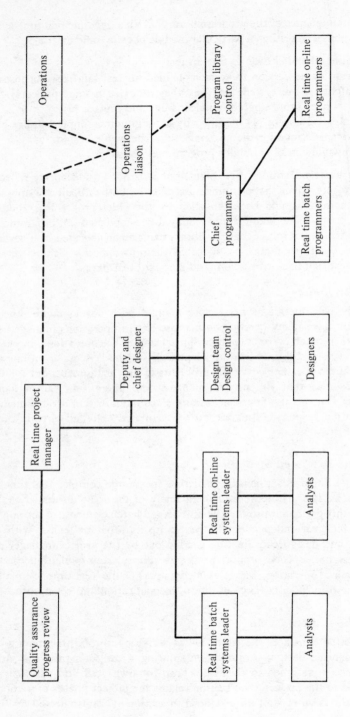

**Fig. 4.4** A large project structure

| Skills | Feasibility | Systems analysis | Systems design | Program specification | Programming | Testing |
|---|---|---|---|---|---|---|
| Business analyst | 3 | 2 | | | | 2 |
| Real time systems analyst | 3 | 3 | 2 | 1 | 1 | 3 |
| Real time systems designer | 2 | 2 | 3 | 3 | | 3 |
| Software expert | 1 | 1 | 2 | 2 | 1 | |
| Expert assembler programmer | | | 4 | | 4 | 4 |
| Programmer | | | 1 | 3 | 3 | 3 |
| Real time operation liaison | | 1 | 2 | | | 3 |

Entries indicate:

1 — useful
2 — important
3 — essential
4 — project dependent

**Fig. 4.5**   Staff skills by phase

Figure 4.5 is provided as a summary of staff skills by phase. The reader will recognize that some of those skills may well exist in one individual, e.g., a particular systems analyst may have the relevant experience to communicate properly with senior user management—the business analyst skill—and carry out the detailed analysis for a real time system—real time systems analyst.

### 4.4.1   FEASIBILITY STUDY

Staffed by at least the chief designer and a senior analyst with some software programming assistance. Project manager assigned and closely involved.

### 4.4.2   SYSTEMS ANALYSIS

The system team is established to carry out analysis, technically guided by the chief designer. The design team is built up during early weeks. Design control should have been first established against the feasibility study conclusions and outline design. The project control and assurance offices are set up in early weeks of this stage.

Operations liaison is established and the chief programmer assigned before end of stage.

### 4.4.3   SYSTEMS DESIGN

The main activity is headed by the design team supported by analysts. Other analysts begin planning and initial work on user procedure documentation, user education and systems testing. The chief programmer is closely involved with design and establishes his controls and standards for the programming stage. Various control procedures, set-up and testing mechanics need to be agreed with operations. Design control will have been updated with the outline designs used to complete the analysis and applied during design. Quality assurance will have checked out detailed systems work and rechecked design calculations and assumptions. Programmers may be seconded to write test or measurement routines.

### 4.4.4 PROGRAM SPECIFICATION

Senior programmers are assigned and liaise with the designer and analysts on the completion and acceptance of detailed specifications. Design control and quality assurance will continue. Analyst and designer tasks concerned with testing and implementation will proceed simultaneously.

### 4.4.5 PROGRAMMING

The programming team is active while the designers prepare for comprehensive link testing, extra module test aids and the start of systems testing. The systems team with possibly some staff released, continues on user aspects and preparation for systems testing and cut over. Operations provide normal module test services, but operation liaison are preparing for complications on link testing, version control and on line testing.

The installation of any new hardware is nearing completion for the first phase of testing and live running. (Software set up has been included here with design and programming for simplicity of description.)

### 4.4.6 TESTING

Testing control progresses from programmers to design team to analysts. While the control moves closer to the user, again more staff become involved, because of the extra implementation tasks, until program stability permits a run down of programmers on the project. Testing and cut over (see chapter 8) consist of a highly critical set of steps, but call for no particular change in the project organization until initial live running.

### 4.4.7 LIVE RUNNING

Live running often falls into two time periods—'live' and OK. The fragile boundary is when system failures drop to the unusual rather than the regular. Real time systems often call for an on-line controller and support team beyond that normally associated with batch operations. Certainly in early weeks the key designers, analysts and programmers need to be near at hand for handling real time failures, as well as longer term repairs and maintenance.

## 4.5 Summary of Project Structures

While the project structures described for real time could be applied to batch projects, the reverse is less often true in practice. A well-run real time project requires a carefully established structure with real time skills in key staff, greater control and planning, and an awareness of the difference from batch.

Project oriented teams are certainly the best way for an installation to start with the first real time system. However, for that team to be successful, time needs to be allocated early in the project to establish the right disciplines, *controls* and techniques.

# 5. Monitoring Development

If one looks back at the development of the techniques of control and management in data processing, many techniques can be seen to have developed from projects that were in large scale or used new technology. Many have survived the test of time, because though developed under the extra pressures of such projects the benefits are equally applicable to smaller systems. In the same way, the disk brake, originally developed for racing cars, fast became standard equipment for family saloons.

Real time projects frequently fall into this category, as often real time is a new technology for the installation and the integrated nature of the design can tend to produce large programs if not large systems. In this chapter, we are particularly concerned with those techniques for the control of real time systems development that are essentially different from common batch practice. Other techniques not covered in the chapter but which are good batch practice (such as formal business reviews at the end of each stage of development) of course remain important.

## 5.1  Important Conventional Techniques

Thorough project planning and control is essential for real time projects, and well-established methods of planning and control, already used in many data processing installations, can be applied with success. Many data processing projects have benefited from 'network or PERT' based planning systems and/or from 'phase/task' based project control systems. It is the authors' experience that real time projects need both.

PERT type planning is needed to establish the inter-relationship of the many parallel tasks that can arise in a real time project while the main process of systems development, and, indeed, much of the activity of the data processing department, is best controlled by phase/tast planning methods.

In real time systems there tend to be three main inter-related sub-projects to consider in the overall plan. These are:

Systems Development  – The conventional systems development cycle as applied to the real time project.

| | |
|---|---|
| Implementation | – User training and systems implementation, including the installation of remote terminal operations. |
| Installation | – Physical planning and installation of new central equipment, networks and terminals. |

Figure 7.1 in chapter 7 illustrates the systems development sub-project for a typical real time project, but in any particular situation the practical approach is as follows:

(1) ensure that the project team is already familiar with, or adopt effective project planning and control techniques including:
   – Network/PERT/CPA planning,

| Task no. | Task Description |
|---|---|
| 3 | Recovery design |
| 4 | File design – subdivided as below |
| 4A | Control prog (M&P) |
| 4B | Message file |
| 4C | Print stack |
| 4D | Printed messages |
| 4E | Transaction file |
| 4F | Validation tables |
| 4G | Terminal control table |
| 5 | Task breakdown and functional specification of tasks |
| 6 | Task interface design |
| 23 | Dry test of module breakdown |
| 7 | Design specification – MCP |
| 8 | Design specification – JST – Command |
| 8A | Design specification – recovery |
| 9 | Design specification – GET TCAM |
| 10 | Design specification – MULTI SCREEN |
| 11 | Design specification – PUT TCAM |
| 11A | Design specification – Display |
| 12 | Design specification – Validation |
| 13 | Design specification – Edit |
| 13A | Design specification – Look-up routine |
| 14 | Design specification – Create look-up file |
| 15 | Design specification – Main look-up file |
| 15A | User specification – Maintenance of look-up file |
| 16 | User specification – File driver |
| 17 | User specification – Print stacker |
| 18 | User specification – Stack reporter |
| 19 | User specification – Print program |
| 20 | User specification – Stack dump |
| 21 | User specification – Stack restore |
| 22 | User specification – MICR plug |
| 24 | Design specification – MERGE-EXTRACT |
| 25 | Design specification – ENTRY GENERATION |
| 26 | Design specification – SORT |
| 27 | Design specification – DAY COMPACTING |
| 28 | Review of design specifications |
| 29 | Programming – MCP (including module testing) |

(a)

| Task no. | Task Description |
|---|---|
| 30 | Programming – JST |
| 31 | Programming – GET-TACM |
| 32 | Programming – MULTIPLE SCREEN |
| 33 | Programming – PUT-TACM |
| 33A | Programming – DISPLAY |
| 34 | Programming – BASIC VALIDATION |
| 35 | Programming – APPT-EDIT |
| 35A | Programming – LOOK-UP ROUTINE |
| 36 | Programming – CREATE LOOK-UP |
| 37 | Programming – UPDATE LOOK-UP |
| 38 | Programming – FILE DRIVER |
| 39 | Programming – PRINT STACKER |
| 40 | Programming – STACK REPORTER |
| 41 | Programming – PRINT PROGRAMS |
| 42 | Programming – STACK DUMP |
| 43 | Programming – STACK RESTORE |
| 44 | Programming – MERGE-EXTRACT |
| 45 | Programming – ENTRY GENER. |
| 46 | Programming – SORT |
| 47 | Programming – DAY CONTRACTING |
| 48 | Linkage testing of RT part – PREP |
| 48A | Actual testing |
| 49 | Volume testing of RT part |
| 49A | Actual testing |
| 50 | Recovery and reconfiguration tests |
| 50A | Actual testing |
| 51 | Linkage testing of print part |
| 51A | Actual testing |
| 52 | Linkage testing of batch part |
| 52A | Actual testing |
| 53 | System testing of system |
| 53A | Volume testing of system |
| 54 | VDU operator's manual preparation |
| 55 | VDU operators training |
| 56 | Management manual preparation |
| 57 | Console operator manual |
| 58 | System recovery manual |

(b)

**Fig. 5.1**   First draft task list

– A DP project control system suitable for the systems and programming cycle; preferably task/phase oriented;

(2) progressively refine formal plans, but set as much detail (best estimate first) as early as possible;

(3) at each major project check point (phase/stage) explicitly review the formal plan and set a hard plan for the next phase/stage;

(4) monitor progress against plan by a numeric control system taking steps to ensure tasks are being completed in a qualitative sense;

(5) plan and control the overall project as a central phased development plan for systems development, with implementation and installation tasks built around the central development, as a network.

This chapter assumes the reader has completed step 1 above and will therefore interpret 2–5 against that background.

Those readers who are not familiar with good data processing project planning and control systems, and therefore do not meet (1) from past experience, further study is recommended on network analysis (PERT), and perhaps the use of 'BIS control' for activity control and business review.

Real time systems do not need new tools for project control. However, real time projects can less often afford to ignore those tools that already exist. Thorough and detailed project planning and control is essential. The time spent in such planning and administration will always be paid back in a more efficient project.

Too many real time project managers have avoided making plans for later stages, during the early stages of the project (feasibility, studies, systems analysis, and design). Often this is because they (rightly) recognize the possible high range of uncertainty in their estimates. However, in all such cases they equally do not recognize when they are beginning to drift off course.

Careful planning with open recognition of high potential inaccuracy is a much better base for the control of successful projects than just hard work and target dates, instead of detail plans. Figure 5.1 illustrates a typical task list prepared during systems analysis for the latter stages of development. The example is a first draft task list and illustrates the level of detail to which *early* estimates should be made.

## 5.2 Technical Design Control

The needs of earlier real time systems identified a further level of project control that has since been applied in a wider context to data base systems and overall systems planning (now referred to as configuration planning and control, CPC). This further level of control is concerned with the planning and progressive monitoring of the projected and actual performance of the final system in operation.

Whereas project control is primarily concerned with estimating, planning and control of the use of men, money and machine resources during project development, technical design control (TDC) is concerned with controlling the hardware resources used in the operational running of the new system. Such control is first applied during development and therefore acts as a control against the prediction of systems performance characteristics as well as eventual operational performance.

An important feature of a technical design control system is the ability to cope with estimates and predictions that vary in levels of detail and accuracy during the progress of the project. Variance from the planned or projected performance requires to be highlighted as soon as the symptoms become apparent.

Just as project control systems should be easy to use and help individual team members so should a technical design control system assist in the rapid evaluation of design options.

### 5.2.1 TECHNICAL DESIGN CONTROL AND THE IMPACT OF MINOR CHANGES

One of the key reasons for the need for technical design control in real time is the non-linear effect of errors in calculation or prediction on the resulting performance. Consider a simple model of a sub-system where the designer has been particularly concerned in the use of a disk file in random access mode. This example will illustrate how several minor errors (5–10 per cent) can quadruple queueing delays. Loading on the disk (see chapter 15 on Timing) may be defined in terms of average values as:

$$\rho_d = n \times l \times p \times t,$$

Where $\rho_d$ is the percentage disk loading
   $n$ is the expected message rate
   $l$ is the number of logical record accesses per message
   $p$ is the number of reads/writes of indexes, data, etc., necessary to achieve a logical access
   $t$ is the physical access time of the device.

In a sample case average values may be:

$n = 12\ 000$ messages per hour
$l = 2$
$p = 2\frac{1}{2}$
$t = 40$ ms.

Thus the file access rate $(ln) = 6\frac{2}{3}$ records per second, and the average access time $(pt) = 100$ ms. Now consider a number of example variances arising in the design process.

The system is further defined to provide for operator correction of errors and the resultant re-entries increase one message type from contributing 10 000 of the original total to 10 500. An increase in the volume of activity on the other message type brings the total message rate $(n)$ to 12 600 messages per hour. Closer analysis of message paths shows $l$ is nearer $2 \cdot 1$. Further analysis of disk overflow shows the possible average value of $p$ to be $2 \cdot 7$ and further study of head shift overheads causes the designer to adjust $t$ to 45 ms.

Most of these changes are small (of the order of 5–10 per cent) and as such if identified in the progress of work on the various elements of the system they might be ignored. However, let us consider the overall performance of the files. Utilization will increase by a multiplicative effect of error, i.e., $\rho$ goes from

$$\rho = \frac{12\ 000 \times 2 \times 2 \cdot 5 \times 40}{3600 \times 1000} = 0 \cdot 66$$

to

$$\frac{12\ 600 \times 2 \cdot 1 \times 2 \cdot 7 \times 45}{3600 \times 1000} = 0 \cdot 90 \quad \text{approximately,}$$

and a simple queueing model would indicate queueing delays rising from $0 \cdot 3$ s in a moderately *stable* queue to $1 \cdot 2$ s *in an unstable queue*. Thus a series of 5–10 per cent drifts in one sub-system's detailed timings have increased its contribution to response times by 300 per cent.

The example above illustrates how minor variances can cause problems if the combined effect is not monitored. In practice, the variances are often much more substantial in detail, and still are not detected early enough when no control system is used. The reader need only consider one or two large real time systems that he has heard of where there has been a late increase in hardware!

### 5.2.2 TECHNICAL DESIGN CONTROL AND RECOGNIZING THE IMPLICATIONS

One of the other problems of developing systems without the disciplines of technical design control is that precise program mechanisms often do not get studied in detail. In the example above, if the initial model is assumed, development can proceed with the view that the file access time is 100 ms (*pt*).

Without close control the file structure could be developed in such a way that, say, $p$ rises from $2 \cdot 5$ to 4 or 5 from indexes and overflows, or $t$ rises from 40 to 100 ms because an over optimistic layout was earlier assumed. The net effect is 100 ms, rising to 500 ms and often not detected because no one has had to quantify the performed characteristics of the design. Perhaps the reader's reaction is to feel that such gross change in one element could not go undetected? Regrettably the history of real time projects, past and recent, indicate the contrary. For example, in one situation the authors were called in to impose technical design control and forecast operational usage in a project already in early testing. The project was led by staff who were not novices in real time systems development, yet early program tests had indicated possible loading problems. The development team had not used any form of technical design control.

In imposing technical design control the detail implications of the designs were forced to the surface, and even at that late stage it was found that the team's assumption on disk service times were as far as $9:1$ too low, and the practical effect of the file structure could result in well over 10 disk accesses for certain single logical tasks. In this case, the lack of formal control (technical design control) during development had meant both the combined and individual effect of detail designs were not seen until testing.

### 5.2.3 TECHNICAL DESIGN CONTROL AS A DESIGN AID

The above examples illustrate the need for a control mechanism in order to identify variances that occur as the design process leads to greater levels of accuracy and in some cases (not shown up in the example above) to greater levels of detail in the breakdown of the elements of the system.

One of the facets of the design process is the number of iterations that can take place. Designers will postulate one possible solution, calculate the performance and then wish to re-calculate performance for a slight variance in design, say, to change of a transaction profile, different assumptions on message rates, change of disk design, change of file overflow, etc. Therefore, as well as a control mechanism, there is a need for a similar working process by which the designer can carry out his calculations, make his minor changes and rapidly recalculate the resulting performance.

Technical design control is not only an effective method for the control of physical resources, but also can be implemented in a form that provides a useful tool for a designer as outlined above. It can provide the methodology which enables changes to be made and their effect to be rapidly assessed by an easy change in the already established documentation.

### 5.2.4 APPLYING DESIGN CONTROL

The precise form of design control used for real time projects is highly dependent on the scale of the project and on the constraints imposed. A low activity rate real time system being loaded into a machine which is largely batch oriented may not be CPU sensitive, but because of the breadth of the application may be very memory sensitive. Equally, another system, with very simple transactions and a very high activity rate, may be performance sensitive if it is the main activity in a small processor. Experience in using design control as consultants working with many clients has shown the authors and their colleagues that once the basic approach is understood a suitable format can be readily devised to meet the requirements of each individual project.

The first step in setting a design control procedure is to recognize how the system can be broken down into logical components. There is a choice of views, so it is important to select a consistent approach across the project. The accuracy of the projected use of resources in the computer will tend to develop in the course of the project in three dimensions, i.e., the dimensions of detail, the dimension of dependence and the dimension of time (see below). In general, the best starting point is to consider a message and associate with it a number of characteristics: its activity rate, the hour of the day, and its need for computer resources (lines, memory CPU time, files, tapes, etc.). Then define the message profile under each of these headings. Now consider the development of information during design under each of the three 'dimensions' mentioned above.

### Detail

As part of the development process from feasibility study through to live operation, the message will become defined in more detail. A main message type used at the beginning of the study may later be defined in terms of several subsidiary types. A major processing routine may be re-defined as sub-routines and later on each of these into sub-routines. This is a practice applied in batch systems for years and clearly fits very well into the transaction environment of real time systems.

At each level of design, calculations or assumptions will be made. If satisfactory performance is achieved, then any subsidiary design of the sub-elements must start off with the objective of meeting an individual performance target compatible with the overall figure at a higher level. For example, suppose resident routine 'A', has a design profile of average path time of 10 ms and memory residence of 60 000 bytes. Then, before design starts on its three sub-elements AA, AB, AC, design targets should be set, e.g.,

(1) The number of accesses of each routine per access of the main routine are:
         AA  0.5
         AB  2
         AC  3
(2) Core resident requirements are: AA  10 k
         AB  30 k
         AC  20 k
(3) CPU processing time targets are: AA  10 ms
         AB   1 ms
         AC   1 ms.

These figures are set as targets for subsidiary level design and are recorded as part of the technical design control process.

If AA, AB, etc., do not meet the criteria, then further detail re-design may immediately be carried out. If the designs come up with performances that are within the criteria or even significantly below the target, then these will be fed into design control and eventually will show up as greater slack within the system. If the variances are outside the performance target, they may be considered to be satisfactory for the time being, but again, their combined effect will show up through design control as shown in the example earlier in this chapter. In this particular case, the combined effect changes in AA, AB, and AC will first show the effect in the predicted performance of the overall module A. In many cases, it is better to review the combined effect before too much re-design to meet more detailed targets. The design can therefore be directed to those areas likely to gain the most benefit.

*Dependence*

As the design progresses, messages will be identified as requiring common resources, such as common routines or access to common file or disk. While the use of such common resources needs to be recorded in the relevant message profiles, the 'resources' themselves need to be developed further once only.

This inter-dependence can be quite complex and can occur at several hierarchical levels, e.g., in one system the following could occur:

– several messages use common sub-routines;
– several routines require logical accesses to the same file;
– different logical accesses to the same file require different mixes of physical accesses;
– physical accesses to different files may use a common disk.

The extent that each level in this hierarchy is reflected under technical design control is very situation dependent. For example, in the illustration above, the disk utilization could be calculated and recorded under each message type, or the logical accesses could be recorded by message type, and independently the physical accesses per logical access could be recorded by access type.

The right choice depends on the nature of the project, and therefore it is important that the whole project team establish at the beginning of the project the approach that they intend to take.

### Time

Apart from the breakdown in detail noted above, detailed estimates change as the system moves from the designing stage to writing modules and eventually to testing. Estimates at any particular level increase in accuracy and progressively move towards a greater certainty. This is no longer a process of

CPU USAGE                    CPC 6/1    Page _____ of _____

                                        Date: _____

PROJECT NAME: _____    Prepared by. _____

        CODE: _____       Reference: _____

| PROCESSING MODULE / MESSAGE TYPE (TT/MN) MSECS | | | | | | | | | CPU USAGE DUE TO FILE ACCESSES | TOTALS |
|---|---|---|---|---|---|---|---|---|---|---|
| | | | | | | | | | | |
| | | | | | | | | | | |
| | | | | | | | | | | |
| | | | | | | | | | | |
| | | | | | | | | | | |

COMMENTS:

References:

**Fig. 5.2**  Sample TDC form—CPU

56

<u>ACTIVITY RATES</u>          CPC 8/2          Page _____ of _____

PROJECT NAME:_____          Date:_____

        CODE:_____          Prepared by:_____

TRANSACTION TYPE:_____          Reference:_____

AVERAGE ACTIVITY RATE:_____per minute

PEAKS OF ACTIVITY:

                  DAILY beginning at ___ for ___ minutes with ratio to average of____

            SECONDARY DAILY beginning at___ for ___ minutes with ratio to average of____

            DAY OF WEEK _____with ratio to average day of_____

            DAY OF MONTH_____with ratio to average day of_____

            DAY OF QUARTER_____with ratio to average day of_____

            DAY OF YEAR_____with ratio to average day of_____

SEASONAL FACTORS:          MONTHLY – _____

                      QUARTERLY – _____

NUMBER OF TERMINALS FOR THIS TRANSACTION TYPE:___ on average;___ at peak

THEORETICAL ACTIVITY PEAK (PEAK NO. OF TERMINALS FOR THIS

            TRANSACTION TYPE ALL OPERATING AT ONCE):_____|per minute

QUOTED ACTIVITY PEAKS –          DAILY:_____|per minute

                          WEEKLY:_____|per minute

                          MONTHLY:_____|per minute

                          QUARTERLY:_____|per minute

                          YEARLY:_____|per minute

        MAXIMUM RATE USED IN SUBSEQUENT CALCULATIONS:_____ per minute

DAILY – HOUR BY HOUR AVAILABLE:

                References:

**Fig. 5.3**   Sample TDC form—transaction

formal breakdown in the design, but a situation of change arising from a later view as results are progressively measured rather than calculated or predicted.

## 5.2.5 ESSENTIAL ELEMENTS OF DESIGN CONTROL

Technical design control becomes part of the standards of the installation or the project and as such needs to relate to other standards such as project control, documentation, methods, and techniques. However, as for most standards, there are common problems and solutions that can be carried across projects. The essential characteristics of a technical design control system include the following:

— formal standards for documentation and recording, including standard forms;

DISC FILE USAGE          CPC 10/1    Page _____ of _____

PROJECT NAME: _____          Date: _____

CODE: _____          Prepared by: _____

FILE NAME: _____          Reference: _____

FILE CHARACTERISTICS:  SIZE _____ CYLS _____ TRKS

BLOCKING FACTOR _____ ;  BLOCK SIZE _____

ORGANIZATION _____ ;  NO. OF RECORDS _____

NAME OF BACK UP FILE (IF ANY): _____

| MESSAGE TYPE | NO. OF ACCESSES PER MESSAGE | | | COMMENTS |
|---|---|---|---|---|
| | READ | WRITE | R/W | |
| | | | | |
| | | | | |
| | | | | |
| | | | | |
| | | | | |
| | | | | |
| | | | | |
| | | | | |

Reference:

**Fig. 5.4**   Sample TDC form—disk

Resource: Disk

Project: GDT7

Version: 2

(All figures are percentages)

| | Time Slot | | |
|---|---|---|---|
| | 8–11 | 11–5 | 5–6 |
| Total | 63 | 42 | 40 |
| Messages update | 3 | 11 | 33 |
| Enquiry | 59·4 | 30·2 | 6·2 |
| Modules   A | 15 | 10 | 10 |
| C | 2 | 8 | 25 |
| BA | 28 | 14 | 3 |
| BB | 4·2 | 2·1 | ·4 |
| BC | 9·7 | 4·9 | 1·0 |
| BD | 3·5 | 1·7 | ·3 |
| BE | — | — | — |

**Fig. 5.5**   Sample TDC entry—disk

— forms that are simple to use as a record during the design process of an element of the system. This record at the end of the design feeds into the overall procedure;

— the approach to transaction breakdown in 'detail', 'dependency' and 'time' is established at the start of the project;

— design control is established immediately after the feasibility study and best estimate/guesses are made for all aspects;

— each breakdown in detail is preceded by an assignment of resource and time targets of the higher level to the sub-elements, so that they properly combine to meet the higher level targets; these then become subsidiary design targets for the next level of detail;

— variances detected at each level are resolved at that level or fed up through the design control system until the variances reach a level where they are either disregarded because their accumulated effect is slight, or they are found so significant that a new design or a new project plan has to be established;

**59**

– technical design control reports are used within the team and are summarized for reporting outside the project.

Examples of technical design control forms are included in Figs. 5.2–5.5. The
examples are typical project tailored forms, and are selected as an illustration, not a
sample set.

### 5.2.6  IS IT WORTH THE EFFORT?

The potential problems of not applying technical design control have been identified; what about the costs? In order to achieve the right form of control for
the first time, a project team must budget either for support by a consultant to
establish the system fairly quickly by drawing on his corporate experience, or
spend several man weeks of design team effort in creating their own controls.
As with project control, the latter approach can be very expensive in effort and
have high risk of only partial success if technical design control experience does
not already exist in the team. However, the benefits of using technical design
control is certainly worth the cost and effort needed to establish it.

The savings arising from early detection of potential failure to meet performance objectives or other design problems can exceed the cost of administration of technical design control and the set up costs. Indeed, the benefits are
more immediate still in that technical design control is also a valuable aid to the
designer in his day to day work.

Consider a typical case. In this project, the wider configuration planning and
control (CPC) system had just been established across the installation and
technical design control was being applied as a sub-set of configuration planning and control for a major real time development project with severe timing
constraints. Technical design control was taken on in the project after the
feasibility study and used from the start of the main development cycle.

At the start, technical design control appeared as an overhead. For example,
an initial design task concerned with handling very heavy loads on the disk
system was expected to take two days but took three days to carry out and
document under design control. However, the results were dramatic. The stage
of development was such that new designs were being evaluated frequently,
and under the old (and common) ways of doing the work it was expected to
take designers about half to one day to review calculations for each of the options. Through the discipline of design control reflected in the initial recording
and the layout of information, designers on this project found they were doing
the necessary re-designs in times varying from a few minutes to an hour, thus
saving about three hours every re-calculation. In the course of the project the
overall savings were significant and clearly the extra control was achieved at a
saving rather than at a cost. The ease and speed of re-calculation additionally
meant that more alternative designs were considered, thus contributing to the
quality of the final design.

**60**

## 5.2.7 WHEN IS TECHNICAL DESIGN CONTROL NEEDED?

In discussing and illustrating design control, it has been necessary to talk about complex situations and increasing levels of detail and complexity in the three dimensions of 'time', 'dependence', and 'details'. Design control can, however, be just as powerful if applied to a few initial elements in a simple system. In another actual case, the design control was chosen only to be applied to main memory utilization. The application was mixed with existing batch work, and was rapidly determined not to be CPU or peripheral critical, but a memory upgrade was close for the installation as a whole, with the real time system likely to tip the balance.

It so happened that in the course of the project the installation, for reasons not connected with this particular project, decided to change its main disk system. The implications were not realized at the time. A minor change in manufacturer's software was required and this led to greater core utilization by resident software and the batch programs. Quick analysis through the help of design control showed that while the real time system was still going to be able to fit into its original target of main memory, the machine was going to be core overloaded because the other elements had expanded. The choice was a cutdown in the batch programs or real time. The usual reaction would have been to try to cut down the batch systems, but as there was no mechanism of control and as several batch systems were involved, the problem appeared quite massive and not capable of solution at reasonable cost.

Fortunately, the design control mechanism in the real time system identified quite clearly where it most used core and the effect of possible increased overlays could be measured. The final decision was to reduce the real time core residence and the change was accomplished successfully with all systems actually fitting into core and without undue increase of real time loadings.

Design control contribution was three-fold:

(1) it identified positively that the real time system (then still in development) would not fit in the reduced core (thus avoiding the 'wait and hope' syndrome);
(2) it readily provided the detailed figures on which to evaluate the implications of different approaches to increased overlay;
(3) the designers, under the discipline of design control, had already included flexibility to change the number of resident modules.

## 5.2.8 PERFORMANCE MEASUREMENT

Early design predictions will be built on the designers' best views of such facets as average instruction speeds, memory usage and file handling mechanisms. Many real time development projects have hit problems because the basic assumptions were based on false premises.

Where such facets are indicated as being critical by technical design control, then special attention needs to be paid to the precise basis for the estimates. Often the performance of software (such as file handlers, operating system calls, etc.) can be interpreted if examined in terms of its specification and description of implementation.

As part of the design process, real time designers are recommended to develop and use measuring techniques to determine, *during* development, the performance characteristics and then update technical design control entries produced from the first designs.

A typical test on, say, an index sequential system, may involve a dummy program issuing several thousand accesses to a suitable dummy file. Another may use sophisticated hardware/software monitors to determine other characteristics. In this context, experimental measurement of sub-system performance is part of design. Waiting until the testing phase is too late.

**Part 2**

# Stages of development

# 6. Systems Analysis in Real Time

The use of the terms 'systems analyst' and 'systems analysis' without definition often leads to misunderstanding, because installations have different definitions of the analyst job specification and of the analysis phases of a project. The tasks involved in analysis, both in the feasibility study and in the systems analysis phase itself, are broadly defined in chapter 4. Within this book the term systems analyst is used to describe the staff responsible for carrying out the tasks described in that chapter.

The term 'designer' is used to describe the role of those staff responsible for the project phase after systems analysis—computer systems design. However, as discussed in chapter 7, designers may assist in feasibility studies and systems analysis. Thus, for the purposes of this chapter it is assumed that the analyst is concerned with all project development activities outside of computer system design and programming. More detail of the activities involved are shown in Table 6.1.

Figure 6.1 illustrates in outline the interaction between these related activities for one project, commencing from the start of systems analysis. The other staff roles and activity involved with that of the analyst are also identified.

#### Table 6.1   Activities of the Analyst

— Identifying and surveying opportunities for benefit from computerization with the user.

— Carrying out a feasibility study to determine the economic viability of the system and the techniques to be used, including the applicability of real time.

— Carrying out the systems analysis phase.

— Liaising with designers during computer system design.

— Planning and carrying out system and acceptance testing.

— Planning and assisting in file conversion.

— Specifying and implementing new office procedures.

— Planning and carrying out user training.

— Planning and assisting in control of cut-over and phasing in of the new system.

— General activity in liaising with the user during all project phases.

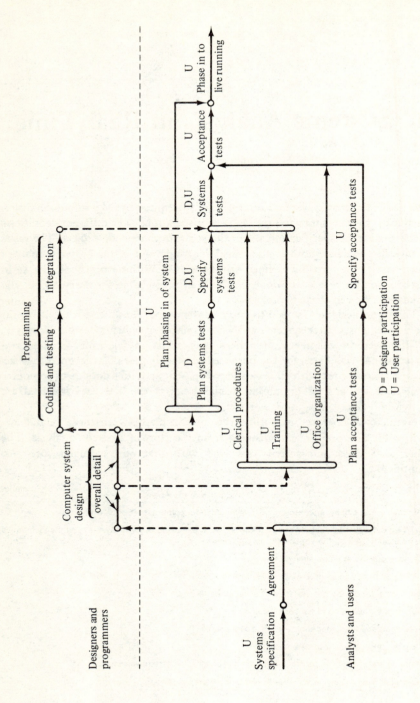

**Fig. 6.1** Relationship of analyst responsibilities

This chapter covers the analyst's activity prior to the start of the system testing phase. Chapter 8 deals with activities which follow the completion of a computer system design phase, many of which also involve the analysts.

## 6.1 Feasibility Study

When a system, for which real time is a potential technique, is being studied there are often also several other options to be considered, ranging from normal batch processing, through remote job entry, and terminal based data collection, to full real time updating. In any such system there is usually an optimum mixture of these techniques. For example; updating via a remote job entry link, with corrections of exceptions only via interactive terminals.

The feasibility study can therefore be seen to have several objectives. First it must provide a basis for user management to evaluate the project; thus it must communicate effectively to non-computer people. Also it must determine whether the project will bring benefits and is cost justified, before significant expense is incurred. Further, it must establish whether the project is technically feasible and achievable within projected costs, and finally must set a general project framework in terms of systems definition and outline design as a basis for the systems analysis phase. This means an initial determination of the complexity of use of real time, and the mix with batch, and other techniques.

**Table 6.2**   Activities in the Feasibility Study

— Definition of scope of system and its objectives.

— Study of existing system.

— Identification of its deficiencies.

— Outline specification of new facilities required.

— Identification of the potential system solutions.

— Outline design and costing for each solution.

— Choice of preferred solution.

— Costing of preferred solution in more detail.

— Costing of next project phase (systems analysis).

— Provisional costing of subsequent project phases.

— Statement of benefits of new system.

— Preparation of feasibility report.

A typical feasibility study can take 6–12 man months with two analysts involved, both very experienced, and at least one with real time computer system design experience. They obviously require a good knowledge of the business area which the system is to serve. In addition to analysts, it is desirable to have a member of the team who normally works within the user area.

Actual involvement of a user helps to overcome one of the common problems which occur in real time systems, that of lack of understanding by the user of the techniques involved. A potential first time user often becomes enthusiastic about using terminals within his environment, and intuitively thinks of a full real time updating system backing that part of the system visible to him. The feasibility study provides an opportunity for a user representative and the data processing department jointly to investigate and understand the real business justifications for the use of real time, and to evaluate the benefits it will bring.

The feasibility study involves the broad activities given in Table 6.2. Table 6.3 gives a list of contents of a typical feasibility report.

**Table 6.3** Typical Feasibility Report Contents

Management summary

Scope of the study

Benefits of the system
    Cost saving
    Profit generating
    Improved resource utilization

Costs
    Hardware and software
    Ancillary equipment
    Development
    Implementation
    Operating
    Comparison with existing

Existing system
System requirements
System approaches considered
    Brief description
    Comparison
    Conclusion and choice of potential system

Potential system
    Description
    Outline specification
    Implications for adjacent systems
    Organization and staffing
    Equipment
    Security and standby
    Rejected options and reasons

Development plan

In investigating the existing system, the analysts will be carrying out much the same activity as in the normal systems analysis phase. If the feasibility study is to be cost effective it naturally must not go into as much detail. The effort is best limited to study of the transactions which occupy most clerical time, or are of high volume (these are often synonymous), since these will have major impact on terminal operator and computer utilization. Fortunately, in many cases the selection can in this way be limited to 10 per cent of all transaction types. Similarly, large bulk, and frequently accessed files receive the most attention. The processing of the high volume transactions must also be specified in sufficient detail to enable a degree of computer system design to be carried out.

**68**

It is of particular importance to identify known deficiencies in the system, and to discuss and agree potential new system facilities with the user. These can sometimes have an important bearing on the cost of the eventual system. For example, if a weakness of a given system were the user's inability to make rapid enquiries of stock levels, it might be decided that these should be provided via terminals in the new system. In this case the new enquiry itself may well be a high volume transaction with great effect on the cost of the system. Unfortunately, the volume can only be estimated, but it is better to estimate than not to take account of the transaction at all. It is sometimes helpful to set a range in which the volume is expected to fall, and to carry out costing for both extremes to determine the sensitivity of the cost to the accuracy of the figures. If the cost is very sensitive to the amount of use of such a facility, it may be possible to set a policy which limits its use to a certain level.

In determining the potential system solutions, it must be emphasized that it is worth spending some time and research in first setting out a complete set of options. These should include those which appear more mundane (and achievable!) as well as the more obvious, such as full real time updating. The first list can usually be pruned to a short list for more detailed study. This can be illustrated as follows.

If increased accuracy has been defined as an objective, because of existence of a complex coding system which generates costly error correction procedures, any potential solution not making significant impact on accuracy will be discarded.

For each solution in the identified short list, computer system design is carried out to sufficient level to achieve a realistic assessment of performance and costs. This activity is discussed in more detail in chapter 7.

The cost of the next project phase—systems analysis—can be estimated with some accuracy. Subsequent phases should be estimated to give a budgetary indication of the overall project cost. To carry out these costings, those transactions, files, and processes not studied in detail must at least be identified. Costs can be estimated by judging complexity, size, and volume in comparison to those studied more fully.

Because of the importance of the decisions resulting from the Feasibility Study it follows that analysts of high skill and proven achievement must be employed. The qualities relevant to carrying out the systems analysis phase itself are important—for example, patience, persistence, attention to detail, and knowledge of business. However, in the feasibility study, the analysts also require wide knowledge of possible techniques, imagination in applying them to the problem, and sound judgement in assessing the benefits to the business.

## 6.2   Systems Analysis Phase

The systems analysis phase is concerned with investigating in detail the existing system (data gathering and consolidation), analysing its shortcomings, and developing a new or modified information flow for the application in question. This flow is documented in the system specification, which forms a vehicle of communication and agreement with both users and computer system designers.

### 6.2.1 DIFFERENCES FROM BATCH PROCESSING

Systems analysis as defined above is not different in principle to a common procedural approach in batch systems development. The separation of systems analysis and computer system design is not novel. But in real time systems development, this separation is fundamental. Many installations produce successful batch systems by combining what have been called here the systems analysis and computer systems design phases. In fact, the term computer systems designer has no significance in such installations. The analyst might even produce program specifications as his first major output document. Where this works it is a tribute to the experience of the analyst! The chances of short cutting in real time, however, are very much reduced due to the relative shortage of skills, and the wide range of complexity of systems which can be created to give the same visible results.

The division between analysis and design is thus important in order to place the proper emphasis on design in real time systems. However, the flow of development must be smooth and therefore design aspects must be borne in mind during analysis. A good feasibility study that has included an effective broad initial design can provide the framework needed. Some further design work may also be desirable in the systems analysis phase. The part that design plays in these earlier project phases is discussed in chapter 7, but briefly the main objective is to narrow the attention of the designers in the computer system design phase to carrying out detailed work on the system option which is best fitted for the given application.

The analysts in the systems analysis phase thus have the job of providing the detail of the new information flow required of the system, within the general technical framework identified in the feasibility study.

It is true of many batch systems that there can be a great deal of tolerance in the quantitive information which an analyst defines, with little change in the system performance. For example, in straight forward COBOL written systems using fixed format records, if the analyst gets the maximum field size right that is all that is necessary. Similarly he can sometimes be quite casual about determining the average number of occurrences of a field, so long as the maximum is known. Both for input and output, the timing of the transfer may be entirely independent of the actual number of occurrences, e.g., it takes no more time to output a full line than a few characters on the normal line printer.

This quantitive aspect of analysis is the biggest difference between batch and real time analysis. Quantitive information typically needs careful determination in real time systems, particularly for critical aspects of the system. The analysts therefore need some real time system design knowledge, or preferably, a participating team member or close adviser who has done it before. In this way they can avoid wasting effort in obtaining detailed figures for non-critical aspects of the system, for fear of missing key data. Some examples of these considerations are given later in the chapter.

## 6.2.2 SYSTEMS SPECIFICATION

An example systems specification contents page is given in Table 6.4. This section deals mainly with that part of the specification which specifies the information flow of the systems, since this is most different from normal batch practice. First, an outline of a documentation technique is given, followed by discussion of the quantitative aspects which are particularly important. An example is used to illustrate both.

**Table 6.4**  Typical Systems Specification Contents

Management summary

Scope of systems analysis and specification

System requirements

Proposed system
  Summary flow diagrams
  Non-computer system details
  – Logical inputs
  – Logical outputs
  – Main processes
  – Logical files
  – Controls
  Interface to other systems
  Organization and Staffing
  Legal and privacy aspects
  Subsequent development

Cost and benefits
  Development costs
  Running costs
  Benefits
  – Calculable
  – Intangible

Development plan
  Detailed estimates for system design phase
  Indicative estimates for other phases
  Schedules
  Personnel and equipment needs

Conclusions and recommendations

## Example System

The system is a mail-order processing system in which the orders are raised by agents by reference to a standard catalogue. Items are coded to a high level only, since experience has proved that the error rate is unacceptable if the users are asked to code to a low level. So, for example, a code for 'Shoes, Oxford' is provided, but coding of colour and size is not. Details such as the latter are entered as part of the description by the person ordering.

To enable a specific order to be completed at the centre, the clerks must first see the range of possibilities and their codes within a certain overall product code, together with the stock availability, since popular products often sell out. They can then input a firm order, completely coded, against known availability.

*Documentation of Information Flow*

In the example system, the analyst knows from the feasibility report that the use of video terminals is recommended. However, he concentrates at the systems analysis stage on establishing in detail the information flow required by the system. So, for the order transaction, he specifies the logical message pair structure (later computer system design work might decide that the actual physical number of message pairs, imposed by terminal characteristics, is greater). This structure is documented as in Fig. 6.2 together with the number

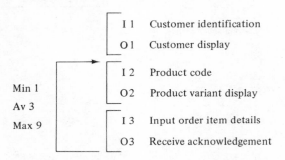

Fig. 6.2   Message structure of order transaction

of iterations within the transaction caused by multiple order items being ordered. The figure also identifies the input and output specification sheets. In the example given, the number of logical message pairs is dictated only by the required information flow at the terminal. Customer credit worthiness and validity of identifier must be established first. Then all possible varieties of a product must be displayed to the operator to enable him to separately code each item. Figure 6.3 shows the inter-relationships between all the specification elements in the transaction. Again it must be stressed that the analyst should not be required to make the processes correspond to actual processing modules, or file groups to final physical files. Only the logic is being established definitely at this stage. Some outline examples of the specification sheets are given in Figs. 6.4–6.6.

The documentation so far described specifies all normal messages. But messages also need to be sent to inform the terminal operator of error conditions. To avoid complication in the message structure definition, the error messages can be kept as a simple list which is referenced by the procedure specifications (P1–3). At analysis stage only error messages for data errors are defined. Messages informing of hardware or software malfunction, and recovery messages, will be specified during computer system design in consultation with the analyst.

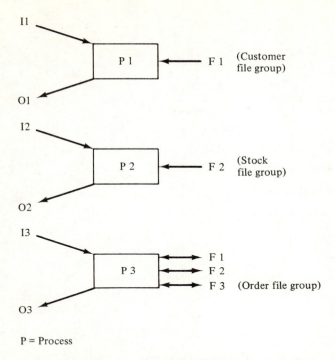

P = Process

**Fig. 6.3**  Documentation relationship for order transaction

| I3 Order item detail | | | | | | |
|---|---|---|---|---|---|---|
| Level | Field name | Type | Occurrence | | | Comment |
| | | | Min | Av/Abs | Max | |
| 2 | Order item | | | 1 | | |
| 3 | First choice | | | 1 | | |
| 4 | Product code | | | | | |
| 4 | Sub-code | | | | | |
| 3 | Second choice | | 0 | 0·1 | 1 | |
| 4 | Product code | | | | | |
| 4 | Sub-code | | | | | |

**Fig. 6.4**  Example of input specification

O 2 Product variant display

| Level | Field name | Type | Occurrence | | | Comment |
|---|---|---|---|---|---|---|
| | | | Min | Av/Abs | Max | |
| 2 | Product header | | | 1 | | |
| 3 | Code | | | 1 | | |
| 3 | Description | | | 1 | | |
| 2 | Product variant | | 1 | 20 | 50 | |
| 3 | Sub-product code | | | 1 | | |
| 3 | Description | | | 1 | | |
| 3 | Price | | | 1 | | |

**Fig. 6.5** Example of output specification

F2 Product file group

| Level | Field name | Type | Occurrence | | | Comment |
|---|---|---|---|---|---|---|
| | | | Min | Av/Abs | Max | |
| 2 | Product header | | | 1 | | |
| 3 | Code | | | 1 | | |
| 3 | Description | | | 1 | | |
| 2 | Product variant | | 1 | 14 | 50 | |
| 3 | Sub-code | | | 1 | | |
| 3 | Description | | | 1 | | |
| 3 | Price | | | 1 | | |
| 3 | Free stock | | | 1 | | |
| 3 | Location | | | 1 | | |

**Fig. 6.6** Example file group specification

## Sensitive Statistics

In any system the analysts must take special care in gathering statistics which are likely to have considerable bearing on the amount of software and machine resources required. Real time design experience in the analysis team is an asset in concentrating attention on the really essential statistics. In the example system as described above, the statistics of importance are as follows:

(1) number of order transactions in peak day;
(2) occurrence of line items within the order (Fig. 6.2);
(3) occurrence of product variants within the product file group (Fig. 6.6);
(4) occurrence of product variants within the product variant display (Fig. 6.5);
(5) number of products and volatility.

On the other hand, it is unlikely that it is worth a lot of effort to refine the occurrence of second choice within the order item input details message, since, even if the average given were 100 per cent out, a relatively small difference in transaction time would result.

For item (3) and possibly (4) above, minimum, average and maximum occurrence is probably insufficient to enable detailed design choices such as block size to be made. The actual distribution is probably required. Figure 6.7 shows an example for the occurrence of variants within the product file groups. If the file is volatile (i.e., many deletions and insertions) an estimate of how the distribution might change in time is necessary also, probably based on historical performance.

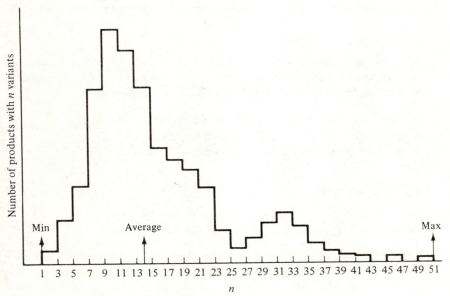

**Fig. 6.7**  Distribution of variants

The average number of variants in Figs. 6.5 and 6.6 are different. This can happen in any system, but is particularly important in real time systems. The average 14 (Fig. 6.6) is the simple average of the number of variants for all the products. The average 20 (Fig. 6.5) is the average of those that are to be displayed. The increase means that the more popular and thus more frequently displayed have a greater number of variants. These 'dynamic' averages are often the most difficult to establish. It may well be necessary to work through several typical days' transactions, noting the record which each requires to access, and the number of variable items (e.g., product variants) which would have been output in each case. These are then averaged and the distribution is detailed in a similar way to that in Fig. 6.7.

In the example system we are considering, transactions arrive by post. It is thus important to know the relative numbers in first and second posts, and delays caused by necessary clerical handling.

For other types of transaction, such as those originating over the telephone, the distribution of arrival rate throughout the peak day must be measured. In determining the peak load, not only the transaction rate is of importance. In the example system, the peak day could be two weeks before Easter if judged from the point of view of numbers of orders coming into the system. It is possible that another time in the year, perhaps just before Christmas, may have a higher load because the number of line items per order increases. This might arise because the products suitable for small gifts are ordered much more frequently at this time. This product popularity shift could also be accompanied by a shift in the average number of product variants to be displayed.

The analyst obviously needs to choose shrewdly where he directs the majority of his effort in establishing volumes of transactions and their constituent parts.

## Other Specification Details

The specification should give an indication of response time requirements for each transaction, but should avoid being too restrictive on the designers. A statement of response requirement, as follows, is an example.

| TRANSACTION | REQUIRED RESPONSE |
|---|---|
| Order entry | average of seconds |
| Order hard-copy | minutes. |
| Etc. | |

This is far better than,

| Order entry | 98 per cent in $\leqslant 4$ s |
|---|---|
| Order hard-copy, etc. | average 1·5 min |

which could result in the designers' wasting resources in trying to achieve such over-stringent objectives which, having been agreed with the user, are thus regarded as inviolable. The specification should also contain an appendix which gives envisaged designs for illustrative purposes only. These, particularly in the case of terminal layouts, can be a useful source of discussion with the users and designers, but should not be regarded as binding on the latter at this stage. The need for computer system design within the systems analysis phase is discussed further in chapter 7.

## 6.3   Office System Design

The systems specification is used by the designers, first in establishing the overall computer system design, and then in detailed design as described in chapter 7. After overall computer system design has been completed, the analysts can commence office system design, since by then the shape of the system has been established. Of course, some details will need to be filled in during and after detailed design.

Office systems design (and office is used here to include any premises where terminals are to be installed) involves those activities concerned with organization of staff, office layout, and the clerical procedures associated with the new system.

### 6.3.1   OFFICE ORGANIZATION

The advent of the new system changes the emphasis of many existing functions and probably introduces new ones into the office. The structure of the new organization and description of the new and redefined functions needs to be decided well in advance of the live date. In setting down the new organization, it is essential that management and supervisory personnel are responsible for determining the new organization, but considerable discussion with the analysts is necessary so that they can become fully aware of all that is involved.

There are three basic reasons for establishing the new organization early. These arise from the need to allocate existing staff in advance to their new function, so that they have time to become familiar with their new roles, recruit new personnel if existing staff cannot be converted to new roles, and set up and monitor training for the new roles.

In some cases, negotiations with unions or staff associations are necessary. Such discussions can take appreciable elapsed time and are best started early to prevent them from falling on the critical path to live running.

Similarly, training (which is discussed in more detail in chapter 9) can take considerable elapsed time, and cannot be started until the new organization and function have been mapped out, and staff allocated or recruited.

### 6.3.2   MANUAL PROCEDURES

Separate written procedures should be produced for each terminal based function associated with the system. Only those transactions appropriate to a given function should be included for that function. In this way, a measure of security is provided quite apart from that designed into the computer system. The procedures carried out by clerks not directly associated with terminals should also be specified.

The procedures for terminal operators are best indexed by transaction type. Within each, the main path through the transaction should be given in detail, specifying what fields should be keyed at each stage, what output to expect, and what checks should be applied, or what decisions need to be taken. Any branches within the logical flow of the transaction should be specified, together with the means of deciding which to take. It is probably better if all error messages are listed alphabetically or by identity number at the end of the transaction description, with subsequent actions specified for each.

As well as specifying the above details, it is desirable for the procedures to describe in layman's terms how each transaction affects the files in the system, and its relationship to other transactions within the sphere of operation of the operator concerned. The clerical procedures should most certainly be completed before system testing starts, so that all transactions can be tested by following the instructions laid down in the procedure manuals.

### 6.3.3 OFFICE PHYSICAL DESIGN

The new system, with its introduction of terminals, involves considerable changes in physical layout and necessary services. Amongst the factors to be considered are the following:

- furniture for terminals and operators,
- power supplies,
- cabling, modems, concentrator housing,
- operator telephone facilities,
- standby telephone facilities,
- document stands and trays,
- quick access manual files,
- document storage space,
- engineering access,
- sound insulation (for character printers),
- lighting,
- flow of documentation,
- postal services.

Often, many of these aspects are ignored until far too late. Early planning is important to ensure that lead time for order and installation of facilities is sufficient. Frequently, other departments in the company are involved who perhaps have never dealt with anything like this before. The necessary communication by the analyst can take considerable time. For example it is a fundamental consideration if a complete new office is required by the new system. It is not until detailed physical planning has been carried out that this can be built, or if built to an approximate specification of requirement, fitting cannot be started until such planning is completed.

The impact of the new system on the behavioural aspects of office procedures warrants close attention. Special emphasis should be placed on the initial implementation.

# 7. Computer Systems Design

Computer system design is of paramount importance in achieving the objectives of a system within limited resources and for reasonable cost. The history of real time projects suggests that those projects that neglect design are likely to:

- achieve the approximate system originally defined, but perhaps with considerable growth in hardware costs, development effort and elaspsed time or, a little worse,
- reduce objectives mid project, but still with growing use of resources or, at the worst,
- be cancelled mid-project.

This contrasts with batch situations, where design is an important discipline but not designing at all is less often a disaster. However, batch only installations are increasingly recognizing design as an important stage in development, and that attitude must be carried forward to real time projects, perhaps with greater emphasis.

While often the natural inclination of those working in real time for the first time is to rush design (and get on with the programming) the opposite should be the case. Good careful computer systems design (and associated planning and control) has consistently been reflected positively in later stages of the project by smoother development and fewer surprises, easier interpretation, less error in performance projection, and greater ability to cope with externally injected problems.

This chapter first looks at when computer system design should be carried out and its objectives. It then examines the organization and control of the computer system design phase of a project. In considering the design phase, the chapters which relate to design activity are identified and set in context.

## 7.1 Computer Systems Design and Project Phases

The main computer design effort is applied during the design phase of a real time project. However, to ensure a smooth development cycle and a sound basis for successive agreement and authorization at major check points, some

**79**

design is also required in earlier phases, e.g., as part of the feasibility study, and before completion of the system analysis phase.

The main difference in the real time computer system design work as applied in these three stages is in the depth of detail. The overall approach remains the same. The variation in depth of design arises out of the different design objectives of each stage.

### 7.1.1 OBJECTIVES IN THE FEASIBILITY STUDY

The structure of the feasibility study has been discussed in chapter 6, where the need to investigate and cost various possible alternative systems was identified.

The need to identify a complete list of possible system solutions was established. Apart from identifying how well these satisfy fundamental system objectives such as speed and accuracy, it is necessary to establish the cost in equipment, development, and production running. It is obviously impossible to do this without carrying out computer system design to a certain level. This level must be carefully balanced to minimize the cost of the feasibility study, while at the same time enabling the costs of the alternatives to be determined sufficiently accurately for a selection and the cost-benefit analysis to be valid.

The objective in the computer system design must be to establish technical feasibility, cost the hardware and determine other operating costs, and enable estimation of the cost of development and acquired software. The amount of detail will need to be judged within this context.

In establishing technical feasibility, the computer system design must be sufficient to identify the type of hardware and software and degree of technical complexity required by the system alternatives. This must be judged within the policy constraints and available skills of the particular installation and its users.

Given that the solution is technically feasible, the cost of hardware is determined by carrying out further computer system design. The major influences on hardware cost are the higher volume transactions, the larger and more frequently accessed files, the software used, the fail-soft technique, and the number and remoteness of locations. The design will follow the general principles of overall design in the computer system design phase. Exact specification of field layouts is not important unless it would affect the cost. For example, a display to a video is sufficient if designed to the level which enables it to be determined that it will occupy, say, one screen display, and will be readable and understandable by the user.

Utilizations of main storage, disk storage, disk channels, etc., are estimated as described in chapter 15, to check that the hardware capacity is adequate.

Thus, to complete the feasibility study, a computer system design (even if only in outline) must be established. The system is then timed using identified data volumes to establish that the hardware/design meets required performance criteria.

## 7.1.2 OBJECTIVES IN SYSTEMS ANALYSIS

In the project structure discussed in chapters 4 and 6, the systems analysis phase is directed at specifying the applications system in detail. Chapter 6 showed how this involved identifying the interactions required at the terminal and defining in detailed logical terms the input and output messages, the processing logic, and the file content. The main purpose of the systems analysis phase is to specify in detail the information flow required to meet the application requirement in logical terms. However, some degree of physical design—computer system design—is necessary or desirable during systems analysis. It is required in order to improve communication with the user, bring the cost/risk/time predictions up to date, and then re-check the economic feasibility of the project, and, finally, to evaluate alternative approaches to systems elements.

For the first of these three reasons, the computer system design is mainly concentrated on the interface to the user. It results in a set of provisional designs for transaction sequences as they will appear on the terminals. The presentation is most understandable when actual examples of typical transactions are used and are thus easy to visualize. These are not to be regarded as binding on the computer system design phase itself, and are normally not complete definitions of the transactions, but very useful feedback from the users can result. An actual mock-up of these transactions on the terminals to be used is very often most effective in achieving the appropriate dialogue between the analysts and users.

For the second reason, computer system design is used to revise the feasibility study designs in the light of the better information available, and so will be concerned with all areas of design. Again the level must be restricted to limit the work while achieving reasonable confidence in cost predictions. If, for some reason, a full feasibility study were not carried out, this design work is all the more essential, and must be done for all systems alternatives. Of course, it is better to carry out systems analysis within the context of one, or at most two, system alternatives previously decided upon in the feasibility study, since the specific information required usually differs in certain areas, at least in emphasis, for different alternative solutions.

For the third reason the analyst will need to establish systems features at a detailed level (one at a time) with an understanding of the design and hence cost implications. Chapter 2 identified some trade offs from a user's view. Clearly the design view of these features need to be established during analysis.

All computer system design carried out during systems analysis should be documented and included with the systems specification. It is best presented as an additional report or an appendix, and should be regarded as indicative rather than binding on the computer system design phase which is to follow.

Firm estimates for the resources, time scales and cost involved in the computer system design phase must be made at the end of systems analysis. The detailed planning of the design phase is, however, best left until the initial tasks of the phase have been carried out.

## 7.2   The Computer System Design Phase

While all project phases are important, it is the computer system design phase which is fundamental in ensuring success of a real time project. Because of the complex interactions between the various parts of a real time system, it is essential to ensure in advance that the parts fit together in a composite whole which is achievable within available or planned resources.

This complexity also demands that the overall system be broken down into discrete yet compatible sub-systems which different people can develop. If the computer system design is good, the sub-systems can be integrated together smoothly after separate development and testing.

The difficulty and slowness of programming and testing often historically associated with real time systems arises from bad computer system design. The problems have often arisen, not in developing sub-systems, but in the redesign and re-development which stemmed from difficulties encountered when these sub-systems were put together. One example of this was a system in which the transaction processing and recovery logic were incompatible. The transaction processing logic wrote input messages to the log tape on the assumption that in recovery these were picked up and reprocessed. The recovery logic, on the other hand, worked on the assumption that it picked up updated file records on the log, aligned the files to point of failure, and requested re-input of messages from terminals which had not completed an update at that time. Both sub-systems worked fully, within the assumptions of the designers, before integration was attempted. Obviously, if a composite design had been established first the delays, arguments, and redevelopment which resulted in this case would have been avoided.

### 7.2.1   STARTING POINT OF THE COMPUTER SYSTEM DESIGN PHASE

In view of the need to achieve compatibility across the system, the computer system design phase is ideally carried out as a period of intensive activity within the data processing department, with no reference to the user until it has ended. Apart, that is, from liaison and discussion which is aimed at maintaining the essential user involvement. But a minimum of discussion about the required information flow of the system should be necessary in the ideal. Such discussion is disruptive because it interferes with the design work and also shifts the ground on which the design is based. An agreed system specification which fully documents the required information flow is thus essential before the computer system design phase is started.

But back in the real world, as discussed in chapters 2 and 6, the design phase can identify systems facilities that are non-feasible or very costly to implement. In such cases, the designer must refer the facts to the analyst or user rather than striving in isolation to provide the facility by a complex and unnecessarily costly design.

One of the great advantages of using computer staff with real time design experience and analysis skills in the early project phases is that the preliminary designs carried out during the feasibility study and system analysis tend to resolve the majority of these cases at the right time.

## 7.2.2 PLAN FOR COMPUTER SYSTEM DESIGN PHASE

The broad tasks involved are as shown in Fig. 7.1.

---

Starting Point:

System specification

TASKS:

```
 (1)  Planning for CSD
 (2)  Overall CSD
 (3)  Document overall CSD
 (4)  Timing
 (5)  Set objectives for detailed CSD tasks
 (6)  Detailed CSD
 (7)  Produce system design specification
 (8)  Final timing
 (9)  Plan for next phase
(10)  Review costs
(11)  Presentation
(12)  Agreement
```

---

**Fig. 7.1**   Summary plan for computer system design

The objective of overall computer system design is to establish a coherent framework within which the detailed tasks of computer system design are controlled. Tasks 2, 4, and 5 are discussed in section 7.2.3, while tasks 6–12 are investigated in section 7.2.4.

The planning task (1) involves the following:

— Setting up of the core of the team.
— Familiarization and clarification of the systems specification.
— Investigating the hardware and software existing and planned within the installation.
— Deciding on adequacy of standards and if necessary defining appropriate extensions for the computer system design phase.
— Planning the staff required and arranging for training in areas where it is needed.
— Broadly scheduling staff.
— Setting up project control, technical design control (if not established in earlier phases), management reporting, team communication procedures and overall estimating for the computer system design phase.

In selecting the design team and in particular the chief designer (see chapter 4) the right type of design experience is more important than detailed knowledge of, say, a given communications software package, since part of the team's work should result in the choice of the specific techniques to be used. Often it pays to consider options beyond those offered immediately by the main frame manufacturer, as with terminals or real time software packages.

The core of the team should be involved during the computer system design phase and beyond, and thus forms the main vehicle for communication and control throughout.

Project control is set up during project planning, but since the first task—overall computer system design—determines the specific tasks in detailed computer system design, the lower level tasks appropriate to the latter can be set up and estimated at that level only immediately prior to the start of detailed design.

### 7.2.3 OVERALL COMPUTER SYSTEM DESIGN

The objective of this task is to establish a design which is cost effective and achievable within the available resources. The level of detail to which it goes is determined in general terms by the need to set a framework for detailed design which is self consistent, and which will provide guidelines for subsequent design so that:

- design can proceed in detail in discrete areas like terminal network design without invalidating work in other areas by producing logical incompatibilities;
- physical restraints on use of resources can be realistically set to give a means of controlling the tendency for cost-drift during detail design.

The overall design should consider the following main areas:

*Transaction Handling*

Logical transactions are broken down into physical messages as they appear on the terminals, not to character detail but identifying such prime aspects as means of achieving continuity within the computer and at the terminal, error control, position of recovery, start and end-of-day messages, transaction numbering, batch control techniques. Maximum degree of compatibility in layouts and sequence between transaction is achieved to reduce operator training and programming costs. Associated clerical activities are identified.

*Processing*

The processing routines required to match the terminal sequences are identified and described in outline.

*Data Files*

All main files, system files such as logging and terminal context maintenance files, temporary work and core files are identified. Medium, access method, organization, blocking, key structure are decided for each file.

*Fail-soft*

Logging methods, data and media, are set. Outline plans for batch and on-line recovery programs, file integrity assurance programs, redundant hardware, and necessary software are also established.

### Program Structure

Communications and real-time program organization software packages to be used or requirements for own written versions are identified.

### Overlaying Technique

Decide whether standard manufacturer's software is adequate or own system is to be used. Outline own system.

### Testing and Integration

Choose standard testing tools or define requirement for own. Check that integration of parts of program is achievable under test harnesses.

### Timing

Initial timings are carried out on the design so far to test that the system is achievable within cost justified resources.

### Security

Outline system file access requirements, and their effect on transaction design (e.g., passwords).

### Interface to Batch Processing Outline Design of Batch Suites

Break down supporting batch processing into suites. Identify programs, with brief descriptions of program logic.

The overriding aim is to achieve the simplest possible design compatible with the application requirement. Obviously, the real time elements of the system are minimized at this stage. Also, potentially expensive areas like fail-soft are carefully considered. If, for example, recovery can be achieved by simple batch programs instead of the complex solution and on-line recovery processing, the system will be much cheaper and less risky.

Documentation of the overall computer system design needs to be as brief and understandable as possible in view of its important function as a central means of communication. It is suggested that maximum use should be made of diagrams which link related aspects of the system together. Figure 7.1 illustrates in outline a useful charting technique. Apart from diagrams of this type the documentation can be a simple narrative description of the functioning of the various aspects of the system.

Following the completion of the timing activity, the resource utilization of some parts of the system can be determined and recorded. Occasionally, a decision on a specific technique may not have been taken because detailed design is necessary for a final decision. However, the alternatives should be timed to the most accurate level possible at this stage. Subsequent detailed design can then be controlled against these physical criteria using TDC.

During the documentation of the overall design a comprehensive framework should have been established for later technical control (see section 5.2).

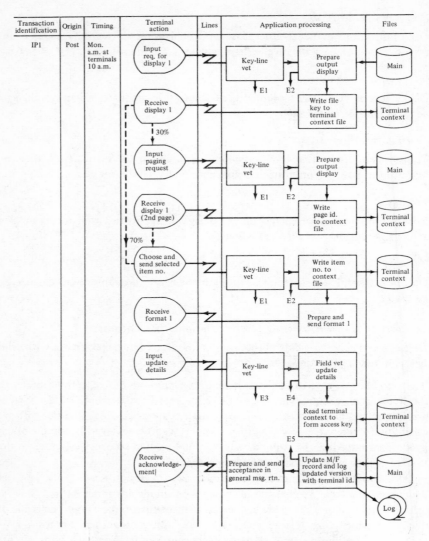

| Transaction identification | Origin | Timing | Terminal action | Lines | Application processing | | Files |
|---|---|---|---|---|---|---|---|
| IP1 | Post | Mon. a.m. at terminals 10 a.m. | Input req. for display 1 | | Key-line vet | Prepare output display | Main |
| | | | Receive display 1 | | | Write file key to terminal context file | Terminal context |
| | | | Input paging request | | Key-line vet | Prepare output display | Main |
| | | | Receive display 1 (2nd page) | | | Write page id. to context file | Terminal context |
| | | | Choose and send selected item no. | | Key-line vet | Write item no. to context file | Terminal context |
| | | | Receive format 1 | | | Prepare and send format 1 | |
| | | | Input update details | | Key-line vet | Field vet update details | |
| | | | | | | Read terminal context to form access key | Terminal context |
| | | | Receive acknowledge-ment | | Prepare and send acceptance in general msg. rtn. | Update M/F record and log updated version with terminal id. | Main |
| | | | | | | | Log |

**Fig. 7.2**  Overall computer system design diagram

At the end of overall computer system design, the detailed computer system design tasks can be determined and staff scheduled specifically. Areas of interface between teams, identified within overall computer system design, should be specified in detail by agreement before the further design tasks are commenced.

### 7.2.4  DETAILED COMPUTER SYSTEM DESIGN

The overall plan shown in Fig. 7.1 can now be expressed in more detail. Main task 6 might be broken down into sub-tasks as follows:

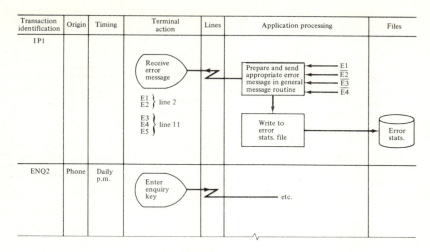

| Transaction identification | Origin | Timing | Terminal action | Lines | Application processing | Files |
|---|---|---|---|---|---|---|
| I P1 | | | Receive error message | | Prepare and send appropriate error message in general message routine ← E1, E2, E3, E4 | |
| | | | E1, E2 } line 2 | | | |
| | | | E3, E4, E5 } line 11 | | Write to error stats. file | Error stats. |
| ENQ2 | Phone | Daily p.m. | Enter enquiry key | | etc. | |

**Fig. 7.2.**  *Continued*

- file design;
- terminal layout and sequence design and application processing;
- line network design;
- real-time program framework and testing technique design;
- batch processing design.

In all cases such sub-tasks exist, but it depends on the size of the system whether separate individuals or teams need to be assigned to them.

The detailed computer system design to be carried out is discussed area by area in later chapters (10–14 inclusive). It is desirable in some cases to design a simple system which may later be enhanced to take account of increased load or facility requirement. However, compatibility of all other areas which will remain unchanged must be assured during design.

At the end of detailed computer system design, the system is again timed to check that it is still within previously set resource constraints. If not, the possibility of hardware enhancement, or partial or complete redesign, must be investigated and a choice made. Such an uncomfortable discovery is made much less likely by monitoring the use of resources while the design is still being carried out. Timing is discussed in detail in chapter 15, and the procedures for resource monitoring—technical design control—in chapter 5.

The content of a typical computer system design document is shown in Table 7.1. Individual standards vary, but in a real time system it is likely that the computer system design document will go to a lower level of detail than is typical in batch systems. For example, individual application processing routines and recovery programs will be specified in detail. If the design work is carried out well to this level, program specification, and programming of individual routines or programs is very little problem. Consequently in this book these project phases are

**Table 7.1** Typical Contents of System Design Document

TITLE PAGE

TABLE OF CONTENTS

INTRODUCTION

A brief description of the computer system, its objectives, processing frequency and recipient departments, abstracted from the system specification.
The target date for the implementation should be stated.

OVERALL SYSTEM DESIGN
A flowchart or schematic representation and description of the complete suite of programs, batch and real time, including short descriptions of each program, giving all names of programs and files.

DETAILED DESIGN
One chapter per program or real time program function is included in this part of the document. Each chapter will include the following:

- name and short description;
- details of input referring to card, tape layout, message control block format, etc., by form reference number;
- output, referring to report, layout file record, etc., by form reference number;
- processes; logically structured description of processing within functions;
- controls;
- flowcharts or design language for more complex routines;
- definition forms applicable solely to this program.

SYSTEM SECURITY
Details of the security system applicable to this suite will be given. If standard software (e.g., MONITOR) facilities are to be used state which and how.

RESOURCE UTILIZATION
Statement of run times, device utilizations, resource requirement, e.g., main storage on-line disk space.

PLANNING REVIEW
A detailed review of planned effort for the programming and subsequent activity, in the light of the more detailed information now available.

APPENDICES
All file and record definition forms which are common to more than one program will be held in the Appendices, for ease of amendment. Each document type will be held in a separate chapter, within the Appendix.
For all multiple-use files a 'where used' list should be given.
Details of special processing routines, e.g., check digit verification applicable to several programs, will be in an Appendix.
A description of the daily, weekly and periodic processing schedule should be given, defining who is responsible for initiation of the runs.

---

much less considered than others. The problems begin again when the individual elements are being integrated together (project phases following computer system design are dealt with in chapter 8).

At the end of computer system design, various further activities are necessary. These are planning of the next project phase, reviewing implementation plans, costing the system with current information, presenting and agreeing the design with user and computer management (including operations), and planning extra system test data to add to that produced in systems analysis to take account of, for example, the need to test paging technique at the terminals.

Presentation of the design is important to achieve the maximum communication. There will be several different types of reader of the design document and its layout needs to be aimed at reconciling their different skills and objectives. The types of reader are split between users and development staff. On the user side are users responsible for agreeing systems features established during design, e.g., use of terminals, cost levels, service levels and time scale, and those responsible for scheduling/allocating resources for use during later stages of development and at time of cut-over. Within the data processing function, there are analysts who will participate in later testing stages, programmers who will implement the designs, operations management who must judge the ability of the planned configuration to provide the necessary resources, and senior development management, including quality assurance.

# 8. Design to Live Running

Systems analysis lays the foundation for an effective system. Computer system design is crucial in setting the framework for an efficient and achievable system within the available resources. But those stages subsequent to this—from design to live running—in which the system is turned into reality are those which consume the majority of resources. Consequently, careful planning and control of these are essential to avoid grossly inflated costs and continuously receding end dates.

To recall chapter 7, the problems associated with inadequate computer system design can be summarized as

- logical: incompatibilities show up in, for example, the programming phase causing effort to be wasted;
- physical: during latter stages of testing, a deficiency of some physical resource such as main storage is discovered, causing at best extensive tuning, and at worst radical redesign.

However, even with a good design, success is not guaranteed, since there are many other factors to consider. A number of subsidiary techniques such as program testing tools are required for rapid implementation, and a complex structure of inter-related tasks needs to be brought together smoothly and at the right time to enable inplementation timetables to be planned and maintained according to schedule.

These factors are dealt with in this chapter, which deal with each of the project phases following computer system design in turn, through programming and the various testing stages, to live running. Aspects concerning real time alone are considered. Although real time systems have a large batch processing component and, of course, timely implementation of this is crucial to the overall success of the project, the aim here is to bring out the essential differences in real time which need consideration.

The basic starting point for these later project phases is a sound, logically consistent computer system design specification (chapter 7), which has been shown to be achievable within specified physical resources (chapter 15), and to provide for the user requirement with the minimum of complexity (chapters 2 and 3). Coupled with this should be an agreed system for monitoring the overall use of physical resources throughout the rest of the project, so as to prevent unnoticed drift from the design requirement (chapter 5).

## 8.1 Programming

One of the still-current myths associated with real time programming is that it is slow and painful, and requires extremely high skill. Programming rates as low as two–five instructions per day have been quoted as typical. This impression almost certainly derives from the early days of real time, when all control software had to be created as well as the application code. It is made worse in situations where poor design forces much code to be re-written, after incompatibilities have shown up, and where inadequate testing techniques cause extended program development time.

In more recent, well-planned projects, the contrary situation has emerged. Coding rates for application code have been found to be in excess of those typically experienced in batch processing, and relate more closely to rates achieved in a good structured or modular coding environment.

### 8.1.1 PROGRAMMING OF THE REAL TIME FRAMEWORK (MONITOR)

It is rare in current practice for it to be necessary for a project team to design and program software for network management. At the very least there is a communications package which assembles a queue of messages for the user program to access without being synchronized to network events. This software also usually accepts requests for output to terminals for subsequent action. Consequently, this area is not dealt with in detail.

As an extension to, or as an addition to, this communication software, normally a framework (MONITOR) is required for the application code. This MONITOR, as described in chapter 14, has various forms, but in general provides an easily learned interface from application code to various service functions such as file access, communications handling, and main storage management. Increasingly, this framework too, is provided as standard software by the hardware manufacturer, or an independent software vendor (e.g., IBM CICS, ICL DRIVER, Cincom ENVIRON 1, TSI Taskmaster).

If the MONITOR is provided, the choice of which and the facilities which it is relevant to use for a given system will have been determined during design (or before, if a choice for multiple projects was necessary). There is then a need to train programming staff in the use and maintenance of the monitor, particular attention being paid to choice of facilities. It is often useful if an extremely simple application system is quickly defined and programmed to run under the monitor. The objectives are both to train the systems programmers, and to exercise all relevant facilities, so checking that they perform in the manner expected. More detailed testing will be done in conjunction with the actual application system to be implemented.

If a real time program monitor is to be created from scratch, some difficult programming is obviously necessary. However, the need for this will have been determined during computer system design, and the detailed facilities which it is to offer will have been determined. For example, the part of the MONITOR dealing with file access will have been specified to the level where, for instance, the following details are known:

- files to be accessed and software to be used;
- buffering strategy;
- method of dealing with simultaneity;
- logical access functions to be provided for application code;
- interface to other service routines.

So, although the programming may require, say, skill at handling file access at a low level, the problem is contained to one of reasonable scope. Similar definition of the logical functions to be provided, and design concepts for the other service functions, will have been determined at design stage. The problems arise mainly from acquiring or training programmers to deal with new or unusual software interfaces. In particular, gaining the expertise to handle the detail of the interface to communications software often takes time. The real time monitor often needs to be programmed in a low level language to achieve the necessary timing efficiency or ability to, for example, handle dynamic file buffer pools.

In summary, programming the real time program monitor is more difficult than the application code, but given that the skills discussed above are available it can be accomplished at rates comparable with those for complex batch update programs. This is possible only if careful computer system design has preceded the programming phase. The main reason for avoiding such programming, however, arises from the difficulty of complete testing of the separate service functions together, and in conjunction with the application code (see section 8.3).

### 8.1.2 PROGRAMMING OF APPLICATION CODE

If the application code has been specified in the computer system design phase in the way described in chapter 7, few problems should be expected in the actual programming. One project achieved on average over the whole team the remarkable performance of 100 COBOL statements per day written and individually tested. This rate is far higher than typical batch programming performance, and although productivity was helped by the fact that there were only six programmers in the team, two of those were trainees. High rates of coding should be expected in this area if design has been taken to a relatively low level (e.g., specifying a routine which carries out the update of a single file for one transaction, after receiving a validated message, passing data to a subsequent reply-formatting routine). The logic is then simple and is carried out to a simple uniform interface, all in main storage. Knowledge of the machine, apart from certain aspects of terminal hardware, or real time concepts such as multi-threading, and store management, are required only as background.

Programmers who have the ability to code within a batch processing modular programming environment are thus capable of carrying out the application coding in a real time project organized this way. As with any new situation, there are basic rules to be learned, such as the layout and use of interface areas to the monitor, and certain standards which ensure efficiency. A possible example is a rule that states that if a file record is flagged in a return code as being locked, all other locks for the transaction should be relinquished and the terminal operator informed of a temporary delay. These rules, although simple, need to be observed meticulously. Careful dry running of code produced by programmers new to the environment, by someone experienced in interfacing to the monitor, eliminates most problems of understanding in the early stages.

Within a given installation, the rate of application coding to be expected, if carried out to the design level described above, would be approximately the same as achieved for simple modules in a typical batch program.

In the design, the decision of which program language to be used and its relationship to the program monitor, will have been taken. The decision relates to the languages the monitor provides for, the skills available, and overall efficiency considerations.

Although high level languages such as COBOL may require two–three times as much main storage and run time for a given routine as a low level language, the gain in programming productivity, bearing in mind available skills, can often be worth it. The design must, of course, have estimated resource utilization for the chosen language, and have determined which routines have most influence on efficiency. These routines, if particularly critical in use of resources, may well be programmed selectively in a low level language. Thus it is possible, and advisable if appropriate, to mix programming language rather than to write everything at a low level—another myth of real time programming.

### 8.1.3 DESIGN CONTROL

As modules are coded, their projected performance should be evaluated against targets set at the end of the design. Performance variances so identified should be fed to the technical design control system (see chapter 5).

## 8.2 Testing

Following completion of coding of application routines and monitor service routines, there are various levels of testing required before the system is ready for introduction to live running. Bearing in mind that in real time the user is in intimate contact with the system, it is of fundamental importance to ensure testing to a very high standard.

If a batch system malfunctions it is often possible to trap the consequences of the error, and to correct it and re-run before the user sees the results, even if this means a delay. The user is to an extent decoupled from the computer procedures, and can often carry on with other activity while awaiting the results. In the best case he may never know a fault has developed at all.

By contrast, in real time, for any system failure, be it hardware, software, application code, or machine room operator error, the user may well know of it before anyone in the computer centre. In addition, much clerical work may be held up, pending correction or by-passing of the fault, because the terminal operators now depend on interaction with the computer system at an individual transaction level. There is thus greater emphasis on thorough testing for real time systems.

### 8.2.1 LEVELS OF TESTING

The testing levels are similar to those applied in many batch systems, although the degree of thoroughness needed is typically greater and some new techniques are necessary. The levels of testing are broadly as follows:

- program logic testing and integration;
- system testing;
- system load testing;
- user acceptance testing.

A feature of successful testing for real time is the extensive use of batch testing aids for the first three categories. These testing levels are considered in more detail in subsequent sections.

### 8.2.2 CREATING THE RIGHT TESTING ENVIRONMENT

In achieving testing within the minimum time scale and cost, it is not only the use of appropriate techniques and careful planning of the tests which are required. It is worth summarizing the activity prior to the testing phases which contributes to this smooth implementation at minimum cost.

In the analysis phase, when the facilities required by the user of the system are being considered, it is important to remember that every inessential facility which has been incorporated will have far greater resource implications when the testing phases are reached. Any facility interacts with others and all interactions need testing. There is thus an effect on testing which is not directly proportional to numbers of facilities. Particularly important here is real time updating, which introduces extra complexity in recovery processes and their testing. One large organization wasted millions of pounds and failed to achieve its goals, when the need was limited to daily data collection, overnight batch updating, and dissemination of data next day. This was primarily a failure in the analysis phase.

The second important preventive measure occurs in the computer system design phase. If carried out thoroughly, problems in testing caused by logical or physical incompatibilities will be minimized. It is frequently such problems which prolong the testing phases rather than actual testing. The delays are caused by hasty redesign and re-writing of parts of the system.

The later phases of testing before live running begin to involve the user heavily in operating terminals, providing test data, and accepting the system. All three require a high degree of involvement and training in the overall system, its facilities in detail, and the hardware. Frequently, problems and delays arise during the introduction of systems, because the user is not ready for this involvement. A loss of impetus and possible redeployment of project team members can as a result exacerbate the delay. Preparation for these later testing phases needs early planning by the analysts and sometimes requires that facilities for terminal training are provided ahead of the availability of the system in its final form (chapter 9).

## 8.3    Program Testing

Perhaps the most surprising rule for program testing of real time programs is that it is best carried out in batch mode. This arises from the fact that testing at terminals requires high machine overheads, owing to the need for a full software framework and frequent large compilations. Work at one terminal can easily interfere logically with tests on others, and slow keying of transactions and on-line thinking time causes throughput to be extremely low.

Because of these constraints a system tested wholly on-line is likely to be inadequately tested. By contrast, batch testing enables the effect of a much higher number of possible combinations of condition to be examined, and facilitates testing at a low level before progressive integration of elements to form the complete system.

This section looks at the various levels of testing. For illustration purposes, testing techniques for a program structure like the MONITOR (chapter 14) are described. Very similar considerations apply to other forms of program organization. Figure 14.4 shows a MONITOR structure with the principal service elements. A number of applications routines are shown interfaced to the service elements.

### 8.3.1    TESTING INDIVIDUAL APPLICATION ROUTINES

For a given transaction a set of application routines may have been defined and coded as follows:

- transaction code validation and route switch (used in common with other transactions);
- data validation;
- file update;
- preparation of reply format;
- error handler (used in common).

The first stage of testing is to prove the logic of each of these in isolation from the others. To do this a batch program is required as shown in Fig. 8.1. This Level 1 test aid enables individual application routines to be compiled into it and interfaces to the application routine via the message block (MB)—in exactly the same way as in the real time program. In addition, the way in which the routine records its data in the appropriate area and makes logical service calls, by passing control to the request analyser, is also the same. Initiation of the routine is carried out by the dummy Sequence Monitor in exactly the same way

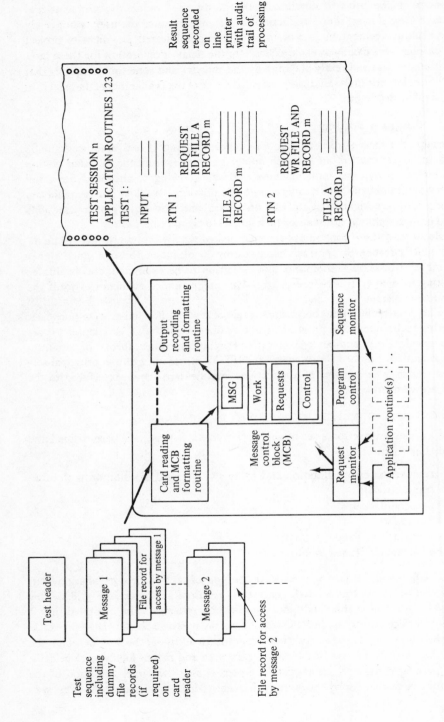

**Fig. 8.1** Program testing: Level 1

as in the real time monitor. The test aid operates by reading a card or a sequence of cards which specify data to be set up in the MB, corresponding to a single possible entry condition to the routine. The routine is then actuated by the Sequence Monitor, and it carries out the necessary processing before setting up the final service call in the appropriate data area, and passing control to the Request Monitor. The Request Monitor validates the request, and then causes the request and the appropriate areas of data in the MB to be recorded on the line printer. The next card or sequence representing another data condition is then read, processed, and the results recorded, and so on. As many data conditions as are required to test the routine fully can be rapidly run through the routine in this way, and the results recorded. It is convenient if the input conditions are also recorded on the line printer, and associated with the corresponding results. In the above example transaction, if the routine which carried out data validation were being tested, the input conditions would be various messages, and the output conditions would be logical requests for file access, or parameters for the error handler.

This level of test aid can have various formatting facilities on input and output which make easier the specification of data conditions and the checking of results.

For example, in recording output to terminals, simulated on the line printer, it is helpful to format the results in a way which represents as closely as possible the visual appearance of the data on the actual terminal, rather than as a character string which incorporates various terminal function control characters. Those characters which cannot be represented on the line printer can be represented alongside the appropriate line. For example, flashing fields on a video terminal are represented with an explanatory code, and start and end character counts. The amount of effort spent in designing, writing, and testing such extra facilities must obviously be weighed against the amount of time saved in testing.

Proprietary MONITOR software often has a matching level of test aid similar to that described above. The function of this test aid is analogous to the individual module test harness used in batch program testing.

### 8.3.2. INTEGRATION OF APPLICATION ROUTINES

After individual testing of application routines they can begin to be tested together, simulating the processing of complete messages or transactions. It is not necessary to test all combinations of processing within each routine again, but the interface conditions between routines need to be tested throughout the full range of possibilities. In this way, any differences of specification of routines or understanding between programmers will be detected.

The level of tester described above is an appropriate tool for testing at the transaction level. Instead of repetitively testing the same routine, it must be set up to switch control to the next routine, as requested in the appropriate area in the MCB by the previous routine. Any further input data, such as those resulting from a file access request, are read from cards and set up in the MB before control is passed on. Thus each routine works on interface data supplied by the previous one, and data which in live running would come from terminals or files are supplied from the card deck, which is set up in the right sequence. The testing tool ideally needs to be able to recover from such errors as looping around the same application routine, using the same data because a routine has erroneously nominated itself in the interface, looping within a routine because of a logic error, and errors in setting up the test data.

The action required to deal with the above is for the tester to record diagnostic information 'regarding the type of error and current content of the MB' at the appropriate point in the transaction sequence printed record. Following this, the data areas should be reset and the subsequent message set up and processed, if the error is recoverable, such as for missing test data.

Each transaction can be fully tested in this way. Transactions which are made up of multiple message pairs, with temporary status data stored in the processor, or on a backing file, must obviously be tested in their entirety. It may be necessary to simulate access to such temporary data by setting them up to be read in from the card deck, if the tester does not automatically allow for this. Alternatively main storage can be used in place of backing storage.

These extra facilities in the Level 1 of type of tester are often made available by the supplier of the real time monitor. The facilities it provides need to be investigated carefully before tests are planned.

There are limitations to the testing which can conveniently be carried out by the Level 1 tester. For example, the testing of recovery routines would be laborious. The content of a log tape resulting from a sequence of transactions could be inferred by examining the printed test record. It is much more convenient, however, for recovery testing to use live files with test data which are actually altered by the transactions, and an actual log file generated as processing proceeds. Then recovery can be tested by arbitrarily stopping processing at various points and recovering the files, using the log file. The restart conditions arising from the recovery run can then be checked to ensure that, for example, no double updating of files has occurred.

So to facilitate testing with live files, another type of test aid is required. This tester, referred to here as Level 2, injects input message information into the program by reading cards, and records the corresponding outputs on the live printer. Thus, it interfaces to the Communications Handler (using MONITOR again as an example) and provides and accepts messages and status information as if it were the communications software. The Input/Output Handler accesses live test files using standard software as in live running—Fig. 8.2 illustrates the Level 2 tester.

The Level 2 tester can thus be used in place of Level 1 for transaction integration, and facilitates testing outside that of pure application logic, such as recovery. In addition, other areas, such as correct use of overlay facilities in the MONITOR, unlikely to be provided for in the Level 1 tester, can be tested. Testing tools similar to this are not universally provided by suppliers of MONITORS. Packages, such as IBM CICS, where the communications

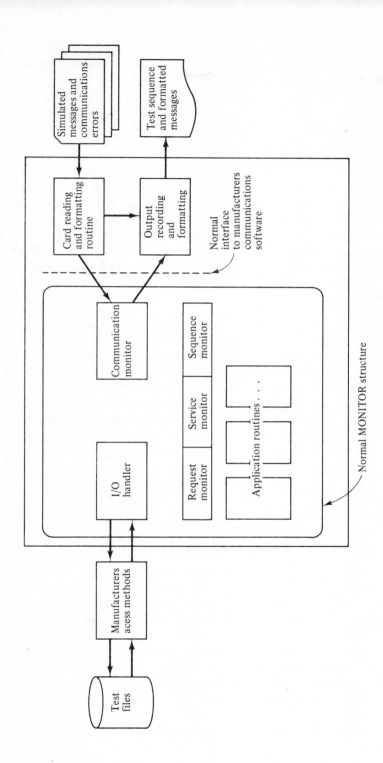

**Fig. 8.2** Program testing: Level 2

software and the real time organizational framework are intimately bound up, do not provide an easy interface to which such a tester can be written if the supplier does not provide one.

The biggest advantage of the Level 2 tester is the potential ability to test the entire real time program in batch mode, and then to interface it to the communications software without recompilation. All application routines are progressively integrated with the actual monitor to be used for live running. Any problems arising from incompatibilities between actual service facilities and design assumptions can be quickly shown up.

Certain valuable physical information can also be gathered by normal machine performance measurement tools, e.g., the number of overlays or paging accesses required by a known set of transactions, given that the core is restricted to that available for actual live running (allowing of course for the absence of the communications software). This information can be used to refine performance predictions made during the computer system design phase, and if necessary tune the system before live running.

### 8.3.3   TESTING THE MONITOR

Less emphasis in the chapter is given to this topic, since real time project teams are increasingly using monitors provided by their hardware manufacturers, or by an independent supplier. Where there is a genuine reason for developing a monitor for a particular installation, such as to achieve an exceptionally high message throughput, or if no software is offered  for a particular machine, it must be done. Such development is far less predictable than other aspects of real time, particularly when it comes to testing, owing to the interactions involved between different parts of the monitor. Many of the combinations of conditions which arise by chance in live running are difficult to simulate in testing.

Testing must be broken down to handle individual service routines. Using the MONITOR structure (Fig. 14.4) as an example, the I/O Handler, Communications Handler, and the combination of Request Monitor, Sequence Monitor and Service Monitor, must each be tested in isolation before combining them.

For each, special testing harnesses or dummy application routines need to be designed and written, to enable testing to be carried out. To use actual application routines would not be sufficient, even if it would work, since it would be unlikely that all conditions of the service routines would be tested. A batch testing tool such as the Level 2 tester described above is useful for testing these routines.

First, central switching routines (Request, Sequence, and Service Monitors) can be tested by constructing a framework of dummy service and application routines. The amount of code involved in these central routines is, however, quite small, and might be exceeded by the special test code. It is likely to be easier to exceptionally carefully dry run the code, and then to link it to the Communication Handler for joint testing. The latter is used initially in the most straightforward way, testing with simulated simple error free messages until the central switching routines are proven. Very simple dummy application routines can be used under the service structure to generate the full range of service calls, and thus exercise all possibilities of switching control from one routine to another. Since the I/O Handler routines are not present at this stage, any input or output calls will be simply recorded, and control passed on, by a dummy I/O Handler.

Having tested the kernel of the real time program, full testing of the Communications Handler can take place. All error conditions can be simulated by the Level 2 tester and the responses to these checked. A dummy application routine can be designed to generate successively all possible output request types to all relevant terminal types (the message content can of course be very simple). Similarly, a full set of input message types can be injected into the Communication Handler, which is then used to set up the MB, and control is passed to another dummy application routine. The latter can record each resultant occurrence of the MB by directly writing to a peripheral device, so that the format can subsequently be checked. Although it is bad practice in actual real time code to have direct access via the operating system to peripherals, this can be very useful in testing.

Similarly, dummy application routines can be written to test the I/O Handler. In this case the use of actual test files on disk or tape is probably easiest. The test sessions can test access from these dummies progressively by request type and by file.

Combination conditions are tested last. Particularly difficult is testing of code for handling conditions such as interlocks caused when a record is accessed by more than one routine simultaneously, and access request queue handling. Certain combination conditions arise by chance if the MONITOR structure has been generated with multiple MBs, but it is difficult to force a specific condition to occur. This art arises from the need to synchronize the timing of requests originated from dummy routines with the access times of the files, so as to produce the appropriate coincidences of request.

The above discussion illustrates the considerable ingenuity required in the design and carrying out of testing of real time monitors. Other service routines such as main storage management are just as difficult to test.

Meticulous planning and control of testing is required to ensure that each part of the monitor is produced and tested at the right time for integration with other parts. As an illustration of this, Fig. 8.3. shows in outline the interrelationships of activity required for a simple MONITOR. In this case Communication and I/O Handlers had to be written and interfaced to a simple application.

8.3.4  PROGRAM LOAD TESTING

If the system is known from earlier manual timings to be critical in certain parts, it is desirable to test the program—now completely integrated and

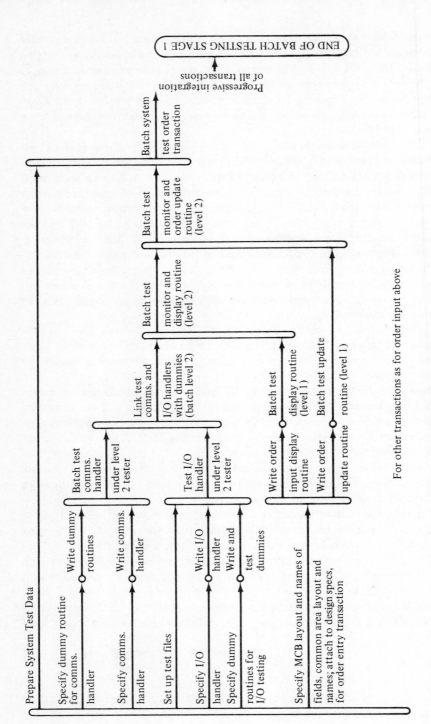

**Fig. 8.3** Production of a real time monitor

logically sound—under load. This is done at program testing stage using relatively crude data and using techniques discussed in section 8.4.4.

### 8.3.5 COMMUNICATIONS COMMISSIONING

As a separate activity from batch and real time program testing, and prior to live testing, communications hardware and software and the real time monitor, if used, must be proven to work according to manufacturer's specification.

With a complex network make up of a number of different terminal types, a communications multiplexor, and network control software, there are too many possibilities for error for it to be feasible to carry out their testing in combination with a new set of application code. It is thus advisable to design and carry out a separate testing procedure with the supplier of the facilities, to agreed acceptance criteria. With multiple suppliers this procedure is more difficult, but since the opportunity for error is greater it is proportionally more important. Even with a simple system a check of communications elements separate from the application is desirable.

Everything externally supplied should be included in this commissioning testing. If an outside monitor is to be used, this should be demonstrated to work in conjunction with the equipment to be used. Each terminal and line type should be tested in conjunction with the communications controller under control of the software. Line switching, and the consequent software table adjustments, need to be tested, as do automatic dialling, or remote control of peripherals on terminals.

Communications software and real time monitor packages are often macro generated. The commissioning tests should seek to ensure that the version required for the application has been generated, and in particular, no facilities have been omitted. The tests should also be designed to fully test the software, since regrettably bugs can quite frequently appear.

The overall objective of commissioning testing is to ensure that when live testing of application programs commences, only problems arising in the latter will have to be dealt with. Errors which could either be in the application, or in the communications hardware and software, cause frustrating delays, since each party typically blames the other. It is not until a conference of experts in all aspects of the system can be forced together that any worthwhile diagnosis can take place.

### 8.3.6 LIVE PROGRAM TESTING

It is a strange paradox that in real time systems actual live testing is best kept to a minimum. The reason lies in the difficulty of achieving high enough throughput via terminals to enable testing of the large number of combinations of conditions necessary for complete testing. On-line testing time is also expensive: thus it should only be used for that testing which is not possible to carry out in batch mode. Often, also, sufficient terminals have not been commissioned to allow all programmers free access to the machine, particularly during early stages of testing.

If testing has been carried out to Level 2, as described above, the need for on-line testing is limited to checking that the interface to communication software performs exactly as assumed in the artificial interface to the testing package, validating that software, communication controller, network and terminals perform together as expected, and checking that message sequences on the terminals are actually as predicted by the batch techniques.

Frequently, at this stage, errors of assumption become apparent. For instance, misconception regarding the function of a single control character, built into both the application logic and formatting routines of the tester, will not show up until now. Similarly, the operation of details of communications protocol can prove to have been misunderstood, or to be wrong. Hopefully, if separate commissioning testing has been carried out, the latter will be infrequent.

Consequently, although examples of each message type should be tested, it is not essential to test all data combinations. Even so, there will be many tests to be carried out and careful preplanning of the sequence is needed. The most time-consuming part of such testing is in assessing the accuracy of contents of output messages. To read, and check thoroughly against a specification, 2000 character messages takes a long time, and should be done off-line. A single lens reflex camera pre-set, or an instant print type of camera, are convenient for quickly recording messages. Alternatively a print sub-routine can be built into the real-time program at the communications interface. As an output message is passed across the interface it is also recorded on the line printer using this tool.

One problem, which has shown up in projects which relied heavily on on-line testing, is that the elapsed time of testing increases drastically as the throughput problems show themselves. Simultaneously, many errors are detected, some of which interfere with testing of other parts of the system. This, in turn, creates a heavy amendment and recompilation load which competes for use of the machine. One project resorted to patching machine code to reduce the compilation load. This expedient cost a great deal during initial live running, since the system became almost impossible to maintain.

After the inital system goes live, it may be impossible to carry out live tests on new releases in parallel with a complete test version of the system. In this case, it is convenient to test within the framework of the actual live system, given the right facilities. Basically, the program needs to be capable of differentiating between test and production terminals. The routine which normally routes on transaction type also routes according to terminals. Thus, two separately relevant and similar versions of the same transaction logic can be in use at the same time. On completion of testing, the production terminals are switched to the new code.

In summary, the problems caused by having to plan and carry out controlled testing, through the various levels described, are small compared to those encountered later if it is not done. The exhilaration of testing on the terminals early soon fades as the tenth all night testing session draws to an exhausted end!

## 8.4 System Testing

The objective of system testing, as always, is to test the suitability of the system from the user's point of view. Programming might have faithfully delivered what was specified in the computer system design document. But was this a true reflection of the need? With good project phase control and agreement procedures, this is much more likely, but obviously still needs to be checked out. In particular, the interface to external procedures and computer systems must be thoroughly validated. Normally, it is necessary to set up a team of analysts, and designers and programmers who are dedicated to system testing. To achieve an even workload, it is often convenient to overlap program and system testing for different parts of the system.

### 8.4.1  SYSTEM TEST DATA

Ideally, the analysts would set their own test data at the end of the system analysis phase. The designers would subsequently create their own test data and so would the programmers. To rationalize the testing stages, the middle one is often split between the other two. So the system tests contain some tasks which are included to test the effect of certain physical restraints imposed by the computer system design.

The analysts and designers between them plan the sequence of system tests to match the envisaged sequence of production of the various parts of the system. In this way, system testing can overlap with program testing. They also try to ensure that the sequence is such as to minimize extra work in doing testing, e.g., if a batch program is used to create, update, and delete records in a master file which is interrogated in real time, the batch program would be tested first and used to set up the file for system testing the real time transactions.

Within this overall framework, the analyst first creates files and transactions which are thought to cover the business variations documented in his specification and product output. For example, in a given order processing application, he might want to have on file examples of customers with various requirements:

- invoice to delivery address;
- invoice to regional headquarters;
- invoice to headquarters;
- statement to headquarters, invoice to delivery address;
- pre-invoice;
- post-invoice;
- any combinations necessary.

All variations for input, output and processes need to be covered. Despite aiming at complete logical cover, the further aim should be to keep the volume of test data down. No fresh information is gained if more than one test, testing a certain combination of conditions, but with different data values, is used. The checking becomes more tedious and is more likely to be skimped.

After the analysts had completed the test data, looked at from the point of view of the external system, the designer adds in any further tests necessary for conditions which are imposed by the computer design system. An example taken from the system described in chapter 6 might be as follows.

The analyst asks for the set up of a record in the product file with the average occurrence of product variants (14). The designer has decided on a block size such that a maximum of 25 variants can be accommodated. Any products with greater than 25 variants have overflow blocks chained to the prime block. Thus the designer specifies that there should in addition be products with 25 and 26 variants in the test file, so that the logic which accesses the overflow blocks will be tested.

In a similar way, in the knowledge that only five variants per video screen can be displayed at one time, the designer also ensures that a product with only five variants will be on file as well as those which require several video 'pages'. He will thus be able to test the paging logic in the program.

### 8.4.2 BATCH SYSTEM TESTING

Given the necessarily high volume of data used in system testing, the remarks made about testing with terminals in real time program testing are even more relevant. Here, batch testing is almost essential to achieve thorough proving of the system. The term 'batch testing' means here the batch testing of real time programs.

The test aids described in section 8.3 can equally well be used for system testing. The Level 2 tester which allows normal access to files is particularly appropriate. Using this, thorough testing of the system from the analysts'/designers' view can be achieved. The system will almost certainly be tested in discrete logical parts, in step with handing over of these parts from program testing. It is not important at this stage that the interface between these parts is properly tested.

### 8.4.3 SYSTEM TESTING VIA TERMINALS

In system testing, much greater emphasis on terminal use is necessary than in program testing, because the logical interface to external clerical systems, and the suitability of the system for the actual users, are being evaluated.

Prior to this stage of testing the production of user instruction manuals for terminal operation and the training of sufficient operators in the system and operation of the terminals (see chapter 9) must have been completed.

Initially, the analysts carry out tests at the terminals using a sub-set of the batch test data, in conjunction with the user manuals. Subsequently, trained users are used for such tests, since they can often identify problems which the analysts have missed. It is of little use selecting only these users who are particularly able. Some of the least able of the likely group of final operators should also be selected. The latter may well uncover some flaws in design, or the instructions, which the others might unconsciously correct for.

It is important in system testing to test the system with a representative group of terminals, distributed geographically as they will be in live running. This could, for example, show up a lack of messages giving appropriate information to one location about completion of work by a separate function elsewhere. A simple omission like this could have been completely overlooked when testing in a single location where such messages are unnecessary.

It is vital during final system testing to test fully the recovery procedures routines and programs. These should be rehearsed with normal terminal and computer operators so as to check out the operating instructions. To simulate error conditions is often difficult, and may necessitate help from a computer engineer, who can perhaps create to order a store parity error, for example.

### 8.4.4. LOAD TESTING

An important system testing step, in a system known to be critical in the use of physical machine resources, is load testing. Typically, a heavily loaded system has many terminals. Owing to the way in which such systems are phased into live operation it may be many months or years before full loading is achieved in the normal live use. It is then rather late to discover that the system will not support the load.

If technical design control (chapter 5) has been applied to a project, there will be few surprises at this stage. The fully tested programs might also have been load tested before handing over for full system testing.

Ideally, what is required for load testing is software which injects messages into communication software as if they had come from terminals. This software could operate by reading pre-prepared and time-stamped messages in blocks from disk. The messages are then injected at the appropriate time followed by normal processing through the system. Resultant output messages are again time-stamped and accumulated on disk. The message handling software and disk accessing obviously needs to interfere as little as possible with normal processing. A subsequent analysis program can, for example, print out statistics on response time by transaction type. To make operation of this technique more convenient, it is desirable if the initial test data can be re-used as originally specified to simulate progressively higher and higher loads, by a simple change of a parameter. For realistic simulation, the messages should be distributed in time as they will be in live operation (e.g., Poisson distribution if this is appropriate—see chapter 16). Further it is very convenient if the initial program which sets up data on the disk automatically carries out the distribution by appropriately time stamping the messages according to the specified distribution and average arrival rate. The set-up and analysing overheads need to be outside the real time load test program.

Unfortunately, simulation software is rarely provided by manufacturers or software suppliers. However, if a system is likely to be time critical, and considerable savings in hardware could be achieved by controlled tuning, the expense in writing such a package could well be justified.

Otherwise, some improvised means of load testing will need to be devised. With perhaps 10 per cent of the eventual numbers of terminals connected, a load approaching the final level can be achieved by one, or a combination, of the following techniques:

- continuous input of transactions where there would normally be gaps between them;
- reducing transaction times by restricting terminal work merely to input and output of messages, leaving out all associated clerical functions such as checking data, reading displays, signing documents and looking up codes;
- pre-preparing input messages on a storage medium such as paper tape or magnetic tape cassette at the terminals; these are then injected into the system at the required rate;
- inserting a routine in the program at the communication interface which reduces the output message size to a fraction of the actual size which has been prepared by the application logic, or multiplicates input messages;
- use of a programmable front-end processor to read messages from disk to be passed into the main processor for processing, subsequently capturing the output messages again on disk.

The disadvantage of all load testing techniques is that they leave part of the system not fully tested, or load another part unrepresentatively. For example, using the third of the above potential approaches, the software load in polling the terminals will be less than as in the final system, but the line loading will be greater. To counteract this, more lines with fewer terminals per line than for the final system is desirable, but not necessarily easily achievable in practice.

Consequently, the technique chosen needs to be intelligently related to the information on probable loadings generated by the theoretical timing carried out during the system design. The technique is directed at testing parts of the system identified as being most loaded initially.

## 8.5 Acceptance Testing

This phase of testing is aimed at providing the user with the basis on which he can confidently accept that the system represents what he wants, out of a true understanding of what the system actually does. The techniques are many and include the following:

- user re-checking of system test data;
- parallel run with existing manual or computer systems;
- run of a complete business cycle with data provided by the user;
- cutting over to live running in a small volume location;
- combination of the above;
- taking the analyst's word for it!

The analyst must plan, in consultation with the user, exactly what form the test is to take at systems specification time. They need to agree formally what the precise responsibilities of each party are. The analyst will inevitably have a considerable part in the planning of the acceptance tests. However, he should not provide any of the test data (if these are required). Any help in this direction should be in checking that the user has covered the full spectrum of combinations of data conditions. Planning of acceptance tests can start while computer system design is being carried out, since details of system design do not need to be known, only the general 'shape' of each transaction as given in the system specification being necessary.

On the techniques listed above, the following observations can be made. User re-checking of system tests does not give the same degree of commitment on his side, since he is not responsible for the data as in the third technique. In the latter, the volume of data should be much less than in a normal business cycle. For this reason, it is possible to re-run from the beginning each time a fault is discovered and corrected, until a completely faultless run is achieved. This ensures that no unexpected side effects are caused by system and program corrections.

Parallel running is superficially attractive, but can be unsatisfactory in some cases owing to: an excessive volume of results to be compared, time differences of data in the two systems which can appear to indicate logic errors, non-existence in the current system of new facilities offered by the new one, and a large staff requirement.

The fourth alternative, in which a small physical part of the system is put in first, has the advantage of requiring few resources. The biggest danger, if it is not used in combination with other techniques, is that without formal scrutiny of results some errors or shortcomings in the system are not discovered.

In any event, users, particularly if new to real time, cannot be expected to take the initiative in deciding on the form and content of acceptance testing. As a result, the analysts have to give them a lot of help in this phase. This help should stop short of actually carrying out the tests for the users. This would achieve no more than system testing has already done. The users should feel confident in the operation and facilities of the system to a very detailed level before accepting it.

In one company the computer department insisted that the users of a system should carry out a full acceptance test before starting live running, despite thorough and successful systems testing. One month before the system was due to go live the users realized that they were not ready to carry out those tests because they did not understand the system well enough. This had the undesirable result that the system was put into operation several months late. On the other hand, however, it went live very smoothly in the hands of a satisfied user who was confident in his own understanding of, and ability to use, the system.

## 8.6  Version and Release Control

A typical well planned real-time system may have at one time different sub-systems in different stages of testing. For one sub-system individual application routine testing may be in progress, while another may be in full system testing via terminals. At the same time various amendments to specifications may be coming through. Total confusion will result if these, or amendments correcting errors detected at various stages, are applied to a sub-system after, say, system testing upon it has commenced. To avoid this, formal versions and releases are very useful.

Releases are used to control the phased introduction of systems facilities, much as is the practice in manufacturer software releases. Versions are basically copies of code within the same release, but at different stages of testing.

Releases are conveniently used to incorporate non-urgent amendments, such as slight format errors which do not affect the use of the system drastically. Any amendments discovered during programmer system testing which are urgent, of course have to be corrected within the current release. This system of controlling application releases and versions is primarily aimed at controlling the logical state of a system, but enables better control over the physical use of the machine.

With several levels of testing which progressively involve larger and larger compilations and volumes of test data, the availability of machine time becomes critical towards the later stages of testing. This is to be expected, since if a machine is configured to run a given real time system with a normal maintenance load, at later testing stages it will be running a large sub-set of the system in real time, as well as a heavy compilation and batch testing load. The more effective the development planning—with perhaps interleaved program and system testing—the higher the density of machine use tends to be.

The need is thus apparent for very careful planning of the way in which the system is integrated and tested. This planning should be carried out in outline during computer system design to verify that the techniques envisaged are workable. It should then be completed, and a standard procedure issued to all concerned prior to the start of programming. Obviously, this plan needs to be related to the testing techniques which are to be used.

The extent to which different versions are used depends on the size and complexity of the system. For a very simple system, a single version number of all code could be used for all program and system testing, with perhaps a sub-version indicator used to signify that the code has been copied and renamed for system testing. In this way, any subsequent changes made to the original code—perhaps adding facilities for subsequent release—would not affect the system testing.

For a more complex system it may well be convenient to copy and rename all basic routines as they pass a given testing stage. In some cases, minor code changes are required anyway to fit in with the environment for the next testing level, and it is desirable to rename to avoid confusion. For example, using the test sequence described earlier, the identification of one specific routine (e.g., the output formatting routine for a given transaction type) might be as follows:

- in coding and individual routine testing using
    Level 1 tester,               Version 1/1;
- in individual transaction testing,   Version 1/2;
- in sub-system testing
    Level 2 tester,               Version 1/3;

**110**

| | |
|---|---|
| – in live program testing, | Version 1/4; |
| – in batch system testing under Level 2 tester, | Version 1/5; |
| – in live system testing, | Version 1/6; |
| – in acceptance testing, | Version 1/7; |
| – in live running, | Version 1/8. |

The sub-version number indicates the progress of the routine through its various stages and prevents changes being made in error. For example, even if a programmer makes a change to a routine after it has been released for system testing, he cannot inadvertently destroy the copy being used for the purpose.

Errors detected at any stage are recorded against the version number and stage of testing. A new version is created, say Version 2/1, which clears these errors, and it proceeds up through the testing hierarchy. However, if this were done in isolation for each routine, the progressive overhead in compilation and testing as it became integrated and retested at the various levels would be prohibitive. Consequently the retesting of groups of routines and transactions must be carried out together. To control this process the higher levels of code integration also needs tight version control. For example, the control record for a given version of the batch program, comprising the real time program bound into the Level 2 tester, might be as follows:

Version 3/5 Level 2 test Batch system test

| Order transaction | – key line validation | Version 1/5 |
|---|---|---|
| | – data validation | Version 2/5 |
| | – update | Version 1/5 |
| | – output edit | Version 3/5 |

Enquiry transaction, etc.

This would indicate that errors requiring amendment to at least two of the routines had been found previously.

It is apparent that a very high excess cost can result from lack of control during testing. To avoid this,

- when choosing or designing monitor software and associated test aids, as much care must go into investigating the convenience of integration of the program as in the live running facilities;
- a 'production control' function should be created which controls the assembly of a real time program against the pre-defined system with as much care as is normally considered necessary for a complex manufactured product;
- for a complex system a quality assurance function is desirable, making spot checks on detailed quality of coding and thoroughness of testing, as well as maintaining records of where errors are arising, and the efficiency of their elimination in subsequent versions.

111

– very good operations procedures are required for dumping and restoring program libraries following a fault, otherwise considerable programmer and analyst time is wasted in re-amending versions if recovery is not completely up to date.

## 8.7 Phasing in the System

After completion of all stages of testing, and acceptance by the user, the system must be put into actual everyday use ('cut-over'). Real time systems are rarely cut-over overnight. The system is carefully introduced over a period of perhaps 6 months. The analysts must plan carefully in advance exactly how the phasing in is to be accomplished. In a typical project this planning starts after computer systems design is complete.

This will hold for many systems, but in some exceptional cases partial plans must be made for phasing in the systems before even systems analysis starts. Systems with very large manual files fall into this category. It is necessary to estimate what file information will finally be required to allow time for the data to be converted to a computer held form. There have been some systems requiring far more effort in converting and maintaining files than in implementing the rest of the real time system. Obviously, the analyst has to recognize such a need in very good time. As an alternative, it might be possible to go over to live running with skeleton files which contain no historical data if this caused the problem of volume, thus reducing considerably file conversion problems. In this case, a manual system must co-exist with the real time system to deal with transactions which require data which are currently not on file. This course of action is particularly convenient when, by normal running of the system, files become progressively up to date.

Systems may also be phased in by:

– application, e.g., customer order processing before re-order on suppliers;
– transaction class, e.g., enquiries before time critical and high security updates;
– segment of file, e.g., in a group ledger system, one company is put on at a time;
– location, progressive introduction of terminals, starting with those nearest the computer.

In any scheme for gradual introduction of a system, the analyst must be very aware of seasonal changes in business volumes. A system for dealing with the supply of home heating oil might be impossible to implement during the months of November to March, because the user has no spare resources to deal with the extra work cut-over temporarily creates. Thus, phasing in, in this case, would need to be planned for the period April to September, and if the project runs late by one month, the effective delay could be up to one year, unless an extended period of working with part of the system unconverted can be contemplated during the peak business period.

112

The analysts need to review carefully the plans for phasing in the system with plans for the following;

- training;
- office organization;
- clerical procedures (interim manual systems also require documentation);
- system testing;
- acceptance testing;
- hardware and software delivery schedule.

It is worth spending considerable effort in planning the introduction of a system. For a large system, a number of strategies should be examined and costed. Alternatives which are equally logically sound can differ widely in resource implication and thus cost. Quite apart from cost it may be impossible to provide the resources in the appropriate time scale. As an extreme example, one real time system was abandoned after the files had been built up to half their maximum size prior to live running. By this time it was realized that the comprehensiveness of data aimed for was impossible to achieve. It was far too costly to keep up with the amendments to data already on file while waiting for the real time systems to complete development.

# 9. Real Time and The User

In any well-developed computer system, the user has an important role to play. This is particularly true in real time systems, especially in cases when the advent of the terminal makes a direct impact on the user department's method of operation. This chapter considers the user's role during development and in going live, and discusses the training that needs to be provided for users from management through to operational staff.

Initially it is worth considering a few of the reasons why the user's role in a real time system is subject to different stresses from those experienced in the batch situation. The placing of a terminal under user operational control not only affects the system designer, but obviously the user as well. The need for user staff to be taught the details of terminal operation and transaction procedures is clear. However, the impact is far wider than learning to handle terminals as opposed to paper.

First, the user operators are readily aware of many computer events not previously visible outside the computer department. This includes such examples as operator (computer room or terminal) error, software failure, hardware failure, line failure, and system overload.

Second, several features within the computer system are of greater personal importance to user management. This arises because of the user's responsibility in the operation and his possible greater reliance on the system. The features include such aspects as priority, security, and recovery procedures.

In an ideal world, the user assisting in the definition of a real time system is already experienced in the use of real time. In practice, this is seldom the case, and those users who have worked with batch systems may even start at some disadvantage as their understanding needs some change. It is therefore important that those responsible for the development of a real time system carefully review the user's roles that apply in their situation so that the user can be guided appropriately.

## 9.1 The User in Development

In chapter 2 we examined a number of application aspects that directly im-

114

pacted upon the designer, and therefore had to be carefully considered from both a business and a technical view point during development. Because of these facets, smooth systems development calls on the user staff responsible for liaison and agreement with the data processing development team, to face three main tasks:

## 9.1.1 TASK 1: COMMUNICATE REQUIREMENTS

'Participate with the project team in evaluating different systems options.' Each option relates to a different level or form of service, with its associated development and operational costs. In the course of the project, the user needs to evaluate options beyond a simple management summary level, such as considering individual transactions in terms of their complexity, response times, recovery, etc.

While the people in user management do not need to be concerned with the technical choices corresponding to the various options in such debates, they do need to recognize the range of cost in development and operations, and the elapsed time and risk of development associated with each choice. The requirement is two sided. The user's willingness to work with the data processing team in evaluating the value to him and the priority associated with each option is important. On the other hand, the data processing team's role in estimating the cost, time scale, and risk of the various options in terms meaningful to the user, is equally vital.

Such discussion is most effective if first carried out at the working level and not left to the critique stage of a written system proposal (a systems specification). Whilst the evaluation of the relative priority of two transactions or the benefit of a real time (as opposed to overnight) solution can be well covered by the user's own experience, other evaluations will benefit from advance discussion and education in the ideas and concepts concerned. This education should be carried out before specific topics are discussed and first and possibly emotional views become frozen.

Furthermore, while the team is concerned with evaluating systems requirements in terms of the user's responsibilities, the nature of the task is such that the user may need to examine his work in a form that he has not considered as explicitly before, e.g., the cost of a three minute, as opposed to a forty minute loss of service after a real time systems failure.

To meet both these needs, the user requires a general appreciation of real time systems and particularly four key areas, namely:

– transaction response times;
– files and degree of timeliness required;
– security;
– reliability and recovery.

These four are expanded further in Fig. 9.1.

| RESPONSE TIME | Need for criteria such as average time or specific proportion in a given time (e.g., 95 per cent with 10 s) |
| | Irritational/behavioural effects of delays |
| | Loading and exponential deterioration |
| | Immediate/delayed responses—Amount of work necessary within response time, e.g., |
| | — message recording only |
| | — message validation |
| | — reading of files only |
| | — updating of files |
| FILE TIMELINESS | Relationship of last transaction to external sequence |
| | Few seconds out of date (i.e., to lost transaction) |
| | Minutes out of date |
| | Overnight updated |
| SECURITY | Value/benefit to security breaker |
| | Cost/problem of broken security |
| | Different levels for different data |
| | Relationship of computer security to existing manual systems |
| | Cost of providing security (level dependent) |
| FAILURE/RECOVERY | Range of levels of failure |
| | — disturbance—seconds |
| | — disruption—minutes |
| | — major impact—minutes to hours + |
| | Range of frequency of failure |
| | Range of time of recovery |
| | Responsibility for recovery |
| | — automatic |
| | — computer |
| | — user |
| | Integrity and levels of choice |

**Fig. 9.1** Check list—user understanding

### 9.1.2 TASK 2: AGREE SPECIFICATION

As with any system, the user team needs to agree a systems specification which reflects many of the issues discussed in task 1 above. As discussed in chapters 4 and 6, the analyst faces the problem of defining the system as precisely as possible while leaving design options open. From the user's view, the need is to be able to accept the specification although the fine details are missing.

In a batch system, the logical content of the computer input is sufficient definition for most user situations, with perhaps the physical design or layout on, say, the punch card, being of little interest to the user department. The layout of the punching document is of importance to the user and for data preparation, but not to the program. However, in a real time situation, the layout on a VDU screen, while properly left for the design stage, is of importance to the user, who is concerned with the detail of his terminal operations.

### 9.1.3 TASK 3: REFINE SPECIFICATION

Having authorized his specification, the user's responsibilities in the definition process must continue in the real time system. Within the constraints of the logical definition set out in the systems specification the designer will wish to

**116**

develop his design, setting out precise definitions of the system as seen by the user. Aspects being defined at this stage include (see chapter 7) the following:

- physical input/output formats at the terminal;
- detailed security system and associated specific user procedures;
- detailed recovery system and associated user procedure;
- detailed user action in case of failure at the terminal (note that the user sees failure in almost every case, whatever the cause).

To ensure a proper balance between the technical and development aspects of design, and the increasing detail of the systems definition, the designer needs to discuss the options in further detail with user staff responsible, even if this is done through the analysts working in the development team.

During the design process, the designer is developing a system to meet technical as well as business and application criteria. Given that the preliminary designs, developed during analysis, are of necessity broad based and that the requirements are critical on computer performance, then there remains a real possibility that design may prove that earlier broad design assumptions are invalid. In this situation, one of the paths open to the designer is to re-challenge the systems specification. It may appear poor public relations for the data-processing department to say 'It cannot be done for the price', but probably it is in the organization's interest to re-challenge the system specification if it is found to be based on a false technical premise. The significance to the user is the need for him to recognize the nature of the environment in which he is working, so that he will *positively* contribute to later debates on such questions, rather than relapse into a critique of the data processing team and react with the thought 'Why didn't they get it right during analysis?'

## 9.2   The User's Role in Going Live

In this chapter, so far, we have interpreted the user's role in development as being concerned with his responsibility to discuss, specify and agree the system. The user department also has a role to play in testing, establishing the new system and finally taking over the operational role.

In planning user activity during this later period, the project manager faces two conflicting pressures. The first is a desire to involve the user staff at the earliest opportunity to ensure maximum familiarity with the system before live operation. The second is a desire to keep user involvement to the minimum in order to mask the errors and problems that are shown up in testing, and to complete development with a tightly scheduled team. Unfortunately it is too easy to get the balance wrong. Frank education of user management and staff in the subject of real time systems is necessary if early user involvement is to be achieved without disruption to the project.

Readers may be familiar with situations in which systems, although developed to a satisfactory level, still do not get implemented. Sometimes the system is openly 'placed on the shelf'; in other cases the user finds cause for further testing, parallel running or minor amendments. The user's fear of operational responsibility for the system can be a major factor in delay after the system is available (i.e., after *genuine satisfactory* testing by the development team). The close relationship between user staff and the terminal in a real time system tends to increase this natural fear.

The effect of this situation is felt by the project team during the latter stages of testing. Therefore, there is a need for careful planning to take account of this fear, and to take educational steps to minimize the chance of the situation arising. In setting the project plan, it is a useful discipline to classify the purpose/objective of assigning a task, at the testing stage, to users. Possible reasons are as follows:

| | |
|---|---|
| User necessary | — for example, preparation of key file data or test data. |
| User important | — for example, user action on this task will provide different situations or a different perspective from that provided by the development team. Test operating of terminals or preparation of test data are examples. |
| User training/ education | — not itself a task in the development process, but necessary for successful operation, or earlier user contribution to development. It includes many of the activities discussed in the latter part of this chapter. |
| User familiarization normal or User familiarization (overhead) | — in planning the project, it is often useful to assign tasks during testing to user staff rather than the development team, with the objective of helping those assigned to become familiar with the system at the earliest opportunity. Such allocation may be a reasonably efficient alternative to allocating a member of the development team ('normal'), or one where the overall benefit of user training outweighs the relative inefficiency in that (and associated tasks) that arises from assigning user staff ('overhead'). |

During the later stages of a real time project, the user's scheduling for his involvement may be more complex than in similar batch systems. For example, with batch systems, no matter how heavily involved in testing, parallel running and take-on, the user management people always have some flexibility in scheduling the operational work of their staff and the support to the new system. Early tests can always be spread out to allow enough spare time for turn round, and daily systems can be run once per week in certain stages of testing. However, in the real time environment each test session is subject to greater constraints because of the *real time* environment.

Certain preparations can be carried out by the user in slack periods or by overtime worked in advance. However, the on-line testing, itself a slow process, needs the user's involvement during the test session, which may well be forced to a fixed period of the day due to other loading on the computer or on the user department. Consequently, as user involvement in final testing or parallel running becomes heavier, it may be necessary to work unusual hours to have access to test time. The alternative is to carry out normal activities outside the normal working day with testing being done during the day.

These problems are themselves very dependent on the conditions that apply to the particular situation, but on the whole remain reasonably straightforward to solve. However, the key lesson is that they need to be recognized at the earliest stage in the project and planned and established in some detail. Then, the user's role in going live can be *costed, scheduled* and *negotiated*.

Figure 9.2 illustrates a typical task list for user involvement at this stage of the project. Each heading on this list can involve a number of sub tasks and several user staff.

---

Note: Tasks listed might involve user staff with or without the development team. Check list excludes training.

Prepare test file data ⎫ Program testing
Prepare test data       ⎭
Review message formats on screens
Vet user manual
Operate terminals during early test
Support link testing
Prepare test data against user manual
Operate system against user manual
Test failure conditions, procedures
Assign bad operators to use system
Attempt to break security
Test apply management/supervisor controls
Test daily start-up and close-down
Check results from early tests
Plan formal acceptance tests
Prepare for formal acceptance tests/systems tests
Check results from systems tests
Plan phased implementation
Arrange accommodation for terminal operators and clerical support
Liaise with line engineers
Prepare main file data
Correct new master files
Organize overtime, etc., to handle peak department loading during testing/parallel running
Agree new operator job specifications, salary scales, etc., as appropriate
Schedule staff off normal work and for support to testing and for training
Establish operational links with data processing department

---

Fig. 9.2   User task check list—going live

Eventually, the well planned system reaches the point at which the data processing department is sufficiently confident in the system to ask the user to take over in live operational mode. If there are no external pressures forcing the system on the user by some fixed deadline, this is when fear may give birth to delay. Careful planning, involvement and education as discussed earlier contributes to minimizing this fear. However, the planning for cut over to live operations should also take this potential barrier into account. Phased implementation helps to improve the user's confidence, especially if the early stages are absolutely basic to the user's responsibilities. In such situations, the early steps may be more readily accepted and form the basis of greater confidence in more significant elements. This subject has been discussed in chapter 8.

## 9.3 User Training

The examination of the user's role has already identified some of the training needs. In general terms, user training can be related to three levels of user staff seniority:

- directors and senior management    (direction);
- middle and junior management    (management);
- operational staff    (operations);

and further related to the stage of development of the system, as follows:

- agreement to specifications    (policy);
- participation in development    (development);
- operational use    (operational).

A series of real time user management and staff courses is set out below and summarized in Fig. 9.3. Figure 9.3 reflects 'training needs' and may therefore be achieved by fewer courses. Several of the topics are generally available as publicly offered courses; other topics require tailored project-oriented presentations.

| Course Code | Topic | Attendee |
|---|---|---|
| 1.1 | General real time appreciation | D |
| 1.2.1 | Full real time appreciation—senior management | DM |
| 1.2.2 | Full real time appreciation—managers, supervisors | M |
| 2.1 | Systems overview | MO |
| 2.2 | On-the-job participation | MO |
| 2.3 | Pre-operational details | MO |
| 3.1 | Operational system overview | DM |
| 3.2 | Supervisor's control | M |
| 3.3.1 | Operator system overview | O |
| 3.3.2 | Keyboard | O |
| 3.3.3 | Specific terminal | MO |
| 3.3.4 | System details | MO |
| 3.3.5 | Simulation—tape | O |
| 3.3.6 | Simulation—on-line | MO |
| 3.3.7 | Live—pre-cut-over | MO |
| 3.3.8 | Live—training mode | MO |
| 3.3.9 | Terminal guides | MO |

Possible attendance    D — Directors and senior managers
M — Managers/supervisors
O — Operations

Fig. 9.3   User training courses

### 9.3.1   POLICY TRAINING

To allow directors and senior line management to best play their role in the development of a real time system, there is a need for *early* senior management training to be organized to provide a greater understanding of the methods, problems and advantages associated with real time.

In agreeing systems definitions, whether early broad-based studies or detailed specifications, project plans and budgets, it is important that management recognize the significance of the system. To this extent, initial training should start before systems development so that the lessons can be learned in the general case, thus avoiding the emotional impact of the specific. Topics that should be covered include the following:

- general appreciation of real time and its technology;
- the need for design targets and the user role in agreeing practical targets;
- the development cycle and its impact on the user;
- user staff contributions to testing and system cut-over to live running;
- the need to agree the specifications at more than one level.

Such training may be too broad to be covered at a single session, say before a feasibility study is complete. A more practical plan is to organize a fairly short introduction (course 1·1) once real time is identified as being a possible solution and a further, more detailed session (course 1·2) once the first project has been quantified, approved and authorized to proceed to systems analysis.

Like many computer systems, the systems specification may require agreement at several levels of detail. In this case policy training (course 1·2) is best divided into two sessions, one (course 1.2.1) being concerned with an overview of the system, the applications logic and the implications of the budget, user staff resources, etc., and the second (course 1.2.2) is more concerned with the operational aspects relevant to those who need to discuss and agree such system details as VDU screen layouts.

One international group rightly considered senior management education for advanced systems (real time and data base) sufficiently important that it commissioned the preparation of a studio-filmed course for general distribution to their operating management.

### 9.3.2 DEVELOPMENT TRAINING

There is a limited need for formal training of user staff during the development cycle, other than that covered in section 9.3.1, with the possible exception of detailed briefing with regard to specific tasks, e.g., how to prepare test data. Those user staff assigned to specific tasks during the development cycle will be better motivated if they have some appreciation of the overall system under development. This can be achieved through a short course (course 2.1) on the system, its main features, the computer and the overall plan.

We have already discussed (section 9.2) how some of the activities of systems testing can be assigned to user staff as a part of their training programme as much as part of the development cycle. When such tasks are allocated for training purposes, even with the limited objective of increasing confidence, then as previously suggested they should be recognized as such, but also monitored and controlled as such. Those user activities in the development programme that are part of the process of full user training, we will group as a course (course 2.2) for the completeness of Fig. 9.3.

Where selected user staff are allocated to assist in the testing cycle, they may often need to obtain basic operational skills before the general operational training is established. To meet such circumstances, some special one-off pre-operational training may be required (course 2.3).

### 9.3.3 OPERATIONAL TRAINING

The day to day operation of the real time system requires knowledge and skills possibly not already present in the user departments. However, while the initial training of existing staff may be clear, it is equally important to plan from the start for the training of new entrants to the department. Very often operational manuals, and on the job guidance by (then) experienced staff will cover the later arrival. Nevertheless, it must be planned from the start as a specific training activity.

The training for operational use falls more clearly into the three staff levels discussed in section 9.3 above.

### 9.3.4 OPERATIONAL MANAGEMENT TRAINING (D)

Whilst directors and management may have agreed a systems specification in the course of development, it is also necessary to provide a clear presentation of the operation of the system as finally developed. The theme of the seminar would be 'This is what we have' and 'This is how you control it' (course 3.1).

### 9.3.5 SUPERVISORY/MIDDLE MANAGEMENT (M)

Management more closely concerned with the day to day operation needs to be updated on the general system and also learn sufficient details of the system to operate special supervisory controls and to assist operators with their problems. The need is more concerned with a good knowledge of 'what to do' than with the manual dexterity and fluency as required by an operator. Courses required are a management overview (repeat course 3·1), systems overview and details (see operator training, course 3.3.1), and supervisor's controls (course 3·2).

### 9.3.6 OPERATOR TRAINING (O)

In planning operator training, the team needs to provide both practical training in operational details and material which aims to change attitudes, so important where a major change of job role is concerned.

It is at this stage that plans need to be set for the difference in the potential training environment that applies to the training of:

(1) operators involved from the start,
(2) operators involved in later phased take-on,
(3) operators recruited in later years.

**122**

## System Overview (Course 3.3.1)

This course is similar to course 3.1, but aimed at operational staff rather than managers. The objective is to increase confidence in the new environment by providing an introduction to the whole system.

## Keyboard (Course 3.3.2)

Operators adjusting to keyboards for the first time may require keyboard dexterity training. Training organizations which specialize in the development of keyboard skills can be of assistance even where their courses are not computer terminal oriented.

## Specific Keyboard (Course 3.3.3)

When purpose-built keyboards are involved, or the terminals have different keyboards from those previously used, separate dexterity or familiarity training may be required on the terminal device itself.

## System Detail (Course 3.3.4)

Operators need classroom training in the explicit details of the system. Such training, in a large system, may be divided into groups organized by operator duties. This training covers all of the essential 'rule book' of operator actions and integrates with practical experience on the terminal. The next few course references are concerned with different approaches to this practical training.

## Tape Simulation (Course 3.3.5)

Many projects have successfully achieved practical test use of terminals, before being able to link them to the computer, by simulating the line with a tape recorder. A standard audio tape recorder can provide limited facilities for the operator to call up pre-set formats on a screen. It is more useful, however, if it acts as an input medium recording a string of input messages. Following a training session, the operators performance can be analysed by the 'tutor' playing back the tape. The linking of the tape and terminal can usually be achieved by an engineer with a basic understanding of terminals and modems, etc., and with the assistance of computer and terminal manufacturers. The author's experience is that although tape simulation is limited, it is very cheap, simple, and effective at the start of the project.

## On-line Simulation (Course 3.3.6)

When training is needed before the live system is available, benefit can be achieved by the simple development of a cut-down simplified system. This version of the system may handle only major transactions, have no optimization, no recovery facilities and use small simple files. Such exclusions allow it to be developed relatively economically, but it is an overhead to be set against the user training budget. In some cases, such a basic training system can provide useful early programming experience on the communications software. The cut-down system is used for early practical training of operators, and it has the added advantage that it can be loaded onto any suitable hardware, with one or two terminals, at any time.

*Full System—Pre-live Operations (Course 3.3.7)*

Once a 'version' of the system is well tested and reasonably stable, it can be released for training purposes, possibly with reduced files and a few terminals, while full testing and final development progresses. This training version, being the first full environment for operators, should not be used too early, since the faults they may find in it may cause trainees to lose confidence. Nevertheless, it is a valuable training tool, but it is only a tool, and the training sessions still need organization and preparation in exactly the same way as any other training sessions.

Preparation tasks may include the following:

– organize machine time and terminals;
– load and control the training version of the system;
– plan training session sequence;
– prepare training files;
– prepare test transactions;
– supervise the session;
– analyse data input and response;
– recapitulate with trainees.

The overheads on the development budget may look high, but if more than perhaps six operators are involved, the returns in speed of learning and improved performance usually justify the preparation.

*During Live Operation (Course 3.3.8)*

With normal clerical turnover rates, well over 50 per cent of operator training takes place after cut-over throughout the life of the system. Yet no one wants to risk the danger of trainees' corrupting operational files, and duplicate real time systems are expensive to set up just for training.

This problem has been very successfully solved on many systems by incorporating, or enhancing, a central security system. For example, every operator signs on at the start of a day (or change of status) as 'operational' or 'trainee'. 'Operational' operators operate in full system mode with all normal facilities. In 'trainee' mode, the system restricts the file access used.

There are two basic choices: in one version the trainee is steered to a special training version of the file; otherwise he may use all facilities of the system. In the second version the trainee has freedom to read main files as a normal 'operational' operator but all 'writes' are written to a training log. Both approaches have their contrary advantages and disadvantages, dependent on the application, but are simple for designers to implement.

With the training mode facility, new operators can be trained when required, but using the live system. Alternatively, with the availability of several experienced user operators, new recruits can be trained on the terminal in training mode, by informal guidance from experienced terminal operators or supervisors.

*Systems Guidance*

While the systems analyst and designer should develop the system to simplify the operator's task and provide guidance by such techniques as formatted displays, further assistance can be provided via the terminal.

The need for the operator to call for the displays of 'instructions' to enable him to carry out his work depends on the nature of the job. A casual user of the terminal needs guidance when the need arises. In this class are nurses using hospital systems, and managers initiating enquiries; both of these are casual users.

On the other hand, a regular terminal operator expects to learn in advance as reflected in this chapter. Regular operators might include such examples as airline reservations clerks, order processing clerks, data input terminal operators and foreign exchange dealers.

However, in those cases where guidance through the terminal may be valid, the requirements need to be determined early in the systems development cycle. As such, the 'training' element becomes incorporated in the systems specification (course 3.3.9). The range of guidance can be quite wide, from question and selection guidance at one extreme to the ability to call up a list of standard transaction codes at the other.

## 9.4   User Training Overview

User training is important and the author's experience is that the training objectives are best met through carefully prepared training sessions followed up by relevant on-the-job comment and guidance. Data processing systems have a history of problems arising as much from users as from the development team. The costs to all concerned from poorly educated and trained users certainly can run to substantially higher levels than the cost of preparing the training programmes suggested above.

For convenience, each training need identified in this chapter has been coded as a course summarized in Fig. 9.3. This also indicates which courses each of the main groups of users may attend.

In practice, the number of training sessions may be very different from Fig. 9.3, which should, therefore, be used as a planning check list. In cases where different operators handle different transactions, courses 3.3.4 and 3.2 may run in several versions. Equally, in a project involving few users at management or operational levels, many of the courses may be merged or similar material used with different stress according to the variable audience needs.

9.4.1   COURSE CONTENTS

In planning user training, especially in the latter stages, it is often found that too little emphasis is placed outside the basic application. Training must cover the following:

- standard operations and transactions;
- data correction by the operator;
- recovery from operator error input to the computer terminal;
- systems recovery procedures at the terminal operator's end;
- start day, end day, end batch, etc;
- security;
- associated clerical activities.

## 9.4.2 SCOPE OF TRAINING

Those readers who are concerned by the stress placed on user training will find the following case study of operator training of interest.

The proposed system involved converting the existing clerical section to the use of terminals. Early experience showed that keyboard training for a clerk who had never handled terminals before took twenty hours on the keyboard. The learning of each transaction type in the system by practice on the terminal took three hours on average to achieve 70 per cent of his final speed. For the 20 transaction system, the learning time was thus 80 hours, during which time he fully occupied a terminal. Even if five terminals were available to enable training in groups, it would take about a year to train the 100 operators required, only to the point where they could carry out each transaction confidently. Further training in the relationship between transactions, and between the real time and complementary system, was necessary.

In the example given above, it looks as if there was a need to start practical training one and a half years before live running start date. In a system of average complexity, full definition of the design might well still not be complete at that time. Thus training of all operators before live running was impossible. Fortunately, the training problem was recognized early, and other factors soon led the team to consider a phased take-on of the system.

To meet the staggered cut-over requirement and the considerable volume of operator training, the final training programme provided for an increased level of training facilities as the project progressed, with a balance between 'on and off terminal' training in order to avoid a situation in which the training terminals themselves become the bottleneck. The solution would not have been determined early enough in the development cycle had the project manager not placed great emphasis on planning the user training.

In another case, a large scale national network had led to the demand for a large training programme. The final training was achieved by installation teams visiting each site and training operators on site on their eventual operational terminals in step with the commissioning rate of these terminals. Such projects have inevitably had a training mode facility, and the installation team members often themselves have been trained for that job (i.e., were not part of the development team). Again, analysis of the particular case showed real benefits in implementation and the need for early planning.

**Part 3**

# Design techniques

# 10. Terminal Network Configuration

Certainly the most unfamiliar aspect of real time systems to the installation new to the subject are the network components and the software which supports it. All other topics covered elsewhere in the book have some link to previous experience in batch systems. The network is totally new. Bearing in mind that the total cost of a real time system can be dominated by network costs, making the right choice of equipment and techniques is of the utmost importance. It is also this part of the configuration which is most intimately experienced by the users. They are likely to judge the effectiveness of the systems principally on how well the terminals and associated equipment meet their needs. As a result of all this, considerable development effort needs to be directed into this area.

In this chapter, first the components of the terminal network are reviewed. These are terminals, communications controllers, communications software, and data transmission components.

No attempt is made to describe any particular manufacturer's hardware or software. In this field, announcements of new equipment occur with ever increasing frequency, so the aim is to review the general characteristics of what is available. The intention is to provide a background against which detailed investigation of specific equipment or software can be made, and to provide a basis for appreciating the techniques of network design. Both of these topics are covered towards the end of the chapter. The main objective is to introduce commonly available facilities and to discuss the way in which a typical installation will utilize these in implementing a system. Such installations normally have to develop sufficient skills in the appropriate techniques, without the availability of experts in communications. The expected increase in use of terminals over the next ten years is some ten times the current level. Consequently, many more existing data processing staff will have to acquire fluency in terminal network configuration.

## 10.1 Terminal Types

In this section, terminal types are reviewed. Consideration of specific manufacturers' terminals is outside the scope of the book. In any case, before carrying out detailed evaluation of terminals, it is important to establish the general characteristics suitable for the application. Consequently, here the emphasis is on the categories and discussing their characteristics. First, general purpose terminals are considered, followed by some examples of special terminal types. Finally, considerations of compatibility are discussed.

### 10.1.1 GENERAL PURPOSE TERMINALS

The principal types of general purpose terminals are covered in turn as follows:

- hard copy terminals;
- video display units (VDUs);
- intelligent hard copy ('banking terminals');
- intelligent visual display units;
- remote batch terminals;
- remote clusters of these.

### *Hard Copy Terminals*

Characters are generated by key-depressions on a keyboard similar to that of standard typewriters (hereafter referred to as a QWERTY keyboard, those being the first six alpha characters as they appear). The keyboard has in addition special control keys, used, for example, for generating the start of message characters, and may also have a separate block of numeric-only keys. As each character is keyed it is transmitted to line, consequently special keys are often provided to generate cancellation of characters already sent. Keyed messages are printed simultaneously with keying on stationery advanced by operator control. The return messages are printed as they arrive from line on the same stationery, or on stationery on a seperate platen; in either case the line spacing is controlled by characters in the message stream. Peripherals for temporary storage of messages, or for reading to line semi-permanent data such as product descriptions, are common. Examples are paper tape punch/readers, and magnetic tape cassette recorders. The extent to which these devices are capable of automatic control by program varies. Typical line speeds are 10–30 characters/second; although speeds up to 120 characters/second are available for non-continuous use. Lines utilized are telegraph, switched public telephone network (SPN), or leased, the choice being dependent on speed and convenience of use. On some devices message buffers are obtainable, thus providing for sharing of lines between a number of devices by polling techniques, and for a degree of message editing before transmission.

### *Video Terminals (VDUs)*

These devices are normally provided with a message buffer. Messages are keyed into this buffer from a QWERTY keyboard (plus sometimes a numeric key block) character by character, and simultaneously displayed on a cathode ray tube as normal text. The next character position for entry is shown on the screen by a visible mark (the cursor) which advances to the next available position as the character is keyed. Screen capacity is usually in the range 240–4000 characters, commonly in lines of 80 characters. After composing the message, the operator actuates a 'transmit to line' control, and the message is read onto the line at the appropriate line speed. A typical speed is 300 characters/second, with a maximum of the order of 1200, and minimum of 50/100 for simple devices intended for straightforward teleprinter replacement. Return messages start at the top of the screen or can often be addressed by the main computer program to any point on the screen (cursor addressing). Some other particular features often provided are as follows:

| | |
|---|---|
| Message editing | — Editing of message content by operator, or by program to cancel or insert individual characters or sequence of characters keyed in error, or no longer required. |
| Format feature | — For operator guidance, fixed headings may be displayed on the screen by program, usually on request from the terminal, providing in effect a form with blank fields to be filled in by the operator and subsequently transmitted, the form being retained for repeated use if required. |
| Null character suppression | — Ability to send only those characters from a format which the operator has entered even if the space provided for the field is greater. |
| Processor override | — A facility in which the central program can force the terminal to accept an urgent message (sometimes onto a pre-defined line) even if the terminal is not in the 'receive message' state. |
| Local hard-copy | — Attachment of a local hard-copy device for copying current screen contents on command by the operator. |
| Character presentation | — Various character presentation such as, upper/lower case, italic/roman, constant/flashing, and normal/reduced brightness. |
| Local file validation | — Ability to restrict field type in the format, for example, to numeric only. |
| Light pen | — Facility for the operator to select a displayed item by touching the screen surface with a light-pen in a designated position instead of keying a character. |

*Intelligent Hard Copy Terminals*
This type can be viewed as an extension of a buffered hard copy terminal, as

131

described above. The additional facilities are provided by means of a small processor built into each device, or shared by a group of devices. It is possible to program this using a manufacturer-provided language to enable local error checking of, for example, range, type of character, check-digit and batch total. The program may also give operator guidance by positioning the print head at the appropriate position on the stationery and control peripherals attached locally to the terminal without operator intervention. To limit the amount of control data to be sent with each message, formatting of received messages by program is often possible. Because of the local intelligent capabilities, standby operation by collecting validated data on a storage medium local to the terminal, for later transmission to the centre, is often possible. This could, of course, be the normal mode of operation if the data are not time critical to the minute. Line costs could be reduced by the use of switched lines in many cases. The device, if powerful enough, could ultimately be used as a small, free-standing processor.

This type of device is becoming available with increasing local power, and, at the upper levels, provides a powerful mini-computer configuration with disk storage. Programming by high level language such as COBOL is also becoming more common, or by special high-level languages provided by the manufacturers.

*Intelligent Video Terminals*

The video terminal, as described above, forms the basis for this type of terminal. Extra facilities are provided by adding a mini-processor for data and program storage, typically of 8K 8-bit characters and upwards. In addition, backing storage is often provided by means of magnetic tape cassettes or floppy disk recorders, and for the larger devices, normal disk drives.

The processor provides the possibility of local error checking in a similar way to that described for the intelligent hard-copy device, and storage of more data than can be accommodated on the screen, thus allowing for local paging by the operator. The control of the attached peripheral devices is carried out by the processor, thus reducing device knowledge required in the operator. Line control procedures to match communications software provided with the main frame, or front-end communications processor, may be simulated by program, and several transaction control procedures may also be resident in the main storage of the terminal.

The backing storage devices used in conjunction with the local processing power enable data collection local to the terminal, for later transmission to the centre, to be a normal mode of operation if central processing is not urgent, or allow for stand-by operation while the main computer is out of action. More transaction sequences than can be accommodated in the terminal may also be stored ready to be called in when required (random access being preferable for this purpose if transactions cannot be easily sorted by type prior to processing). Backing storage further enables reference data required at the terminal, either for enquiries, or needed for processing of the data, to be held locally.

132

High level programming languages for writing transaction sequences are commonly offered. It is preferable if the standard video features, such as format and editing, are provided by hardware logic, and do not have to be accomplished by the user by detailed low-level programming.

*Remote Batch Terminals*

For running normal batch jobs at a distance from the main computer a remote batch terminal (RBT) is required. A basic RBT (sometimes called RJE terminal) has a controller which interfaces to the line and carries out communications control and monitoring procedures, and controls the operation of the attached peripherals. To this are attachable a variety of peripherals which operate typically at low to medium speed as compared to main computer peripherals, examples being paper tape reader and punch, card reader, line printer and magnetic tape devices. For local control, the RBT has a hard copy or video control console for controlling the sequence of input and output, and interrogation of job queues in the central machine.

Line speeds vary from 1200 to 9600 bits/second. It is the line speed which limits the obtainable speed of peripheral devices in many cases. For example, at 4800 bits/sec, 600 characters/second are possible, which is equivalent to 300 lines/minute for printing full 120 character width lines. The maximum printer speed could be of the order of 1000 lines/minute. Consequently, additional facilities for tabulation, or space suppression, are sometimes provided to reduce the number of characters required to transmit space fields.

Other facilities which can be important for control of RBT's are remote dialling, start-up and close-down, and sensing of peripheral conditions such as low paper on the printer.

This type of terminal is also sometimes provided with a built in mini-processor, which provides for adaptation to different line control procedures, greater compaction, expansion and formatting of data and user programmability. This gives the capability of carrying out local validation or even complete batch runs for simpler systems using the terminal's peripherals. High level languages such as COBOL and RPG may also be provided for carrying out this user programming.

*Remote Clusters of Basic Terminals*

Many of the basic types described above are offered as groups of the same or a mixture of types, connected to the same control unit. Some examples are:

- video clusters with one or more hard-copy terminal;
- intelligent hard-copy devices with video terminals connected;
- RBT with added video terminals for data preparation or enquiry;
- intelligent VDU with additional VDU's under control of the basic mini-computer controller.

Intelligent terminals as discussed already can often form the basis for such a terminal cluster. These clusters can usually be configured in modular units to suit a given application requirement. At the upper end of control unit power, when considerable programming facilities may be offered, these configurations of terminals become comparable in power to small main frame computers used in this way.

## 10.1.2 SPECIAL TERMINAL TYPES

As the range of applications of terminals progresses and the potential of hardware technology increases, very many special terminals are appearing on the market. These are often oriented to particular industries, and frequently aim to reduce the complexity of terminal operation because of the twin needs of limiting the required operator skill in the type of application, or keyboard manipulation and achieving high throughput. Some of the terminals available are reviewed briefly in this section.

### Shop Floor

Used for data capture in a particular environment. Data is entered by pre-punched cards, badge readers, directly from transducers connected to, for example, a weighbridge, and via simplified keyboards. The terminal may be connected in clusters to a local intelligent controller which checks and stores data for forwarding to a central point.

### Stock Control

Portable terminals, battery driven, which record data on a magnetic medium. Stock identifiers and re-order quantities may be read from pre-prepared labels at each stock location. Labels are read with a 'wand' attached to the terminal which reads the magnetically or optically encoded information. Exceptions can be entered via a simple keyboard. Connection on-line (using an acoustic coupler) to send the data to a central point may also be possible.

### Point of Sale

This is intended for rapid production of documents for, or capture of data from, a customer at the time a clerk is dealing with him. Standard information, such as account numbers and product identifiers, may be read automatically by a magnetic or optical code sensing device. A keyboard special to the business may be provided, possibly accompanied by visual display of the significance of the keys for each specified transaction. Sufficient intelligence to carry out calculations, such as for invoices, may be provided. Often by-product information is produced for later processing in such forms as magnetic tape cassette or machine readable tally-roll. The option to use the terminal, directly or occasionally on-line, or completely off-line, is also provided in some cases. At the upper end of the scale, these terminals are connected locally to a mini-computer. This allows processes like checking customer credit-worthiness and rapid stock monitoring to be carried out.

### Cash Dispensers

This is intended to enable common banking transactions to be carried out directly by a customer at various locations. Account identification data are read automatically from a magnetically encoded card. Variable data, such as transaction type and amount, are inserted via a simple keyboard. The terminal may check a status file held locally or at the centre before carrying out the transaction, and acting upon it.

## Optional Mark or Character Readers

These are small readers sensing optical marks or hand-printed stylized characters at typical speeds of 600 documents/minute. May be connected directly on-line, but more often to another terminal such as an intelligent video, which checks and enables rapid correction of doubtful characters and field content. Used, for example, in order data capture, when rapid processing is required at the point of origin of the data, and the product range can be conveniently pre-printed or encoded onto the source documents. One reader terminal can service orders prepared by many clerks in this way.

## Touch-tone/Voice Response

A touch-tone telephone (using keys instead of a dial) is the complete terminal. The keyboard is used to generate a normal telephone number and so connects into a special controller on the main computer. Encoded messages are then sent using the keyboard. A reply is prepared by the program and is translated by the control unit to normal English words, by access to standard messages pre-recorded on a special drum. The reply is received as in normal operation via the earpiece of the telephone. The use of this technique is currently restricted in some countries such as the UK to non-PO lines.

## Simultaneous Display

For rapid dissemination of data simultaneously to various locations. Data are stored at each location in a buffer and displayed there on one or more TV monitors. Changes to these data are generated by one message from the computer to a special control unit, and are then electronically reproduced simultaneously on all the lines to the remote displays. The use of the buffer at the terminal end allows normal telephone lines to be employed.

### 10.1.3   COMPATIBILITY

With a rich variety of terminals to choose from, many of them from other sources than the supplier of the main computer, the establishment of compatibility is an increasingly common problem. An installation purchasing very many terminals may be in the fortunate position of forcing the computer manufacturer to make his equipment and software compatible with the terminals. However, a more typical installation is normally looking for the terminal to be compatible to the hardware and software used to control one of the main manufacturers' terminals. Table 10.1 shows some aspects of compatibility. The characteristics for an imaginary manufacturer's terminal are contrasted to those for a possible replacement terminal from a 'foreign' manufacturer. The first four would probably require hardware changes. The next two might be solved by software changes, but the need for recognition by the communications equipment of particular control character could require hardware alterations. Even the seventh could require at least changes to translation tables in the software.

Table 10.1  Compatibility Comparison

| Characteristics for manufacturers terminal | Aspect of compatibility | Characteristics for 'foreign terminal' |
|---|---|---|
| (1) EBCDIC | line code | ISO7 |
| (2) Cyclic parity | error checking | two-coordinate parity |
| (3) 2400 bits/second | speed | 2400 bits/second 1200 in stand-by |
| (4) Synchronous | timing | asynchronous |
| (5) Single poll message | line protocol | poll status then poll message |
| (6) Automatic | error action | notify operator re-transmission is required |
| (7) Standard | special features | magnetic tape cassettes in addition |

This is deliberately chosen as a bad case, but illustrates the possible hidden cost in an apparently cheap alternative terminal.

10.1.4  GENERAL CONSIDERATIONS

There are often many versions of each type of terminal available from a number of manufacturers. The facilities of terminals described by a generic classification, such as point of sale, can vary widely. In the future, this diversity will certainly increase. Choice of such terminals cannot be made on the basis of a simple view of the application, such as, 'The terminals are for a production system so shop-floor terminals are required.' Nor can it be made from a knowledge of the market gained in the past. In addition, the terminal characteristics need careful evaluation from the compatibility view-point. In a year, the possibilities can change dramatically. Consequently, a formal selection process as described in section 10.6 is desirable.

## 10.2  Communication Controllers

To relieve the main computer of much of the detail of interfacing to lines, including the extremely high overhead of the bit manipulation involved, a communications controller is connected between a channel on the main computer and the line equipment. This section discusses

– single line controllers;
– multi-line hardware controllers;
– multi-line software controllers.

10.2.1  SINGLE-LINE CONTROLLERS

A single-line controller carries out various monitoring and control functions for a single communication line. It also breaks down characters into bit streams

**136**

and assembles them again as characters as appropriate, and examines characters for special significance. A fuller list of functions is given in Table 10.2.

**Table 10.2**   Functions of a Single Line Controller

- Interface to the main computer, similarly to any peripheral control unit, in transferring characters or words across the channel, under control of the channel program.
- Code conversion.
- Breaking characters down to bit serial form for transfer to line.
- Providing the appropriate physical line conditions, e.g., communication with the modem.
- Assembling bits received from line to character form.
- Transmitting and receiving bits at the appropriate line rate.
- Stripping off and generating bits and characters used for character framing or synchronization.
- Checking of parity and informing the main computer of errors detailed.
- Recognition of special control characters such as ETX (end of message).
- Interrupting the central processing unit within the main computer on completion of a message or detection of a fault condition.

The communications techniques implied by these functions are discussed in chapter 17.

### 10.2.2   MULTI-LINE HARDWARE CONTROLLERS

These controllers, sometimes called character multiplexors or scanners, carry out similar functions to those described above, but for many lines. Normally, a mixture of types of line and speed is possible, either within the same controller, or by connection of a group of controllers each providing for one type and speed.

In addition to the single line functions, the device maintains character registers for each line. Apparent simultaneity of all lines connected is possible, because a fast electronic scanning device is provided which deals with lines in a cyclic fashion. The scanning logic is rapid enough to service each line interface more frequently than the bit rate, so data flows can be maintained on each line in parallel. The scanning logic takes into the registers any bits received by the line interface since last checking that interface, or for transmission sets up the next bit to be sent. The precise timing of reception or transmission is controlled by logic associated with these line interfaces.

The controller in interfacing to the channel has to identify characters (or words as appropriate) by line. For transmission, the characters are then stored in the register appropriate for the line. For reception the characters, after passing across the channel, can then be stored by the software in the computer in sequence with characters previously received from the line. Obviously, the stream of characters across the channel consists of characters interleaved from many messages. This creates an extra overhead, since the channel program has

**137**

to transfer characters at random to or from different areas in main storage. A further overhead on the channel is the need to pass all the messages associated with line control, such as polling of terminals, in addition to the data themselves.

Hardware multi-line controllers can normally handle all lines allowed by the configuration rules, working simultaneously at the rated speeds. In other words if every line were sending a continual stream of data, the messages would all be received intact. Timing problems certainly can arise, however, within the main computer.

### 10.2.3 MULTI-LINE SOFTWARE CONTROLLERS

Sometimes referred to appropriately as front-end processors, software controllers have hardware interfacing to the lines which is similar to a hardware controller as described above. In addition, there is a separate processor interposed between this hardware and the channel of the main computer. Some of the functions described above as being effected by hardware, such as code recognition, might be carried out by software in this case.

The communications software which manages the network, described further below, resides in the front-end processor. This lifts the overheads of transmission control messages from the channel. Message buffers are contained in the storage of the device, and it is only when a message has been successfully received that it is passed over the channel. The software would normally also handle any retransmission requests. Since messages, or segments of messages, are transferred over the channel, the latter no longer has the burden of dealing with a mix of characters in random order by line.

Software controllers are sometimes used in an interim manner to simulate a hardware controller. In this case many of the advantages in reduced overheads may not be realized.

Some software controllers are connectable remotely from the main processor. In this case, the controller is connected to a telephone line instead of the channel. The line is then connected into a further controller local to the main processor.

Additional potential advantages of software controllers are the capability of message switching between terminals without intervention of the main computer, and message buffering on disk to deal with overloads, or to enable collection of data when the main computer is down. Also possible is the validation of message content by user-written routines. These potential advantages, of course, are realizable only if the software from the controller supplier provides for them.

## 10.3 Communications Software

It is normal for software to be provided by the main computer manufacturer or from an outside supplier so that the burden of detailed handling of terminal traffic is removed from application programmers. This section introduces the

138

environment into which this software fits, and then considers the attributes
required of such software, before looking at some problems of these packages.

### 10.3.1 COMMUNICATIONS SOFTWARE ENVIRONMENT

Figure 10.1 shows the environment of communications software. The communications software, in controlling the network, accumulates a queue of
messages for the application program (the IN Q). After processing, the program
requests the software to output a message to a given terminal, and it is placed
on the OUT Q (actually one queue for each line). The software is either all resident within the main computer, or mainly within the multi-line software controller. In the latter case, there are extra routines required to control the flow of
messages across the channel between the queues and the software controller.
The manner of working of the software is otherwise similar in the two cases.

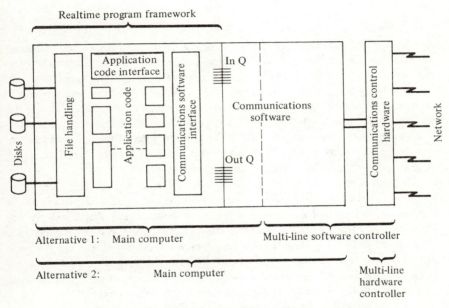

**10.1** Relationships of communication software to the system

Since input and output messages are communicated to the application
program via queues, the latter can carry out its processing without being synchronized to communications events. Nevertheless, as discussed in chapter 14,
there is often the need for a framework of service routines within the program.
This framework, illustrated in Fig. 10.1, provides for very simple logical
application codes to be written, and manages the interface to manufacturer's
software, including communications.

Sometimes the real time program framework and communications software
are provided as separately identifiable packages, and the programmers are

aware of the message queue interface (As for ICL 1900 Communications Manager and DRIVER). The two may be combined, and the message queue handling is embedded in the software. (As for IBM CICS.) The trend is towards provision of both as an integral part of the machine operating system. (As for Executive B in ICL 2900 series.) Whatever the software situation, it is convenient in outlining communications software requirements to discuss the software as if it interfaces to message queues as shown in Fig. 10.1. In most cases such queues actually exist, even if unknown to the programmer.

## 10.3.2 COMMUNICATIONS SOFTWARE REQUIREMENTS

In this section an imaginary communications software package (CSP) is described, to illustrate some important facilities of such software. Not all actual packages have these facilities, nor do all applications need them. There are also additional facilities provided in some available software.

### Line Control

A communications software package stores in tables, hardware addresses of terminals within line address (the physical connection location on the communications controller). It carries out a control conversation appropriate for the type of terminal, as in the example in Fig. 10.2. In this case each terminal is addressed in turn, requesting transmission of a message if ready (polling). If a terminal has no message it responds with a NAK character; otherwise it sends the message from the terminal buffer. The CSP puts such messages onto the input queue, unless an error is detected by transmission control checks, in which case it requests a retransmission (up to three times).

While messages are being processed in the program, polling continues, restarting at the next terminal in the table following the one which has just sent a message. A terminal awaiting a reply is not polled again until the reply has been sent. To limit software overheads for a lightly used system, a delay may be specified between polling the last terminal in the table and starting the cycle again. Before each polling message, CSP looks at the output queue for the appropriate line to see if there is a message awaiting output. If so, it stops polling and transmits the message to the appropriate terminal (selecting).

This conversation can be carried out by CSP for all lines connected, apparently simultaneously. Because of its high speed of processing relative to times between communication events it can, for example, send polling messages down all lines and be ready to receive a reply wherever it originates, without delaying that line.

### Message Buffering

Messages are stored in main storage as a dynamic pool of message cells of prespecified size. In this way, as illustrated in Fig. 10.3, less storage may be provided than the theoretical maximum required if all lines simultaneously sent maximum size messages. The storage size may be pre-calculated to cater for

**140**

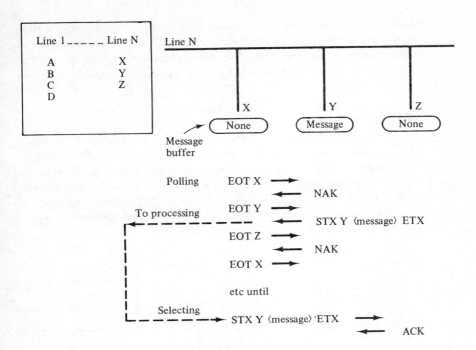

**Fig. 10.2** Terminal control conversation

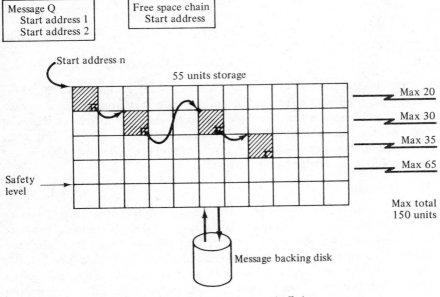

**Fig. 10.3** Dynamic message buffering

the majority of probable cases. To prevent loss of data in overload, after a safety level is reached messages are written to a backing disk. The chronological sequence is preserved for presentation to the application program by reading the earliest message, whether it is in main, or on backing, storage, when an input request is received.

### Several Programs

A communications software package interfaces to a number of separate programs (mutually store-protected by the operating system), as shown in Fig. 10.4. Terminals may be allocated to any program when the software is generated. This allocation may be switched via the network controllers console during live running. Messages are routed by CSP between programs if required. This method of working is convenient if groups of terminals are permanently occupied with a particular application.

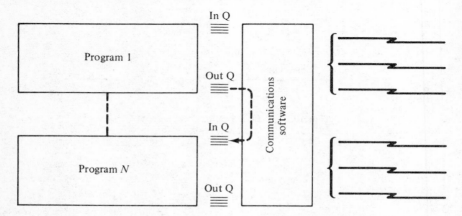

Fig. 10.4   Multi-programs with line allocation

If terminals require to interface to a number of applications, CSP routes the messages by message code. It analyses the code in a fixed position in each message and queues it for the prespecified program for that code, as shown in Fig. 10.5. Facilities are provided for handling unrecognizable codes. CSP deals with lines on one or more communications controllers, and allows any number of programs to be related to one controller.

### Error Detection

Automatic retries are handled by CSP, if errors are transient. Error statistics are accumulated for interrogation via the network control console. Details of permanent error symptoms are output to the console. To diagnose the fault further, the suspected line or terminal can be isolated from the system by CSP, which can then run diagnostic routines on that element alone, and output further information to the controller. Error reports are fed via the input message queues to the application program.

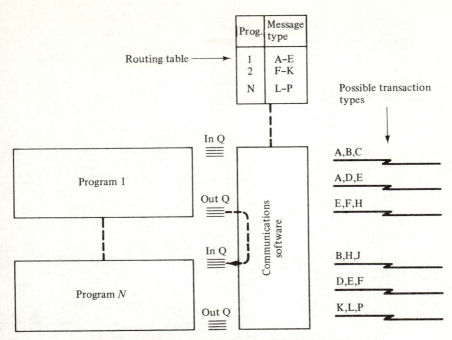

**Fig. 10.5** Multi-programs with message routing by type

## Terminal Reconfiguration

Line tables in the software are maintained by physical terminal address, within line address. Many network failures are possible. Figure 10.6 shows the case of a terminal address C on line 1, which is cut off by failure of the spur connection from the multi-drop line. After dial-up facilities on the modems have been utilized to re-connect to the centre, the line is plugged into line position 50 on the controller. The network controller is able to input messages to CSP to reconfigure the tables to match the physical reconfiguration, as illustrated in the figure. To make such changes to the network transparent to the program, each terminal is addressed by a logical identifier which does not change. When a request for output is made, CSP translates from the logical to the physical address required by line control routines, and vice versa for input. There is a set of such reconfiguration messages to match each possible fault and hardware change. Terminals, when inactive, may also be temporarily withdrawn from a polling sequence by means of the control console.

## Application Program Interface

By using a simple macro, the program accesses the next message (or error report) in chronological sequence. It is placed by CSP into a predefined area in main storage. Similarly, issue of a macro command causes an output message in this interface area to be taken by CSP onto the relevant terminal queue.

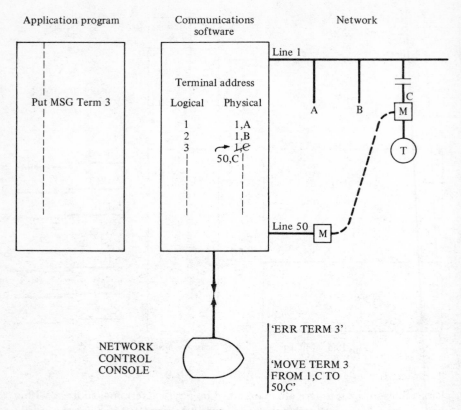

**Fig. 10.6** Software reconfiguration

Details of message length, terminal identifier, terminal type, and other status information are passed through the interface. CSP checks the validity of program commands and the content of the interface area.

The facility of having several input queues of different priority is provided by CSP. Terminals or message types are pre-allocated to the appropriate queue. When the program requests the next message, it is given the next message in chronological sequence from the highest priority queue which contains any messages.

*Generation of Software*

A convenient high level language is provided to enable a user to specify the generation of a particular occurrence of CSP. Thus, facilities not required may be left out to save computer time and storage space. Attributes which are specifiable include

– number of programs;
– queue structure for each;
– amount of message buffer storage;

144

- use of disk-backed message buffering;
- message codes and allocation to programs;
- logical terminal addresses;
- allocation of logical terminals to programs;
- terminal types;
- controller, line, and terminal physical addresses, and the relationship to logical address;
- control conversation structure, and transmission code for each line;
- sequence and priority of polling within each line;
- error statistics required;
- amount of main storage for CSP;
- data logging of input and output messages.

### 10.3.3 COMMUNICATIONS SOFTWARE PROBLEMS

Generalized software packages reduce the user involvement in the detail of network handling, but have some associated disadvantages.

The first is the relatively high machine resource requirement. A package similar to CSP as described above, on one manufacturer's range, can occupy 100–200 K bytes of main storage, and on a medium sized machine can consume 100 ms of CPU time for each message pair.

The second is the lack of required facilities. Since the software is offered as a package it is difficult to tailor for an individual installation to provide for these omissions. As an example, the facility for reconfiguring line tables to reflect a network change, following a fault, might not be provided. Because of the potentially severe consequences of such omissions, there is a need to carefully match requirements against facilities offered in a given package. Even if the communications software is integral with other software, as outlined in section 10.3.1, many of the facilities discussed here are required in the communications handling part, and so all products offered should be evaluated in detail.

## 10.4 Data Transmission Components

Between the controller and the terminals, various transmission components are required. These, in order of occurrence, going outwards from the controller and its line connections hardware, are

- modems (for telephone lines);
- line switching and testing panels;
- communications lines;
- modems;
- terminal connection units.

This section looks at some of the system design implications of these components. The detail of the data transmission techniques involved is covered in chapter 17.

## Telephone Lines

The range of speeds of telephone lines available is typically 200–9600 bits/second. Speeds up to 1200, or even 2400, are possible on good quality sections of the public switched network (PSN). For working reliably at speeds of 1200 and above, leased (or private) lines are still required in many areas. The speed capability of a transmission link is in fact a function of the modem/line combination. Higher speeds than those provided for by modems available from the PTT's (Supplier of data transmission facilities, e.g., British PO, AT & T in the USA) can be achieved by using privately purchased modems, even though the line's characteristics are not enhanced. For example, transmission at speeds greatly in excess of 2400 have been achieved over switched lines (up to 9600 bits/second).

The rate of transmission of user data along any link also depends on a variety of factors other than bit-rate speed. These are number of bits per character, number of control characters, e.g., for polling, and rate of error and thus number of retransmissions. The following example illustrates the effect of these aspects.

| | | |
|---|---|---|
| Number of characters to be transmitted | = | 10 000 |
| Number of data bits/characters | = | 7 |
| Line speed | = | 2 400 bits/second |
| Time to transmit, on a simple calculation | = | 29 seconds |
| Average size transmitted block | = | 500 characters |
| ∴ Number blocks | = | 20 |
| Transmission control characters required per block | = | 10 |
| Actual numbers of bits per character (including start, stop and bits) | = | 10 |
| Line error rate, average | = | 1 bit in $10^5$ |
| | = | 1 block in 20 |
| Actual number of characters transmitted | = | 10 000 data |
| | + | 200 control |
| | | 10 200 |
| | + | 510 error |
| | | 10 710 |
| Actual number of bits transmitted | | 10 710 × 10 |
| Time to transmit allowing for control, error checking facilities, character framing bits | = | 45 seconds. |

This comparison, 45 seconds against 29, slightly overstates the problem, since in practice errors often occur in bursts, thus causing less blocks to be in error than if uniformly distributed (as assumed implicitly). However, it is obvious that significant timing errors can occur from insufficient knowledge of the data transmission techniques utilized in a given system.

A normal telephone line terminates with two wires. This allows for one-way (simplex), or half-duplex transmission. The latter is transmission in one direction followed by transmission in the opposite direction, but not at the same time. For a small extra charge, a leased telephone line may be installed with four wires (switched lines are always two wire). Four wire connections allow full duplex transmission—transmission simultaneously in both directions. This capability is infrequently used by terminals for simultaneity of user data.

*Telegraph Lines*

Telegraph lines are either provided by the PTT as switched connections—the Telex service, limited to a maximum of 50 bits/second—or as leased lines, with a typical maximum speed of 110 bits/second. No modems are required in either case. The same considerations on throughput apply as for telephone lines. Leased telegraph lines provide a full duplex capability. This is sometimes used to increase error checking of input on character printers which do not have full parity checking. Instead of each character being directly printed and simultaneously sent to line as it is keyed, it is only sent to the line. On being received at the communications control equipment, it is simultaneously stored and sent back to the terminal to be printed. Transmission in the two directions takes place along separate parts in the full duplex link. The advantage of this echo checking technique is that if the operator sees a character printed as he intended, there is an extremely high probability that the same character was received by the computer.

Telegraph lines are cheaper than telephone. However, it is not normally possible or desirable to share telegraph lines between a number of terminals using polling techniques. This arises from the low speed and lack of facility in many countries for multi-point lines. As a consequence, each terminal normally requires its own connection to the centre, which can be more costly overall than shared telephone lines.

10.4.2  MODEMS

The modems are selected for a given system with regard to available line grades, speed and timing capability of the terminals and communications controller, the volumes of data to be transmitted, and availability of modems of the required speed.

If modems of high enough speed are not available from the PTT, and it is necessary to obtain modems from an independent supplier, the following points need checking:

— compatibility with the terminals;
— approval by the PTT for connection to lines;
— service and emergency repair;
— who accepts responsibility for a fault not positively identified as being in a specific piece of equipment.

Modems are connected in pairs at either end of a single line. If a multidrop line is used, there must be one modem at the end of each spur connection, and one at the centre.

A small delay in transmission occurs due to the way in which the modems operate—apart from the expected transmission time arising from the number of characters to be sent at the known line rate. For one message pair this may be 150 ms, in total, for a two wire connection within the UK. For intercontinental lines this may be of the order of seconds. This delay (even if only 150 ms) becomes significant when a number of terminals are sharing a line, since it applies equally to the polling requests which result in 'no data' messages, as well as the transmission of actual data. Consequently, in this case, four wire connections are often used, even though data are not to be sent full duplex. The two independent paths reduce the time taken by the modem to make itself ready when a change in data direction occurs. This reduced time is typically 30 ms for lines of a few hundred kilometres in length.

Many modems have provision for stand-by operations, should a leased line fail. This is standard in, for example the UK Post Office modems where a telephone handset and exchange line is mandatory at any location remote from the computer. After failure, the handset and PSN are used to dial the centre, where a temporary connection is made to the normal or a stand-by modem. At this time, it might also be necessary to switch the speed down to that which can be transmitted over the switched line (as an example, 4800 normal, to 1200 bits/second stand-by working). The modem might also require different control signals in normal and stand-by mode because its mode of operation is different. The communications controller and terminal both need to be capable of driving the modem in the two modes. For successful planning of stand-by operation, it is thus necessary to:

- check the hardware facilities of all components to ensure that they can operate in both ways;
- ensure that efficient control over verbal communication and switching of lines and components can be done in one place at the centre;
- allow for the possible degraded speed of operation of the system in standby mode.

### 10.4.3 LINE SHARING

For telegraph lines, line sharing using channelizing equipment is possible. Using a pair of channelizers, one at each end of a telephone line, it is possible to provide for simultaneous transmission of up to 24 telegraph transmissions, depending on speed. Figure 10.7 illustrates the concept. A telephone line is simply substituted for a number of telegraph connections over all or part of their route. Each telegraph wire has sole use of a sub-channel in the telephone link, and can transmit at full speed at the same time as all others connected. The channelizers act as modems, but using a different pair of transmission frequencies for each telegraph channel. The connection at the centre and at terminals is no different from that without channelizers, and there are no message delays associated with their use (except propagation delays measured in milliseconds). For a typical network, line cost reductions of 30–50 per cent can be achieved with this technique. On the other hand, the amount of redundancy of lines is decreased, since telephone line failures stop operation of more terminals. Because this equipment uses the full band width of the telephone line, it is often not possible to use the PSN for standby, because frequencies used for standard control tones in the PSN would be overlapped by data signals.

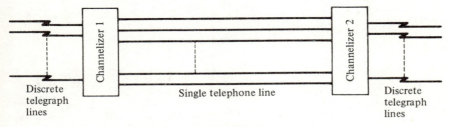

Fig. 10.7   Channelizers

For telephone lines this technique of splitting up a line by frequency division is not normally possible. It requires a wide band line to do this. Instead, the time available on a line is divided up by allowing terminals to use the line in sequential fashion. Each terminal, while transmitting, uses the full band width (or transmission capability) of the line. To make this process efficient, terminals need message buffers, so that the operator can be entering data, or dealing with previously transmitted data, without requiring use of the line. Actual transmission, when required, occurs at full line speed, and occupies a relatively small fraction of the overall transaction time at the terminal.

If terminals are in separate locations, they are connected by a multi-drop line as shown in Fig. 10.8. The main line is connected via exchanges, and each terminal is connected via a modem to a spur line dropped off at the nearest exchange. For standby reasons, the PTT may prefer a route to any given terminal to be via no more than two exchanges (e.g., UK PO). In Fig. 10.8 this would be achieved if all spur connections radiated from exchange A. The main connection between exchanges A and B would also preferably be via a main trunk route. The line time is distributed between the terminals by means of a software controlled conversation such as that illustrated in Fig. 10.2.

For groups of terminals in the same location, whether connected to a direct or multi-drop line, a multi terminal controller is used. This technique is shown in principle in Fig. 10.9. One modem is used for all terminals. The simplest type of controller merely performs the functions of matching the terminal modem interfaces to a single modem, and amplifies signals so that the terminals can be placed at greater distance from the controller than they otherwise would be from the modem. The controller conversation takes place exactly as for separately connected terminals, since the controller passively passes all control or data messages through itself. Thus, if no terminals have a message to send,

149

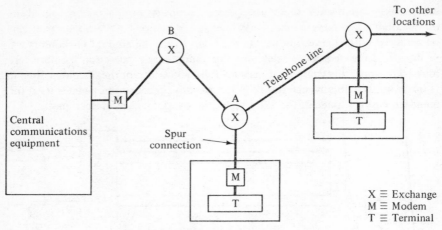

Fig. 10.8 Multi-drop line

they will still all be polled by the software. To overcome this unnecessary overhead, pollable controllers may sometimes be used. In this case, the software interacts with the controller, and not individual terminals. The controller monitors the terminals, and if none have a message ready to send, it informs the software of this with one single message. If there are one or more messages ready, it sends the first according to a predetermined sequence of priority. By using controllers of greater intelligence it is possible to further decrease line time per data message, and so increase the numbers of terminals connectable, by increasing the rate of transmission on the line above the speed of operation of the terminals, and compressing and expanding data. Going further, and in many cases achieving a much greater amount of compaction the controller is used for maintaining local files of, for example, standard formats, and literals such as product descriptions. It then carries out local validation and thus reduces the traffic from error messages and corrections.

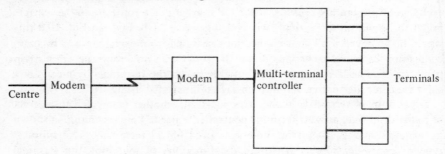

Fig. 10.9 Multi-terminal controllers

## 10.5 Choice of Hardware and Software

Frequently, in the communications area, there is the need to choose hardware

**150**

and software from a range of possibilities. This is sometimes limited to choice within the main frame manufacturer's facilities, but increasingly it is also worth looking to outside suppliers.

The basic aim of such choice should be to identify facilities which are cost effective, judged from the point of view of the foreseen application needs. Too frequently, selection exercises within this area are carried out as academic comparisons, implicitly against some general ideal requirement. It is no good selecting, say, a real time program monitor for its ability to handle such problems as dynamic work storage management, if a simple real time system with a few terminals dedicated to a single application is all that is to be implemented in practice. The cost of the selection exercise should, of course, be related to the potential savings to be gained.

A sequence of activity which has been found in practice to be effective for selection projects is outlined below:

- identify all applications which will require the facility;
- identify all possible sources of supply;
- prepare a brief summary of the requirement and send to all suppliers. Ask for details of experience with, and support for, the facility, other installations, where, engineering and other support services, compatibility;
- assess replies, eliminating obvious non-starters, such as those with no installed facilities, no support in essential areas, incompatibility;
- prepare short list;
- prepare specification for tender providing more detail of application: message types, volumes, processing, etc., specific questions on support, experience and financial viability to be answered in tender, bench-mark or demonstration required;
- brief the suppliers;
- evaluate tenders eliminating errors, over- and under-quoting, and agree changes with suppliers to form a common basis for comparison;
- compare tenders giving most weight to features considered most essential for the application(s). Cost each, ensuring that the cost of providing essential features not offered is included (see section 10.2.2 and Fig. 14.8 for possible features to evaluate);
- choose the overall best offer, or possibly two or three to be finally reduced to one during contractual negotiations;
- carry out contractual negotiations, ensuring that aspects of the facility to which the system is sensitive in cost or performance are, where possible, guaranteed.

For a large installation requiring hundreds of terminals, the opportunities for considerable savings by such selection procedures and for commanding the necessary support, are great. Even a small installation, however, has the opportunity to make useful savings by selection of appropriate communications or real-time monitor software. The difference in machine resource requirements between similar competing products in this area can be significant, even at low message volumes.

## 10.6 Design Approach

Having considered the components which go to make up the network, and their selection, this section goes on to consider the design approach in arriving at a network configuration to suit a given application requirement.

The starting point is a clear definition of the information flow requirements at the terminals in the system specification. The designer's job is to fit these requirements to the appropriate hardware, and calculate loadings so as to define the configuration. In doing so, he has to visualize the transactions from the point of view of the operator. For this reason, there are aspects of the task which depart from exact science or laid-down procedure, and are more in the realm of behavioural science. Qualifications in the latter are not necessary, but considerable imagination and discussion are often needed to achieve the required understanding of the human interface to the machine.

### 10.6.1 THE DESIGN PROCESS

The network need not be designed at the same time as the central configuration, and is best tackled first; thus a logical split of design activity is necessary. This split is along the line shown in Fig. 10.10, just outside the communications control equipment. In the absence of the detail of the central design, an assumption must be made about the response time of the computer. This time, called here computer turn-round time, is the time required to carry out all the processing and waiting in internal queues; i.e. from the last character of the input message arriving to the first character of the output messages passing across the design interface. In interactive processing it is usual for terminal conversations to be carried out as one or more such message pairs. If only one unbuffered terminal is using the line, this is the complete response time as seen by the operator—the perceived response time. For a single buffered terminal, the perceived response time consists of the time from pressing the transmit key to receiving the first output message character. In other words, it is the input message transmission time (during which little of apparent use to the operator is taking place) plus the computer turn-round time. In the case of buffered terminals, sharing the line, as shown in Fig. 10.10, the perceived response time is made up of:

- line delay (wait while terminal is polled);
- input transmission time;
- computer turn-round time;
- line delay (wait before terminal can be selected).

This applies for a polling conversation of the type illustrated in Fig. 10.2, where polling continues while message processing for a given terminal takes place. If the line is held by the control conversation while processing takes place, the second line delay is not present. These line delays occur because, in general, the

152

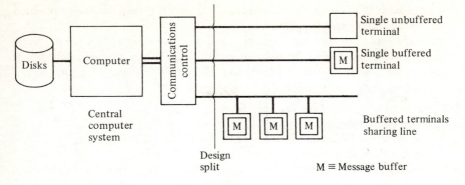

Single unbuffered terminal

Single buffered terminal

Buffered terminals sharing line

Central computer system

Design split

M ≡ Message buffer

Actual configuration

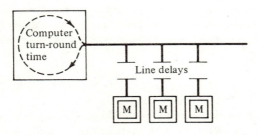

Computer turn-round time

Line delays

Design equivalent

**Fig. 10.10** Separation of the network

line is being utilized for another terminal when a given terminal requires service.

Initially, in network design, an assumption is necessary for the perceived response time (PRT) to allow calculation of terminal numbers to be carried out. Later, when the degree of line sharing is being considered, the line delay or contribution can be verified by calculation. Finally, when the central computer system is designed, the computer turn-round time can be calculated, and its contribution to the PRT can be assessed. Theoretically, if the total PRT varied from the assumption, recalculation of terminal numbers would be required. However, if, for example, an assumption of 5 seconds had been made for PRT, and an average transaction time of 50 seconds applied, any errors in the assumption would be of small overall effect. Further, since it is common experience that an average PRT of greater than approximately 5 seconds causes problems to operators, psychologically they expect an 'immediate response' and as a consequence get increasingly irritated by longer response times. Consequently, a PRT of a given value, such as 5 seconds, is often a design objective rather than merely a temporary working assumption. The degree of line sharing and central computer design must be chosen to be com-

**153**

patible with this, rather than accepting a higher PRT than originally assumed and recalculating terminal numbers.

In systems with very short transaction times, the design objective might be much lower than 5 seconds, because such a value would occupy a substantial part of the overall transaction time, and thus affect throughput substantially.

The network design process is, in summary:

— choice of terminal for the application;
— transaction design;
— transaction timing (in which an assumption of PRT is made);
— calculation of numbers of terminals in each location;
— calculation of number of lines required for each location (in which a line delay compatible with the assumed PRT is achieved);
— allocation of terminals to lines;
— possible iterations around each or all steps.

These subjects are covered in this sequence in the rest of the section. The amount of iteration around a number of steps can in many cases be eliminated by carrying out an initial overall design which sets the framework for the detail (see chapter 7).

### 10.6.2 CHOICE OF TERMINAL

With an ever-increasing range of possibilities, the choice of terminal is in some cases a major consideration. The basic problem, as always, is to balance cost and effectiveness; to decide where extra features costing more are contributing to greater productivity and operator acceptability, as opposed to being just 'nice to have'.

All too often the choice appears deceptively obvious. A few trite (but true) examples, of comments from instant designers are quoted below.

— 'We are a bank, so we need banking terminals.' The application was for relatively high volume file enquiries.
— 'We are dealing with a quick access requirement to main files, so we need video terminals.' The solution later adopted was to use micro-fiche readers, since the files were static between weekly updates.
— 'We need hard copy so we will use teleprinters.' The use of video terminals with attached hard copy devices was finally adopted, since before deciding on information to be printed, a scan through much data was necessary.

Some of the considerations necessary in deciding on the right terminal are considered below.

### Method of Connection

Are the right type of lines available throughout the network? Does the controller provide for connection of this type of terminal and the mix of terminals required in the foreseeable future?

## Compatibility

If the terminal is from an independent supplier, is it compatible at all levels with the communications hardware and software available (see Section 10.1.3)? Even with the range offered by the main computer supplier, an otherwise unwarranted upgrade in operating system could be required to enable a desired terminal to be connected.

## Fail-soft

To what degree does the terminal depend on the main computer to continue in operation? It may be much cheaper to provide intelligence and temporary data storage at the terminal, than redundant hardware at the centre.

## Environment

The cleanliness, humidity, temperature, likelihood of accidental damage, should be related to the terminal's specification. A terminal built for office conditions may not be reliable in, for example, a warehouse.

## Reliability and Field Service

Because the locations are distributed, and probably very dependent on continuing operation of the terminals, proven reliability, fast attendance, diagnosis and repair are potentially of overriding importance.

## Operator Guidance and Checking

This is the most difficult area of choice. The degree of guidance and validation is determined by the transaction diversity and complexity, and the operators' potential skill. Often the operators are re-trained current staff in the function being computerized. The type of terminal and additional features necessary both depend on this aspect.

## Cost

The unit terminal cost is no guide. The transaction time depends, for example, on the speed of operation of the terminal, the local facilities for reducing keying effort and the degree of interaction required with the computer. Each extra terminal requires an operator, which adds to the cost. The degree of sharing of network facilities such as lines and line termination units also can vary with terminal type. Considerable differences in complexity of programming and use of central computer facilities can affect the comparison. Thus, to compare costs of alternative terminal types, some design and overall costing of the network plus operators is necessary.

As an example of this overall costing, see Fig. 10.11. There are three alternative networks shown, using different types of terminals. The transactions are complex and require significant operator guidance, and hard copy of at least selected output information is required. The alternatives examined were:

**155**

- The first used hard copy terminals to guide the operators through question and answer by computer program. Hard copy was a by-product, but not necessarily in the most convenient form.
- The second used video terminals with a format called up to guide input for the whole transaction. The necessary hard copy was sent by program to the shared hard copy terminal, and it was limited to just the information required.
- The third used intelligent hard copy terminals with pre-printed stationery on

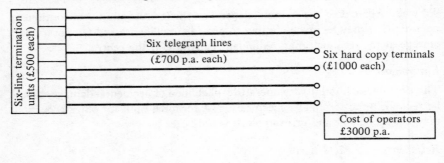

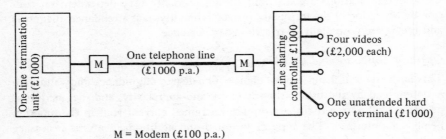

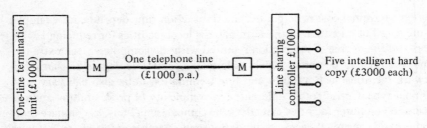

Fig. 10.11 Costing alternative networks

the platen. Operators were guided by local program which stepped the print-head down the form as it was filled in. Hard copy was in a convenient form with some redundant information.

Because of the differences of approach necessary, the terminal numbers, and thus numbers of operators, are different depending on the transaction times

156

**Table 10.3** Comparative Network Costs

| Cost element | Hard copy | Video | Intelligent hard copy |
|---|---|---|---|
| Terminals | 6 000 | 9 000 | 15 000 |
| Line sharing CU | — | 1 000 | 1 000 |
| Line termination units | 3 000 | 1 000 | 1 000 |
| Total capital | 9 000 | 11 000 | 17 000 |
| Annual cost amortized | 2 250 | 2 750 | 4 250 |
| Modems | — | 200 | 200 |
| Lines | 4 200 | 1 000 | 1 000 |
| Operators | 18 000 | 12 000 | 15 000 |
| Total annual cost | 24 450 | 15 950 | 20 450 |

| | |
|---|---|
| Overall cost ranking | Video |
| | Intelligent hard copy |
| | Hard copy |
| Convenience ranking | Video (because of selective hard copy) |
| | Intelligent hard copy |
| | Hard copy |
| Unit terminal hardware cost ranking | Hard copy |
| | Video |
| | Intelligent hard copy |

calculated. The comparative costs amortizing capital at 25 per cent are calculated and compared in Table 10.3. This shows that a simple unit cost comparison would have caused the network of greatest actual cost, and least convenience, to have been chosen. The most predominant cost is that of operators; hence the more advanced terminals, which bring down the transaction times and the number of operators, can be cheaper.

### 10.6.3 TRANSACTION DESIGN

The starting point of transaction design is a specification of the logical content of each transaction. This will specify field types, sizes, and occurrences in the usual way. As discussed in chapter 6, any breakdown of the transaction into logical steps will have been identified. For example:

— input account number;
— receive display of account name and address and credit rating;
— input order details;
— receive order number.

If the account numbers were quoted verbally and could be wrong, and a significant portion of accounts were bad debts, this breakdown would be logically necessary. It would enable the operator to check the initial details before accepting an order.

The object of transaction design is to take these logical specifications, and to define in precise physical terms exactly what will take place for each at the terminal. It involves:

— design of layout of messages exactly as they appear on the terminal, allowing for limitations such as maximum message buffer size;

**157**

- deciding use of ancillary input devices such as optical label reading and edge punch card readers;
- deciding use of ancillary output devices such as magnetic tape cassettes and hard copy printers;
- specifying associated clerical activity, such as looking up indexes, signing, and date stamping documents;
- providing error correction facilities;
- designing the sequence of activity, and branches where change of action occurs at decision points.

In this design, careful attention needs to be paid to minimizing the transaction times, and increasing the accuracy of the operation of the terminals.

*Minimizing Transaction Times*

The major contribution to overall transaction time in many applications is the input keying time, and manual operations like looking up directories or discussions with customer. Input time can be reduced by uniform and clear design of documents so that information is found easily. Also the reduction of characters keyed can be achieved by partial input of key data which is sufficient for the program to identify. It then presents to the operator a range of possibilities from which he selects.

Directory look-up times can be reduced by removing them to a prior manual operation (which does not thus use terminal time), or by inserting an imprecise but readily available key as described above; a possible example is

```
INPUT    1     COLLINS
OUTPUT 1       1 COLLINS A    9 MANOR PK LON
               2 COLLINS G L 5 FOXBOROUGH R
               3 COLLINS S   55 CLOSE AVE L
INPUT    2     2 plus input data, etc.
```

Sufficient data are output to enable a precise identification of the required option to be made by means of an account or other identity number. This technique needs to be controlled to prevent unnecessary iteration with the program. The above sequence would be an example of unnecessary iteration if precise identity was available in the majority of cases. More frequently it appears under the justification of being 'helpful' to the operator by excessive question and answer to elicit the input of data.

*Increasing Accuracy*

Accuracy can be increased by providing for good visibility of output data; ensuring they are not too crowded and follow a sequence natural to the business, and ensuring continuity between message pairs, e.g., in a video application, if data are to be selected from information previously displayed and inserted into a format, both areas should be simultaneously on the screen at the time of input.

Error correction should be simplified by informing the operator clearly what is wrong, and in doing so not obscuring the data in error, and by reducing the number of different procedures associated with error correction and thus the amount of re-keying.

Accuracy is enhanced by minimizing the amount of control over facilities local to the terminal which the operator has to remember, e.g., causing the input of data from a magnetically encoded card to be carried out by program at the right time in a transaction sequence, rather than relying on the operator to remember to command it to happen. Operator guidance should be provided at a more detailed level by giving suitable guidance in the course of the transaction (e.g., by the use of formats on video terminals, and giving the operator advice messages to prompt him as to what to do next), but avoiding too much iteration as discussed above.

Both accuracy and convenience of operation are improved by allowing the operator the opportunity to sequence the flow of transactions at the terminal, e.g., if a batch of messages has been prepared at the computer for a terminal, a single line message only should be sent informing him of their availability. This enables him to choose the time at which he commands full output and prevents corruption caused by clashes of input and output messages (on non-polled lines).

As an illustration of some of the above points, the following example transaction is described. The transaction is used to amend certain account details held on file. Accounts are held by account numbers on the main file, but a subsidiary file giving abbreviated account information held within post code is used to identify the precise account to be amended (in this remarkable system, postcode which identifies the road/street of residence is normally available with the transaction detail, but account number is not). Working from the logical specification, the designer has chosen a video terminal, and established the design shown in Fig. 10.12. (This shows only the main part of the straightforward sequence ignoring errors.) The operator keys and sends the post-code. He receives a list of accounts within the road so identified, from which he selects the one required, adds the account number to the post-code and sends both. He receives a format (format headings shown between parenthesis), plus account details, enters the data to be amended and sends. The resulting message is the actual account key plus the amending details. The contents of the screen remain until either an acknowledgement message clears the screen, or an error message appears on line 4 in the space provided. In the latter case fields in error are corrected and the whole message is sent again. The error correction message is no different to the original, thus simplifying operator action and computer processing.

This sequence covers only part of the range of possibilities. Table 10.4 gives a possible structure for this transaction, identifying decision points, and forced branches in procedure. This implies a number of messages still to be defined, in content, and in their relationship to those illustrated in Fig. 10.12. The further messages, however, could easily be built onto the framework shown in the figure.

159

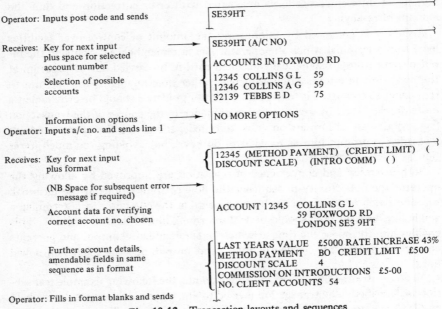

Fig. 10.12   Transaction layouts and sequences

One of the greatest problems a designer faces is that of imagining himself in the operator's seat, routinely carrying out the transactions. A designer, although perhaps more intelligent than the operator, might spend only a few days designing a transaction. He perhaps feels it is complicated, and allowing for the operator's supposed lesser intelligence, he creates a transaction sequence which gives far too much intended guidance to the operator. To counteract this tendency, the designer needs to think of the frequency of a given transaction and its mix with other types. A degree of experimentation on a few major transactions, involving the operators practically, can often be useful to ensure that the sequences are right. Chapter 9 discusses some of the ways of training operators. Some of the techniques can be used to carry out design trials.

### 10.6.4   TIMING THE TRANSACTIONS

Often, transaction timings are underestimated. This arises from two causes. The first is the omission of significant elements of the overall time, and the second is over-optimism in variables such as keying rate and thinking time.

Two broad categories of transaction can be identified. One, where patches of documents are processed at the terminal, and the other, where the operator deals directly with callers in person, or by telephone. These categories, called here pseudo batch and random, respectively, are illustrated in Fig. 10.13. The general headings for transaction elements which consume terminal and operator time for both categories are:

**160**

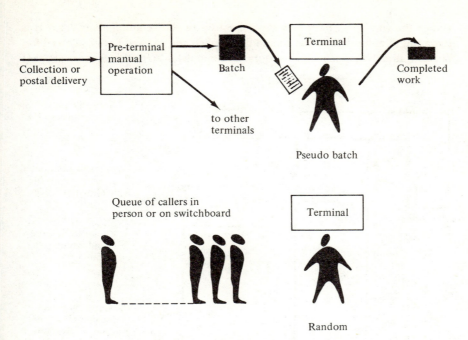

Fig. 10.13 Categories of transaction

- keying time; average number of data and control key depressions divided by average keying rate;
- checking of data input;
- error correction;
- directory or table look-up times;
- perceived response time;
- line time; average number of characters transmitted divided by character rate for the line;
- decision time; assimilating information and deciding action required.

Timing elements, which are often also incorporated in pseudo batch transactions, are (1) document overhead, which is the time to select the next document, decide on required action and put it on to a completed stack; (2) potentially much greater is the time to locate the next field to be keyed—the field search time (this can be considerable for very variable documents coming from a variety of sources); and (3) lastly, time used in document endorsement which can include signing, date stamping and adding a computer allocated transaction number.

For random transactions, there are equivalent additional times such as initial chat time required to establish the action required for the next caller, time for prompt questions; such as 'next item', 'quantity required', and final chat time; for example 'your order will be delivered on Tuesday next'.

These times can be quite extended; the last example could continue as ' . . .

**161**

and by the way how's your new extension to your shop coming along . . . ?' It is tempting to assume that this should not happen and so need not be allowed for, but if it already happens in the equivalent manual system the chances are that

TERMINAL EVENTS                                    COMMENT

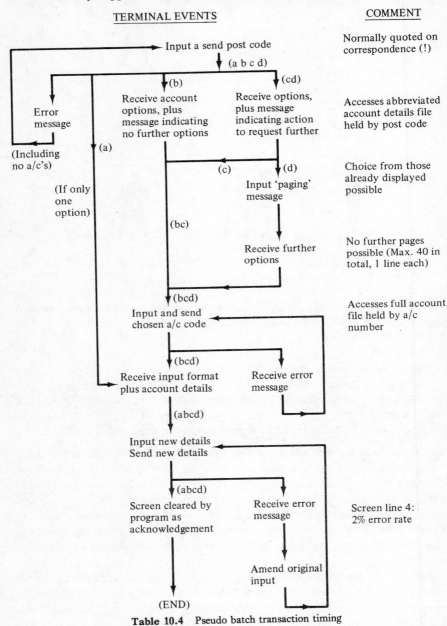

**Table 10.4** Pseudo batch transaction timing

it will continue after terminals are installed. At the very least such activity should be fully discussed with relevant managers and supervisors.

The two categories of transaction can be combined, as for example when a caller arrives with a document in hand, in which case a mixture of the above elements can occur.

In timing the transactions, the precise sequence of activity at the terminal for each is set down, times are calculated for each item and the overall time is accumulated.

It is worth setting down all the elements first before worrying about timings, because this way it is less likely that any item will be forgotten. Often, within a given transaction there are several branches. In the example given in Table 10.4, there are four main paths through the transaction, shown as a, b, c, d (this is apart from the error correction loops). For simplicity, the terminal sequence for each of the four paths would be set down separately, timed, and the overall average calculated according to the probability of each path occurring. This is far less error prone than trying to calculate the appropriate average for each step of the transaction, set out as one sequence. Table 10.4, of course, shows only the interaction with the terminal. Other activity which consumes terminal time, like decision time and document endorsement time, is not shown but would have to be included in the transaction time.

To illustrate the timing of transactions two simple cases are taken. The timings are illustrated in Tables 10.5 and 10.6, an example for each category of transaction. Both are transactions made up of one simple message pair carried out on message buffered terminals. It can be seen that, for each, a large part of the terminal time is made up of items not directly connected with interaction with the terminal, such as finding and using information, discussion, and clerical processes. Although the transactions are theoretical, the timings are from practical situations. At the same time as setting out the terminal time, the required line time is also conveniently identified at this stage. It is used later for calculating the allocation of terminals to lines.

**Table 10.5** Pseudo Batch Transaction Timing

| Timing element | Design assumption | Terminal time (sec) | Line time (sec) |
|---|---|---|---|
| 1  Document overhead | 5 seconds/doc. | 5 | |
| 2  Locate & key input data | | | |
|     Field search time (Average 6) | 4 seconds/field | 24 | |
|     Keying time (Average 40 char) | 2 key dep/second | 20 | |
| 3  Perceived response | 5 seconds | 5 | |
|     (includes 1/3 sec. transmission) | | | 1/3 |
| 4  Receive display (Average 1040 char) | | 8 2/3 | 8 2/3 |
| 5  Assimilate data | 1 second/line | 12 | |
| 6  Endorse document | | 5 | |
| Total average terminal time | | 80 | |
| Total average line time | | | 9 |
| Line rate = 120 character/second | | | |

**163**

In passing, it can be seen that the line times are small compared to the overall terminal time. This is typical and explains why it is feasible to share a line between a number of terminals. In carrying out transaction timing, it is important to record assumptions made about times, volumes, and rates. If these are clearly documented it is easy to rework the calculation later in the light of changes caused by better information. (See Section 5.2.)

**Table 10.6** Random Transaction Timing

| Timing Element | Design assumption | Terminal time (sec) | Line time (sec) |
|---|---|---|---|
| 1 Initial chat | 10 seconds | 10 | |
| 2 Interaction with caller | | | |
|   Prompt questions (average 4) | 10 seconds/q | 40 | |
|   Keying time (average 30 characters) | $1\frac{1}{2}$ key dep/second | 20 | |
| 3 Perceived response | 5 seconds | 5 | |
|   (includes 0·1 s transmission) | | | Negl. |
| 4 Receive display (average 1500 char) | | 5 | 5 |
| 5 Discuss display with caller | 10 seconds/item | 50 | |
|   (average 5 items) | | | |
| 6 Final chat | 10 seconds | 10 | |
|   Total average terminal time | | 140 | |
|   Total average line time | | | 5 |

Line rate = 300 characters/second

### 10.6.5 CALCULATION OF TERMINAL NUMBERS

Having established the time for each transaction, and knowing the volumes for each, the numbers of terminals required in each location can be determined. The calculation differs depending on the category of transaction.

*Pseudo Batch*

The terminals can be assumed to be fully loaded, so long as there are documents available to be processed. The number of terminals required ($M$) is found from

$$M = \frac{n_1 s_1 + n_2 s_2 + \cdots}{\text{time available}}$$

where $n_1$ and $s_1$ are the number and average transaction time for transaction 1, and so on.

As an example, we take the case of a two transaction system in which all documents are available at the start of a day. The clerical day is 7 hours, and all documents must be processed within the day of availability. The two transactions are as follows:

Transaction 1     $n_1 = 200$ on the peak day, $s_1 = 2$ min
Transaction 2     $n_2 = 500$ on the peak day, $s_2 = 1\frac{1}{2}$ min

**164**

$M$ is given by

$$M = \frac{200 \times 2 + 500 \times 1\frac{1}{2}}{7 \times 60} = \frac{400 + 750}{420} = 2 \cdot 7.$$

Thus, the number of terminals required is 3.

This situation, in which all work has to be carried out within the day of availability, is common. However, the simple view taken above is frequently not valid. The effective clerical day may be reduced by non-productive operator time; organization and methods estimates vary, typically in the range 10–25 per cent. In addition, documents may not be available at the start of the day. Pre-terminal clerical processing, such as batch totalling or adding missing information, could mean that the effective start of day is 2 hours after the start of the clerical day; unfortunately this delay is worse at peak times. And finally cut-off times: the work may be required to be completed before the end of clerical day to enable subsequent processing to be completed.

The effect of these can be mitigated by sorting documents into those requiring urgent processing, and those which can be used to fill what would otherwise be gaps in terminal work. For example, if the urgent transaction in a system is order input, which can start at 10.00 hours following off-terminal clerical activity, and must be completed by 16.00 hours to enable loading instructions to be completed, the calculation could be as follows. Calculate the number of terminals on the basis of the number of orders to be handled in this six hour period. Check that the capacity is then available to deal with the less urgent transactions, before and after this period, and if necessary adjust the numbers accordingly.

This leads to the concept of developing a work schedule at the locations to optimize the business objectives (e.g., processing orders fast) and the use of the terminals. Scheduled breaks such as lunch hours need to be taken into account, possibly staggering the hour for different staff, or bringing in relief operators at the appropriate time.

### Random

In this case, the terminals cannot be assumed to be fully loaded, since arrivals are not constant, and service times (i.e., transaction times) in general are varying. A queue of arrivals awaiting attention will occur, and although this fluctuates with random changes in arrival and service time, some average level of service must be maintained. Queueing calculations, as discussed in chapter 16, allow account to be taken of these variations and the need to maintain a service. The result is that the average utilization of terminals is less than 100 per cent. Another way of looking at this is that documents can be stacked so that the operator always has work available to do, but people have a finite tolerance of queues. In practice average queue sizes are typically short, say, 2 to 5 people. Because of the variations in arrival rate and service times, there is a significant chance that there will be at certain times no work for the operator to do. This is a partial, but useful, rationalization which explains the need to plan for a terminal utilization less than 100 per cent.

In calculating numbers of terminals, the first step is to determine the maximum rate of arrival within the peak day (if it is intended to provide the specified level of service at that time). This is the rate of arrival, smoothed to damp out the effect of random variations.

In a specific system, with two transaction types, the rates for a number of consecutive half-hour periods in one location might be as shown in Table 10.7. The figures follow the business trend. Looking only at transaction rates, it appears that 11.00–12.00 a.m. is the peak in the system, with a total of 9 transactions per minute. But when weighted by transaction time, the peak load is seen to be actually 3.00–3.30 p.m., even though fewer transactions (7 per minute) are occurring.

**Table 10.7**   Variation in Random Load

| Time | Transaction 1 Rate of arrival $n_1$ | $n_1 s_1$ | Transaction 2 Rate of arrival $n_2$ | $n_2 s_2$ | Overall load |
|---|---|---|---|---|---|
| 9.00 – 9.30 | 1 | 2 | 1 | 1/3 | 2 1/3 |
| 9.30 – 10.00 | 2 | 4 | 2 | 2/3 | 4 2/3 |
| 10.00 – 10.30 | 2 | 4 | 3 | 1 | 5 |
| 10.30 – 11.00 | 2 | 4 | 5 | 1 2/3 | 5 2/3 |
| 11.00 – 11.30 | 3 | 6 | 6 | 2 | 8 |
| 11.30 – 12.00 | 3 | 6 | 6 | 2 | 8 |
| 12.00 – 12.30 | 3 | 6 | 3 | 1 | 7 |
| 12.30 – 1.00 | 2 | 4 | 2 | 2/3 | 4 2/3 |
| 1.00 – 1.30 | 1 | 2 | 1 | 1/3 | 2 1/3 |
| 1.30 – 2.00 | 1 | 2 | 1 | 1/3 | 2 1/3 |
| 2.00 – 2.30 | 2 | 4 | 2 | 2/3 | 4 2/3 |
| 2.30 – 3.00 | 3 | 6 | 2 | 2/3 | 6 2/3 |
| 3.00 – 3.30 | 4 | 8 | 3 | 1 | 9 |
| 3.30 – 4.00 | 2 | 4 | 1 | 1/3 | 4 1/3 |
| 4.00 – 4.30 | 1 | 2 | 1 | 1/3 | 2 1/3 |
| 4.30 – 5.00 | 1 | 2 | 1 | 1/3 | 2 1/3 |

$s_1$ = transaction 1 average time = 2 mins
$s_2$ = transaction 2 average time = 1/3 min
Rates of arrival ($n_1$ and $n_2$) (number per minute)

Having determined the peak in this way, a preliminary estimate of terminal numbers can be obtained by using the formula,

$$\rho = \frac{n_1\ s_1 + n_2\ s_2 + \cdots}{M},$$

where $\rho$ is the facility utilization of the terminals, $n_1$ and $s_1$, are the rate of arrival and transaction time for transaction 1 (and so on), and $M$ is the number of terminals.

The first estimate of $M$ is obtained by choosing its value such that $\rho$ is no greater than 0·7 (utilization of 70 per cent). For the example just considered, the calculation would be

$$0·7 = \frac{(8 + 1)}{M}.$$

Thus $M = 12·9$, which must be rounded to 13.

**166**

In practice this simple calculation, using the 70 per cent rule, gives an overestimate of the numbers of terminals required, and the degree of error becomes greater as the number goes up. This arises from the fact that for increasing numbers of terminals the safe utilization also goes up towards 100 per cent. Also the 70 per cent rule is providing for an unknown service level. Instead of working from a service criterion such as 'the average queue length should be 3', it is providing for a 'reasonable', but unknown, service level.

To calculate numbers from a specification of service level, and without the over-estimate noted above, the multi-server queueing theory graph given in chapter 16 is used.

### 10.6.6 LINE CALCULATIONS

After the number of terminals required in each location has been calculated, the next step is to calculate the line requirement. There are three basic situations to consider, as follows:

— terminals which can only be connected one to a telegraph line;
— single terminals in each location with low volumes, and the possibility of connecting to the centre for limited periods only via a switched telephone line;
— message buffered terminals which require connection for extended periods, and can share a line (almost universally in this case a telephone line).

*Telegraph Terminals*

If a multiple number of such terminals is required in a location, they can be connected typically up to 12 per telephone line using channelizing techniques, as described in section 10.4.1 and Fig. 10.7. The maximum of 12 applies for 110 bits/second terminals, and a normal transmission quality telephone line. The terminals each use a discrete sub-channel which is capable of taking transmission at the full rate irrespective of any transmission occurring in the other sub-channels. Consequently, there are no delays before transmission can start, and the PRT consists only of computer turn-round time. For this reason, no line load calculations need be carried out. The hardware configuration rules of the channelizer used will ensure that the system operates satisfactorily. The calculations which are required are to decide whether the channelizers are cost-justified for a given location. For example, suppose between a given location and the centre, a telephone line costs 1000 units p.a., telegraph lines cost 700 units p.a., and a pair of channelizers cost 3000 units p.a. With capital costs amortized at 25 per cent the telephone line and channelizers would cost 1750 units p.a., so a saving will accrue if three or more telegraph lines (costing 2100 units p.a.) would otherwise be required.

*Single terminals using switched telephone lines*

The minimum period acceptable for the terminal to be connected to the centre is decided upon. This may, for instance, be because that period is the time when random enquiries occur. Or it could be the time taken to process a batch of documents after preparation. The cost of the switched connection is calculated for that period. If it is less than the cost of the equivalent direct leased line, it is worth considering. If however, a number of such locations could be connected on a shared multi-drop line, this overall system should be evaluated and compared to the cost of connection of each terminal separately by switched lines, before the decision is taken. The shared line system is considered further below.

## Message buffered terminals sharing a line

The first step is to calculate how many lines are required for each location. This is done by carrying out load calculations.

For both categories of transaction—pseudo batch and random—messages become ready for transmission at random times, depending on the instant of each operator pressing the send key. Sometimes several are pressed together, and at the other extreme there may be no outstanding messages at a given instant. The calculation in either category requires the use of queueing theory.

The line transmission time is calculated for each transaction as illustrated in Tables 10.5. and 10.6 (by dividing the number of characters transmitted by the line character rate). The peak transaction rate for each transaction is also known or can be calculated as a result of previous work. For the random category, this is determined in a similar way to that illustrated in Table 10.7, but in this case transmission times, not transaction times, are used. In the pseudo batch category the appropriate peak rate is similarly determined. Rate of arrival is synonymous, in this case, to rate of processing of documents at the group of terminals within the location.

A first idea of the number of lines required can be obtained from

$$\rho = \frac{n_1 \, s_1 + n_2 \, s_2 + \cdots}{M},$$

where $\rho$ is the facility utilization of the lines, $n_1$ and $s_1$ are the rates of arrival and transmission time for transaction 1 (and so on), and $M$ is the number of lines.

$M$ is first chosen such that $\rho$ is $0 \cdot 7$ or less. For example, for a single transaction system, where

$$n_1 = 10 \text{ per minute}, \qquad s_1 = 9 \text{ seconds},$$

the value of $M$ is given by

$$0 \cdot 7 = \frac{(10 \times 9)}{60M} .$$

Thus $M = 2 \cdot 1$, which must be rounded to 3.

As for terminal calculations, more complex queueing theory can be used to

168

calculate the numbers of lines required. The number of lines which would give a specified average line delay could be calculated, allowing for the effect of having a finite maximum queue length (owing to the fact that if all terminals are waiting for service no further messages can arrive at the line). Unfortunately, the lines do not conform well to the multi-server queueing model used in the commonly available equations. The queues are not FIFO or LIFO, or any normally assumed dispatching discipline. The polling rule takes messages, if available, in cyclic (or a more complex) order, and also consumes extra line time in handling negative responses. There are other transmission effects such as modem delays to be taken into account also. Because of this, simulation is a much better way of calculating line requirements, because then an exact model can be constructed. Some computer manufacturers supply, or allow the use of, packages to do this. Full simulation packages allow for the timing effect of all parts of the central configuration within the same run. A more convenient and cheaper form is the package which simulates the mechanisms on a single line, and uses as parameters assumed computer turn-round time for message pairs, and a message load and distribution. With this type, a close approximation to numbers of lines required can be obtained before the full system simulation is run.

Whether by calculation or simulation, an estimate of line delay is obtained. This must be checked for compatibility with the assumed value for PRT used in terminal calculations. If the assumed PRT is in itself a design objective, of course, the line delay when added to the other components must conform. If it does not, the number of lines must be increased accordingly. If the PRT used was merely a working estimate, and the now more precisely calculated PRT is acceptable, an interation on terminal calculation must be carried out because transaction times will be greater.

By this stage in the network design, the number of terminals required in each location and the number of lines required have been determined. The simplest way of connecting terminals to lines is by providing one modem per terminal, and connecting the modems to a shared line as a special case of a multi-drop line (special because all spur connections are within the same premises). However, this costs more where there are a lot of terminals than using terminal controllers (as described in section 10.4.3.) These allow a number of terminals to be connected to a single modem at the terminal location.

If, in a given location, a requirement of 11 terminals and 2 lines has been calculated, the terminals are split 6 and 5 across two controllers. Since the line calculation, initially at least, would have assumed even distribution of transmission, the calculation is repeated to check that the line with 6 terminals will support $\frac{6}{11}$ of the load and, if necessary, the number of lines is adjusted accordingly. The other check to be carried out is that the maximum number of terminals per controller allowable by hardware configuration rules is not exceeded.

As discussed in section 10.4.3, some terminal controllers modify the transmission load as received from the terminals by increasing the transmission rate on the line to the centre, or by compaction/expansion of data. The transmission time required per transaction in this case must take account of these facilities. It is not calculated simply from the number of characters and character rate handled by the terminals.

10.6.7   DESIGN UNCERTAINTIES

In almost any design, there are uncertainties in some of the variables used in the calculations. The more important of these must be identified, and if possible better quantified at an early stage in the project. Problems usually arise from a lack of information about timing of individual elements in the transaction sequences (such as the time to look up a customer directory) or in the frequency of certain transactions.

The timing problem is dealt with by establishing the detailed sequence of activity as described in section 10.6.4, and then, having assigned times to each element with the best information available, determining to which elements the calculation of terminal numbers is particularly sensitive. In the example given in Table 10.5, the predominant timing elements are field search, keying, and assimilation of data. All three are examples of times which are often guessed, because of lack of hard information. If the transactions were of low volume compared to others, the transaction time, whatever reasonable assumptions were used, would not have a great weight in determining numbers of terminals. However, if it were of high volume, these sensitive elements would need experimental measurement.

Items like looking-up directories, and signing and date stamping a document, can easily be determined by simple measurements using a stop watch. On the other hand, items such as keying rate and manual file search time require more elaborate evaluation. Using techniques as described in chapter 9, complete or partial transactions can be simulated or actually programmed in a simple way on the machine. All the real life details of processing the transaction within the machine do not have to be provided for. The important thing is to supply to the operator responses which realistically represent what happens at the terminals. Before carrying out such experiments, a representative selection of operators should be trained in use of the terminals. This is important, because the relevant times to be measured are those which occur when operators are carrying out the transactions in a routine fashion. Such experiments can also be helpful in measuring how long it takes the operators to reach a uniform average rate of performance.

The other major uncertainty which can occur is the transaction volumes. For systems which duplicate an existing manual or batch processing computer system, the problem is not too great. The greatest uncertainty is in estimating growth over the expected life of the system. This is best done by reference to the corporate plans for growth of the particular business area, but there are still some uncertainties. For example, in an order processing system, a company might be aiming for an increase in volume of sales of 10 per cent per annum. However, this does not necessarily mean a growth in 10 per cent of order transactions, because the company may at the same time be aiming at increasing sales to large customers at the expense of the others, since in this way unit costs will be reduced. As a consequence, the number of line items per order may increase, but not the number of orders. Or in the extreme, both may stay the same or even decline and the quantities ordered increase. The effect on terminal load is different in the three cases. But at least the most likely change can be established, and the system checked for adaptability should the changes be different.

It is transactions which were not possible before, or on which the previous system imposed a severe constraint, which cause the greatest volume problems. Enquiries are often of this nature. Even if they were possible before, say, by overnight batch file interrogation their availability within seconds in a real-time system could increase volumes by several orders of magnitude. The eventual volume, given no constraints, is unknown. More to the point, the benefit of unconstrained enquiry can also rarely be determined. Usually it is necessary to take a view on just how many enquiries will be allowed for in the new system. The volume could be limited by giving enquiries low priority within the program, but this adds overheads, and the possibility of unavoidable interference with other transactions. A better and simpler solution, in many cases, is to limit the number of terminals available for enquiry. Thus, the system can be designed with knowledge of the maximum number of transactions which can be put through these terminals. Future increases can be controlled by increasing the number of such terminals, having examined the business justification for doing so.

In view of possible uncertainties in earlier phases of a project, the maximum opportunity must be taken for recording and analysing statistical information on what is actually occurring in the system. For systems which are implemented in progressive stages, evaluation of these results should take place after every stage. The implications on the rest of the system can then be determined while there is still time to make adjustments.

The possible uncertainties make it even more important to use the techniques of technical design control (chapter 5) because these give the maximum opportunity to predict potentially embarrassing excess loads.

# 11. File Design

File design has always been one of the critical areas of computer system design. For batch systems, decisions on the information to be held in the different files and the methods by which the files are to be accessed, related and matched, are usually taken early in the design process. The resulting file structure has a considerable impact on the suite/program breakdown, on the complexity of coding needed, and, since batch programs are frequently I/O-bound, on system performance. File design is similarly critical to the performance and indeed viability of real-time systems, but for somewhat different reasons. The problems encountered and techniques used are also different from those relevant to batch files. These differences are examined in the section 11.1.

This chapter then describes the file organizations available to the designer, ranging from the simple techniques common in batch systems where timing is frequently non-critical, through to more complex organizations tailored to the critical requirements of individual real time systems. Subsequent sections deal with file structures, methods by which records may be related to other records in the same or different files, and with design optimization techniques. Finally, a design approach is presented which relates file design to the overall process of system design in a controlled design environment.

## 11.1 File Design Objectives

This section examines the objectives to which the file designer works, expressed in quantitative terms as design criteria. The importance of these criteria, and indeed of the designer's success in achieving them, is illustrated in Fig. 11.1. This example system is fairly typical. It is a single-threaded system, in that it fully processes one message, including the CPU work and disk accesses required, before starting on the next message. In this situation, the computer is acting as a single server, servicing a queue of messages, and its utilization is simply the sum of the utilizations of its components, i.e.,

Utilization (computer) = utilization (CPU) + utilization (disk) = 66 per cent.

(Tape processing is ignored for simplicity in this example.)

| Hardware item | Unit of work | Units per minute $n$ | Service time $s$ | Number of items $m$ | Percentage utilizations |
|---|---|---|---|---|---|
| Terminal | transaction | 50 | 2 mins | 150 | 67 |
| Line | message pair (2 per trans- action) | 100 | 2 secs | 15 | 33 |
| CPU | message pair | 100 | 50 msecs | 1 | 8 |
| Disk | access ($3\frac{1}{2}$ per message pair) | 350 | 100 msecs | 1 | 58 |

Percentage utilization $= \dfrac{n \times s}{m} \times 100$ ($n$ and $s$ adjusted to common time units)

**Fig. 11.1** Example Real Time System Utilizations

Since the response time (made up of the service time and queueing time) of the computer increases rapidly for utilizations over 70 per cent, this system is near to being critically loaded. Since, in this example, 58 of the 66 per cent utilization is disk utilization, the importance of file design is clear. If, by optimizing the design, the average file access time can be reduced by, say, 10 per cent, then the overall computer utilization will drop to 60 per cent. Compare this worthwhile gain with the result of considerable effort being expended on coding optimization; a 10 per cent reduction in CPU time reduces the overall computer utilization by only half a per cent to 65·2 per cent.

The effect is even more pointed if looked at the other way. If the service times in Figure 11.1 are design targets, and the program designers/coders miss their 50 ms target by 10 per cent, the resultant computer utilization is only half a per cent up at 66·8 per cent. But if the file designer misses his target of 100 ms by 10 per cent, the resultant utilization is 72 per cent, which will measurably impact the average computer response time. Worse, the system may now be critically loaded, in that small fluctuations in message load cause wide variations in response time.

These relative loadings are fairly typical of those found after initial designs, and thus file design has a strong impact on central processor timings. It is also important because file bottlenecks often cannot be relieved by simply spending more money. This constrasts particularly with the terminal network, where if all else fails, a high utilization may frequently be reduced by getting more terminals or lines or upgrading line speeds.

The prime objectives to which the file designer will work are:

— handle a random demand for access to the file;
— minimize file access times;
— make the files as secure as possible, and as easily and rapidly recoverable as possible;
— make the design flexible, so that an increasing load and/or increasing file sizes are accompanied by only a smooth and gradual increase in response time;
— minimize run time costs.

Secondary objectives are

- minimize backing storage space required;
- minimize main storage requirements, for indexes, look-up tables, buffers, etc.;
- minimize the development effort and hence cost;
- enable the files to be used for batch processing, if required;
- minimize the amount of off-line batch processing made necessary only by the file organization, e.g., reorganizing the file or regenerating an index.

The task of ensuring the integrity and recoverability of files is crucial to real time design. Real time files are accessed randomly and updated in place, so that the previous version of the record is immediately lost. As a result, the security techniques used differ considerably from those usual in batch work. Security, integrity and fail-soft are fully discussed in chapters 12 and 13, but design work on file access and file security must proceed in parallel.

The objectives listed above are also those generally applicable to file design for batch systems. However in batch systems, access time is not automatically a prime objective. Any of the objectives listed may be the most critical, depending on the applications and the installation. For an archive retrieval system, minimizing disk space may be the prime aim; in one installation, core storage may be a configuration bottleneck, while in another, short of programmers and testing time, reducing development effort may be crucial. With highly loaded real time systems, the secondary objectives may similarly vary in relevance, but the prime objectives are usually overriding. If the file access times are too high, then the system simply will not run.

In this respect the design process is somewhat easier for real-time files than for batch files. Not only is the time objective dominant, but many real time systems have a small number of transaction types which make up a high proportion of the volume. The timing of these transactions dominates the average timings over all transactions. Under these conditions, the designer can focus on one problem: to devise a structure which yields reasonable access times for these few transaction types. When this is achieved, the task of ensuring that the design covers all objectives over all transactions is essentially one of extension and optimization. This is an easier design problem than that often encountered in batch/general purpose data base design, where no single problem dominates.

However, the central problem of designing a file structure with the necessary speed of access may be a difficult one. Another characteristic of real time file design is that the design can, and often must, take full advantage of the particular characteristics of the dominant transactions and the way in which they generate file accesses. For highly-loaded systems, the use of generalized file access methods and packages is thus often impracticable.

## 11.2 Basic File Structures

The main file devices and basic file structures available to the real time designer are discussed in chapter 19. The file structures described are

Sequential files     — tape or disk based.
Direct files         — key gives direct disk address.
Randomized files     — key converted to disk address.
Unordered files      — records stored in available space.
Indexed files        — including index sequential.

The designer carries out his design (see section 11.6) by evaluating the performance of each structure against the systems requirements. There are however certain general comparisons that can be made to illustrate why these structures do not always provide sufficient choice. A set of comparisons are summarized in Fig. 11.2 with a numeric scale to indicate relative strengths and weaknesses.

| Files<br>Facilities | Sequential | Direct | Randomized | Index<br>Sequential | Unordered |
|---|---|---|---|---|---|
| Disk space | 3 | 1–3 | 1–3 | 2 | 3 |
| Software overheads | 3 | 3 | 2–3 | 1–2 | 3 |
| Access time | 1 | 3 | 2–3 | 1–2 | 1 |
| Insert time | 1 | 3 | 2–3 | 1–2 | 3 |
| Time drift | 3 | 3 | 1 | 2–3 | 3 |
| Need to tidy | 3 | 3 | 3 | 1 | 3 |
| Serial processing<br>(for batch systems) | 3 | 1 | 1 | 2 | 1 |

Evaluation   1 poor to 3 excellent

**Fig. 11.2**   Real Time File Structure Comparison

None of the structures is the ideal for real time in all circumstances. The use of direct access is frequently prevented by the file's key set; randomized files are wasteful of disk space and cannot be used for sequential processing without sorting, and index sequential files are slow, particularly for files with a high insertion rate. Index sequential packages can also create undesirable 'waits' (see chapter 14).

The designer may therefore wish to consider further structures such as combinations of these basic file organizations.

### 11.3   Combination File Structures

The objective of combining file organizations is to achieve different characteristics that better suit the needs of a particular real time file design situation.

Index sequential, although described as basic because of its common usage, is itself a combination of sequential organization and indexes. Three further combinations are described as a representative sample of the considerable variety possible.

*Indexed Unordered*

All data records are kept in an unordered file. Either the bit map or chain method can be used to control the file's free space. Record addresses are obtained from some form of index, which is often itself index sequential. Since the records in the index consist only of key and address, the file is small, which alleviates considerably the usual index sequential problems. If a few fields in the data record are in particular demand and reasonably short, they can be kept with the key in the index record. This saves an access for requests needing only these fields, while adding little to the access time for requests needing the complete data record.

*Random-Index Unordered*

This is a special case of the indexed unordered organization, in which the index is a randomized file. The sequence of events for a read is thus to randomize the key; the resulting bucket address is then accessed, and the index record read; this contains the address of the data record in the unordered file, which can now be read.

*Indexed Random*

The file is split into a number of sub-files, each of which is a randomized file. These files may be on separate disks and may use different randomizing algorithms. A main storage limit index is used to determine in which sub-file a requested record is located. This is clearly a convenient way of spreading a file over a number of disks, as the main storage index may be readily adjusted, on an empirical basis, until the access loads are similar on each disk.

These structures require additional development effort, since they are not generally supported by standard file handling software. However, many projects have provided these and similar tailored structures, with benefit, by building on the basic software file handlers.

If the combined organizations are also compared with regard to access time, disk space, and the other criteria listed in Fig. 11.2, it is found that the combination file organizations are neither more nor less effective overall than the simple organizations.

Each real time system presents a different set of problems to the designer, who needs as wide a selection of organizations as possible that can be adapted to fit. The combination techniques are valuable in that they are better in certain ways, and thus extend the designer's repertoire. Each was originally developed to meet the demands of a particular real time application, and thus illustrates the flexibility with which the file designer must approach real time design.

## 11.4   Linked File Structures

The previous section was concerned with the problem of storing and retrieving records whose logical key was known; for example, retrieving the product record of product 101432. This section is concerned with the situation where the logical key is unknown: for example, for an enquiry which quotes an order number only, retrieving the product records of all products ordered on that order. The requirement is sometimes described as 'search on content'.

Such requirements can be met using a variety of software techniques including secondary indexes and pointer chains; all of them use the concept of linking records together with pointers, which can consist either of physical disk addresses or logical keys, see Fig. 11.3.

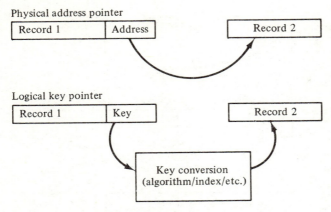

**Fig. 11.3**  Pointer types

The pointers mentioned in section 11.2, e.g., free space chains, were of the physical address type. These are faster, since no key conversion (which may require an index access) is necessary, but less robust. If the file containing record 2 is re-organized, record 1 must be updated if it contains an address pointer, but not if it contains a key pointer. In a large-scale, complex, data base environment, robustness is at a premium, and key pointers may be preferred. For real time, access time considerations often demand the use of address pointers.

### 11.4.1 CHAIN STRUCTURES

The basic concept is to link a set of records together in a chain; one record, the head of the chain, is known as the owner or parent record. Examples of such sets might be a set of orders, the owner being the customer who originated those orders, the set of staff records of the staff in a particular department, the owner being the staff record of the department's manager, or the set of order lines of an order, the owner being the order record. In the first and third examples, the owner and member records are of different types, but in the second example, the record types are the same and are probably in the same file. Order line records might well be kept in a 'chain file', i.e., a file which can only be accessed via address pointers from records outside the file, in this case order records and possibly product records. Chain files generally have the unordered organization described in section 19.2.6, or are secondary structures built on another file organization.

Figure 11.4 shows a selection of chain structures which provide different facilities from the straight chain in various ways. A minimum addition is to join the chain into a ring (b); this enables the owner record to be accessed from any

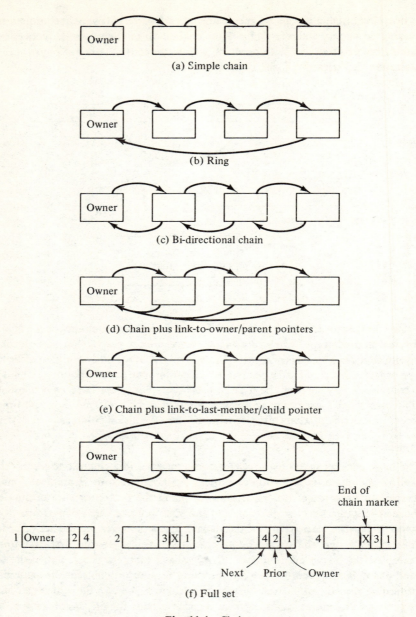

(a) Simple chain

(b) Ring

(c) Bi-directional chain

(d) Chain plus link-to-owner/parent pointers

(e) Chain plus link-to-last-member/child pointer

End of
chain marker

1 Owner 2 4    2 3 X 1    3 4 2 1    4 X 3 1

Next  Prior  Owner

(f) Full set

**Fig. 11.4**  Chains

member record. To do this in one access (rather than following the chain),
owner pointers are needed as in (d). Backward pointers (c) are useful when a
record needs to be deleted without breaking the chain. Link-to-last-member
pointers (e) are useful if new records are to be added to the chain on a FIFO

**178**

basis. However, each new pointer type increases the chain maintenance overhead, so the exact selection of pointers should carefully reflect the processing volumes of the different access types.

Chains can be used both for linking related records and for storing variable length records in fixed blocks on a non-sequential basis.

### 11.4.2 POINTER LIST STRUCTURES

An alternative to the chain method of linking together a set of records is the pointer list. The owner record holds an individual pointer to each member record; this normally implies that the owner records will be variable length. Frequently each member holds a single, owner pointer. This structure is more difficult to implement than the chain structure, because of the variable length problem, and is no faster if all the records in the set are wanted. However, if only one specific record is needed, then it can be obtained in single access, whereas the chain structure requires an unknown number of accesses.

### 11.4.3 INVERTED FILES

An inverted file is a file which has every field indexed. As such it is rare, but it is more frequent in the 'partially inverted' form in which several but not all of the fields are indexed. The indexes may be basic indexes, or they may consist of the owner records of pointer list or chained sets. Figure 11.5 is an example personnel file, and Fig. 11.6 shows the file indexed, as an example, in each of these ways:

- *the main index* is basic (no synonyms);
- *the department index* is basic, extended to a pointer list;
- *the grade and salary indexes* are basic, extended by chains. Only the first entry in each chain is illustrated. In this example chains for grade 41 and salary < 4 500 (implied > 3000) are 3 long.

The example also shows the inverted file being used as a look-up table. Instead of holding the long names in both the main file and the index, the name is held in the index only, and the main file points to the index. This technique is primarily relevant for name fields with many common entries. Inverted files are fast for retrieval purposes, using any of the indexed fields as key, but they are very slow to update. For example, the addition of a new record to the file

| Block No. | Man No. | Name | Department | Grade | Salary |
|-----------|---------|-------|------------|-------|--------|
| 4254 | 376 | Smith | 104 | 45 | 4500 |
| 4255 | 104 | Brown | 192 | 39 | 2600 |
| 4256 | 252 | Green | 192 | 41 | 3100 |
| 4257 | 492 | Black | 192 | 41 | 3200 |
| 4258 | 151 | Jones | 163 | 41 | 3600 |
| 4259 | 305 | White | 104 | 37 | 1800 |

Fig. 11.5   Part of a personnel file

179

Name index

Block No. | Name | Address
--- | --- | ---
2061 | Black | 4257
2062 | Brown | 4255
2063 | Green | 4256
2064 | Jones | 4258
2065 | Smith | 4254
2067 | White | 4259

Department index

| | | |
--- | --- | ---
104 | 4254 | 4259
163 | 4258 |
192 | 4256 | 4257 | 4255

Group index

| | |
--- | ---
37 | 4259
39 | 4255
41 | 4256
45 | 4254

Salary index

| | |
--- | ---
<2000 | 4259
<3000 | 4255
<4000 | 4258
<5000 | 4254

| Block No. | Man No. | Dept. No. | Grade | Salary | Name Ptr. | Grade Ptr. | Salary Ptr. |
| --- | --- | --- | --- | --- | --- | --- | --- |
| 4254 | 376 | 104 | 45 | 4500 | 2065 | – | – |
| 4255 | 104 | 192 | 39 | 2600 | 2062 | – | – |
| 4256 | 252 | 192 | 41 | 3100 | 2063 | 4257 | – |
| 4257 | 492 | 192 | 41 | 3200 | 2061 | 4258 | 4256 |
| 4258 | 151 | 163 | 41 | 3600 | 2064 | – | 4257 |
| 4259 | 305 | 104 | 37 | 1800 | 2067 | – | – |

**Fig. 11.6** The personnel file inverted

requires five accesses; updating one indexed field can include three updates (one main file, one index delete, and one index insert).

### 11.4.4 MULTI-KEY RETRIEVALS

Some real-time enquiry and retrieval systems have the problem of efficiency satisfying large numbers of requests involving multiple keys, such as:

- list the man numbers of men over 40 earning less than £8000;
- list the customer numbers of customers in South West region, with a turnover last year less than £100 000, who last year ordered more than £20 000-worth of goods.

Such requests can be satisfied without file scanning only if the file is inverted with respect to the criterion fields. One method is to access each record which satisfies one of the criteria. These records are selected by a secondary index, chain or pointer list. Each record accessed is examined against each of the other criteria, and extracted if appropriate. This method is faster than a full file search. It must be used if any of the criteria are indexed using a chain. It is convenient to maintain a count of the members on a chain in the owner record, so that the shortest chain (i.e., the most selective criterion) is accessed. A corollary of this is that it is not worth indexing or chaining very unselective fields (e.g., customer type if there are only three possible types).

If all the criteria are indexed by an index or pointer list, it is possible to access only the records which satisfy all the criteria. This involves extracting the relevant record addresses from multiple index files, which may be sequenced randomly with respect to record address. If the criteria are

**180**

sufficiently selective, the collections of record addresses extracted from each index as satisfying one criterion will be sufficiently small for the subsequent compare and extract manipulations to be handled in core. This is the fastest method; it requires the file to be inverted using secondary basic indexes or pointer lists. If, however, the file is very large and the criteria not very selective, the individual collections of record addresses may be large in themselves. In such cases it is convenient to maintain each index in record address within index key value sequence. This has the disadvantage of increasing the processing for updates, but for retrievals, it saves sorting the record address collections before matching and comparing them.

### 11.4.5 NETWORKS AND DATA BASE SYSTEMS

If the data files for the real-time system span a number of business functions and areas, the different record types are linked, using the methods described in the preceding sections, in many different ways. This reflects the inter-relationships implicit in the real data in its business context. The term data base may be used to describe such a collection of related data; related in order to reduce redundancy of data, and related to enable data access by a variety of

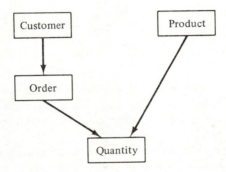

**Fig. 11.7** Example data base schematic

different paths. An example data base is shown in schematic form in Fig. 11.7, and the way a few of the records might be chained together in such a data base is shown in Fig. 11.8.

This network-structure data base contains no redundant data and can answer queries of the following types without file scanning:

– list the orders placed by customer $N$;
– list the products ordered by customer $N$, with quantities;
– which customer placed order $N$?;
– list the orders outstanding for product $X$, with quantities;
– list the customers who have ordered product $X$, with quantities;
– list the products required to fill order $N$, with quantities.

**181**

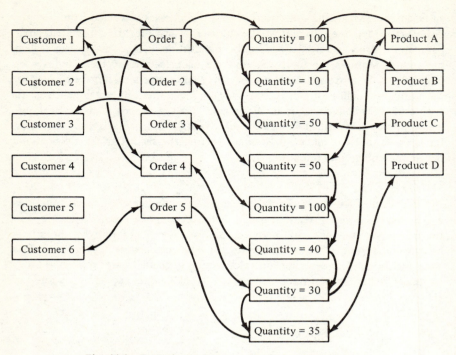

**Fig. 11.8** Example data base, sets linked by ring pointers

Not only may the data base needed specifically for the real time system be a network of linked records (as in Fig. 11.7), but it may be desirable for the real time system to access a multi-purpose data base serving other applications, both real time and batch.

The programming effort involved in maintaining such a data base can be enormous. A considerable amount of design and code is needed to access the data base, follow the chains, and insert records into multiple sets:

- to maintain the integrity of the data base in a multi-access environment against double-updates, interlocks, etc.;
- to provide privacy facilities;
- to back-up and recover such a data base, on a centralized basis.

There have been several projects where access efficiency needs have led to the development of tailored file handlers. However the development of data base software is such that real time designers lean increasingly towards the use of standard data base management packages.

### 11.4.6 USE OF PACKAGED SOFTWARE

The extent that particular file structures can be achieved by standard software varies with computer manufacturer and time. Several of the access methods described—sequential, direct, index sequential, data base—will instantly be reorganized as being matched by manufacturers' software, and therefore their implementation risk can be reasonably judged.

Where standard software exhibits shortcomings, the consideration of other methods may mean a need for some software level programming. However, this is not always the case. Many of the structures described in this chapter and chapter 19 can be implemented by a competent programmer building upon the standard manufacturer access method. For example, secondary indexes can effectively be built in index sequential files, using logical addresses under normal programming languages. Other structures may make use of the more basic file handling software, but this software still masks the user from channel/device level programming.

Whatever the historic experience in an installation, it can be cheaper/more effective to look beyond the standard structure. However, low level file channel program manipulation should be avoided when prior experience of programming at that level is not available.

Whatever the software interface chosen, the designer must understand not only the logical action carried out by the software but also the physical implementation. Otherwise, he will not be able to predict the performance of his design. Many real time performance predictions have been wrong because the team made a wrong assumption on how the file handling software performed *in detail*. For example, one index sequential system involved an extra disk access per file access when the input area was assigned as virtual storage, even when the area was resident in main store.

Where more complex structures are identified, a data base management system may be the right design solution. Data base management systems (DBMS) enable applications programmers to access complex data bases using simple commands (usually extensions of the high level host language, e.g., COBOL, PL/1) and facilities are probably provided as part of the package, covering integrity, privacy, security, etc.

Nevertheless, the designer must use DBMS packages with caution. The activities of chain maintenance, index searching, privacy lock checking, interlock list maintenance, logging, etc., are transparent to the programmer, but they are still happening. Worse, these functions are generalized and therefore inherently less efficient than a tailor-made system specific to the real-time application. Worse still, the complex mechanisms of the package make system timing difficult to calculate.

The need for quantitative file design for real-time systems is therefore increased if a DBMS is used, and certainly not reduced. The designer must understand the DBMS mechanisms, ensure that only the facilities necessary for the applications are used, place considerably less reliance on timing calculations, and simulate the system, using the DBMS, earlier in the development process.

## 11.5 File Optimization

This section discusses methods of optimizing file access performance. The starting position is a design within reach of handling the required throughput, but with a utilization of each device which is still too high. (For more detail on utilization calculations for file access devices, see chapter 15.)

### 11.5.1 REDUCING ACCESS TIME

Given an intial design, several techniques are possible to reduce access time. The value of each is situation dependent. Some useful techniques include:

Change access method    — index to randomized algorithm;
  — index to direct algorithm. Application numbering systems have been altered, with effect, to achieve a near direct algorithm.

Hold index in core or part index in core.
Use look aside buffer for index or data.
Increase number of levels of index (avoid long serial index searches).
Reduce number of records per block and hence transfer time.

If the choice of access method is apparently circumscribed, by a requirement for the file to be accessed by batch sequential applications, the possibility of having a separate real-time file should be considered. The file can be converted before and after the batch run. Overall, the machine time involved may be considerable, but if it reduces the file utilization in the critical real time shift, it may be justified.

Allocate file space to reflect activity. (Using Pereto 80:20 principle.) Often file accesses are very asymmetrically concentrated over the file keys, so that 80 per cent of file accesses are to only 20 per cent of the keys. In one manufacturing firm listing 20 000 products, the distribution of customer orders is such that 10 per cent of the products account for over 90 per cent of the orders by volume (though not by value). The principle is to hold certain index records in core and to always access these records first; if the record is there, an index access has been saved; if not, the time cost is insignificant. Alternatively, actual records can be held in core. Figure 11.9 shows how the mean access time can be reduced. The selection of records to hold in core can be determined daily, calculated from access statistics kept by the real-time system the day before. A similar effect can be achieved dynamically, using a look-aside buffer pool.

### 11.5.2 REDUCING THE FILE SIZE

The objectives of file size reduction can be to reduce access time or save space. The main impacts on timing are as follows:

— reduce record size; this leads to faster transfer of data;

**184**

File has 20 000 records. Each record is 200 bytes long; the basic index record length is 10 bytes. Mean access time is 30 ms (index) + 50 ms (record), total 80 ms. 10K bytes is available to hold frequently accessed records.

(a) Main Storage Index Records

1000 index records can be held in 10K. This is 5 per cent of the file; statistics show that this accounts for 80 per cent of accesses.

Mean access time = 0·8 (50) + 0·2 (30 + 50)

$\qquad\qquad\qquad$ = 56 ms

Percentage
  reduction $\qquad$ = 30

(b) Main Storage Records

50 records can be held in 10K. These 50 records statistically account for 20 per cent of accesses.

Mean access time = 0·2 (0) + 0·8 (30 + 50)

$\qquad\qquad\qquad$ = 64 ms

Percentage
  reduction $\qquad$ = 20

**Fig. 11.9** Reduction of Access Time Using the Pareto Principle

— reduce file size; this can lead to less cylinders and hence reduced seek time. If indexed, fewer levels of index, or larger percentage increase in core.

File reduction techniques include the following:

— where a file is required by both batch and real time procedures, the separation into two files enables the real time record to be reduced to only those fields needed in real time. Several bank systems have used this particular technique. The cost: overnight twin file maintenance;
— make use of variable record length structures. Solution depends on software constraints and the actual distribution of record lengths.

Techniques include:

— multiple-record-length files;
— multiple files fixed length, e.g., short records in one file and long records in a second file;
— fixed cell files with records chained across cells.

*Field Compression*

Fields can be shortened by using binary numbers instead of packed decimal, and bit indicators rather than character indicators. Long character fields can be coded, using a look-up table. Data compression techniques can considerably reduce the length of some data. Before writing a record, it is passed to the compressor routine to create a shorter record, which will vary in length according to the data values. This is then written away. Immediately after reading a record, the decompressor routine decodes it before passing it to the application program. Compression therefore uses CPU time, but in return reduces file sizes. For real-time systems, this can be a useful exchange. Figure 10.10 gives some examples of data compression.

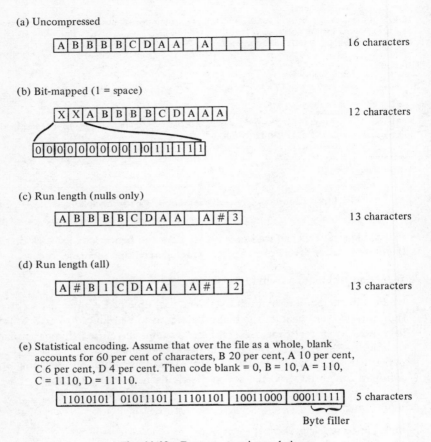

(a) Uncompressed

16 characters

(b) Bit-mapped (1 = space)

12 characters

(c) Run length (nulls only)

13 characters

(d) Run length (all)

13 characters

(e) Statistical encoding. Assume that over the file as a whole, blank accounts for 60 per cent of characters, B 20 per cent, A 10 per cent, C 6 per cent, D 4 per cent. Then code blank = 0, B = 10, A = 110, C = 1110, D = 11110.

5 characters

Byte filler

**Fig. 11.10** Data compression techniques

### 11.5.3 MULTI-SERVING DISKS

To reduce the disk utilization, the real-time files may be spread over multiple disks. If the disks are to act as independent servers, the following points must be observed.

— It is the access load, not the files, which must be evenly spread over the disks. Thus, the access method must not include a disk bottleneck (for example an index). The distribution of accesses across the file key ranges

**186**

must be reasonably predictable, or if not, the system must be capable of flexible re-allocation of files or sub-files.

- If a single file is to be spread over more than one disk, the manufacturer's software must be able to support multi-pack files.
- The disks must either each have their own control unit, or more likely, be capable of simultaneous off-line seeking under the control of a single shared control unit.
- The real-time system must not wait for one access to be completed before initiating the next; if it does, then only one server can work at a time. This means that the real-time system must be multi-threaded (or multi-programmed or multi-asked).
- The disks used must be dedicated to the real-time system or subject to a low level of interference from other programs; if they are not, the multi-serving disk timing calculations presented in chapter 15 are invalid.

When timing files, the disk drives are the usual bottleneck, since each access has a greater disk service time than control unit/channel service time; particularly if disks capable of rotational position sensing are being used (see chapter 15). If, however, channel utilization is a problem, the service time can be reduced by decreasing block lengths; failing this, the disks must be split over two controllers and channels.

### 11.5.4 FILE ACCESS SOFTWARE

The structure of real time programs is discussed in chapter 14. One of the common features of these structures is that application routines do not access files directly, i.e., they do not interface with access routines in the operating system software. Instead, the application routine returns control to the monitor middleware with a request to read a file or write to a file. This means that all access requests, for all files within the real time system, pass through a common I/O monitor routine. This has a number of advantages:

- File access in real time is frequently complex. Tailor-made index structures, randomizing algorithms, data compression, look-aside buffer pools, chain structures, privacy look-up routines, all require a considerable amount of logic that is certainly best shared by all applications in common routines. These routines may be executed sufficiently frequently that they may best be written in a low-level language.
- Certain real time file functions, for example, lock-list routines, statistics-gathering routines, logging, require that file accessing be centralized. It is important that the system be capable of collecting statistics on file usage, in order to monitor the assumptions made in the design process with regard to access key distributions, incidence of overflows, etc.
- If all file accesses are processed by a single I/O monitor, the monitor needs to be capable of queueing requests (unless the system is single-threaded). This queue of requests may be used to optimize individual access service times. If the software calculates the disk head position needed to satisfy

each request, and knows the current head position, it can service requests not on a first-in, first-out basis but on a least-head-movement basis, with a potentially considerable decrease in average seek time.

## 11.6   Approach to File Design

As chapter 7 has already discussed, real time system design is a top-down iterative process. This is true equally of real time file design, being a subset of system design, and Fig. 11.11 summarizes this approach as applied to file design.

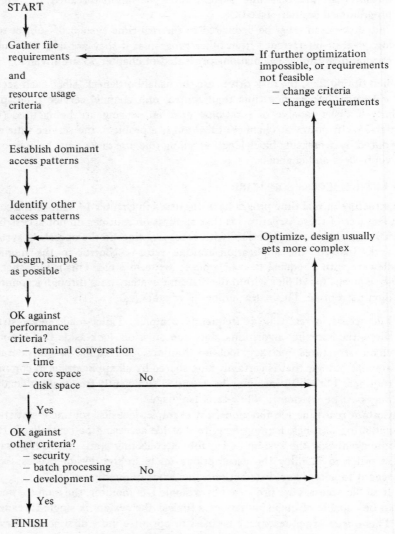

**Fig. 11.11**   File design approach

188

As has also been previously discussed, file design and security, integrity and recovery sub-system design cannot be divorced. Security is therefore included as a criterion in Fig. 11.11, since the file design is complete only when security design is complete. It is pointless refining a file design until it meets all criteria, and then starting on security sub-system design. It may prove impossible to reload the files from tape sufficiently fast to meet the recovery elapsed time criterion; additional audit trail data may need to be held at block level for integrity purposes; certain data items may need to be stored in a separate physical record for privacy reasons (see chapters 12 and 13).

## 11.6.1 FILE REQUIREMENTS

It is essential to enter the design phase with a clear specification of:

- the data to be held on file;
- the relationships between the data items;
- the sizes of the data items;
- the volumes of data;
- particular security requirements of the data such as access restrictions to data items.

These static data requirements must be supplemented with the dynamic data requirements, namely, for each transaction:

- transaction frequency;
- file data to be read;
- file data to be updated;
- particular relationships between transaction and file, such as the distribution of required accesses by a transaction type across the file's key range.

The information listed above is gathered during the preceding systems analysis phase, and should be specified at a logical level, i.e., in a format that does not pre-empt the design process by presuming technical solutions to the analysed requirements. However, certain volumes may be dependent on the final message pair design within each transaction.

Data items, along with relevant size, type and security information, can be conveniently grouped as normalized relations, which provides an unambiguous method of identifying data relationships without presupposing physical file and record formats. The dynamic data requirements may be documented in the form of tables of transaction types against relation and/or data item names, the table entries consisting of read, update, etc.

## 11.6.2 RESOURCE USAGE CRITERIA

The other essential input to the file design process is a set of design criteria, defining the resources available to the designer. The elapsed access time criterion may be specified in terms of service (access) times, response (processing and service) times, and/or utilizations.

A single system criterion may be given, with or without criteria for each message type. For single-threaded systems, file response times are equal to service times. However, response times plus utilizations must be specified when the real-time system is to share either disks or channels with other applications (particularly disks).

The designer must know the exact disk and channel configuration available and the loads imposed on the configuration by other applications, if any. There is often a disk space criterion, expressed in cylinders or packs, particularly if the files are very large, or alternatively the configuration very small, so that the disks are shared. He should also be aware of the disks on which program overlays, operating system macros, system queues and terminal conversation scratch pad areas are stored; these contribute significantly to the disk and channel utilizations.

A main storage limitation is normally essential, to cover buffers, in-core indexes and look-up tables. The designer may have non-real-time system limitations imposed on him, e.g., that a file must be capable of being read sequentially in a certain time, or alternatively that only a certain time is available at night for reorganizations, etc. A designer's desire to use specially written routines may be thwarted either by development time or cost limitations, or by a lack of main storage space for the routines.

## 11.6.3 ACCESS PATTERNS

Armed with the file requirements, documented during the analysis phase, and the design criteria, the designer begins by identifying the dominant access patterns. In doing so, he is essentially determining the line of attack to be followed in the design, for a design that meets the criteria for the high-volume transactions can usually be modified and extended to cater for the bulk of transaction types, which are low-volume.

The designer therefore concentrates on the few high-volume transactions, grouping the data accessed by these transactions into physical records and files. These act as a starting point for the selection or design of file access methods, record chain linkages and the rest of the detailed design.

## 11.6.4 DESIGN ASSESSMENT

The initial design should be as simple as possible. Subsequent design proceeds in a number of iterations, each iteration usually being more complex than its predecessor, but not getting more complex than is necessary to meet the criteria. When the design is satisfactory for the initial set of transaction types, further transactions are brought in, the design modified and re-assessed in an iterative fashion until all transactions are satisfactorily handled.

The design is thus repeatedly assessed against the design criteria. For this assessment, the physical performance criteria, timing and space utilization, are examined first. These are often the hardest to satisfy, and can be assessed by calculation. Chapter 15 discusses file timing calculations.

**190**

## 11.6.5 NEED FOR OVERALL DESIGN

Although file design, like other sub-system designs, can be approached independently at some stage, the design must be integrated into the whole system: The early impact of security and fail-soft has already been discussed, and in some systems the design of the operator conversation may also have an impact. Thus a good designer must carefully judge when to concentrate on the basic application and when to consider other aspects during the file design process. There is no simple guide, but to illustrate the problem a fairly typical case is described in summary below.

(1) The designer is provided with basic design criteria:

| | |
|---|---|
| file data | — logical structure, static volumes; |
| transaction data | — content, relationship to files, volumes; |
| performance targets. | |

(2) The file is an accounts file, with several 'sales' recorded against each account holder. The file structure can be summarized thus:

| | |
|---|---|
| header fields | — approximately 200 characters; |
| sales fields | — average   4 sets per account, maximum 30 sets per account. |

One sales set is 200 characters.

(3) The main transaction logic is concerned with updating the sales sub-records and follows the sequence:

- select and display accounts record;
- input and update sales set(s) (the actual sales set(s) is selected by inspection).

To proceed with his design, the file designer requires several further questions to be answered (or at least postulated).

- The distribution of records between 0 and 30 sales sets per record.
- The dynamic distribution of transaction across records between 0 and 30 sales sets per record.
- The operator's method of searching down the list. If 7 sales sets are displayed at a time this may mean 4 file accesses for sets of 28 if the file designer chooses his block sizes accordingly (1 block = 7 sets + chains). If 2 sales sets are displayed at a time, this might better suit the operator and give the file designer the choice between temporary core storage of a partial record (core terminal slot for *every terminal*) or 14 file accesses if the data are blocked in 2 or more sales sets sub-records per block, and no core terminal slot provided.

Therefore what is the message pair sequence and layout?

– Can the sub-records be sequenced (say overnight) to improve chance of required sales sets being in the 'front' of each account record?

Some questions can be answered by analysis (but need to be answered in detail only if file design is overflow sensitive). Others require iterations with the terminal conversation design, and in that context initial best designs will be needed for different broad options. Chapter 7 outlines an approach to the solution of this problem in reference to broad design and detail design.

### 11.6.6 DESIGN CONTROL

If the designer is unable to solve the design problem, or in other words cannot produce a design which meets the requirements within the specified resource usage criteria, two options are open. It may be possible for the criteria to be relaxed. Section 5.2 describes the concept of technical design control, used to control resource usage on a top-down design project. While the file designer is struggling, the program designers may be keeping easily within their resource limitations, in which case more time, or core, can be allocated to the file design. (The converse is equally important, if the file designer finds his resource criteria generous, he must report this to the design controller, who can then relax the criteria elsewhere.) If the criteria cannot be relaxed, because there is no slack in the system, the alternative is to cut down the requirements. This means going back into analysis and consultation with the user. Nevertheless, this may be well worthwhile, for the designer can identify the particular requirements which are causing the problem, and it should be possible to place an incremental cost on these requirements. This can powerfully concentrate the mind of the user.

A maxim to remember is *'only real essentials in real time'*; there is a tendency to overload the real time system with tasks that could be carried out in batch mode, just because the terminals are convenient in the user environment. Incremental costs of particular requirements, produced during the design phase, are a powerful means of separating the essential from the desirable or merely 'nice'.

As has been illustrated earlier in this chapter, file performance depends on many factors. Given a selected design, then such factors that may not be totally clear to the designer are:

– real mechanisms within the software;
– static distribution of actual data in the file, e.g., inserted/deleted records on file; variations in record lengths;
– dynamic distribution of access to data.

Therefore the careful timing of designs is important, as is the determination of the sensitivity to variants in design assumptions. Design control will play an important role as designs develop and dynamic and static distributions and their effects become clearer.

Unless the team has very precise information of the performance, it is worth while writing dummy programs of file accesses at an early stage in development. The timing of a simple program that consists mainly of a loop of file reads/writes can provide significant evidence on the performance of software commands. This approach can be extended as the system's development proceeds, and further tests can be made on the more critical aspects.

Another approach is to develop simple batch programs to test real time file systems. Again the objective is to provide early evidence on the file system's performance.

# 12. Fail-soft

One of the consequences of implementing real time systems is the increased impact on the user of systems failures. A 10 minute down time on a computer providing a batch service with a turn round of hours may be unnoticed by the user, but 1 minute off the air is likely to disrupt many users in a real time environment. Given that the failure rate of hardware and software is sufficiently high to be important, the designer of any real time system needs to consider the effect of failure and what steps can be taken to minimize the consequences. The solution is highly situation dependent. Many simple systems have included little special provision accepting occasional failure as a reasonable risk, while others have rightly invested considerable sums on reserve equipment and special procedures and software.

The subject of failure and subsequent recovery can conveniently be divided into two sub-topics: 'fail-soft' and 'security and integrity'. This chapter, on fail-soft, is concerned with facilities and procedures aimed at minimizing the operational effect of failures and restoring partial and/or full service at the earliest opportunity. Chapter 13 covers the subject of security and integrity, which is more concerned with the prevention of deliberate or accidental acts of damage to hardware, software, or data and the recovery of the data from any failure.

There is some practical overlap between the methods needed to maintain the integrity of data in these two situations, and the reader is advised to read these two chapters in conjunction with one another.

Causes of failure and methods of recovery are dependent on the whole system, i.e., hardware and software. This chapter therefore first considers hardware fail-soft in isolation, and then considers the make up of a complete fail-soft design. The design approach to fail-soft is next examined, followed by a number of important techniques. The chapter is concluded by a review of the user's role and an outline case study.

## 12.1 Hardware and Fail-Soft

The basic objectives in fail-soft hardware planning are to minimize the chance of failure and to minimize the time required to re-establish a workable con-

194

figuration after any failure. The first is concerned with the intrinsic reliability of the hardware (and later software) and the latter with the speed of diagnosis, isolation of fault, repair or replacement, i.e., 'recovery'.

## 12.1.1 RELIABILITY

98 per cent+ availability may be a reasonable target for a batch installation, but there are many unlucky data processing managers who have had to make the most of a somewhat lower performance. What may be a headache in batch mode can be highly disruptive to the users in real time mode. Thus where hardware selection involves providing for a real time system or vice versa, strong emphasis should be placed on unit and system reliability, both in supplier evaluation and in contract terms. Once the hardware is selected, a similar approach needs to be taken with the reliability and environmental quality of the computer room. Environment, in this context, includes such facets as dust filtration, corrosive gas (ozone given off from static based dust filters has been known to corrode CPU components), temperature, power supplies and fire and flood precautions.

## 12.1.2 RECOVERY

In hardware terms, a measure of recovery capability can be expressed in terms of the time to establish a minimum configuration for the real time job in hand after a failure. The main facets outlined in section 12.1 can then be grouped as 'diagnosis and isolation' and 'repair and replacement'. The latter points are considered first.

Waiting for maintenance engineers to repair hardware faults before initiating system re-starts is usually found an unacceptable delay in terms of the fail-soft performance of a real time system's central hardware. However, as mentioned in the introduction to this chapter, that is occasionally the right answer. In other cases, repair time remains as an essential part of fail-soft planning, especially if the repair process causes disruption, or needs computer resources, or means temporary lack of stand-by against the event of a second failure.

Replacement of the faulty item is the normal approach to overcome extensive repair times. In computer terms, this means alternative hardware, switchable under the control of the operations department or software.

The question facing the designer is 'given that a certain configuration is needed for the real time task, what equipment should I provide as reserve against failure?' The question is further complicated by the use or lack of use that can be made of spare equipment on other tasks, such as testing or batch systems.

Simple duplication of all items of hardware is a possible approach to improving availability, but in practice the money is sometimes better spent in a more selective manner. The question posed should then become 'How should a given level of expenditure be best allocated to reserve equipment to maximize availability? and what balance between extra cost and improved availability is justified for this project?'

### 12.1.3  FAIL-SOFT CALCULATIONS

To assist the designer in deciding on the impact of different configurations, some method of calculating the effect of the reserve is required. The design cycle is then

(1) Postulate configuration with a level of reserve.
(2) Calculate level of service and cost.
(3) Modify level of reserve and restart.
(4) After several cycles select best cost/performance.

Possible calculations can be based on one of two measures—'MTBF' and 'availability'—and the approach is set out in detail in chapter 18.

The MTBF is the mean time between failures of a component (or the whole) of the real time configuration. Formulae in chapter 18 show how MTBF's for units can be combined to calculate the MTBF for a configuration. A designer looks for the largest MTBF for his configuration when selecting between types of unit (disk, tape, etc.) or between suppliers. However MTBF is awkward to use in calculations involving alternatives (e.g., two disks provided, one needed, one spare). 'Availability' is easier to use and is calculated from MTBF's and mean time to repair (MTTR) as follows:

$$A = \frac{\text{MTBF}}{\text{MTBF} + \text{MTTR}}.$$

The definition fits the common-sense view, and can be used more simply to compare alternative sets of reserve equipment. In general, the MTBF reflects frequency of failure, and availability, the up-time. While for initial calculations, hardware MTTR can be regarded as the time from notification of error to correction, a more refined view is required later. Chapter 18 covers the wider definition, including communicating and isolating the error.

### 12.1.4  DIAGNOSIS AND ISOLATION

We have identified that part of the time to recover from failure is concerned with diagnosis and isolation. This is a subject that has raised much debate with those concerned with the choice of hardware architecture. Often such debates are strongest among manufacturers, new range planners, and designers, but it is equally pertinent to the user who is choosing his hardware for a real time project or has chosen a product that still provides him with choice after choosing the manufacturer, e.g., a multi (2) processor configuration that can run as two independent processors or as dual processors.

The basic choice arises between two extremes of 'isolation' and 'integration'. Before examining these further let us first consider the practical situation.

(1) A failure occurs somewhere in the system which eventually is detected. But where is the fault located?
(2) The failure is detected by a terminal or computer room operator.

(3) The operations team enter recovery procedures. (See later in this chapter.) In order to restart and continue processing, the *cause* of the error needs to be isolated. Therefore sufficient diagnosis is required to determine where the fault lies. For minor failures such as transient hardware errors, and software interface errors, the source of error is often difficult to trace.

(4) Having detected the cause of the error, recovery needs to be initiated as quickly as possible. The relative rate of recovery follows a hierarchy of

- hardware oriented (e.g., hardware error correction);
- software oriented (programmed recovery procedures);
- operator oriented.

In general terms, 'isolated' designs are good for step (3) and 'integrated' designs are good for step (4); in certain job mixes, the integrated approach can provide a less expensive solution. These approaches are described in more detail below.

### The Isolated Approach

The isolated approach is to keep all reserve hardware separated from the main real time processor. In that case, after an un-diagnosed failure, the restart procedure can certainly be initiated using the spare hardware with the knowledge that the fault will continue only if it lies in the software or in the data files. The latter two can also be changed to prior (different) versions if so required.

The system is most secure with a completely duplicate real time configuration, and in that case the designer and management will be looking for other interruptable work that can use the spare machine during normal operation. The isolated approach might be found in real time systems based on say Univac 315, IBM 360/370 series, ICL 1900/S4, and DEC PDP 11.

### Integrated Approach

The integrated approach requires the environment of a multi-processor structure, where the system is designed for ease (and hence speed) in re-configuration and re-start, possibly without re-loading the system. Potentially, the system can be designed to be responsible for recognizing certain faults and reorganizing accordingly, e.g., core module failure. The practical difficulty with this approach occurs when, for any reason, the installation suffers a relatively high rate of errors not easily diagnosed and performance is severely degraded over a long period. The problem in the integrated approach is isolating the un-diagnosed fault.

Systems which have followed this 'integrated approach' may be found in, e.g., the B6700 and the ICL 2900. However, having chosen such hardware, the user still has the final choice of use as 'integrated' or 'isolated', depending on the precise configuration ordered.

### Integrated or Isolated?

There is no general answer. Each supplier decides his philosophy against the current state of his applied technology and his interpretation of market demand. The user can only judge the merits of either approach against the particular needs and features of his system.

### 12.1.5   HOW FAR WITH HARDWARE?

Fail-soft design is a complex task, and for that reason the designer benefits from dividing the work into two steps. In the first step he considers only the hardware configuration, and gains an understanding of the hardware's contribution to failures and to their recovery.

In the second step he works on the overall system. At this stage, the wider considerations often lead him to change views taken at the end of the first step—hardware-only fail-soft design—such change must be expected, but the two-step approach is nonetheless worth while.

The type of change that arises can be illustrated by a simple example. Take a disk with a MTBF of 500 hr and MTTR of 2 hr (on site engineers). Availability (see chapter 18) is 500/502 or 0·996, and two disks in parallel may raise the figure to $1 - (0·005)^2$ or 0·999 + . After considering costs, the designer may consider a reserve disk in his fail-soft design.

However, systems considerations could drastically change the situation. With software faults, the disk failure rate plus data errors from programs, or, say, CPU failure, may lead to a MTBF of 100 hr, and file re-creation on a simple recovery plan for a large complex file may average 5 hrs. Thus for 1 disk, availability $A = 100/107 = 0·934$. For 2 disks, the switching is not immediate, as files need re-creation, so the second disk only reduces effective MTTR to 5 hr; thus availability $A = 100/105 = 0·952!$ The overall effect of the second disk is thus less dramatic than suggested from the hardware only analysis.

The practical situation is more complex still, but in the final analysis it is systems performance as a whole that matters; hardware calculations are only a first step in the direction of designing adequate fail-soft facilities.

### 12.1.6   THE COMPUTER ROOM

The general organization of hardware inside the computer room falls outside the scope of this book. Nevertheless, in planning the fail-soft facilities of a major real time system, the design team need to cooperate with operations management to ensure a viable system.

A check list is provided in Fig. 12.1 as a guide. Each of the items in the list can be a major design/implementation topic in its own right, and project teams may need to take specialist advice. For example, in considering power supplies, where the need is to ensure both smoothness of supply and continuity, the solutions that have been used in practice usually involve a mixed supply, with options including such techniques as mains supplies, filters, alternators, motor generators, floating cells and automatic cut over. In such a case, the project team need to set objectives and compare performance or cost, but specialists are needed to prepare the best alternative solutions.

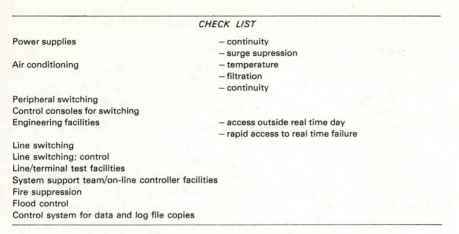

Power supplies    — continuity
    — surge supression
Air conditioning    — temperature
    — filtration
    — continuity

Peripheral switching
Control consoles for switching
Engineering facilities    — access outside real time day
    — rapid access to real time failure

Line switching
Line switching; control
Line/terminal test facilities
System support team/on-line controller facilities
Fire suppression
Flood control
Control system for data and log file copies

**Fig. 12.1** Computer room—fail-soft planning

## 12.1.7 COMMUNICATIONS

In planning the fail-soft factors of the communications network, similar approaches can be taken, as with the central hardware. However, in this case the availability for any one terminal is determined only by considering that part of the network required for its work. Therefore 100 per cent network availability is seldom of interest, rather the view from individual terminal operators.

Failures affecting the operator's view of reliability at the terminal arise in the terminal, local line sharing adaptor, modem, line, central communication processor and the central system.

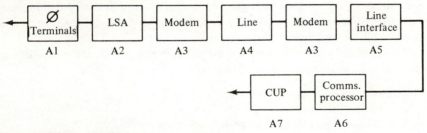

An = Availability of module *n*

**Fig. 12.2** Availability model for one terminal

Calculation of performance and the impact of different reserve circuits and units can be carried out against the simple model in Fig. 12.2 for each terminal or centre. It is important for the designer to determine at an early stage precisely what options he has in terms of switching between lines, modems, interfaces, controllers, etc. The options open to him very much depend on the constraints imposed by the local telephone authority, the line speeds he uses, and the manufacturer's own facilities. The method of switching or replacing units in the communications link from terminal operator to main processors can have

**199**

major impact on price and availability. Experience unfortunately suggests that a 'first view' solution does not always work in practice.

For example, in Fig. 12.2, an exchange facility between the lines and the central modems would permit the re-routing of both terminals and lines to reserve modems and CPU interfaces on the failure of modems, interfaces or the communications processor, and also the re-routing of modems and CPU interfaces to spare lines.

The implication of this approach is a reserve modem connected to each spare line interface, reserve modem/interface pairs available to each spare communication processor, and reserve terminal equipment (unless such units could be re-plugged). Placing a switching system between modems and the line interfaces increases flexibility at that level but ties modems to lines. Some large systems have used both levels of switching. This approach improves flexibility but is complicated to design and operate. The choice between these options can only be resolved by detailed costing and reliability calculations after the detailed feasibility of the proposed connections has been validated.

## 12.2 Systems Availability

Overall, the systems performance can be measured or predicted in a similar manner to hardware alone, but as in the example in section 12.1.5 above, disk failure may now be considered as 'file failure', where the MTBF is made up of both hardware and software causes, and MTTR is taken from the accumulation of the hardware switching or repair time and the time to recover the file logically.

However, recovery procedures are now much more complex than just switching equipment, and this section therefore considers the types of solution that can be applied. Figure 12.3 provides a check list of system fail-soft areas that must be considered by the designer. The areas are dealt with further in section 12.2.1 onwards.

The fail-soft system eventually developed is dependent on the environment, which may be classified under the headings of:

(1) batch single programming,
(2) batch multi programming,
(3) real time—simple—file interrogation (see chapter 20),
(4) real time—simple—data capture,
(5) real time—complex,
(6) real time—complex 24 hour service.

The further down the list, the more complex the problem, and this chapter is written against the needs of item 5, i.e., real time-complex with file updating. The reader is assumed to be familiar with the batch systems covering 1 and 2. Items 3 and 4 fall between batch and real time in terms of the resulting solutions.

Twenty-four hour systems are a special case, as preparatory work for fail-soft cannot be carried out between real time shifts. A number of techniques

Prevention
Preparation
Detection
Reaction
Diagnosis
Isolation
Reconfiguration
Rescheduling
Re-step
Re-process
Re-start
Re-institute
Maintenance

**Fig. 12.3**   Fail-soft steps

have been proven for this special case and usually involve provision for

(a) dynamic switching of disks, files, program modules,
(b) incremental dumping and logging.

### 12.2.1   PREVENTION

The old adage 'prevention is better than cure' is particularly pertinent to fail-soft design. Prevention in real time systems probably is better interpreted as 'minimize frequency or impact of failures'. The project team's ability to 'prevent' falls under three heads.

### Products

Given that many errors are induced by hardware or manufacturer's software, any team with a tight fail-soft specification to meet needs to place more emphasis on high product reliability/availability than for batch work. Thus, reliability requires careful probing and evaluation of hardware and software at the selection stage, whether for new equipment or added units, or new software for an existing configuration.

### Data

With the increased scope in message format provided by a terminal over, say, a punch card, the design team need to take greater care to ensure that messages in error are trapped by the system and do not cause system failure. While the normal design processes should define procedures to trap such faults, a data error that on some terminals can cause problems is where the operator fails to insert message end characters. Designers are advised to check out the effect on the chosen communications software as well as their own program logic.

### User Code

While data induced failures (excluding valid message with incorrect data) may be few, failures of the users' real time programs can be high. When availability is important, so is the thoroughness with which testing is carried

**201**

out. Most installations need to test real time systems to a greater level of perfection than has historically been applied to batch systems.

Most fail-soft planning and design decisions are difficult to subject to simple value judgements. With regard to the question 'Why is it worth spending extra on testing the system to get it near perfection?', there are two benefits to be considered: (1) the subsequent reduction in bugs to be cleared in early months of operation, and (2) a reduced frequency of operational failure in early years. The greater the project team's justified confidence that errors will be relatively infrequent, the less complex (and less expensive) can be the recovery systems.

### 12.2.2 PREPARATION

Preparation refers to the tasks carried out by operators, users and software, on a regular basis in preparation against a failure. Thus preparation tasks are concerned with safeguarding data and preparing information for later analysis. Such analysis may be required either to diagnose the cause of a failure or to decide on the recovery path.

Preparation is the bulk of the regular fail-soft overhead of the system. Preparation techniques and related recovery procedures are discussed further in sections 12.3 and 12.4.

### 12.2.3 DETECTION

The sooner failures are detected and reported to 'those responsible for operational control', the faster the recovery can be initiated and the sooner the corruption of data can be prevented.

Failures can be detected by program traps, user observation, or computer room staff. In each case, the project team needs to establish the procedure for both logging and communicating the fault. With users and within the computer room, the procedures may be fairly straightforward, but the method of dealing with remotely detected failures needs careful design. Many of the possible faults, such as communications control failure, computer failure, or even line failure, cause many terminals to see the same symptom of error, i.e., no response when attempting message input or no reply from the last message. If they all then call the centre, most will just get an engaged tone because it is not possible to deal with them all at the same time. Therefore, not only should the centre plan for such an avalanche of calls, but also establish methods by which the centre can be sure of being able to call the remote locations to initiate action when they are trying (unsuccessfully) to get through to the centre, e.g., by providing more than one line.

In many cases, the operations team can get the terminals operational again, e.g., by switching to a stand-by controller without verbal contact being necessary. Subsequent recovery action may be communicated via the terminals.

While outside the computer detection is procedure oriented, internally the designers may have some choice on the level of self-checking they impose within the system, and on the extent to which the hardware and software permit options for failures to be trapped and perhaps recovered by software.

In the first case, experience has shown the value of imposing validation routines not only on input but also between modules in the system. Such validation may increase overheads, but as program error rates reduce with time, such checks can easily be removed if modularly implemented.

## 12.2.4 REACTION

(This and the following fail-soft steps are presented as if they occur serially. While that is the usual situation after failure, there are occasions when parallel activity or loops are appropriate.)

Once failure is detected, immediate reaction is required to prevent the error propagating, to initiate the recovery, and to initiate later diagnosis and repair.

Prevention of propagation is generally controlled by stopping the system or sub-system. The objectives of ultimate fault correction are often different from that of the recovery procedures, especially where the type of failure does not indicate the cause. For fault diagnosis, the best action is to determine as much information about the fault immediately, by taking main store dumps, for example, for later use.

In many error conditions, a rapid re-start can be achieved without completing a full diagnosis of the cause. Simple restarts eliminate nearly all errors caused by transient hardware faults, chance combinations of events or logic faults in little-used software or applications code, and thus provide efficient immediate recovery (but without determining the cause).

## 12.2.5 DIAGNOSIS

As indicated above, diagnosis can be divided into two phases:

— Diagnosis of symptom and/or cause of failure sufficient to determine immediate recovery action. This process must be planned to identify/eliminate any serious hardware errors and then to identify sub-systems as OK, at fault, or unknown. Sub-systems in this context include software and user programs. It is the difficulty of establishing the cause of a failure (particularly after a transient hardware error or a software fault) that frequently encourages many designers to plan for re-starts to be based on separate hardware.
— Full diagnosis to determine long-term course of correction to software or hardware. One of the designer's objectives is to take this action out of the critical path to system re-start. In hardware terms, this means reserve equipment. In software terms, the need is for certain basic dumps and checkpoints before recovery is initiated. Such checkpoints can be provided partly by the fail-soft preparation procedures in the operational system (e.g., transaction logs) and partly *computer room* and *user* post-failure disciplines.

In the history of data processing, there have been too many situations where this full diagnosis has been on the critical path to recovery. The main reasons are poor hardware performance with unsuitable conditions, poor development and testing, and poor recovery/diagnosis design.

Full diagnosis is the responsibility of an operations support team who clear a back-log of faults, possibly grouped, in parallel with continuing operations. Many bugs need to be avoided in the interim. This can be achieved through such expedients as temporary constraints on the applications system.

## 12.2.6 ISOLATION

The recovery plan takes shape after reaction and initial diagnosis. At that stage, hardware items known or thought to be at fault, or software whose faults are highlighted by the current data, may be removed from the available configuration or library.

After isolation, the recovery process starts—the next five steps. In planning fail-soft systems, it must be remembered that recovery is often initiated without knowledge of the fault. In these cases, the procedures established for operations are on a trial and error basis, the initial actions chosen being the ones most likely to clear most faults. In the absence of hard evidence on diagnosis of error, a possible sequence may be as shown in Fig. 12.4. In this example, the plan is developed to simplify operator decision. If the first restart fails, the second restart is initiated on a reserve configuration. This seeks to avoid any hidden hardware errors. The third try seeks to avoid chance coincidence of events or messages that have detected programme errors.

The final attempt seeks to avoid software library errors arising from premature issue of enhancements or chance faults in the operating system copy.

## 12.2.7 RECONFIGURATION

In order to initiate recovery, a suitable configuration needs to be established both in hardware and software terms. This can range through such options as

- no change of hardware—restart real time programme without change of software;
- no change of hardware—re-load software and re-start;
- switch reserve peripheral to replace failed unit;
- restart on reserve configuration.

Where plans involve multi programmed background work or twin configurations and batch work on the second machine, planning needs to take into account lost time arising from the forced halts and subsequent re-starts of that batch work.

In developing the fail-soft system, reconfiguration needs to be considered as

- a time factor in recovery;
- a cost of recovery;
- a set of procedures that require pre-planning as part of the development process;

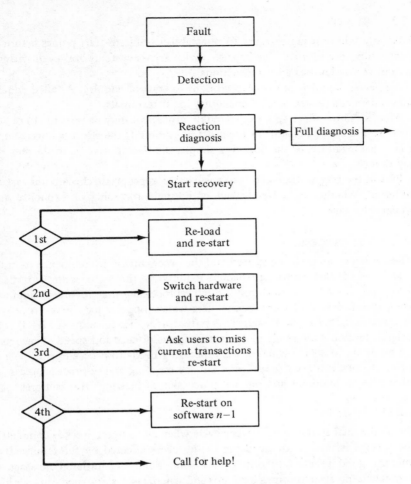

**Fig. 12.4** Illustration—operator recovery plan

— controls to enable the system to recognize changes in configuration; this
particularly applies to changes in the network after a single line failure,
where the whole system should not be brought down.

### 12.2.8 RESCHEDULING

Rescheduling is an extension of reconfiguration where the failure has reduced
available hardware. Rescheduling in the real time system can involve such
techniques as a change in priority of some transactions, or manual procedures
to inhibit less urgent work being input to the system. Background batch
processing, affected by the transfer of equipment to the real time configuration,
requires rescheduling to reflect the reduced capacity available. As with
reconfiguration, rescheduling needs to be considered in plans for recovery in
terms of time, cost, procedures, and controls.

### 12.2.9 RE-STEP

After any failure it is necessary to re-establish stable re-start points before re-establishing the service. The process varies across systems and even within a system across failures and transactions.

A rejected enquiry can re-step straight to start of enquiry. A failed enquiry sub-system can re-step to start of enquiry for all terminals.

After a failure affecting a single update process, it may be possible to re-step for that process to the start of the last transaction. If the effect is uncertain, or it is a major failure, or the design is simple, the re-step may be to the start-of-day dumps.

Part of the preparation step is to ensure that appropriate check points are established, whether as a by-product of normal processing or explicitly as a preparation task.

### 12.2.10 RE-PROCESS

When a major failure has occurred and the processing is to commence from the established re-start points, provision is required for the reprocessing of transactions input since the re-start point. Such reprocessing may involve re-input by users, re-processing of transactions off a transaction file log, or re-processing file updates from file status snapshots (after image file; see section 12.4.4). The designer faces a wide range of choices in terms of cost and speed of recovery, and he needs to decide whether the processing needs to proceed prior, post or during the rest of the day's real time run. Re-stepping and re-processing can involve a lot of computer and manual processing of files/logs/transactions.

### 12.2.11 RE-START

This is the final step in the recovery cycle when all recovery work is completed. The service is now made available to the users affected by the failure. It is generally good practice to provide for some computer-initiated message to users when the system comes back up (and where necessary when the user logs back in). This may need supplementing by a voice or telex communication link outside the computer network.

When particularly fast recovery is important, designers can speed up re-instatement of certain services before all correction, re-stepping and re-processing is complete.

### 12.2.12 REPAIR

Although procedures can be established in order to restart the system without repairing the fault, this task still needs to be carried out. Both hardware and software faults should be corrected urgently as the situation may be complicated by secondary failures. However, in some cases, software faults can be by-passed by placing constraints on which systems facilities may be used. For hardware, this means that thought needs to be given at the design stage as to how an engineer can gain access to the necessary equipment and processor power to repair, test and run up the failed unit. While any unit is at fault it is not in reserve.

### 12.2.13 RE-INSTITUTE

Depending on the environment it may be desirable to bring failed equipment back into the real time system immediately on repair. For example, a two-disk system runs on one disk when one of the disks fails, another system uses a 'slow' disk file when the real time 'drum file' fails, or another loads less tables to core after a core module failure. Each of the reduced configurations may lead to a degraded performance.

Designers need to provide facilities to bring the repaired equipment back into the system in a tidy manner without returning to full systems re-start. Such tidy 're-institution' often proves difficult to provide if identified only after the first few failures.

On 24 hour systems, facilities to upgrade hardware units or software modules, or to reload restructured files fall under this context.

### 12.2.14 MAINTENANCE

Several real time systems have suffered in operational use from poor maintenance planning. Maintenance and repair planning should be carried out together. Consider a typical case where insufficient planning was provided.

A large network of 100 terminals was connected to a twin processor installation with a complex data base. Operational plans involved shift working with a long real time day shift, and night batch shifts. Maintenance was scheduled daily between shifts and at weekends.

Over a period of time the failure rate of the system was high (software, hardware, programs).

The following problems arose:

(1) Engineers were unable to repair by day because no processor available to test—partially rectified by *buying more* equipment.
(2) Real time and batch restarts took up all spare capacity. No float left for engineers to take more than their allotted maintenance time.
(3) Maintenance standards dropped.
(4) Improvements to software and user program failure rates were off-set by increased hardware failure rates. Continued pressure on time available for maintenance.

This situation continued for an extended period and is not an uncommon one. More careful planning at the start could have avoided the problem by the provision of such features as:

— More hardware to increase capacity. If maintenance needs $n$ hours per day, there is no way to avoid that proportion of capacity being lost or covered at a cost.
— Greater engineering cover and more on-site test equipment and space.

Such extra hardware and maintenance costs should have been included in the systems costs before reviewing the justification and specification of the system.

## 12.3 Design Approach

The design of a fail-soft environment is difficult to subject to a fixed discipline. However, there is a basic flow as illustrated in Fig. 12.5.

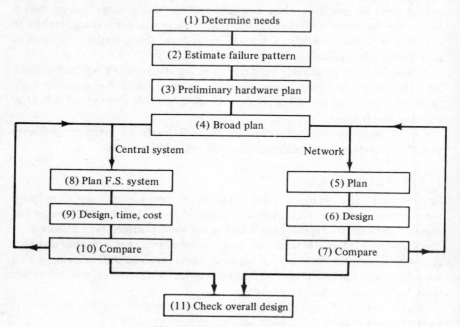

Fig. 12.5   Fail-soft design flow

The main steps are:

(1) Determine the needs from the systems analysis stage. This is one of those areas where the desirable precision is not attainable in practice. However, some attempt to ascertain acceptable performance levels, or the cost/effect of failure at different levels of loss of service, is needed.

(2) Based on systems designs and plans, estimate causes and frequency of failure. These will arise from the central site, lines, network devices, software and user programs. Try to determine some view of the frequency of the different types of symptom, i.e., halts, line out, halts with clear hardware failure, etc.

(3) Plan provisional hardware fail-soft configuration.

(4) Provide a broad plan of the relationship between the network, and central system, fail-soft designs and procedures. Set fail-soft design targets for the network and the central system so that the combined effect is acceptable at each terminal.

**208**

(5–7) For simplicity the network recovery procedure can start design separately. The design process (5–7) follows similar steps to those for the central system, i.e., steps (8–10), i.e., plan network fail-soft, design the detail, predict performance.

(8) Plan central fail-soft, i.e., all except the physical network. The first step is to postulate the preparation and recovery approach. This is a design process that may require several iterations, and designers are advised to start with the simplest approach first. Later iterations evaluate alternative designs, both for reserve hardware, software and manual procedures.

(9) Design the detailed implications of the chosen approach. Check out the effect on timing of the use of the computer in regular processing and delays at point of failure.

(10) Match the design against potential failures identified at (2), and compare the cost of development and running the proposed solution against level/speed of recovery offered. Compare against earlier iterations (8–10), and eventually select 'the design'.

(11) Check that the network and central system designs are still compatible, jointly meet overall recovery targets, and cover each of the fail-soft areas of Fig. 12.3.

The big step in this cycle is postulating the design (steps 5 and 8). There is no easy answer except to follow the check list in Fig. 12.3 and start with a simple approach. Generally, evaluations of the initial designs will themselves then suggest the lines of change to reduce overheads on regular processing and to speed recovery from failure.

## 12.4 Fail-soft Techniques

A number of techniques are available to meet the fail-soft objectives of real time systems. Once the level of reserve hardware and maintenance-plans are resolved, these can be generally classified as

– action during real time day, carrying out the 'preparation' procedures;
– action during normal work, out of real time, in 'preparation';
– action in diagnosis for recovery;
– action in recovery.

These are illustrated in Fig. 12.6.

The design process of section 12.3 can then be seen to be one of determining a balance between *running* and *development* costs concerned with all the steps of fail-soft, the risk associated with the solution, and recovery times for each class of failure.

Apart from techniques implied in section 12.2, several other techniques are often used. These techniques are grouped under:

– transaction recording—logging;
– file protection;
– others.

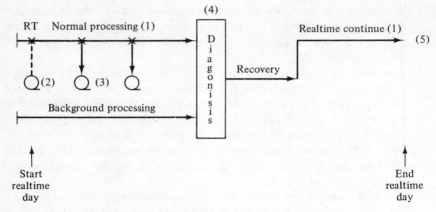

*Notes* (1) Normal processing and logging
(2) End or start of shift file dumps
(3) Mid shift log change
(4) Point of failure
(5) Overnight procedures

**Fig. 12.6**  Fail-soft cycle

## 12.4.1  LOGGING

Logging is a process of writing each message to a computer medium as a continuous record of transactions. Logs as such provide

- input to recovery procedures;
- possible evidence on point of failure;
- computer record of days (shifts) transactions;
- statistics for performance analysis;
- possible input to other procedures.

Several variants of logging are discussed below, where generally the variants provide a range of information stored, a range of risk of loss of some transactions, and variations in the overheads on CPU, disks, tapes, etc.

Given that the log is the sole computer record of a transaction (other than the related updated files), many fail-soft designs lead to duplicated logging.

The following variants of logging may be applied in combination. It is assumed that basic logging consists of writing one copy of the essential data of each transaction to a serial file at a fixed point in the message path, and also that all messages are allocated a system identity number.

### Log Timing

On recovery from a complete shut down the point in the message cycle at which logging takes place relative to the file update (i.e., before or after—sometimes in parallel) may impact on the interpretation of the log. Where pin-pointing message progress is important, message may be logged in full on arrival and the progress reported to the log at key steps in the processing cycle.

**210**

## Log and Status

When each message is logged, additional data are read from tables in the processor and written with the log message. Such data may reflect status of other messages or general statistics.

## Block Logs

Log messages are built up in core into a block to optimize use of the logging device and decrease overheads. The resulting risk is loss of all logs in the block at the time of a CPU failure. This is often acceptable when the information is only for statistical purposes, e.g., for enquiries.

## Cycling Logs

Log messages are written to a disk or drum such that the $n$th log record overwrites the $(n - r)$th record (cycle of $r$).

If associated with block logging, this covers for loss of logs in a block log, after CPU failure. The block must be smaller than $r$ logs.

## Terminal Slots

Each terminal has its own working storage on backing store. Messages are stored by terminal number until processing is complete on that transaction. This may cover several message pairs. This is a variant on cyclic logging and achieves similar objectives.

In certain applications, where transaction processing involves several message pairs, such terminal slots can be organized to carry data between message pairs or to carry transaction and file data, the main files only being updated when all messages and processing on a transaction are complete. This approach seeks to avoid the unpicking of incomplete file updates and generally requires the program to re-read master file records just before the final update. When the final update involves several records, failure can still occur part way through that final series.

## Front End Processors

Communications processors can play a role in logging messages. A cyclic log held in core in the communications processor provides economic cover for the build up of block logs in the main processor. The same technique can be applied with back end file processors. Both the above assume an applications programmable hardware/software environment.

## 12.4.2 FILE DUMPING

When planning to dump real time files, the designers must consider both frequency and format of the dump.

The relative merits of each contribution of frequency and format can only be determined by projecting the costs and speed of recovery associated with each case. In general, the more the overheads in regular processing, the faster the recovery when recourse to dumped files is required.

File dumping and possible associated re-structuring (for example with heavily updated index sequential files) will be scheduled outside the real time day and can become a heavy overload on the total capacity if daily dumps are considered.

With daily dumps, the average number of transactions to be recovered after file failure is half a day, and the maximum is nearly one day's work. Dumps less frequent than daily are possible, but are not often suitable if recovery specifications are tight. Thus, while postulating the form of dumping may be easy, the evaluation of costing and scheduling needs are not.

Moreover, even with daily dumps, file recreation can be too slow to meet design targets when achieved by updating the dump file from the transaction log.

In such cases, there are two approaches to improve the recovery performance from this basic approach. The first is concerned with minimizing the range of failures that necessitate complete file recreation and the relevant techniques are described further in section 12.4.3. The second approach is to speed the post-failure file recreation process; techniques aimed at this objective are covered in section 12.4.4.

### 12.4.3 AVOIDING FILE RECREATION

The need for file recreation can be reduced by increasing information on file status, post-failure, and by providing the means to carry out a partial or temporary correction. Techniques available include the following.

*Snap Shot*

Provide application or special recovery routines to enable the operations team to rapidly display selected file records. Selection may be by operator selection or analysis of the log.

*File Correction Transactions*

After certain failure conditions, file errors may be such that records are difficult to correct by the use of applications transactions. This particularly applies when controls become inconsistent. Special file change transactions which permit individual fields to be altered without effecting any others can aid recovery, but need treating with care as they can create further errors or can be used to break security. Special recording of the use of such transactions can provide necessary controls and protection.

*Block Header*

The form of this technique is dependent on the software interface. Each time a

212

block (or record) is written, status fields are updated to reflect the update. The usual significance of the status fields are as a cyclic record of the last $n$ (2 or 3) transactions that updated the block. This information can later be compared with the most recent messages on the log tape to determine success of updates.

## Block Flags

After post-failure analysis, certain file records may be in an uncertain state. As an alternative to recreation of the file, block flags are set against those records whose contents are in doubt. The application system is designed to enter an error routine if a block flag is found when records are being sought. (Note that if the problem was a possible error in the write process, the flags need to be set to apply to all records in the block in doubt.) The error routines may notify the user of the record's special status.

Thus, say, 99 per cent of transactions may continue without the delay necessary for full file recreation. Block flags can be dynamically removable if later analysis removes doubt or corrective action is taken.

## 12.4.4  FILE RECOVERY

The simplest, and at failure, slowest, technique is updating the dump file from the subsequent transaction logs. Faster recovery techniques include the following, but should only be used if this time for recovery is unacceptable.

## Batch Files

Where recovery time from file failure on overnight dumps is too slow a process, it is possible to progressively update the dumped file in background batch mode, probably on the reserve configuration. If the real time system is enquiry or 'read' dominated this need not be a heavy background task.

Procedures are required for dynamically opening new logs, closing old logs and transferring them to the batch machine, or background partition.

## Before and After Images

A different form of dumping is to include updated file records on a log file. Images of affected file records can be written as before images (before update) or after images (after update) as part of the log. Thus, after failure, a suspect master file can be checked against recent after images, or back tracked to some mid run check point on the basis of before images, or the dump can be more rapidly updated from after images than from re-processing whole transactions.

## Duplication

In extremes of reliability criteria, main files can be maintained in duplicate. The cost is in update processing as well as the media itself. However read access need not be duplicated if the main purpose is to maintain an up-to-date standby file. Some designers have organized 'reads' from alternative files to spread the load.

### 12.4.5 OTHER TECHNIQUES

*Multi-programmed Checks*

Background low priority programs are run to carry out validations on contents, consistency and structure of real time files. Again, such checking can be carried out overnight in batch mode.

*Lock Out*

In a multi-threaded environment the system is occasionally set to a lock-out condition. All messages in progress are cleared before any new messages are accepted out of the communications buffers. A special log comment is recorded to mark this 'stable' point. Full processing then continues. Note that the delay is of the order of double the response time, each time it occurs, or less if it can be initiated at an instantaneous low load condition.

*Hostility*

All routines are written in a manner that carefully checks requests from other routines. These hostility checks can be removed when the system has been running for some time. (Removal usually coincides with rising system loads; see also chapter 7.)

*Limited Service*

After a failure resulting in less hardware capacity being available after recovery, a full service can be maintained to important messages if less important messages are delayed (given lower priority) or cut out altogether.

## 12.5 The User in Recovery

Many recovery systems can be achieved by calling on the user to play his role in recovery, thus simplifying computer solutions and reducing costs of preparation. Whatever procedure occurs at the centre on recovery, the user ideally should restart near the point of failure and not re-input much of his day's work on a terminal. The user's re-start point preferably will be at a transaction boundary rather than at a message pair, in the middle of a transaction's sequence.

When the terminal includes some recording device (paper tapes, disks, cassette), the transaction log may be held by each user. As a general principal all significant transactions (i.e., excluding enquiry only) should be explicitly numbered, and if that number is generated in the computer, the operator should be required to record it on his own documentation.

## 12.6 An Overview

The fail-soft designer has a potentially complex task. For this reason, the initial understanding can be difficult. To assist the reader, a reasonably simple but typical system is described below as a case example. The description is broad and concentrates on the fail-soft elements rather than the application or other design elements. The case is described in a form independent of whether suitable redundant hardware is available or whether the operators need to await repairs. Techniques employed include logging, after images, terminal slots, operator involvement, and transaction level recovery.

### 12.6.1 SYSTEM OVERVIEW

The main hardware components are VDU's, network, main processor, disk work file, disk main file, and logging tapes. The application can be considered as a single transaction made up of two (or more) message pairs each of which updates the main file. Exception paths are not described.

### 12.6.2 NORMAL OPERATION

The code is explicit from the transaction data themselves. It determines the by a piece of paper in the VDU operator's procedures. Had message pairs been chosen as the recovery level, the terminal operator would need to identify his progress to an intermediate point in the cycle of handling the input documents (transactions). The system flow was designed with this recovery level in mind. See Fig. 12.7. The results of the processing of the first message are written to a work file (terminal slot) and are not used at this stage to update the main file.

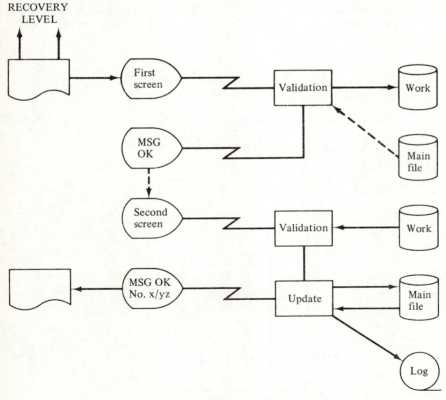

Fig. 12.7   System flow

**215**

The processing of the second (final) message pair includes abstracting data from the earlier pair(s) from the terminal slot, and carrying out the final main file updates. The log file is only updated on this final pair. (Earlier messages can also be logged for statistical reasons if so required.)

If the operator wishes to terminate a transaction at any stage before the final message, the appropriate code causes the terminal slot to be cleared. At this level, the system thus provides for simple cancellation, part way through a multiple message pair process.

A simple system would lock out the main file record when first read and release it on the final update. As this locks the record for the period of the conversation, it might not be suitable in some systems. In such cases, the programs may be written to re-read the main files again before the final update. The lock would then only apply during the up-date cycle on receipt of the final message.

### 12.6.3 END OF CYCLE

Figure 12.8 represents the processing at the end of each transaction after receipt of the last message:

- the terminal slot (work file) is read;
- application processing is carried out with associated main file records being read;
- the main file is updated;

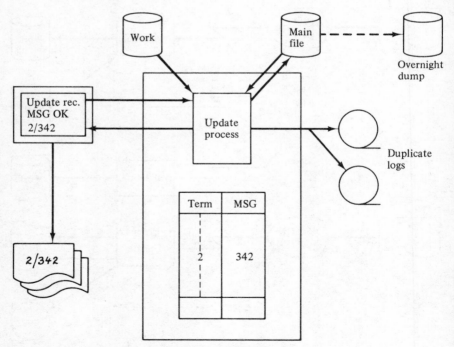

**Fig. 12.8** End of cycle

- the message and main file after image are logged;
- the terminal/status table is updated by incrementing the entry for that terminal by 1. Under this system the transaction number is 'terminal number/sequential number.';
- the acknowledgement is sent to terminal with transaction number (in Fig. 12.8. it is 2/342);
- the operator concludes the transaction cycle by writing the transaction number onto the related document.

### 12.6.4 END OF DAY

The main file is dumped to another replaceable disk in the same format.

### 12.6.5 RECOVERY- (RE-STEP AND RE-PROCESS)

After any failure (other than terminal failure; see section 12.6.7) the system is halted, and after taking dumps of core for subsequent investigation, a recovery program is loaded. See Fig. 12.9.

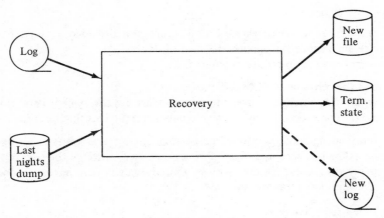

**Fig. 12.9**  Recovery

The capabilities of this program include the following:

(1) Copy log to new log.
(2) Copy dump main file to new main file.
(3) Update new main file from after images on log.
(4) Update, in main storage, the terminal/message table from the log.
(5) Write complete terminal status table to disk and close program.

In those circumstances where simplicity of operation is the aim, the operator's action would always be the same, i.e., re-start after any failure by initiating the complete program (all failures treated as major loss of files). If the designers wanted to give the computer operator more responsibility, then he would be

**217**

| Failed item | Procedure no. | | | | |
|---|---|---|---|---|---|
| | 1 | 2 | 3 | 4 | 5 |
| CPU halt | | | | ✓ | ✓ |
| Log tape | ✓ | | | ✓ | ✓ |
| Main file | | ✓ | ✓ | ✓ | ✓ |
| Total system | ✓ | ✓ | ✓ | ✓ | ✓ |

Fig. 12.10    Selection of recovery procedures

directed to choose the appropriate procedures depending on his diagnosis of the failure.

Figure 12.10 tabulates the form of selection made. In the table 'Procedure number' refers to (1)–(5) above.

### 12.6.6    RESTART

The real time program is reloaded with an operator-provided parameter to indicate re-start mode (as opposed to start of day).

An extra restart procedure is entered, to

– read the terminal status table into core;
– transmit a message to every terminal indicating the system is on the air, and the last successful transaction number accepted for that terminal.

The terminal operator continues processing on the next transaction to that notified as the last accepted. Even if he was part way through the next transaction at the time of failure the recovery procedures will only have re-processed up to the nominated transaction.

### 12.6.7    TERMINAL FAILURE

When a failure occurs that affects a terminal or line but does not bring down the system (trapped by the communications software) the following applies:

– terminal re-instated or noted 'out of the system';
– if required, a new terminal/line is connected and communications software adjusted by complete operator input;
– whosoever takes on the processing work of the failed terminals enquires of the system the latest entry in that terminal status table. The operator can then continue with all outstanding work beyond that notified. See Fig. 12.11.

### 12.6.8    THE WHOLE SYSTEM

This case has been described at an overview level. The solution is simple,

**218**

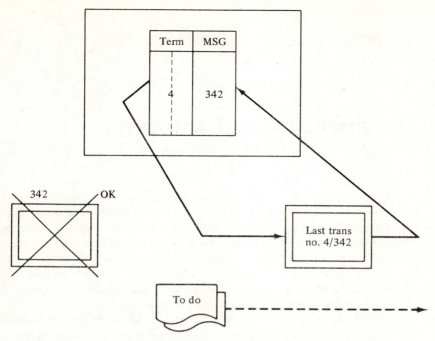

**Fig. 12.11** Terminal/line failure

moderately slow but effective. Its slowness is partially offset by the speed with which it can be put into action, because of the almost complete lack of operator decision time once stable hardware is established.

Many systems' fail-soft requirement could be met by a design similar to this; however, it is stressed that the overview was aimed at illustrating a simple system and so did not cover every possible event or necessary facility.

# 13. Security and Integrity

A terminal network offers the possibility of access to the files to many people. The accessors potentially include both fraudulent and careless operators. Whatever its other advantages, this immediacy of access by-passes the protection which is possible through a conscientious clerical control section. No one can, for example, examine a transaction and verify its origin according to the seal of the bag it came in, and the signature on it. Nor is it possible to check the validity of results before they are passed to a user.

Since these functions can no longer be carried out external to the machine, they become an integral part of the computer system design. So far as the user is concerned, he sees little direct benefit for the costs associated with these extra facilities. Consequently, there is a need to limit this hidden cost to the minimum consistent with adequate protection. The arguments in this respect are very similar to those for fail-soft (see chapter 12).

This chapter deals firstly with the real time aspects of security—prevention of deliberate damage or fraudulent access to files—and secondly with integrity—ensuring that accidental damage can be rectified. (Recovery from major damage is considered in chapter 12.) Finally, the design approach to both aspects is considered.

The protection of the system against fraud or attack by programming is not considered in this chapter. While important, the subject is considered to be equally relevant to batch installations and broader than the scope of this book.

Programming through terminals is a special case, where the designer of the multi-access or RJE system faces a problem not particularly relevant to 'commercial' real time system (section 20.1).

## 13.1 Security

### 13.1.1 PHYSICAL SECURITY

Much has been written and discussed regarding physical security for computers. A variety of schemes are available for preventing unauthorized access to the machine room and other parts of the installation. The purpose of this section is not to review these in detail, but, assuming that an adequate physical security system can be provided, to relate its use to needs in real time systems.

As will be detailed below, achieving security against unauthorized access via terminals requires the design, programming, maintenance and running of routines that access various tables held in the computer. Operators or terminals are identified either directly, or implicitly, by physical position.

The greater the amount of collusion that is required between different individuals to defeat the security system, the more secure it is potentially. For example, in a given case, in order to gain access to a certain file, it may be necessary to connect a terminal physically to a specific line, discover the appropriate line identity and alter polling tables at the time of connection of the terminal so as not to cause error notices from the software. With the connection thus established, it may still be necessary to obtain a badge with an appropriate code, and obtain a valid password for the transaction, before unauthorized accessing of information.

An alternative to obtaining valid identity codes is, of course, to alter the security software tables. If all these activities were carried out by different people or functions, who individually could only enter the appropriate part of the installation, a large amount of collusion would be necessary for the fraud. Such a degree of collusion would make the fraud very difficult to keep secret.

To force the need for collusion, in the example given above, programming could be banned in the machine room. Network controllers only could be allowed into the modem and line switching room. A senior manager allocates security codes via a terminal set aside for the purpose, itself physically protected. A quality control section checks design and maintenance changes and enhancements, none of its members being allowed to carry out programming or operating functions. These are but a few examples in which use of physical security enhances the effectiveness of the overall security system.

13.1.2  RUN-TIME SECURITY

To prevent access to the files from unauthorized terminal users, an on-line security technique is required. In this, certain attributes associated with each message are matched against tables in which the security rules are embodied. The basic attributes which may be associated are

— user identity;
— location;
— transaction code;
— file level;
— file access type.

Some, of course, may be omitted, for example, location and user identity may be alternative ways of achieving the same end. If both are used, it is normally only to decrease the chances of fraud. Similarly, file access type is often omitted. However, this implies that all users would be allowed to update any records which they could access.

## User Identity

This may be established by simply using names. In a supervised environment this is good since it is difficult to claim accidental use of another person's identity, as might be the case with passwords. The latter are potentially more secure, but to prevent them becoming known they must be frequently changed. Secret dissemination is then a problem. Techniques for secret entry of passwords to the system need to be considered also. For instance, suppression of printing on a hard-copy device, while entering the code.

Names and passwords may be entered by keyboard or by badge reader. These readers typically accept plastic cards in which the appropriate identity is physically or magnetically encoded. Personal identity is perhaps most secure when such cards are used. Even if lost, or left lying around, it is not immediately apparent what the code is or to whom it relates.

## Location

Location may be established by implication via line number, or terminal identity. Security problems arise when line switching is provided to overcome genuine line failures. To match necessary hardware changes, line tables must be changeable. Hence a network controller could connect a terminal to a stand-by position and present it as a valid terminal which has been re-routed.

## Transaction Code

The code is explicit from the transaction data themselves. It determines the processing which will be carried out on the message, or messages, making up the transaction. The attributes of user identity or location may be linked to transaction code, giving a permission matrix against which each message is checked. Thus, for example, in a sales office, any terminal may be allowed to access data on individual sales, but the terminal identified by physical address as being in the office of the sales manager might be the only one allowed to access sales forecasts.

Access to files may still be limited to a still finer level within transaction.

## File Level

The file levels to which access may be limited may be physical, e.g., to controller or disk drive, or logical, e.g., to file, record, sub-record (group of fields), or field. The finer the level, the more processing is required for the security checks during running of the system.

## Access Type

Access type can be restricted to one or more of the following:

- read, for use in statistical summary;
- read, to output in detail;
- add/delete;

222

- append, i.e., add a sub-record to the main record as a result of a transaction;
- amalgamate, i.e., command a number of appended sub-records to be permanently incorporated in the main record.

These associations of security attributes are held in a number of tables in the program. Table accesses are required to verify the location, identity, and transaction code association, each time a message is received. For each file access, the relationship between identity of operator and file access level and type must be verified. If access level is only restricted by file or record type, detail of file access permission can be held in the program. However, if security were to go to field level it is likely that the map of field within a file, allowed to each accessor, would need to be on disk. After accessing this map, each request would have to be validated against it to ensure that only allowed fields were passed over for processing. Thus, the overheads of security systems can grow to exceed the resources used in actual application processing. The permissible association of security attributes are held as one or more tables accessible to the program. These are referred to as the 'security matrix'.

Each transaction needs to contain password/identity data. The security routines verify whether the combination of location, identity and transaction code is acceptable for each message pair. This requires access to the security matrix.

For each file access, the access request is also checked against the matrix, with identity and transaction type as relevant. File restrictions may also, of course, be tied to a broad level of permission, such as by program. This might be useful if users of different security classifications were tied to different programs. The storage and complexity of the matrix is dependent on the variety of protection required. For optimum efficiency, it should be read into main storage for the real time day. Large matrices may be held on disk, in extreme cases as a segment on every file record.

Security checking has been described as a two-stage process, and as such may be divided between communication and file handlers (see chapter 14).

The specification and implementation of security systems can be logically straightforward for real time systems (see section 20.1.3). However, to provide adequate security without excessive overheads and validating of identity and matrix, verification requires careful evaluation of alternatives.


## 13.2   Integrity

Files are damaged by accident as well as by deliberate act. These accidents can occur because of transient hardware or software malfunction, chance coincidences of events within the program, operator error and application program fault. The effects of such mishaps can go unnoticed, potentially for a long time. A very minor fault, such as a simple corrupted address link, could mean in practice many hundreds of chained records being isolated from their master records. If this type of error were not detected until one year after its occurrence, it might be extremely difficult to correct. The purpose of integrity systems is to prevent, or detect early on, such faults.

### 13.2.1 CORRUPTION FROM CHANCE COINCIDENCES

In systems which are capable of processing more than one transaction or other run-unit at a time, it is possible to get corruption because of an accidental coincidence of events. This happens even if each process is logically perfect and none of the equipment or software is in error (the ideal world!). Figure 13.1 illustrates how this can happen. By coincidence, processes 1 and 2 request an update of the same record. They both update the original version in main store and write back, but the effects are not cumulative. Process 1 might just as well

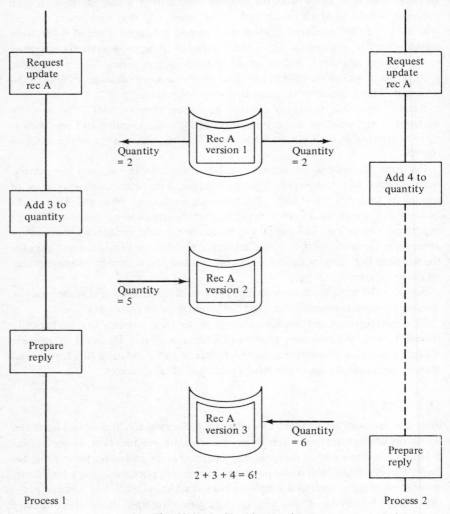

**Fig. 13.1** Accidental corruption

224

not have existed. To prevent this from happening, two courses of action are open. One is to remove the possibility by processing messages, one at a time (single-thread), and the other is to keep a list of records currently being updated, for each current updating process (lock lists).

The single-threading option is by far the easiest, since it removes the problem, but it may not be tenable from the point of view of throughput. The second option requires the use of lock lists. As the records are requested by each process for updating, their identifiers are stored with a process identifier. Any update request for a given record must then be checked against the list, and if the record is already in use, the request is disallowed. Suitable return codes must be provided to enable the user program to take appropriate action. Read only accesses may be freely allowed, since they do not change the record contents. Read locks are occasionally used to prevent other processes changing a record, while one process takes some action based on its contents. This is not normally to prevent logical error, but to save wasted processing or clerical work which would otherwise result.

When the logic of a complex transaction calls for the locking of several records, a further failure becomes possible. Consider the lock lists associated with Processes 1 and 2 as shown in Fig. 13.2. Both processes have an outstanding request held up by the other. The accessing mechanism will give return codes indicating that the records are locked. If both processes then loop on the request, assuming the lock was only temporary the result will be a complete stop in processing. The best standard to adopt is for any process being refused a record to relinquish all its locks, and request a repeat message from the terminal. Coincidences are unlikely to be repeated precisely thus allowing the processes both to be successfully completed.

---

Lock list by process

Process 1     A,    B,    M,    N,    G,    I,

Process 2     K,    L,    E,    P

Request queue

Process 1     Update record L . . .

Process 2     Update record M . . .

---

Fig. 13.2   Deadly embrace

So far, for simplicity, records have been referred to as being locked to processes. However, there are different levels of locking. First, logically; fields, records, files, groups of files can be locked to processes using them. The finer the level, the less physical interference between processes but the higher the processing overhead. Similarly, locking at a physical level can take place by block (hardware record), tracks, cylinder, device or channel.

Locking at a logical level, such as record, can be open to unexpected problems, if the program structure allows multiple blocks to be in course of processing at the same time. By chance, the same block may have been read twice prior to updating by two parallel processes. Even if these processes were updating different logical records in this block, the second version of the block to be written back, as a result of completion of the update of one record, would reset the other record to its former state, overwriting the updated version.

Similar logical problems can arise where more than one program may update the same file. In this case, locking facilities have to be provided within the operating system, and the overheads could well be even higher as a result.

For efficiency reasons, a physical level of locking is often used. For example, after reading a record which is to be updated within milli-seconds, the read-heads are held on that cylinder until the corresponding write has been completed. Thus the whole device is locked out to the updating process and the locking process is thus much simpler.

### 13.2.2 CORRUPTION BY CLERICAL ERROR

A transaction may update many records during several message pairs. If a data error is detected by a program or by the operator, it then becomes necessary to reset the files to their state at the start of the transaction. Two approaches to overcoming this are possible. The easier but not necessarily the more efficient in use of computer resources is to delay making any updates until final acceptance of the transaction. This tends to concentrate file activity into short time intervals. The access pattern is smoother if an audit trail of file changes is kept which enables rapid reinstatement after detection of an error.

The first, being simpler, should be used if possible. It may, however, unnecessarily delay a transaction in the last message pair, if there are many updates to be made. A variant where many changes are being made to the same record (such as successive debits/credits to a given account) is to keep a copy of this record on a work file until the end of the transaction. In this way the operator is potentially able to access the record to see what he has done so far, and may manipulate the record in any way before causing a permanent update. The final update in this example is quick, since it involves access to only one record. This technique also lends itself to simplicity of recovery from hardware or software failure. The particular record must, of course, be locked out to all other processes while on the work file.

In the second approach, each record is updated as early as possible. Hence, if a data error occurs and the transaction is abandoned, an inconsistency remains. To avoid this, a log of the before images of each record is made prior to updating it. This may be the same log as is used for recovery purposes following hardware or software failure. The records are all locked to the process identifier (e.g., transaction serial number or task identity). Should the process be abandoned, a file resetting routine accesses the log file and re-sets the records before unlocking them again.

If a process is long, such as a background sequential update, a very long list of records may become locked to that process. They have to be locked, since other processes updating these records could be negated if it becomes necessary

226

to re-set the records due to data error. To limit the size of such a list, it is sometimes convenient to provide a program function which allows all updates up to that point to be made permanent at any chosen time. Thus, for example, after each batch of input has been agreed to a control total, all updates corresponding to that batch can be made permanent.

### 13.2.3 DETECTING CORRUPTION

Errors on files are detectable by a variety of techniques. The earlier detection occurs after incidence of the error, the more rapidly it may be corrected. Strictly, of course, errors as such are not detected, but symptoms of errors. In general, the earlier detection occurs, the more specific the symptom.

Techniques for detecting symptoms of errors include the following:

#### *Read-after-write Checks*

The record is read again on the next revolution of the disk after completion of writing it back; hardware parity checks are thus carried out before the block could be used again.

#### *Parity Checks*

Hardware parity checks are carried out each time a record is read.

#### *File Dumps*

While dumps are being taken for recovery purposes, every block is read, thus making it highly unlikely that undetected corruption (e.g., following a write fault), has been present for longer than the inter-dump interval.

#### *Structure Checking Dumps*

All pointer references are followed up to ensure that the record pointed at exists.

#### *Hash or Control Totals on Blocks*

Extra fields or records are added to the block, containing control information which has been generated by accumulation of selected fields in each record in the block, e.g., for a block containing invoice records an extra record is present containing fields such as the total of all invoice amounts and the binary sum of account numbers.

#### *Background Audit Programs*

For files which are too large for frequent dumping, an audit program is run at a low priority, sequentially reading through all blocks in the file and carrying out checks on the data.

#### *Hostility*

Every time a record is transferred into main store from a file, full data vet checks are carried out on it.

Whenever an error symptom is detected by one of those methods, notification occurs by software indicators, or the symptom is detected directly in the user program. In either case, complete information on the symptom should if possible be passed to one area of the program, where an error log is written. At the same time an error message should be output to a system controller. He then has the task of carrying out isolation, rapid reaction, diagnosis and recovery, as described in chapter 12. The error symptom log is useful in carrying out this diagnosis.

Detected corruption can be dealt with by going back to a stable dump of the files and reinstating the state at point of failure from the logs. This is necessary for extensive corruption or actual damage of the file medium. However, for corruption which is isolated, it is possible to patch the affected record *in situ*. To do this, utilities which permit display and alteration of any part of the record are desirable. It is also more secure if extensive validation of the records so changed is carried out, including following and checking any linkage fields to other records. This patching technique needs to be restricted to those individuals who are well versed in the system, and this has associated security problems. All such changes should be logged and checked by other responsible individuals.

## 13.3   Design Approach

In common with other service functions like fail-soft, security and integrity systems have potentially high development costs as well as running costs. In design, a compromise needs to be sought between providing an adequate level of protection and incurring unnecessary extra costs.

### 13.3.1   SECURITY

The balance which the designer is aiming to achieve is to make the value to the unauthorized accessor less than the cost of breaking the security.

A financial system which enabled transfer of large sums of money from one account to another, the setting up of accounts, and issue of cheques, would justify considerable expenditure on security. On the other hand, an enquiry-only stock recording system would probably not, because the freedom to manipulate the system is much less and any achievable fraudulent benefits would also probably be smaller.

In any case, the effectiveness of the various possible security measures must be carefully weighed in each given situation. As an example, an expensive security matrix in the real time program against which each transaction is checked does not buy very much security if the personnel at the terminal end cannot be persuaded to be discreet with security codes. It may be just as effective to limit transactions implicitly to person simply by location (implied by line and terminal number). Security then arises from the fact that unauthorized operators have to be physically in locations where they are not allowed, which increases the risk of being caught. This physical security technique would be more effective than a system using logical screening, such as passwords, in an environment where people could be expected to be more careful in locking offices than locking hard copy of passwords in drawers when not present.

## 13.3.2 INTEGRITY

In judging the extent of integrity assurance systems, again, a similar balance must be struck. The overall aim of the designer is to go for the simplest system compatible with the necessary degree of integrity and the timing constraints of the system.

In providing for clerical error correction, it is preferable to suspend all updating until the transaction is known to be acceptable to the operator, possibly using temporary work files while processing is carried out. This is easier and cheaper than the alternative of maintaining a before-image file and providing the routines for using it to correct errors.

In providing protection against accidental corruption by simultaneous updating, it is easier to design the system to carry out updates to one record at a time. No record locking system is then required—the lock is then effectively applied to the whole set of files. Of course this reduces throughput, but the amount depends on the ratio of updates to simple reads, which can still be carried out in parallel. Even simpler, the real time program may be only used for data collection and dissemination, and all updating is carried out in batch mode. The updates are sorted and handled sequentially. This approach, if possible from a response time point of view, is also a considerable simplification for most other areas of design.

Integrity systems intended to detect hitherto undetected corruption can be very expensive in machine resources during real time hours, and also in overnight batch runs. Once more, a balance must be sought between degree of protection and cost. In general, the larger the file and the lower the hit rate, the greater the need for integrity systems. This arises from the fact that very large files take a long time to dump, which is thus done less frequently, and if the hit rate is low, an unsuspected error can go undetected for a relatively long time. In this case, a background program carrying out systematic checks and the hostility technique of revalidating all data transferred may be desirable. But the simple approach of avoiding the problem altogether might pay off. If the hit-rate is low, all records updated during the day could be written to a rapid access random file (changes file) which is sorted and applied to the main file in batch mode overnight. Because of the relative throughput efficiency of such batch processing, much more integrity checking could be carried out in the program. During real time hours, if to answer enquiries required up to date information, the changes file could be searched or directly accessed by record identity, depending on its size.

# 14. Program Organization

During systems development the major portion of the overall design of a real time system is put into effect through programs, and at the heart of the system are those programs and routines operating in real time. Experience has shown that the program structure adopted for the real time system has a major impact on the success of the development, running, and subsequent modification of the system. The operational system consists of both manufacturer's software and user developed routines. Depending on the system and software available, the designer can choose not only what 'software' he uses but also how it fitted together with user routines.

This chapter is concerned with the whole software environment, and while many users take the standard manufacturer's operating system and real time software to make up the majority of that environment, it is still important that designers recognize both what structure would best suit their application and the implications of their final choice. A software package may provide the complete environment, but the performance projections needed during design can only be made through a thorough understanding of the mechanisms in that package and its interface with the hardware and with the user modules.

Before considering the subject further, it is important to stress the difference between communications software and real time program organization. Figure 14.1 illustrates the difference which is discussed in more detail in chapter 10. Communication software is concerned with handling terminals and lines and getting messages in and out of the system (as disk software is concerned with files, or data base software with data base files). Real time program structures are concerned with the whole environment.

Thus we can consider real time systems at three levels:

*Communication Software*

Handling messages and the network (Fig. 14.1 (3)).

*Real Time Operating Environment*

A complete interface to user application modules. Such an interface can be provided by specialized real time software (Fig. 14.1 (1)—(4)), a real time

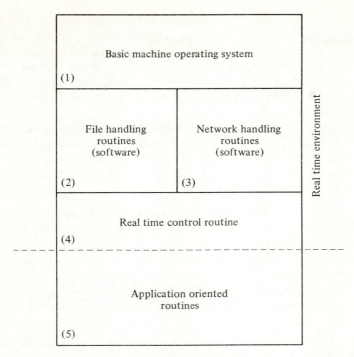

**Fig. 14.1**  Real time program

operating system, or an interface package that integrates the batch oriented facilities of a general operating system (Fig. 14.1 (1) and (2)) with the needs of a real time system (Fig. 14.1 (3) and (4)). (These were provided initially as user's own monitors, then by such packages as IBM CICS, ICL DRIVER, or ENVIRON, and by many alternatives since.)

*Real Time System*

The complete environment including the applications code (Fig. 14.1 (1)–(5)).

Apart from the basic facilities of a 'real time environment', the complete system additionally requires the following:

- the division between complex and simple coding to allow advantages to be taken of both skilled and less experienced staff;
- facilities for simultaneous message processing;
- the use of common facilities between application routines;
- optimization techniques.

## 14.1  Characteristics of Real Time Systems

In order to consider the characteristics and requirements of real time systems, it is worth first discussing those of a batch system so that the differences can be

231

highlighted (certain batch characteristics are so familiar that they are taken for granted). A batch system is typically implemented as a logical sequence of events, where a number of transactions progress together through a series of programs, each performing specific functions on those transactions.

A common pattern of such programs may be: validation and error reporting, sort to main file order, main file update, sort for report production, and finally report production.

To improve the throughput of the machine, operating systems normally supply a multi-programming feature. It is important to note, however, that although the overall throughput often improves using the multi-programming feature, individual programs run longer. The characteristics of the batch system might be:

- the logical flow is reflected by the logic of program sequence;
- programs are independent as units of production and in internal logic, i.e., they are only linked by files;
- efficiency and throughput improvement is achieved through multi-programming and through the sorting of batches;
- a general approach to work and design that considers 'sets of logic' (programs) operating on files (transactions and reference), i.e., run oriented.

With these characteristics in mind, it is now possible to review where a real time system differs.

### 14.1.1 TRANSACTION ORIENTED

A real time program is transaction oriented. Unlike most batch systems where each program performs only part of the total processing required on a transaction, a real time program has to receive and process it completely. The effect that needs to be studied by the designer is both that of a transaction seeking its appropriate code modules and a program handling different transactions.

All routines to process the transaction need to be available to the real time program, leading to potentially larger programs. In an attempt to reduce the size and complexity of a program, a review of the facilities planned for the real time program should be instigated, with a view to determining whether any can be performed in batch mode (see section 2.2.1), or others combined, with perhaps parameters specifying variations in processing for different transactions.

It is normal for a real time program to be resident in the machine for relatively long periods of time, processing the total number of transactions more slowly than if they were being processed in batch mode. These large, and frequently under-utilized, programs lead to the demand for overlaying, either planned or using a virtual operating system.

Planned overlaying involves identifying those routines that are rarely used, keeping them on backing storage and setting aside a storage area to read them into when required. This situation is fairly easy to evaluate, in terms of both storage requirements and transaction processing time. However, the use of a virtual operating system poses different problems. Paging out of frequently used routines can occur in the real time program if a larger virtual store than the available real storage is being used, and there are very active batch programs. Batch programs make frequent and constant demand on resources, whereas a real time program is often just the opposite. These problems can affect the response times of the real time system and make it difficult to predict response times. Design control (section 5.2) is particularly relevant to the management of this situation.

In addition to main storage management the real time program has to control and plan its use of other resources, such as the CPU and peripherals, to allow efficient use of them. Improving the utilization of the files in the system is discussed in chapter 11.

### 14.1.2 SIMULTANEOUS MESSAGE PROCESSING

In heavily loaded real time systems it is necessary that efficient use is made of all the resources available to the real time program. This usually requires the resources to be working concurrently, and this can be achieved in such ways as double buffering, multi-programming, and multi-threading.

*Double Buffering*

Double buffering is the technique (borrowed from batch) of accessing a record from a file for a message whilst using the CPU to process another part of the message. This is illustrated in Fig. 14.2. The approach is to identify as quickly as possible those records to be accessed, and to initiate the access but without issuing a 'wait' command which would allow control to be taken away by the operating system. This allows further processing on the message to continue until it can only proceed when the result of the access is known. At this point the 'wait' command is issued and processing stops until the access is complete. Double buffering is not recommended in real time systems as it can lead to severe constraints on later system enhancements.

*Multi-programming*

A number of communications software packages, as described in chapter 10, are designed to support multiple real time programs, which are multi-programmed under general operating systems. Simultaneous use of resources is achieved in the same way as batch processsing, but this does not usually permit optimum use of the resources and tends to lead to heavy duplication of software overheads. Real time programs can clearly be multi-programmed with background batch systems. However designers are advised to *determine fully* the interference from low priority background batch. Software mechanisms are usually such that the background *does* interfere with the foreground.

Several software systems forces separate networks for each real time program and separate log tapes for each such program. Where such restrictions

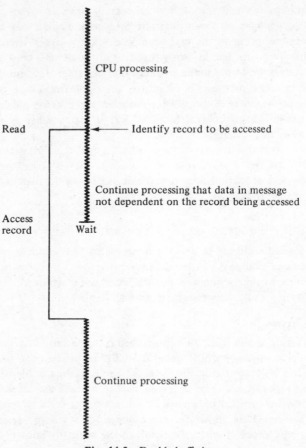

CPU processing

Read ────── ◄─────── Identify record to be accessed

Continue processing that data in message
not dependent on the record being accessed

Access
record        Wait

Continue processing

**Fig. 14.2**  Double buffering

are overcome there usually arise corresponding logical problems like managing access to common files from different programs.

*Multi-threading*

This requires a real time program to schedule its use of resources between a number of messages that may be in the machine together. Increased throughput is obtained in a similar way to multi-programming, but multi-threading does allow for the use of resources to be optimized. It must be remembered that, as multi-programming causes individual programs to run longer, multi-threading may cause individual messages to take longer to process even though overall throughput is improved. Individual messages may gain overall, however, by spending less time in input queues.

To achieve multi-threading, a 'wait' command must not be issued until there is no current message that can use the CPU. Once one message has requested a

**234**

peripheral access, the real time program scans for any other message requiring the CPU or for completion of a peripheral access which will allow another message to continue. When it can identify no further CPU processing for the time being, it issues a 'wait' command, waiting on all peripheral resources in the system. Figure 14.3 illustrates a multi-threading system, where three messages are being processed concurrently. The control of multi-threading can be achieved within a program in a conventional operating system or by a separate real time control package.

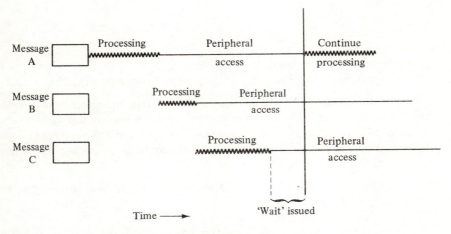

**Fig. 14.3**   Multi-threading

### 14.1.3   SERVICE ROUTINES

There are a number of routines which are essential to the efficient running of the real time program, although not part of the application itself. These routines include file handling, communications handling, fail-soft, and security modules.

The correct program structure can simplify design and programming such that these potentially complex areas can be divorced from the main application logic. Isolating these routines eases, for example, one problem encountered with multi-threading—that of two messages updating the same record simultaneously such that one of the updates is lost. With a centralized file handler, it is easier to recognize this possibility and to control its effect. If the real time program is required to allocate priorities to messages, files or routines, this can be achieved with this type of program structure. In a multi-threading environment, queues build up for the service routines, and it is at this point that priorities can be actioned. The relevant service routine, instead of actioning the first item on a first-in first-out basis, handles the queue on the established priority basis.

The real time environment makes the provision of each of the services very different from the conventional batch approach. Communications handling is, of course, entirely new.

### 14.1.4 MEASURING/TUNING

Despite the results obtainable from simulation programs, the only completely accurate guide to the loading of the system is the system itself. Activity measuring routines can be built in to measure:

- message arrival rate;
- file activity;
- processing activity;
- communications activity;
- average queue sizes and distributors;
- achieved response times;
- other information related to performance and resource utilization.

These routines should record this data for analysis later to indicate whether the resources are coping, and play an important role both in early testing and later operational monitoring. It may be possible to improve the performance of the system by tuning it. This does not only imply examining the coding line by line to identify improvements, but also to:

- increase the total store space allocated to the system, to reduce the overlaying or paging;
- reconfigure files on different devices;
- increase the number of messages that can be processed simultaneously;
- change internal priorities.

These are just examples of the tuning that can be done. The effect of any such tuning is reported by the measuring routines, and eventually the optimum configuration can be reached. However the ability to tune should be built in as part of initial designs.

### 14.1.5 EXPANSIBILITY

It is unlikely that the requirements of the real time program will remain static. Changes will occur to messages, files and record layouts, for example, and the ease with which these are incorporated into the system depends on the program structure. The aim should be to minimize the changes required to existing application coding if, for example, record layouts change or additional record types are added.

## 14.2 Approaches to Real Time Program Structures

Having reviewed the characteristics of real time systems, this section introduces possible program structures open to the designer. Applications vary from relatively simple to extremely complex and the facilities required in the program structure will also vary. No one structure can be said to be ideal for all applications, and the designer has the task of identifying that most suitable to his application and hardware.

The structures introduced in this section are single program (no monitor), multi-program, MONITOR, and tasking—by function or transaction. The latter two are then expanded further later in this chapter, and the idea of monitor software is further explained. Both the latter are designed to meet the requirement of multi-threading several messages within one program.

### 14.2.1 SINGLE PROGRAM (NO MONITOR)

A single program is suitable only for simple applications that will not require future enhancements or undergo major modification. It is written in a serial fashion with all peripheral calls coded in-line, or via a simple module interface.

### 14.2.2 MULTI-PROGRAM

This technique uses the operating system's capabilities of supporting several programs simultaneously, as described earlier. This approach allows distinct real-time programs to run concurrently, but frequently means a duplication of file routines, communication routines and networks, validation routines, logging devices, etc. The interlock problems that arise if two programs wish to update the same file are more difficult to solve. There are a number of advantages, however, in this approach. One of them is the protection afforded between applications. It is unlikely that one application can corrupt the store of another, and if one program fails, the other is unaffected. Another advantage lies in the fact that different applications may be required at different times, and having separate programs avoids unused coding and files being present.

### 14.2.3 MONITOR

This is an approach that is designed to support multi-threading within its own program and is the basis of many of the packages developed to provide a real time environment within a general operating system. Its structure relieves the application coding of communications and file handling, and carries out these functions via a simple interface between the monitor and the application coding. These peripheral handling routines are each called in turn to recognize if any outstanding transfers have been completed or any further requests can be actioned. In order to achieve effective multi-threading, these routines do not wait for a peripheral transfer to complete, but check for completion each time entered. It is therefore necessary to enter each handler regularly.

### 14.2.4 TASKING—BY FUNCTION OR TRANSACTION

Tasking is a general facility provided under different labels and different implementations by computer manufacturers. In simplest terms, tasking is an operating facility that allows the user to establish several controllable elements in one system. 'A task' has many of the properties of 'a program' and as such is under the control of the operating system. Special features associated with tasking are:

- ability to pass messages between tasks;
- code shared between tasks (tasks may be identical in coding terms but able to handle different messages by calling on common code or one appropriate to the current message);
- tasks can be multi-programmed (multi-tasked) together;
- tasks may share data areas.

In real time systems, tasking uses the facility of the operating system to support multi-threading within a program. Tasks within a program are therefore under the control of the operating system and the switching between tasks involves entering the operating system each time. In functional tasking, sometimes known as sub-programming, tasks are related to certain functions, (or sets of code) such as validation, customer file access, etc. In this mode it is important that, as far as possible, each task has at least one peripheral transfer in it and that only one peripheral transfer is actioned by a task for a particular message at one time. When a task actions a peripheral transfer, it waits for completion and the operating system passes control to another task. If there is one ready to proceed it performs a different process on another message.

When a task has completed its function on a message, it passes the message to the next task, via the operating system.

Transaction tasking requires a task for each message being processed. The number of tasks that are set up dictates the maximum number of messages that can be processed concurrently. With transaction tasking messages are processed through the same code, but when a peripheral transfer is required, the wait for its completion is associated with the task and not the actual coding, therefore allowing other tasks and therefore messages to be processed through the same code. This demands pure procedures (re-entrant code). Transaction tasking was the approach used in early dedicated real time software systems, but suffered from its demand for pure procedures, because at that time compilers which automatically produced pure procedures were not available.

It is possible, and frequently implemented in packages, to use tasking in a monitor structure. It is also possible, in a multi-program environment, for each program to be independently tasking or to have a monitor structure. These structures, therefore, are not mutually exclusive but can be used in the combination that best suits the application.

## 14.3 The MONITOR Structure

MONITOR is a theoretical program organization package suitable for real time programs. It is not an actual package, but many packages function in a similar way. Hence, it is useful to describe MONITOR in this section as if it were a package. It performs under, and in conjunction with, the machines' operating system, as a real time operating system. It has the appearance to the application code of performing many of the functions of an operating system. It relays peripheral transfer requests and controls multi-threading by sharing processor time between different messages and overlapping this with the peripheral transfers. Because the control is performed without recourse to the operating system, it is usually more efficient in terms of CPU time. It is within the capabilities of many installations to design and write their own MONITOR, but a secondary purpose for including it in this book is to give an understanding of the mechanisms within available packages and what they are aiming to do.

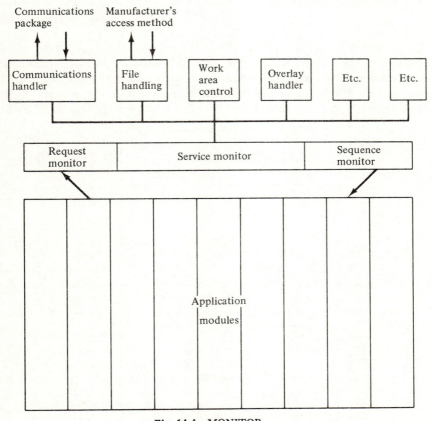

**Fig. 14.4** MONITOR

In this approach, 'complex' functions such as file handling, work area allocation, resource management, and message handling are all performed on behalf of application routines via a simple interface. A block diagram of the structure is shown in Fig. 14.4

Application routines are passed messages to be processed by the Sequence Monitor, and when they require to read a record, for example, they pass a request to the Request Monitor.

This structure, therefore, supports the modular programming concept and the modules consist only of applications coding, anything else being handled via the MONITOR interface. In additon, all application modules are called from one standard interface (the Sequence Monitor) and pass requests to another standard interface (the Request Monitor). This allows one testing harness to be produced that will suffice for all application modules.

It is possible with this structure for different messages to be serviced at the same time by the various handlers as well as the application modules, thus permitting multi-threading. The structure can also support more than one application and permits application modules and handlers to be shared or unique.

### 14.3.1 MESSAGE BLOCKS

An important feature of MONITOR is the Message Block. A typical one is shown in Fig. 14.5. Its precise contents depend on the application requirements. The Message Blocks are normally under the control of the Communications Handler and are resident within it. It is the address of the Message Block that is passed around the system, not the Message Block itself.

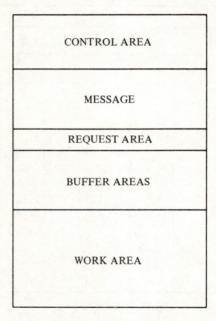

**Fig. 14.5**  A Message Block

*The Control Area*

The Control Area of the Message Block contains addresses for such items as terminal tables, validation tables, error messages, and statistics, which are required by more than one application module. To enable the structure of the Message Block itself to be variable, it may also contain the start addresses of the other areas within it.

240

## The Message

This area contains the message as passed across by the communications software. Once the input message has been processed and no longer required, this area may be used for other purposes.

## Request Area

Applications modules use this area to indicate the handler required, the action required by that handler, and the next module to call depending on the success of the action. A trace can be kept in this area of all modules and handlers entered, and the requests made. This aids fault-tracing if the message is not successfully processed.

## Buffer Areas

Once the File Handler, for example, has read the record specified in the request, it transfers it to this area. Any records to be written are also place in this area.

## Work Area

All application module and service routines, such as the File Handler, use this part of the Message Block if they require work area particular to the processing of the current message. This avoids each routines requiring its own work area permanently allocated and allows the use of re-entrant or reusable code. Although in the MONITOR structure it is sufficient to write only reusable code, in a virtual machine environment, re-entrant code is more efficient. This arises from the need to write out to the paging device any code which might have been changed as the result of current processing. With re-entrant code this is never necessary and the only access to the paging device required is to read in the page prior to processing, if the page is not already present in main storage.

The size of the message block can be either fixed or variable. If additional work area is required, this is obtained via the work area handler.

### 14.3.2   THE PATH OF A MESSAGE

The processing path of one message through one MONITOR cycle is discussed below, without emphasizing the effect of other messages existing within the program. The structure allows for parallel processing of several messages (multi-threading). In this case, the sequence of events for one message is as discussed, but other activity, for other message processing or service activity such as file accesses, can be interposed.

When a message enters the system, it is passed to the Communications Handler, which then places it in a Message Block. This handler decides the first application module required and enters its identity in the request area of the Message Block. The address of this Message Block is then placed on the queue for the Sequence Monitor.

The Sequence Monitor examines the queue and calls the module specified in the Message Block, say, for example, a data validation module, and passes the address of the block to that module.

The application module performs its function, which results in a request for one of the handlers or another application module. This request is again placed in the request area of the Message Block and control passed to the Request Monitor.

The Request Monitor analyses the request area and places the address of the Message Block on the Sequence Monitor's or appropriate handler's queue. It then simply passes control to the Service Monitor.

The Service Monitor is central to the whole structure, but performs no application work. It calls each of the handlers in turn. In certain job mixes, with short processing paths, Service Monitors have been produced that call some of the handlers only every $n$th cycle. Handlers responsible for peripheral transfers check whether a transfer initiated previously has been completed. If it has, it transfers the appropriate information to the relevant Message Block and places its address on the queue of the Sequence Monitor.

The handler then examines its input request area and determines whether the request can be satisfied immediately or not. If it can (such as a work area allocation) the Service is carried out and the address of the Message Block is placed on the queue for the Sequence Monitor.

If a peripheral transfer has been requested, however, it initiates the transfer but retains the Message Block. If the particular file or device is busy, it forms a queue for that resource and initiates the transfer once the previous one has been completed.

A handler, then, can satisfy a request immediately, initiate a transfer, or place the request on a queue. Once it has performed one of these options, it returns control to the Service Monitor.

Once all handlers have been called, the Sequence Monitor is entered to initiate another application module. If there is no message block waiting for a module, then control is returned to the Service Monitor. At this point, it issues a 'multiple-wait' on all events, such as the completion of a read or the receipt of a new message. The operating system then assumes control and allows a lower priority program to have use of the CPU.

When an event is completed, control is returned to the Service Monitor, which then repeats the service cycle around all the handlers.

### 14.3.3 FUNCTIONS OF THE HANDLERS AND MONITORS

The detailed functions of the handlers vary with the application, but broad areas of responsibility are given for the major ones.

*Communications Handler*

(1) Examine queue for output messages.
(2) Pass output message to communications software.
(3) Release Message Block.
(4) Determine whether there is a free Message Block.
(5) If there is, determine whether there is an input message in communications software.

242

(6) If there is, place the message in the free Message Block.

(7) Enter the address of the first application module required.

(8) Place the address of Message Block on the queue for the Sequence Monitor.

(9) Return control to the Service Monitor.

(10) Analyse, and take appropriate action to deal with error indicators passed over by communications software.

*File Handler*

(1) Examine completion indicators set by the operating system, to determine whether a transfer previously initiated has completed.

(2) If it has, place the result in the appropriate Message Block and add its address to the Sequence Monitor's queue.

(3) Examine the file handler's own input area to determine whether there is a new request.

(4) If there is, analyse the request to identify the file or device requested.

(5) Add this request to the internal queue for the file or device.

To optimize file accessing, it is possible at this point to sort the queue for the file or device and thus reduce head movement. To achieve this, the physical locations of the records requested must be calculable from the logical requests.

Additionally, any Message Block designated as having priority can be inserted at the head of the queue for access to ensure a quicker service.

(6) Initiate the access relevant to the first item in the queue.

This process (steps 5 and 6) is repeated for each resource under the control of the File Handler.

(7) Return control to the Service Monitor.

(8) Analyse, and take appropriate action to deal with, error indicators passed over by file handling software.

*Work Area Control*

(1) Examine input area for a new request. If none, return control to the Service Monitor.

(2) If it is a release request, replace store in buffer pool and place the address of the Message Block on the queue for the Sequence Monitor.

(3) If it is a request for more work area, place on internal queue of Message Blocks waiting for work area.

(4) Examine requirements of first Message Block, if present, in internal queue.

(5) If there is enough work area available in the buffer pool for it, attach it to the Message Block and place the address of the Message Block on the queue for the Sequence Monitor.

(6) Examine the requirements of next Message Block in the internal queue and repeat step (5).

(7) When there are no outstanding requests for work area, or there is insufficient work area to satisfy the outstanding requests, return control to the Service Monitor.

Again, it is possible to search the internal queue for priority Message Blocks. It is also possible to satisfy requests lower down the internal queue if they require smaller amounts of work area than the one at the head of the queue and there is not enough work area available for it. There is a danger, though, that when this approach is taken it could take some time in busy periods for enough work area to be released for the request requiring larger amounts, creating an artificially long reponse time for the associated message.

### Request Monitor

(1) Examine the request in the request area of the Message Block.
(2) If the request is for another application module, place the address of the Message Block on queue for Sequence Monitor.
(3) If the request is for a handler, decide which one and place the address of the Message Block on the appropriate handler's input area.
(4) Pass control to the Service Monitor.

### Service Monitor

The Service Monitor, on receiving control from the Request Monitor, calls each handler in turn. When all handlers have been called, it then passes control to the Sequence Monitor. If the Sequence Monitor returns control directly, this signifies that there is no Message Block waiting for an application Module, and therefore no more processing can occur for the time being.

At this point, the Service Monitor relinquishes control to the Operating System by issuing a 'multiple wait'. This 'wait' relates to all possible events that can occur in the real time partition. This avoids the Service Monitor's either analysing what events are outstanding or waiting for an event that may take some time to happen, for example the receipt of a new message.

When one of the events waited for occurs, the Operating System returns control to the next instruction after the 'wait', and the Service Monitor repeats its service cycle, calling each handler and the Sequence Monitor in turn.

The Service Monitor can also be used for trapping any errors that occur and thereby avoiding the automatic cancellation of the program by the operating system. When an error occurs, control can be passed to the Service Monitor by the operating system, and it is then in a position to analyse the error. If possible, it can inform the terminal operator concerned via the communications handler and then release the Message Block. It may call a special routine, via the Sequence Monitor, to perform these operations.

When the system is loaded, either at start of day or in a recovery situation, the Service Monitor calls the appropriate handlers with a parameter indicating all files that should be opened. It may also call special recovery routines, if required.

244

## Sequence Monitor

The Sequence Monitor maintains a table containing an entry for each application module. The entry contains the address of the module and a queue of the Message Blocks waiting for that module. The Sequence Monitor can recognize a priority message and select it for processing in preference to any other. It can also have a priority sequence by application module, with the modules listed in the table in descending order of priority.

When overlaying of application modules is concerned, the module status is reflected in the Sequence Monitor routine table, which indicates the routine's main store start address and overlay file address. When overlays are required (say if core address = 9999999), the Service Monitor can then call the relevant overlay routine.

## Multi-threading

As mentioned earlier, multi-threading is possible when a number of Message Blocks are present in the program. Each time a request is made, a Service Loop is entered. As each handler and the Sequence Monitor are entered, there is a possibility for one message to overtake another which arrived earlier, because the latter is held up for, say, a peripheral action or is of lower priority. To fully appreciate the way in which MONITOR works for parallel messages, the reader is advised to dry-run several messages through the structure as described here.

### 14.3.4   WHY CHOOSE A MONITOR STRUCTURE?

The MONITOR approach has many advantages, mainly associated with its flexibility. The degree of multi-threading is controlled by the number of Message Blocks, which can be increased as the message load increases. Single threading uses just one Message Block.

Flexibility also arises from the use of separate handlers for service functions. For example, the record layout of a file may change because a new application is added to the system. There must obviously be as little disruption as possible to application modules already written, which are based around the old record layout. The file handler, though, can recognize the module making the request and format the record in a manner suitable to that module. Application modules do not need to be re-entrant.

An important element of the maintenance of a real time system is a continual measurement of the performance of the system to ensure that hardware and software structure can support the load, which may be increasing. With the MONITOR approach, the handlers can keep statistics on their activity in terms, for example, of the number and type of accesses to each file. The communications handler can time-stamp the Message Block when a new message is allocated to it and, once fully processed, can calculate the time taken to process the message. These statistics can be written to backing storage periodically and analysed later by a batch program. By extrapolation, early warning is given of a potential overload situation.

245

## 14.4 The Tasking Approach

Not all tasking systems are designed for real time systems, but are by-products of the multi-programming capabilities of a batch operating system. In the same way as there is a limit on the number of programs that can be multi-programmed, there is also a limit on the number of tasks the operating system can handle. There are two basic uses of tasking structures—functional and transaction—and each is described below. A number of tasking-oriented real time operating systems have also been provided by manufacturers, and such systems tend to encourage transaction tasking. Earlier examples include Univac on-line systems and the B6700 stack. ICL's 2900 also follows this approach.

### 14.4.1 FUNCTIONAL TASKING

This type of tasking, also known as sub-programming, requires the designer to break the system down into distinct functions and build separate tasks. Figure 14.6 shows a functional tasking structure. The tasks can be considered as being like programs, in the way processing time is shared between them by the operating system. With older operating systems there is no protection between tasks.

This structure also uses Message Blocks, resident in the Communications Interface Task. When a task completes its processing on a message, it places the address of the Message Block on the queue for the next task. This can normally only be achieved by writing macros that enable application code within a task to activate other tasks or de-activate that task, by calling on operating system facilities.

The coding in each task need not be re-entrant, as a task can only process one message at a time.

### Control Task

The Control Task is analogous to the Service Monitor in the Monitor structure, except that it does not control the sharing of processing power. The switching of control is achieved by the operating system, and the Control Task lies dormant during normal processing.

When the real time system is started, the control task is usually all that is loaded. This then calls initiation and recovery routines as required, and then attaches those tasks necessary for normal processing. As each task is loaded, it issues a 'wait' on its queue. This queue is set up and resides in the Control Task, but is updated by the specially written macros in the operating system.

It is possible in the Control Task to wait on the completion of all tasks attached. In this way, abnormal terminations of tasks can be trapped and the relevant corrective action taken. This can include re-attaching the task and reading in the routines afresh from the library.

### Communications Interface Task

This task performs similar functions to those of the Communications Handler in the Monitor Structure. The multi-threading capabilities are dependent not

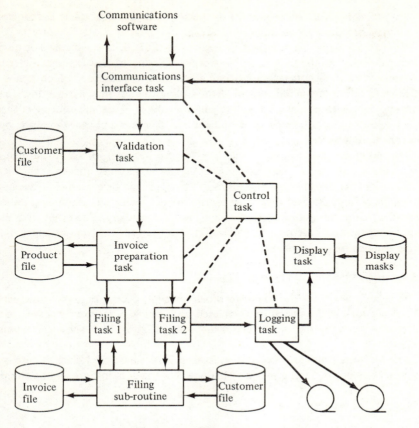

**Fig. 14.6**  A functional tasking structure

only on the number of Message Blocks in this task, though, but also on the number of the tasks in the system.

It is possible to have more than one application in the program, initial routing being performed by the Communications Interface Task.

### Task Structure

It is important that, as far as possible, all the 'waits' associated with different physical devices are distributed across tasks. With applications code (with no waits) there is questionable benefit in division into more than one task. This is shown in Fig. 14.6, where all tasks have either file or communications accesses. The one exception is the Control Task, which is dormant. This allows multi-threading, since when one task is waiting for an access to complete, another task can be processing another message. It is also important not to have too many accesses within one task, as this tends to be a bottleneck in the system. This is because other tasks with fewer accesses would process later messages faster and cause a queue to form for the task with many accesses, thus reducing the multi-threading capabilities.

Figure 14.6 shows an approach to lessen the effect, i.e., to have two or more identical tasks, minimal in size, to process updates to the Invoice File and Customer File. These tasks simply call a common sub-routine, which is not a task itself, but is under the control of the calling task. If this sub-routine is re-entrant, then several tasks can call it simultaneously. This sub-routine is then in a position to form queues for the files it has to access and can, therefore, optimize random accessing.

The previous task causes the address of the Message Block to be placed either on the queues of the tasks in turn or on the shortest queue.

Occasionally, designers of the MONITOR approach face problems, because the file handling software they wish to use forces a wait, thus precluding multi-threading. One solution is to write one's own file handlers. The other is to use functional tasking based on the MONITOR structure with one task per disk drive and one for the devices.

### 14.4.2 TRANSACTION TASKING

This system also uses the Message Block concept, except that this time each Message Block in the system is associated with a task. They are processed concurrently through the same re-entrant code. Figure 14.7 shows a typical system.

The Message Block tasks receive messages from the Control Task. There is a minimal amount of coding in each Message Block task to initiate and terminate

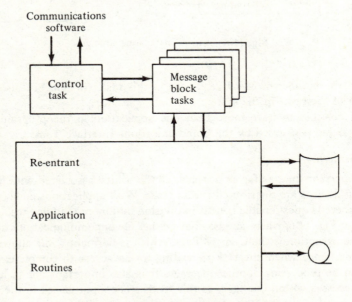

**Fig. 14.7** A transaction tasking structure

the processing of the message. Any wait for the completion of an access is performed in the message control task and not the application routines, so that other tasks can be processed.

## Control Task

The functions of the Control Task include all those listed for functional tasking, but with many additional ones. The Message Blocks can either be attached at the initial loading of the system, and lie dormant until a message arrives, or the Control Task can create and close them dynamically to reflect the message traffic. Often a limit is set, specifying the maximum number of tasks to be in existence at any one time.

This Control Task is frequently made responsible for the interface to communications software. It takes a message from communications, providing either there is a Message Block to receive it or it can set one up.

## Combined with MONITOR

It is possible to use transaction tasking with a MONITOR-like structure, the Communications Handler acting as the Control Task. This has the advantage of a standardized structure, but using the operating system to control switching.

### 14.4.3 WHY CHOOSE A TASKING STRUCTURE?

The advantage of tasking is that much of the control remains with the operating system and there is, therefore, less development effort required. But, because more use is made of the operating system, this frequently results in a greater CPU loading.

The decision whether to choose functional or transaction tasking depends more on the hardware and application than any general considerations. Functional tasking is perhaps easier to understand to those new to real time systems, as modules are linked into logical functions similar to batch processing.

## 14.5 Software Selection

In deciding on the program structure to use, the designer is faced with the question of whether to use a package or develop an in-house system.

### 14.5.1 DEVELOPMENT OF AN IN-HOUSE SYSTEM

This is the one sure way of obtaining a structure that fits the requirements exactly, providing the expertise is available and the requirements are specified in advance. It is a flexible approach and it is likely to be well understood by those people who need to use it, as training is very much simplified. It is less generalized and, therefore, stands a good chance of being more efficient in terms of both space and time.

However, there are a number of disadvantages,

- relevant expertise may not be available;
- its development may well delay the application;
- its development may be more expensive than a package;
- it may never get developed fully and compromises may have to be made.

The same arguments do not apply if the system being developed is a tasking structure. With this type of structure, much use is made of facilities within the operating system, and the designer does not need to consider the detailed operations of switching between resources. The main disadvantage is the overhead occurred in CPU time by referencing the operating system so frequently.

This approach is not recommended unless members of the team or outside consultants bring prior 'own structure' experience to the project.

### 14.5.2 USING A PACKAGE

If the decision is taken to use a package, the question remaining is what package to use. Section 14.1 discusses the characteristics of real time systems, and this can be used as a basic selection check list, together with the features described in the remainder of the chapter.

Additional factors to consider are provided in Figs. 14.8 and in section 10.3.2. This list in Fig. 14.8 is not exhaustive, but gives an indication of the sort of items that should be investigated. The most important consideration, however, is how well the package fits the application and hardware. The

**Supplier**
Basic cost
Secondary costs (options)
Maintenance costs
Cost of likely options
Free support
Free training
Bug correction free
Formal 'fast response' support system
Guarantees
Local customer base
User references

**Managerial**
Ease of installation
Ease of conversion
Ease of operation
Ease of new development
Operating system independence
Documentation quality
Source code availability
Design aids
System modelling aids
Off-line (batch) testing aids
Test mode operation
Trace facility

**Fig. 14.8** Software Evaluation Check List

250

**Fig. 14.8** (*continued*)

**Technical Structure**

Type of architecture (monitor, sub-tasking, etc.)
Flexibility on message control block structure
Option to have programs in different 'partitions'
Ease of communication between programs
Handling of program
Handling of file errors
Inter-program protection
Ability to change programs while processing
Error logging
Ability to start and stop applications independently
Applications multi-threaded
   — re-entrant code
   — multiple copies
Facilities for ensuring/checking high level language re-entrancy
Interlock facilities
Deadly embrace avoidance
Facility to allocate priorities and change priorities dynamically
Ability to write whole application in high level language
Dynamic control over rate of polling and which terminals are polled
Memory queueing with overflow protection (disk?)
Alternative device switching
Option to hold or reject message for non-available programs
Application independent message formatting
Terminal device independence
Broadcast facility general/selective
Overload handling
Transaction logging
Automatic message recovery
Automatic file recovery
Back out from log following data error detection
Check point facility
Ease of recovery
Password protection
Logical terminal facility
Dynamic security under master/control terminal control
Estimated real memory occupancy—monitor
Total estimated real memory all applications
Estimated CPU overhead for monitor
Data compression facilities
Optimization facilities
Dynamic storage allocation
Application/network related

**Technical Facilities**

Statistics produced for:
   Response times
   Message types
   Terminals
   Lines
   Application modules
   Files
   Memory usage
   Other
Ability to vary resources dynamically
Ease of using tuning facilities

Network definition modified by operator
Terminal addition at start-up and while on-line
Ease of adding lines and control units

requirements of the application are paramount, and it is this reason that prohibits any assertion that a particular package is any better or any worse than any other. It is very unlikely that the ideal package will ever be found, and the designer, in his choice of package, has to finely balance what needs to be done against what the package achieves. It is inevitable that compromises will have to be made. Activity on new software products from computer manufacturers indicates an increased level of facility provided by manufacturers' real time oriented operating systems.

Often the packages being considered also include communications facilities, and these have to be measured against the check list given in chapter 10 for communications software.

History has shown the check lists are reasonably time independent, but the significance of items can change with time. If storage drops in price by 80 per cent, for example, the amount of storage the package uses reduces in importance.

The importance of choosing the correct structure and package and then understanding it fully cannot be over-emphasized. The result of the choice can make vast differences in effort and time scale, and therefore any time spent reviewing the choice is more than repaid in implementation.

The MONITOR type structure and its use as described in this book exhibits many of the characteristics of modular programming. The MONITOR is the set of control routines, which, if used written, are tested by the addition of sub routines simulating the application code. The application code is written and tested by batch test harnesses which simulate the effect of the network and the service handlers.

The structure also fits well with Structure Programming ideas. Experience has shown that the application routines are readily—and desirably—written in structural code. The MONITOR structure was described here with the emphasis on friction. The intention was not to indicate coding structure. Suppliers' packages have differing structures, some according to strict structure design ideas, and others not. However, monitor structures can readily be built following Structured Programming design techniques. For example, in a simple COBOL written monitor, the Sequence Monitor and Request Monitor would be part of the same section which consists of two simple CASE structures, occurring in sequence. The application routines would be PERFORM'ed within the Sequence Monitor CASE Structure. On return, the request details would then be analysed by the Request Monitor CASE structure. In a similar manner, the whole program could be designed and written as a composite set of nested logic. This type of design greatly facilitates testing and identification of causes of failure.

# 15. Timing

If a survey were made of all operational batch systems to discover the timing techniques used, many could be found to have been timed empirically during final system testing or parallel running. Previous to this, calculations of elapsed time by timing peripherals only might have been attempted. The result in many cases is no worse than, for example, the main update taking 60 minutes instead of 30. While this approach may explain many premature upgrades to installations, it is rarely disastrous. By contrast, the effect of errors in timing of a critically loaded real time system can be fatal.

A real time analogy to the batch update mentioned above is a system with a measured average response time of half a second during system testing and an infinite response when first fully loaded. The prediction from queueing theory (see chapter 16), that response time approaches infinity as utilization reaches 100 per cent, is unfortunately optimistic. In practice, some resource, such as the main storage allocated to buffering messages, becomes fully committed before this point is reached, and response time thus becomes infinite even earlier.

Timing in real time systems design, then, is very important, and should in practice be done to increasing levels of accuracy several times during the development of a system (see chapter 7). It depends not only on the intrinsic speed of the computer components, but also on the quantity, e.g., size of main storage allocated to the program and number of disk drives. Timing is thus essential in estimating the amount of hardware used, and consequently, if done early enough, can often, by means of a strategic design change, save later forced hardware upgrades, which otherwise might become necessary to buy the system out of trouble.

This chapter deals with the timing of real time systems in stages. First it discusses communications timing, and then describes an approach to timing the central system, i.e., the hardware and software behind the communications processor or multiplexor. The techniques described progress from simple to complex. The presentation is intended to help the designer to stop at the complexity of technique appropriate to the system under consideration. It gives indications at each stage as to whether it is necessary to go to a further level of complexity.

## 15.1  Communications Timing

The timing of the network is dealt with in detail in chapter 10. To carry this timing out in isolation, it is necessary to assume the average response time of the combination of the central system and front-end processor. The separation of the network design and timing from the rest was justified by the likelihood that differences later discovered between the actual and assumed response times would have a small effect on the final network configuration. It is also desirable to establish the physical message pattern arriving at the centre so that specific design and timing can be carried out for the central systems.

The design of the central system can be carried out prior to network design being completed, but the design needs to be more general, and thus more expensive. Extra hardware may also be required, to cope with the inefficiencies normally associated with generality.

When timing of the central system has been carried out as described later, the response time calculated must be compared to the assumption used in network design. If the figures are greatly and adversely different, the network must either be re-calculated using the new figure, or if the assumed perceived response time (see chapter 10) were a specified value for psychological reasons, then the central system must be changed until the response time criterion is met.

### 15.1.1  TIMING OF COMMUNICATIONS CONTROLLERS

In chapter 10, two types of multi-line communications controllers were identified:

- character multiplexors, which operate by hardware logic passing a character at a time into a main frame;
- multi-line software controllers (MSC), which gather complete messages before passing them over the channel to the mainframe and carry out communications housekeeping by software.

The first has no timing problems for the user. Owing to the use of hardware logic, the manufacturer must specify configuration rules which allow the specified maximum number of lines to be all in simultaneous use at maximum speed. The timing problems are all associated with the software and buffering mechanisms in mainframe storage.

The MSC (sometimes called front-end processor) timing, by contrast, needs careful consideration, since the service mechanisms just mentioned are carried out within it. The MSC can be considered to be in two parts: a small mainframe connected to a character multiplexor. The timing of the character multiplexor part is subject only to the manufacturer's hardware configuration rules as discussed above, but this maximum terminal configuration is in most cases unachievable because of the system limitation associated with the software and the available storage. The load increases with the number of terminals to be polled and with the message rate. Thus, one tenth of the maximum number of connectable terminals heavily loaded, might exceed the load imposed by the maximum permissible system load.

The assessment of the adequacy of an MSC to support a given load depends on the internal speed of the processor, its software mechanisms, and the mechanism provided to deal with overloads. Knowledge of any of these, and particularly the latter two aspects, are not usually easily accessible to the designer.

The timing also depends on the number and type of terminals to be handled, the message load at peak, and the processing delay in the mainframe, which are definable by the designer. The designer's part in the timing should be to define this information as described in this chapter and chapter 10 with as much accuracy as possible, and as far into the future as can be estimated. This information is given to the mainframe manufacturer and other possible suppliers, who are asked to propose the appropriate communications hardware. Apart from other contractual points, such as support services, not directly connected with timing, they are asked to propose the power of MSC necessary, the software to be used and its relationship to mainframe software. Size of storage and communications hardware to be connected to the MSC are also requested.

The size of storage is particularly important to watch, since it must be sufficient to handle the peak load without resort to any mechanism for protection against overload if this exists, unless specifically allowed for in the timing calculations. This mechanism is normally invoked when the message storage is nearing overflow and is accomplished either by using disk buffering of messages which occurs after the pre-set maximum limit of message storage occupation has been reached (or worse, all messages are written to disk in case an overflow condition should occur), or by degradation of service by progressively reducing the numbers of terminals polled after the limit is passed. The first can be used to reduce message storage requirements, but needs to be allowed for in the timing. The second is only a last resort to prevent loss of data, and should never be part of normal running.

The manufacturer who is prepared to back his calculations contractually will obviously have more credibility in the eyes of the user. It is also desirable that calculations should be presented in such a way that the result of later changes in message and terminal load can quickly be assessed. At negotiation time, the manufacturer's interest in such calculations are high, but it may not be maintained.

### 15.1.2 COMMUNICATIONS SOFTWARE IN THE MAIN FRAME

The software resident in the main frame broadly carries out the functions of routing of messages, error handling, interrupt analysis, and buffering of output messages, whichever the type of multi-line controller used. If a character multiplexer alone is used, the software also carries out the functions of polling, buffering messages, queueing input messages, overload control, and error control at a character level as described for the MSC (chapter 10).

This software should also be timed by the manufacturer. Often, this is done by using a simulation program. This timing should be based on user-provided information similar to that described above for the MSC.

**255**

The following actual case figures are given as a warning to users who are prepared to guess for themselves, or to accept manufacturers' estimates not justified as described above. The figures relate to one manufacturer's mid-range machine using a comprehensive communication package interfaced to an MSC which was emulating a character multiplexor. On a lightly loaded system, the CPU time to service each single message pair was found to be 100 ms, of which 45 ms was taken up by software time used in accessing a message backing disk 6 times! The disk channel was obviously likely to become critically loaded at quite moderate message rates.

Another more specialized software package from a private vendor was found to service a heavily loaded network with an average CPU time of 15 ms per message pair on the same size machine. The mechanizations were obviously very different and far beyond the capability or inclination of the average user to time accurately. However, without the well-documented experience of another user or reliable simulation, the contributions to overall timing by the communications software alone could make necessary an unexpected and expensive upgrade in power of the mainframe early in the life of a system.

## 15.2   Approach to Timing the Central System

Timing can be a complex exercise, and yet some systems are not time critical, and so do not need much effort in this area. In any case it is vital that sufficient work is done to identify that a system is indeed not critical. The approach described here is designed so as to minimize the amount of calculation required. Calculations get progressively more complex, but before the full complexity is reached, in many cases it will have been possible to determine that a system is not time critical enough to necessitate proceeding further.

The rest of the chapter deals with the subject of timing the central system in progressive steps. Starting with simple disk timing, proceeding through increasingly more rigorous and complex techniques of disk timing, to timing of multi-thread systems. The presentation is such that a number of tests are identified which enable the designer to judge whether he has at that point gone far enough. There is no merit in carrying out timing to an unnecessarily fine level, but it is important to be sure that a sufficient level has been reached. Timings should be recorded under the technical design procedures described in chapter 5.

### 15.2.1   FILES FIRST

In many real time systems, if the message processing pattern is analysed, the percentage of time spent in disk processing is very high. From this, it follows that timing the files in isolation, assuming for the time being that other elements are negligible in effect, at least determines whether the system is possible with a practicable hardware arrangement.

If it is not possible to identify a file configuration which would support the known load, it is of no value to carry out the work of pursuing further timing techniques. The designer's effort is better directed towards reducing the load by modifying the design or negotiating system changes with the analysts.

In some cases, however, the proportion of transaction time required for file accessing is not predominant. As an example, if transactions are broken down into many message pairs, so that progressive terminal operator guidance can be provided by the program, the system timing might be dominated by communications software timing. The contribution of software and application program run time will be important in such cases and should be allowed for as described below. To be absolutely safe, any system which seems possible on file timing should be put through this next timing step.

### 15.2.2  WHOLE PROCESSOR TIMING

The knowledge of the number of disk devices indicates whether, in this step, when other elements are incorporated in the timing, the designer should carry out single-thread timing—i.e., assume the processing of each message to completion before the next is started—or multi-thread timing—i.e., assume the processing of a number of messages in parallel.

In the most critically loaded systems, a simulation is necessary, since the approximations necessary in manual timing become unacceptable. Even in these cases, however, the manual techniques are essential to prove that the necessary effort should be allocated to simulation (even using an existing package requires appreciable user effort), and to establish the starting hardware and software configuration for the simulation if it is proved necessary. Manual calculation also ensures that the designer understands the system and so does not use the simulation blindly.

## 15.3  File Timing

This section deals exclusively with disk timing, starting with a single disk drive/single control unit configuration and proceeding to deal with the multi-spindle/shared control unit configuration.

The timing of disks in isolation can be carried out from a knowledge of the message pattern and arrival rate at the computer during peak times, and the number of disk accesses per message. If the computer and software are to be organized to deal with each message within seconds, then the same peak can be assumed to apply to the disks. So in Fig. 15.1, a message rate of $n$ per second for a single message type is translated to $nx$ disk access demands per second, where $x$ is the number of accesses per message. The analysis in this section assumes objective utilization levels which are consistent with exponentially distributed inter-arrival and service times. In practice, disk access times are often more closely distributed, and the filtering effect of the mainframe and its software tends to make the inter-arrival times at the disks less distributed than on first arrival at the computer. The assumption of exponentially distributed arrivals is thus safe (see chapter 16).

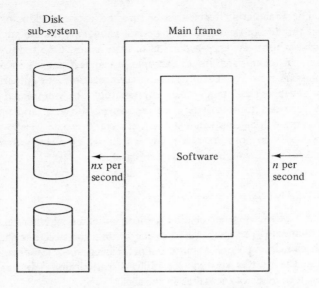

Disk
sub-system

Main frame

Software

$nx$ per
second

$n$ per
second

**Fig. 15.1** Basis for file only timing

### 15.3.1 SINGLE MOVING HEAD DISK DRIVE AND CONTROL UNIT

This analysis applies either to systems in which all files can be held on one drive or those in which, because of size, the files are spread over several drives but only one drive is active at one time.

The first step, as mentioned above, is to identify the transactions, peak rates, files, and the file access pattern, i.e., the average quantity of each access type for each file which each transaction makes.

Table 15.1 shows an example of a simple system with two transaction types, one file, and two access types. The update is a read followed by a write. If other files had been involved the table would have needed extension to allow the load contribution of each file to be assessed separately. This is due to the fact that in general block sizes and thus access times differ. The file access pattern is next translated into a rate of access for each access type (as in Table 15.1). The average time for each access type is calculated from a knowledge of the hardware characteristics and the file organization, as described in chapter 11. The contribution to overall utilization is then calculated for each access type by multiplying the rate by the access time. The individual contributions are then summed to give the total utilization.

From single server queueing theory (chapter 16) the utilization ($\rho$) must not be greater than approximately 0·7 to ensure a stable system. In the example, $\rho = 510$ ms/s, or 0·51. We can conclude for the moment that this particular system is reasonably safe, but is sufficiently near the limit for contributions to processing time other than disk accessing to be important.

If a low utilization of, say, 0·1 or less is calculated at this point, other contributions are unlikely to present problems, and no more detailed timing is

**258**

**Table 15.1**  Calculation of Disk Loading

| Transaction | Rate per second | FILE A | | | |
|:---:|:---:|:---:|:---:|:---:|:---:|
| | | Read only | | Update | |
| | | Per transaction | Per second | Per transaction | Per second |
| T1 | 3 | 1 | 3 | 1 | 3 |
| T2 | 2 | 0 | 0 | 2 | 4 |
| Total rates | 5 | | 3 | | 6 |
| Access times (ms) | | | 40 | | 65 |
| Utilizations | | | 120 | | 390 |
| Total utilization | | | | 510 ms/s | |

necessary unless the processing of transactions is complex or there are many message pairs to each. In general, however, the next step is to proceed to calculate single-thread timing as described in section 15.4.2. For systems where utilization is greater than $0.7$, the file sub-system needs further consideration, as follows.

### 15.3.2   MULTIPLE MOVING HEAD DISK DRIVES—BASIC CALCULATIONS

Supposing the transactions rates in Table 15.1 had been three times the values given, the overall utilization for a single disk drive would have been calculated as

$$\rho = 1.53,$$

which is impossible. To overcome this, the files could be distributed across several disk drives as shown in Fig. 15.2. The program would direct the accesses to the appropriate disk drive. On the supposition above, three drives would have to be used to bring the utilization down below $0.7$. The utilization for each drive would, of course, again be $0.51$. Several points must immediately be noted for this apparently simple solution. It must first be possible to split the file across several drives so that the average activity is evenly spread, and the resulting spare space on the disk drives cannot be used for any other simultaneously active system without invalidating the utilization calculations. Secondly, on the analysis so far, it must be assumed that each disk drive has its own controller, otherwise the simple use of disk drive utilization would be misleading. It is also important to remember that the program must multi-thread, since simultaneous access to all three drives was implicitly assumed in dividing the original utilization by three.

Careful examination of the file organization is needed to verify that the even spread of load is possible. For example, if a file had been organized with list relationships linking records within it, even if activity were balanced for the initial accesses, if secondary accesses generated by the pointers were all to one part of the file, the calculations would be invalid. The more complex the relationships the more difficult it would be to balance activity.

In practice, it is very expensive to duplicate disk drives and control units in

**259**

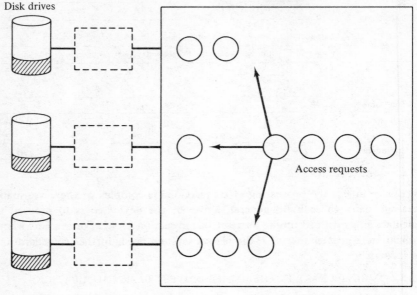

**Fig. 15.2** Distributed disk loading

the way described. There is nothing which can be done in the case of the disk drives, since the access times are inherent in the hardware design. However, by taking advantage of the fact that the controller is not busy throughout the entire duration of each access, a number of disk drives can share a controller. Table 15.2 illustrates why, for the 40 ms read access used as example in Table 15.1. The time for controller involvement, typical for a non-intelligent type, is 15 ms, apart from times involved in initiation and interrupt servicing, which are very small. The corresponding times for the update access would be 65 ms and 30 ms respectively if the average time for updating in main store were 10 ms. If it is now assumed that all three disk drives were connected via the same controller, as shown in Fig. 15.3, its utilization would be calculated as follows (three times Table 15.1 rates).

Controller Utilization = $9 \times 15 + 18 \times 30 = 675$ ms/s.

**Table 15.2**  Read Access Timing for a Typical Moving Head Disk Drive

| Element | Disk drive | Controller |
|---|---|---|
| Initiate seek | small | small |
| Seek to cylinder | 25 | — |
| Interrupt controller | small | small |
| Initiate transfer | small | small |
| Latency | 12·5 | 12·5 |
| Block transfer | 2·5 | 2·5 |
| Total | 40 | 15 |

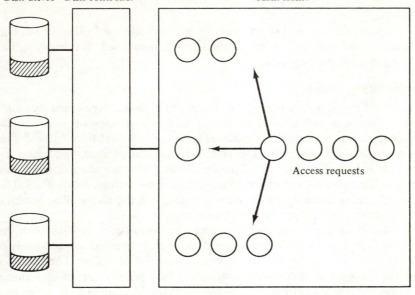

**Fig. 15.3**  Several disks, shared controller

Both the individual drives and the shared controller appear to have safe utilizations, being 0·51 and 0·68, respectively. But this is not so, because they are mutually interfering. For example, when an access to a given drive has been completed, even if there is another request for that drive waiting in software to be started, the controller may be busy servicing another drive, and so there is a wait forced on the first drive. Thus, if initial calculations indicate such high utilization, it is an indication that more detailed calculation is necessary before the system can be proved to be safe.

For utilizations of approximately 0·30 or less, these interactions are so low that they have little effect. For disk drives, this is normally the case only if size of files forces the use of more drives than would be necessary to distribute the loading. At these low utilizations, more detailed calculations would be unnecessary.

### 15.3.3  MULTIPLE DISK DRIVES—DETAILED CALCULATION

In this section a more detailed analysis of the multiple disk drive, shared controller problem is given. First, however, the definition of the model to which the analysis refers is given. An example of some results achieved by its use is considered and its limitation and adaptation to other systems are identified. After this consideration of the use of the model, the detailed calculations for the model are then dealt with. In this way, it is hoped that understanding of the use and limitations of the model can be appreciated before considering the detail. The calculation method is presented as a ready-made technique, rather than as a treatise on the step-by-step application of queueing theory to disk subsystems.

This analysis is applied when using the approach as described in 15.3.2; high utilization figures for the various components have resulted, thus implying that interactions are not negligible.

### Outline of the Model

The model consists of a number of moving head disk drives connected via a simple controller and channel to the computer. The software issues to the drives separate instructions for head movements (seek) and record transfer via the controller. The controller passes on these instructions in negligible time unless it is occupied at the time. Transfers from disk, once started, are passed through the controller and channel into main storage without delay. Blocks (the physical unit of transfer) are of one size throughout the file (or files), which is spread across all drives to give a uniform average access rate.

Whenever an access request is received by software, it is dealt with immediately. If a queue forms for any disk drive, it is handled independently of the others with a first come, first served despatching discipline. The initiation of seeks occupy negligible controller time and have priority over block transfer. If a read request has been performed for one drive which is to be followed by a write (i.e., an update) the read heads on that drive are held until the write has been completed. The analysis caters for simple read, and update accesses mixed in any given proportion. These accesses are direct, i.e., software can identify the hardware address of the record required.

The distribution of arrivals of access requests is assumed exponential. Distributions of various elements of the disk service time are subject to reasonable assumptions given in the detailed analysis. These vary between a constant and an exponential distribution (e.g., block transfer and wait times respectively).

To test the assumptions, calculations using this model have been checked for a range of rates of arrival against a detailed simulation for one type of disk system and found to be within 20 per cent (on the pessimistic side), both for mean and 99 per cent limit values.

### Use of the Model

The approximate number of disk drives is estimated, using techniques described in section 15.3.2. The maximum utilization for this purpose should not be greater than 50–60 per cent, since the effect of enforced waits has been ignored. The block size, and hence its transfer time and the update processing and associated software time, are estimated. Figures for the number of read and update accesses at peak time are established as in Table 15.1. The basic hardware times for the drives are established, and the software mechanism is checked for conformity with the model.

The calculations are carried out as described below for a number of rates greater than the expected rate. In this way, a graph of disk response time can

262

be plotted which, as well as showing whether the currently expected rate is feasible, also shows how far from a critical value the load is.

As an illustration, calculations were carried out and the results plotted in Fig. 15.4 for the following cases:

- file spread over eight drives, unit block transfer time = 3 ms;
- time for update processing between read and write = 10 ms;
- seek time, minimum = 25 ms, maximum = 135 ms, average = 75 ms;
- rotation time = 12·5 ms;
- various rates between 10 and 60 accesses per second were used, firstly assuming they were all reads, and then all updates.

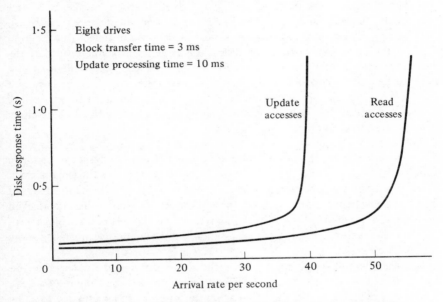

Fig. 15.4  Example calculation for multiple disk drives with shared controller

Obviously, if in a practical case mixed update and read accesses were expected, a single line on the graph would be the result of the calculation. This example shows the extremes. The graph indicates that, for example, if all accesses were updates, and a rate of 35 per second were expected, the system would work, but would be dangerously near the point of catastrophic decline of service.

It must be emphasized that this analysis only caters for disk accessing, and the minimum of processing. In many current hardware/software systems, communications software time alone would prevent the volume of accesses reaching the rate considered in this example.

## Adaptation of the Model to Other Systems

The variations from the model are in three broad categories, as given below, with the suggested approach to adapt the model to fit.

### Head Movement Optimization

The controller or software has the capability to sort queues of accesses to minimize head movement. Simply carry out the calculations as described, for the model, regarding the potential reduction in seek time as an unknown favourable contingency, since the queues for each drive are unlikely to be long enough for large savings to be made.

### Rotational Position Sensing

The drive has rotational position sensing, which allows the controller to service other requests until the drive is within a few milliseconds of the start of block. The latency figures in the calculation should be reduced to reflect this facility. (This will give an optimistic result unless the drive itself is able to initiate the search for record after the seek is complete, since the controller will otherwise need to be interrupted before the search can be initiated, with the resultant extra delay.) Not all software takes, or is able to take, advantage of this facility even if it exists in the hardware. Consequently it is necessary to check carefully in each case. *Accesses are no simply direct.*

This category requires detailed investigation of the way the hardware and software works in combination. Often adjustments to the analysis can be made simply. For example, take the case where the software accesses the start of track block in order to test whether the track is good before the data block itself is read from the track, the access being direct as in the model. If the controller stays locked onto that drive from the time of initiating transfer of the start of track block until the data read is completed, the analysis stands, but the latency is adjusted to allow for the double read.

Index sequential systems are beyond the scope of the model unless the controller stays locked onto the drive while all index accesses and the data access, within one cylinder, are made, when again the latency can be adjusted to allow for the extra time. It is less likely, however, that index sequential will be in use for the high volume systems which require this analysis.

### Detail of the Model

On first reading of this Chapter the reader is advised not to consider the detail of the model. After an overall appreciation of the timing of systems is gained the detail can be read in context.

The model enables the response times for a mix or read and update accesses to be calculated. The assumptions of the model have already been covered.

The times which make up the overall access time ($T$) are as follows, the asterisks denoting quantity to be calculated:

$*t_1$  Wait for disk drive $\left.\begin{array}{l} \\ \end{array}\right\}$ one or the other as appropriate
$*t_2$  Wait for channel/controller

$t_3$ Off-line seek initiation     $t_4$ Seek
*$t_5$ Wait for channel/controller     $t_6$ Latency
$t_7$ Read

If followed by a write,

$t_8$ Process                       *$t_9$ Wait for channel/controller $= t_5$
*$t_{10}$ Latency                   $t_{11}$ Write $= t_7$

$t_3$ is assumed negligible for this analysis

$\left.\begin{array}{c} t_4 \\ t_6 \end{array}\right\}$ are hardware parameters, for a given device

$\left.\begin{array}{c} t_7 \\ t_8 \\ t_{11} \end{array}\right\}$ are determined during System Design

$k =$ number of drives and is a parameter
$n =$ number of accesses per second and is a parameter.

Analysis is for mixed read-only and update (read followed by a write; heads held) accesses. The analysis assumes all accesses are independent and arrive at random. The proportion of the two types of access can be found thus:

$$a \text{ reads,} \quad b \text{ updates,}$$

where $a + b = 1$. Therefore there is a rate of $an$ reads and $bn$ updates, where $n$ is the total number of accesses per second.

The mean service time ($M$) for all accesses is then

$$M = (m_1 + m_2 + \ldots + m_7) + b(m_8 + m_9 + \ldots + m_{11}),$$

where $M$ is the mean value of $T$,
$\quad m_1$ is the mean value of $t_1$, and so on,
$\quad m_3$ is assumed negligible,
$\quad m_4, m_6, m_7, m_{11}$, are known for any specific system,
all times are in milliseconds.

The calculation of the other components of $M$ is as follows:

(a) $m_5 (= m_9)$

The channel/controller utilization ($\rho$) is given by

$$\rho = \frac{n}{1000} [(m_6 + m_7) + b(X - m_7 - m_8 + m_{11}) - bm_5]$$

$$= \frac{n}{1000} [(m_6 + m_7) + b(X - m_8) - bm_5].$$

Where $X$ is the rotation time of the disk

Since we do not yet know $m_5$, it is first assumed zero and $\rho$ calculated.

265

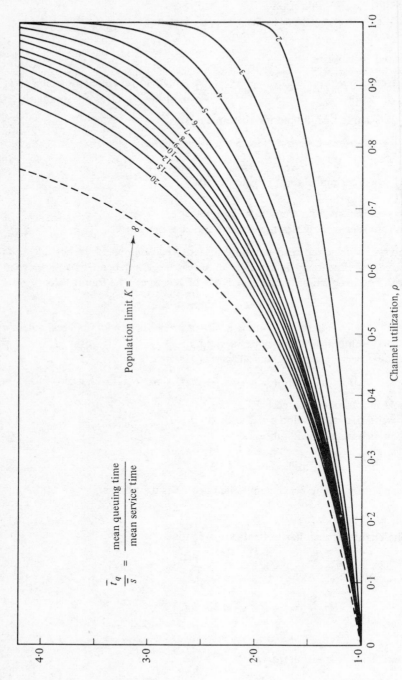

$$\frac{\bar{t}_q}{\bar{s}} = \frac{\text{mean queuing time}}{\text{mean service time}}$$

Population limit $K =$

**Fig. 15.5** Queuing time for limited populations

Channel utilization, $\rho$

Using the graph in Fig. 15.5 for the number of drives assumed, the ratio total queueing time/mean serving time is obtained. Let this be $Q$. Then $m_5$ is given by

$$Q = \frac{m_5 + [(m_6 + m_7) + b(X - m_8) - bm_5]/(1 + b)}{[(m_6 + m_7) + b(X - m_8) - bm_5]/(1 + b)}.$$

The denominator is the mean serving time. Let this be $Y$ (for use in (b)).

$X$ is derived as follows. If

$$0 < (m_7 + m_8 + m_9) \leqslant \text{one rotation } (2m_6),$$

then $X$ = single rotation time $(2m_6)$

$$2m_6 < (m_7 + m_8 + m_9) \leqslant 4m_6, \text{then } X = 4m_6$$
$$4m_6 < (m_7 + m_8 + m_9) \leqslant 6m_6, \text{then } X = 6m_6, \text{etc.}$$

This allows for the possibility of missing one or more rotations for extended times between read and write back. If the wrong assumption about $X$ was made, the calculation is repeated, but in any case $\rho$ is recalculated using the value of $m_5$ found above for greater accuracy. This calculation usually requires no more than one such iteration.

(b) $m_2$

First calculate $\rho_d$, the utilization of each disk drive.

$$\rho_d = \frac{m_d}{1000 \; k/n'}$$

*where* $m_d$ is in milliseconds

$R$ = number of disk drives used, and

$$m_d = (m_2 + m_4 + \ldots + m_7) + b(m_8 + m_9 + m_{10} + m_{11}),$$

$$M_{10} = X - (m_7 + m_8 + m_9)$$

($X$ is as calculated in (a))

$$\therefore \rho_d = \frac{n}{1000k} [(m_2 + \ldots + m_7) + b(m_8 + \ldots + m_{11})],$$

which is an equation relating $\rho_d$ and $m_2$. Then, $\rho_d$ is substituted in the following equation, from which $m_2$ is derived.

$$m_2 = \frac{\rho}{2}(1 - \rho_d) \left[ \frac{3Y^2 + m_6^2}{3Y} \right],$$

where $Y$ is the average channel occupancy derived in (a).

Note that in the above equation for $m_2$, the variance of $Y$ is assumed the same as if the latency were purely random:

(c) $m_1$

The calculation of $m_1$ uses Pollanczek's formula (see chapter 16) which involves $m_d$ and $\sigma_d$, where $m_d$ is as defined in (b) above. $\sigma_d$ is calculated from the relations:

$(\sigma_r)^2 = (\sigma_2)^2 + (\sigma_4)^2 + \ldots + (\sigma_7)^2$    (distribution for read-only accesses),

$(\sigma_u)^2 = (\sigma_2)^2 + (\sigma_4)^2 + \ldots + (\sigma_{11})^2$    (distribution for update accesses),

where

$\sigma_2{}^2 = m_2{}^2$

$\sigma_4{}^2 = (t_4 (\max) - t_4(\min))^2/12$

(i.e., $t_4$ uniformly distributed over the range $t_4$ (min) to $t_4$ (max))

$\sigma_5{}^2 = m_5{}^2$

wait is assumed exponentially distributed—a normally safe assumption)

$\sigma_6{}^2 = (2m_6)^2/12$

$\sigma_7{}^2 = 0$   ($t_7$ constant)

$\sigma_8{}^2 = 0$   ($t_8$ constant)

$\sigma_9{}^2 = m_5^2$   ($t_9 = t_5$)

$\sigma_{10}{}^2 = m_5^2$   (depends on variation in wait time)

$\sigma_{11}{}^2 = 0$   ($t_{11}$ constant)

$\sigma_d$ is then given by

$(s_d)^2 = a\sigma_r{}^2 + b\sigma_d{}^2 + ab\,(m_8 + \ldots + m_{11})^2$

Using Pollaczek's formula with

$\bar{s} = m_d$

$\bar{n} = \dfrac{n}{1000k}$

$m_1 = \bar{t}_q - \bar{s}$

we get :

$$m_1 = \tfrac{1}{2} \left( \frac{(m_d)^2}{1000k/n - m_d} \right) \times \left( 1 + \left( \frac{\sigma_d}{m_d} \right)^2 \right)$$

(d) *M*

All components of *M* are now known or have been calculated and thus *M* can be calculated. *M* represents the response time of the disk sub-system alone for the rate of arrival and number of disk drives assumed. A range of rates can be used in the calculation to test for stability of the system.

### 15.3.4   FIXED HEAD DISKS

Without any form of automatic optimization, the cases of single or multiple fixed head disks sharing a single control unit are both treated in the same way. Accesses, whichever device they are for, can only be handled serially. There is nothing to be gained by initiating more than one access at a time—there being no part of the access (analogous to head movement) which can be overlapped. The control unit utilization is calculated using the formula for utilization ($\rho$),

$$\rho = \overline{n}_1 \overline{s}_1 + \overline{n}_2 \overline{s}_2 + \ldots ,$$

where $\overline{n}_1$ is the average number of accesses of a given type per second, and $\overline{s}$ is the average disk access time for that type, calculated for the device in question. Although if two drives are connected to the same control unit, the utilization of each is half this figure, there is no way in which the unused capacity can be taken up. Either one or the other disk can be accessed, but not both at the same time.

If the disk drives have rotational position sensing, the model is similar to that for the multi-spindle moving head disk, described in section 15.3.2 with the following changes. The latency in that analysis (half revolution) is replaced by the rotational positional sensing latency, and the difference between the half rotation time and the rotational position latency is used in place of the head movement time. The model is less accurate used in this way, because assumptions about the distribution of different variable timing elements do not necessarily carry across.

A more normal approach to optimization of fixed head disks is to provide multiple data paths so that several transfers can be in progress at the same time. These paths are dynamically switchable, as required, to any of the disk units connected (as in the Burroughs equipment). The average data path load is thus reduced by a factor equal to the number of possible paths.

A further optimization is to provide a small processor which stores access requests. After each access is complete, the optimizer calculates for that disk the access which has the least rotational delay before the record can be read, and initiates it. It is difficult to carry out manual calculations for this form of optimization, and it needs to be simulated for each particular case to give accurate results.

15.3.5   KNOWLEDGE OF FILE ACCESS MECHANISMS

It should be apparent from the discussion above that it is vital to know how the disk hardware operates, and its timing parameters. It is also equally important to know exactly how the software drives the hardware.

Failure to fully understand this hardware–software interaction can lead to gross errors in timing. For example, one manufacturer's index sequential software does not take advantage of rotational positional seeking in all parts of the access where there are potential timing gains. The controller stays locked onto a device between the initiation of reading of track indices and reading the data block, thus greatly increasing the controller utilization over expection, if this fact is not allowed for.

## 15.4   Whole Processor Timing

So far, disk timing alone has been dealt with. The way in which other factors are brought together with disk timing is now described. The section deals first with timing of single-thread, and then of multi-thread systems (these are, respectively, a system with a program organization dealing with one message to completion before starting processing the next, and one which is handling the processing of several messages at any time). The file timing will already

269

have indicated whether single threading is possible.

In any case, the same basic data must be available for the system before timing can start. In this section, the timing methods will be related to a program structure like the MONITOR structure described in chapter 14. The treatment may, however, be applied to most common types of structure, since it is basically restricted to utilization calculation. The differences arise usually from the way in which the form of program organization distributes time between various functions. The MONITOR type switches control round all service functions each time application request for service is made by an application routine. Any outstanding service actions are then carried out. A tasking structure, on the other hand, may rely on the Operating System to carry out such switching. Calculations of response time for different transactions obviously rely on the detail of the technique of program organization, but the utilization calculation described in this chapter for the MONITOR structure can readily be adapted to suit other structures. Such calculations are aimed at investigating the overall capability of the configuration to sustain the maximum load envisaged, rather than calculating the effect on individual transactions. In general, whichever organization is used, a detailed understanding of its mode of operation is necessary, so as to be able to estimate CPU and disk time taken up by manufacturer's software. This latter is typically the next highest user of computer resources after application disk accessing.

### 15.4.1 BASIC TIMING INFORMATION

The information is organized in the same way, irrespective of whether single or multi-thread timing is required, on the assumption that, even for single-threading, a MONITOR structure will be used, for ease of production, future compatibility and tunability.

The steps in preparing the basic information for timing are as follows:

**Table 15.3**   Relation of Message Pairs to Transactions

| Transactions | | Message Pairs | | | |
|---|---|---|---|---|---|
| Type | Rate per second | Average number per transaction | Rate per second | Message pair | Comments |
| Enquiry | 0·5 | 1·0 | 0·5 | ENQ I1/ENQ 01 | Enquiry parameter/output page |
| | | 2·0 | 1·0 | ENQ I2/ENQ 01 | Paging request/output page |
| Order | 1·0 | 1·0 | 1·0 | ORD I1/ORD 01 | Format request/format |
| | | 3·0 | 3·0 | ORD I2/ORD 02 | Order details acceptance |
| Status check | 0·1 | 1·0 | 0·1 | STAT I1/ STAT 01 | Status enquiry/output display |
| Other low volume transactions | | | Similar details | | |

**Table 15.4** Timing Statistics

| Message details | | Processing details | | | | File accessing per second | | | | | Monitor requests per sec |
|---|---|---|---|---|---|---|---|---|---|---|---|
| Message pair | Rate per sec | Routine no | Size (bytes) | Run time (ms) | Probability or overlay | Overlay read | Customer file read | Stock file read | Stock file update | Logging file (write) | |
| ENQ I 1/ENQ 01 | 0.5 | 1 | 2.0 | 8 | 0.0 | | 0.5 | 0.5 | | 0.1* | 3.0 |
| | | 2 | 0.5 | 5 | 0.0 | | | | | | |
| | | 3 | 1.0 | 20 | 0.0 | | | | | | |
| ENQ I 2/ENQ 01 | 1.0 | 1 | 2.0 | 8 | 0.0 | | 1.0 | 1.0 | | 0.1* | 6.0 |
| | | 2 | 0.5 | 5 | 0.0 | | | | | | |
| | | 3 | 1.0 | 20 | 0.0 | | | | | | |
| ORD I 1/ORD 01 | 1.0 | 1 | 2.0 | 8 | 0.0 | | | | | 0.1* | 3.0 |
| | | 4 | 0.5 | 10 | 0.0 | | | | | | |
| ORD I 2/ORD 02 | 3.0 | 1 | 2.0 | 8 | 0.0 | | 3.0 | | 3.0 | 3.0 | 24.0 |
| | | 5 | 1.0 | 15 | 0.0 | | | | | | |
| | | 6 | 1.5 | 10 | 0.0 | | | | | | |
| | | 7 | 0.5 | 5 | 0.0 | | | | | | |
| STAT I 1/STAT 01 | 0.1 | 1 | 2.0 | 8 | 1.0 | 0.1 | | | | 0.01* | 0.5 |
| | | 9 | 1.0 | 5 | 1.0 | 0.1 | | | | | |
| Other lower volume messages | | | | | | | | | | | |
| Totals | 5.6 | | | 182.8 ms/s | | 0.2 | 4.5 | 1.5 | 3.0 | 3.3 | 36.5 |

12.5 total

* 10 records/block

- Create a table of transactions and constituent message pairs as in Table 15.3. The rate of each message pair can then be calculated knowing the structure of each transaction.
- Summarize the processing of each message pair in a table such as Table 15.4 (showing the details of the processing routines used, and file accesses made, by each message pair).
- Allow for one service request for each file access, change of application routine, and output message, and thus calculate the rate of MONITOR requests for each message pair.
- List individual application routines in order of rate of use as in Table 15.5. This enables the proportion of routines fixed in main store to those overlayed to be considered (this overlaying is dealt with further below).
  - Overlay accesses are inserted where appropriate into the timing statistics (Table 15.4).
  - Individual file accesses are timed knowing the file organization and basic access time.

Table 15.5    Routine Utilization List

| Routine number | Rate per second | Size (kilobytes) | Overlay area | Used for message pair |
|---|---|---|---|---|
| 1 | 5·6 | 2·0 | — | All |
| 7 | 3·0 | 0·5 | — | Order details |
| 5 | 3·0 | 1·0 | — | Order details |
| 6 | 3·0 | 1·5 | — | Order details |
| 3 | 1·5 | 1·0 | — | Enquiry |
| 2 | 1·5 | 0·5 | — | Enquiry |
| 4 | 1·0 | 0·5 | — | Order format |
| 9 | 0·1 | 1·0 | A | Status check |
| Other messages (total) | 0·01 | 50·0 | A | Other transactions |
| Size in core | | 7·0 | | |
| Size overlayed | | 51·0 | 4·0 | |

This completes the preparation for the timing calculations. The following note applies to the above procedure.

*Note.*    Usually, as assumed here, message pairs are the unit of processing, there being an input message stimulus for each output. Sometimes more than one output message results, in which case a greater load is exerted on the Communications Monitor and Communications Software. To prevent losing sight of this, such a message pair can be represented as in the following example:

BRO I 1/INFO 1 (20)

where 20 is the average number of terminals to which the broadcast information is sent. The actions of the majority of program functions will be as for a single message pair.

*Overlay Technique*

To decide by what method and how much to overlay is one of the more difficult decisions in timing. First, the techniques at the designer's disposal should be identified. For a given machine, the alternatives might be

- leave it to the manufacturer's virtual storage software;
- fix part of the program in main storage and leave the rest virtual;
- use the standard manufacturer's software to provide a fixed size overlay on demand into a dynamically allocated storage area;
- as above into a fixed core area;
- overlaying on demand from a user-maintained object code file into either dynamic or fixed overlay areas.

A completely free choice is unlikely within a given operating system. The choice of operating system should not in general be determined by overlay requirements. The benefits of a virtual system in making overlaying transparent to the user are rarely alone sufficient to justify the overhead of such a system.

In timing overlay systems, it is worth bearing in mind the following points. An all virtual system is not likely to be viable except for very low volume applications. If the manufacturer's software removes control from the user program while servicing an overlay request, multi-threading is not possible during that time with the MONITOR type structure, unless overlays are passed to a separate task. The time taken by many manufacturers' standard overlay systems is large by comparison to a single direct access to the backing storage used, times of 0·5 s being not uncommon.

A dynamic main storage allocation technique means that the overlayable routines are not overlayed each time they need to be used, the more frequent having a higher chance of already being in core.

In the example system considered above, a reasonable decision would be to overlay Routine 9 and all of lower volume into a fixed overlay area of size 4K bytes. The saving of main storage is considerable, with only a small consequent increase in file accessing. By choosing 4K a number of the application routines could be combined into a single physical overlay.

### 15.4.2 SINGLE-THREAD TIMING

In calculating the disk timing alone for the example system, the utilization of a single drive holding all files would have been calculated to be less than 0·5. It would certainly have seemed worth timing on the assumption that single-thread operation might work. In single-thread operation, one message pair is processed to the point of writing the output message back to software before the next one is accessed from software. Processing of different messages cannot thus be overlapped in any way. The whole central system is thus acting as a single server, which is at a given time, processing in main storage, or accessing

**Table 15.6** File Timing

| Item | Rate per second | Unit time (ms) | Total for item (ms/s) |
|---|---|---|---|
| Customer file read | 4·5 | 45 | 203 |
| Stock file read | 1·5 | 40 | 60 |
| Stock file update | 3·0 | 65 | 195 |
| Logging file | 3·3 | 10 | 33 |
| Overlay read | 0·2 | 500 | 100 |
| Overall total | | | 591 |

**Table 15.7** Software and Monitor CPU Times

| Item | Rate per second | Unit time (ms) | Total for item (ms/s) |
|---|---|---|---|
| Communications software | 5·6 | 30 | 168 |
| Communications monitor | 5·6 | 4 | 22 |
| Request monitor* | 36·5 | 3** | 110 |
| I/O monitor*** | 12·5 | 12 | 150 |
| Total | | | 450 |

\* request per:  change of application routine
                file read    file write
                communication write
\*\* request validation plus loop around service monitors  and selection of next routine
\*\*\* including manufacturers' software overheads

disks, or logging, or some other processing action. This is analogous to the several different serial actions which, say, a booking office clerk does in issuing a ticket in a familiar queueing situation.

In single-thread timing, the contributions to overall computer utilization from the separate activities are thus added to give their combined effect. For the example system, Table 15.6 shows how disk accessing is extended to include logging and overlaying. The rate of each individual access is multiplied by the calculated access time and the results for all access types are totalled. In Table 15.4 the average run time of each application routine was given, with the rate of use by each message. These are multiplied up and summed, as for the files, to give an overall CPU (arithmetic unit) utilization. Table 15.7 gives this and

**Table 15.8** Single-thread Timing

| Item | Time (ms/s) |
|---|---|
| Software/MONITOR | 450 |
| Application processing | 183 |
| CPU sub total | 633 |
| Files | 591 |
| Whole computer utilization | 1224 |
| Average/message pair | 219 |

similar figures for software and MONITOR processing. For each an overall CPU utilization figure is calculated. It is essential to understand the program structure.

The result of adding these three contributions to whole computer utilization is shown in Table 15.8. The utilization is somewhat over unity (1000 ms/s) and thus single-threading is impossible. Queueing theory shows that, with exponential inter-arrival and service times, the safe maximum is about 0·7. In practice, the flexibility to go to multi-threading must be built in if utilization exceeds half this value, to allow for under-estimates in the figures used.

In the example discussed here, the total time is split about evenly between files and processing. Of the processing, twice the time is spent in software and MONITOR than in application processing. These relationships are realistic and illustrate the fact that file timing alone is insufficient (cf. batch processing) and that manufacturer's software, being generalized, is often inefficient.

For the example used here, single-threading is obviously not possible. The first tactic is to investigate where, if anywhere, the times can be reduced. Obviously, file accessing and software are the first target. Sometimes an unnecessarily iterative sequence has been adapted at the terminals. Apart from being an irritation to the operators, this approach has a marked effect on the communications software time and introduces extra disk accesses. However, this particular fault is not present in the example system. It will be assumed that no other major timing reductions are possible, thus making it necessary to consider multi-threading, as discussed in section 15.4.3.

For a system which had a utilization below about 0·7, the analysis discussed above for single-thread systems could be extended to calculate response times. Chapter 16 gives the equations to be used, knowing the average of the total processing time and the utilization. By assuming an exponentially distributed processing time, a pessimistic result would be obtained under normal conditions. An exception would be where occasional very long service times occurred amongst service times which were closely distributed and by comparison small. This situation gives a distribution worse than exponential. An example might be an enquiry system where 99 per cent of requests were met by access within one cylinder, while the other 1 per cent required a serial search of the whole file. For service times made up of components whose elements have distributions which are calculable, a more accurate result can be obtained by using Pollanczek's formula (see chapter 16). Further, an estimate can be made of limits such as the time in which 99 per cent of the message pairs will have been serviced. For this, the incomplete gamma function is used in the way also described in chapter 16.

Checking utilizations as described in this chapter is a useful tool for predicting the likelihood of a given system working, but when the analysis is extended to the calculation of response times and their distribution, the effect of distribution of service times becomes important. Consequently, if any accuracy in such parameters is expected, the distributions of the various elements involved in the equations must be accurately measurable or calculable. For example, if a computer has a serving time which is much nearer a constant than an exponential distribution, and the latter has been assumed, a statement (arrived at by queueing theory calculation) that 99 per cent of response times will be less than or equal to 8 s, is very inaccurate. Unfortunately, the statement has superficially an aura of accuracy.

## 15.4.3 MULTI-THREAD TIMING

When a number of messages are being processed in parallel in a program, exact timing by manual means becomes so involved as to be impracticable.

Notwithstanding this, some estimate of the ability of a system to support a certain load can be made using relatively simple techniques.

Given that single-thread operation has been proved unsatisfactory or impossible on timing grounds it is still possible to proceed further by manual calculation. The sequence of activity is as follows:

- investigate whether the file activity can be spread over a number of devices, so as to reasonably uniformly distribute the load;
- check the ability of individual components to support the load, assuming no interaction with other components;
- carry out detailed disk timing calculations as described in section 15.3.3 to estimate the maximum capacity;
- estimate the suitability of the application message profile for overlapped processing;
- approximately estimate number of threads necessary and check if reasonable from the point of view of processing overheads;
- simulate the best guess organization and close variants to check timing.

The example system, described in section 15.4.1, can again be used to illustrate some of these points.

For this system, file timing alone would not have shown the need for more than one disk drive. It is only after trying single-thread timing that it has become apparent that interaction from other elements causes an impossible utilization when processing one message at a time. The file configuration needs further investigation. Looking again at Table 15.6, it is apparent that if the Customer File and Stock File were on separate drives, and overlays were from the system drive, which was itself separate from the data drives, there would be the possibility of simultaneous access by up to four separate message threads to four separate devices. The logging file is separate in any case, because it is on a tape drive. None of these devices would then have a utilization of more than $0 \cdot 25$ (the Stock File).

(Assuming the disks were sharing a control unit, the analysis in section 15.3.3 could be applied, but with such low utilizations much conflict is unlikely. Since a detailed example of the treatment of a shared controlled unit has already been given, it will be omitted here.)

Scope for increasing the throughput of the file sub-system has thus been demonstrated. It might, in practice, still not be necessary to separate the two data files, since they jointly would cause a disk drive utilization of $0 \cdot 46$.

Looking in isolation at the total CPU utilization, as summarized in Table 15.8, it can be seen that the utilization required $(0 \cdot 63)$ is not impossible, given that the CPU is rarely prevented from processing, by queues elsewhere in the system. Even then, it is near critically loaded. The program must thus have enough threads to ensure that it is unlikely that all are held up, for example, for disk accessing.

With the example system message, processing is evenly balanced between file and CPU processing, overall, and within individual messages. It is unlikely that all threads will become inactive simultaneously awaiting file accesses, thus reducing the usable CPU time below 100 per cent.

Calculation of the number of threads required in detail is not possible without making many assumptions, and in any case is very tedious and hence prone to error. An approximate indication can be arrived at, as follows.

1. Decide on a distribution of files to devices likely to work from the point-of-view of timing. Using the timing analysis of multiple disk drives given in 15.3.3 derive the disk response time.
2. Using the calculated CPU utilisation (derived as for the example system in Table 15.8) determine the ratio of time-in-the-queue to serving time. Use the equation

$$\frac{\bar{t}_q}{\bar{s}} = \frac{1}{1-\rho}$$

with terminology as in Chapter 16.
3. Carry out similar calculations for other processing elements like tape drive accessing.
4. Calculate for each message pair the average processor time, average number of disk accesses, and average number of other processing actions (e.g. tape drive accesses).
5. Multiply the CPU time derived in 4 by the ratio derived in 2, giving CPU time plus time spent waiting for it.
6. Multiply the number of disk accesses derived in 4 by the response time derived in 1 to give total elapsed time spent accessing files.
7. Calculate times similarly for other processing actions like tape drive accessing.
8. Add times from 5, 6 and 7 to give an approximation of the average elapsed time of processing for each message.
9. Calculate the number of Message Blocks (MB's) required. Each MB supports a processing thread, and, together they act as multiple—serves with an average serving time of $\bar{s}_8$. $\bar{s}_8$ is the time derived in step 8. They are serving the message queue in communications Software for which the arrival rate is $\bar{n}$. The number of MB's required ($M$) is found approximately by using multi server queueing theory. (Chapter 16)

This is not a rigorous calculation. The effects of interractions between processing elements are not completely taken into account. However, it does give a starting point for more complex timing processes such as simulation.

In many hardware/software combinations available currently, a practical maximum number of threads is of the order of five. If numbers are increased beyond this, the overheads of switching control between the messages begin to outweigh any improvement in throughput.

At this point in timing a system, the software monitor times (Table 15.7 for the example) should be re-examined to check that the times are realistic for the likely number of threads. In Table 15.7, all items except communications software increase with the number of threads.

The system used as an example for timing is obviously critically loaded. In any practical case with such loadings, manual calculations should never be trusted. The next step in timing is to use a simulation package. The manual timing will have indicated which configurations to investigate. In the example system, the configurations to be simulated, arrived at by the above multi thread timing procedures would perhaps be

- all files on separate devices, four threads;
- stock file and customer file sharing a device, others separate, three threads.

In the light of these results, a better guess of the final configuration could be made, and again simulated. The aim is to reduce the number of expensive simulation runs to a minimum. To test the sensitivity of the system, runs at several message rates higher than expected would also desirably be carried out. Simulation is not dealt with in detail in this book, but here some limitations need consideration. When using a package provided by a manufacturer, the mechanisms it simulates must be well understood to avoid erroneous results. Faults in packages or their use which have been discovered in the past have included the following:

- a simulation did not deal with the program structure actually chosen by the user;
- another did not allow for the overheads which increase in proportion to the number of threads;
- two simulation runs for different power machines were run, but for so few messages that a freak result was obtained, predicting a faster response time on the slower machine;
- a simulation was run for a fixed MONITOR-type structure, and the results were assumed to apply to a virtual version of the same type of structure with a resultant error in the CPU time for the monitor of 300 per cent.

All these misuses of simulation resulted in gross errors, which were far greater than for manual calculations carried out for the systems. Consequently, it is very important to fully understand what the simulation package simulates, and how it has been run before trusting the results. While hand timing and simulation are the best tools available and need to be used within the guidelines set down here, their liability to error remains important. Thus, apart from any designer error, technical design control (chapter 5) is also a safeguard against faults in initial timing models.

## 15.5  Summary of Approach

The approach to timing described in this chapter is summarized in Fig. 15.6. The general theme of this approach is to avoid getting involved in unnecessary complexity. For example, if a low utilization on timing a single disk drive is obtained it is most unlikely that multi-disk drive and multi-thread timing will be

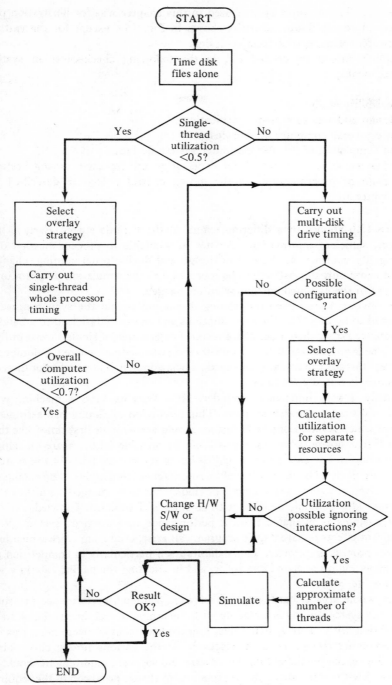

**Fig. 15.6** Summary of timing procedure

necessary. The example system used in this chapter was for illustration purposes, chosen to follow all paths shown in Fig. 15.6 except for the exits to hardware, software, or system re-design.

Timing should be carried out at the following checkpoints in system development:

- feasibility study;
- design addenda to system specification;
- after overall computer system design;
- on completion of detailed computer system design;
- when significant changes from expectation are reported, during system design or programming via the design control procedure described in chapter 5.

Figure 15.6 applies to a differing extent at the various stages. Early in the project, sufficient information may not be available to proceed beyond disk timing. By contrast, at the end of design and during programming, changes might cause only the last step to be repeated, i.e., the simulation program to be rerun with the assumed configuration unchanged.

An obvious lesson from this timing discussion is that the system must be designed to be tuneable, since assumptions and errors in data lead to a band of probability rather than a definitive result. For example, if single-thread utilization is near critical, say 0·60, a multi-thread organization, where the number of message threads can be easily changed, is best adopted. The number of threads, of course, is initially set to one.

Finally, a very important reminder. Most systems share a machine with other real time and batch systems. This discussion of timing has assumed a system which stands alone. Any system should certainly be first timed like this, since if it is not possible alone it will not be possible on the shared machine. The timing in any case gives an indication of the critical parts of the system, which are likely to be most affected by interference from others. The configuration arrived at for the system alone obviously has to be merged with the other systems. This can only be done with confidence if sufficient knowledge of the other systems is available from a performance measurement system. Very significant effects on a real time program can arise, even from work which is at a lower processing priority. This exhibits itself particularly in competition for disk accessing on a shared controller, and in affecting the paging rate in a virtual storage system.

The whole area of hardware and software planning, performance measurement and system tuning is bound up with the timing of real time systems. In an installation with many systems live, a centralized control over these areas is fast becoming recognized as a necessity. At the various timing checkpoints listed above, the predicted future hardware and software requirement should be discussed with a centralized control function to ensure provision of the required resources in the appropriate time scale.

**Part 4**

# Further references

# 16. Queueing Theory and Practice

Chapter 2 identified the problem facing designers who wish to take account of the effect of the fluctuations of message arrival rates and service times without having to determine the precise detail of those fluctuations. The solution is the application of queueing theory, which is well established as an analytical technique for projecting the performance of many queueing situations.

Queueing theory has a complex mathematical basis, and for that reason the real time designer should call in the assistance of an appropriately experienced mathematician if queueing theory is to be used extensively.

However all real time designers can use the predictions of queueing theory to considerable practical effect. Where the designer is not also an expert on queueing theory, he can still use the techniques to:

- determine possible performance on first designs and make initial comparisons between designs;
- determine which parts of a system are heavily loaded and require close study, and which are stable enough to be covered only by the first approximation of basic queueing theory;
- select where to direct further performance evaluation, through further queueing theory studies, simulation, or test measurements.

This chapter is primarily concerned with helping the real time designer to use queueing theory projections in a practical manner. As such, it may be considered to address the topic 'queueing practice' rather than 'queueing theory', because it is the conclusions not the derivation of queueing theory that are presented.

A number of queueing formulae are included in this chapter; before application, the reader must ensure he has correctly interpreted the context in which each formula can be used. Graphs included in the figures in this chapter are for illustration purposes. While their shape is sufficiently accurate for first time predictions, standard mathematical tables and reference graphs should be used for work of greater accuracy.

## 16.1 Basic Queueing Parameters

As already stated, queueing theory permits the designer to work with average values, without measuring the individual fluctuations. There are four basic parameters that arise in most queueing situations: two require measurement or postulation, one is calculated simply and the fourth is projected through the use of queueing theory. For the moment, we will consider these parameters in terms of their average values. (The notation used in this chapter is $\bar{x}$ for the average value of $x$, etc.).

The general queueing situation and the basic parameters $\bar{n}$, $\bar{s}$, $\bar{t}$ and $\rho$ can be represented diagramatically as shown in Fig. 16.1. This simplest model is usually referred to as the single server model (i.e., there is only one unit providing the service).

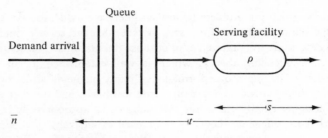

**Fig. 16.1**  Single Server—basic model

The four parameters are further illustrated below by reference to this model and to the example of the queueing situation of airline passengers at a check-in counter at an airport, where the airline in question has several flights per day. The airline has one check-in counter and the check-in facility (clerk + counter) is the single server.

### 16.1.1  ARRIVAL RATE

The arrival rate, $n$, is the rate of arrival of demand for the service under analysis. It is expressed as 'a number per time period', e.g. '$n$ per minute'. For the airline check-in, $\bar{n}$ varies according to the time of day and aircraft departures.

Queueing calculations can be carried out for any period of the day, but for design purposes, the peak loading period is normally selected. Figure 16.2 is a typical plot of arrival rates. The solid curve is $\bar{n}$ observed in intervals of, say, 10 minutes. The dotted curve schematically reflects the instantaneous fluctuations.

### 16.1.2  SERVICE TIME

The service time is the total time necessary to carry out the service concerned, and includes all the period the 'server' is busy. In the airline example this time

**284**

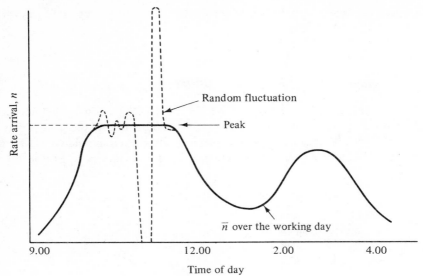

**Fig. 16.2** Arrival pattern

will include all activities in the check-in cycle, e.g.,

- initial conversation;
- check-in procedures;
- final conversation;
- passenger vacates space by the counter.

The service time potentially can vary during the day or year, according to the work mix, and there are fluctuations from one service cycle to the next. The mean service time, $\bar{s}$, must be determined for the same period(s) of day used in determining $\bar{n}$.

In real time systems, servers usually have a variable service time such as caused by the variable head shift time on a disk file.

### 16.1.3 FACILITY UTILIZATION

Facility utilization is a measure of the loading of the unit under analysis, and equates to the fraction of total available time that the resource is busy. Busy, in this context, means not available for any other work.

For example, if the check-in counter clerk is only busy 50 minutes every hour, the facility utilization ($\rho$) is $50/60 = 0.83 = 83$ per cent loaded. For a single server facility, utilization can be calculated as

$$\rho = \bar{n}\bar{s}.$$

*Example*

If a disk file system has to handle a message load that calls for eight file

**285**

accesses per second and the file is capable of handling one access in 95 ms, then

$$\bar{n} = 8 \text{ per sec}$$
$$\bar{s} = 95 \text{ ms}$$
$$= 0.095 \text{ s}$$
$$\rho = \bar{n}\bar{s} = 8 \times 0.095 = 0.76.$$

That is, utilization of the disk file system is 0.76. The designer will normally wish to carry out his designs for the peak period, and it is the peak $\rho$ that is crucial. This may occur at a period where $n$ and $s$ are not individually at a peak (see Fig. 16.3). In any service situation, queues become very large if $\rho$ is 1 or greater.

Fig. 16.3    Variation by Period in Peak $\bar{n}$, $\bar{s}$, $\rho$ – Single-server

| Period | Comment | $\bar{n}$ | $\bar{s}$ | $\bar{\rho} = \bar{n}\,\bar{s}$ |
|--------|---------|-----------|-----------|---------|
| 1 | Peak $\bar{n}$ | 10 | 0.070 | 0.70 |
| 2 | Peak $\bar{s}$ | 3 | 0.120 | 0.36 |
| 3 | Peak $\rho$ | 8 | 0.095 | 0.76 |

In many queueing situations, $\bar{n}$ and $\bar{s}$ may be made up of several discrete pairs. For example, in the check-in case, the airline may be able to identify different patterns at one counter for:

– local issued tickets—own office;
– tickets issued elsewhere—own office;
– tickets issued by another airline;
– charter tickets;
– each of the above for flights with or without check-in seat reservations.

In a real time system, each transaction type has its associated $\bar{n}$ and $\bar{s}$.

In such cases, the 'analyst' may identify $\bar{n}$ as being made up from each type of work, where $\bar{n} = \bar{n} + \bar{n}_2 + \bar{n}_3$, etc., and the 'designer' may predict $\bar{s}$ as being the weighted average of different $s_1$, $s_2$, $s_3$, etc. (i.e., the average $\bar{s}$ of services provided in a period of time). In that case

$$\bar{s} = \frac{\bar{n}_1\bar{s}_1 + \bar{n}_2\bar{s}_2 + \bar{n}_3\bar{s}_3 + \ldots}{\bar{n}_1 + \bar{n}_2 + \bar{n}_3 + \ldots} = \frac{\Sigma\, \bar{n}_i\bar{s}_i}{\Sigma\, \bar{n}},$$

and $\rho$ can be calculated as

$$\rho = \bar{n}\bar{s} \quad \text{or} \quad \rho = \bar{n}_1\bar{s}_1 + \bar{n}_2\bar{s}_2 + \ldots,$$

whichever is the simpler.

*Example*

Two files are held on one disk with average activity rates 10 per second and 2 per second, and file access times are respectively 40 and 100 ms, then for that single server (the disk),

$$\bar{n} = \bar{n}_1 + \bar{n}_2 = 10 + 2 = 12 \text{ per second},$$
$$\rho = \bar{n}_1\bar{s}_1 + \bar{n}_2\bar{s}_2 = 0\cdot400 + 0\cdot200 = 0\cdot6,$$
$$\bar{s} = 0\cdot6/12 = 50 \text{ ms}.$$

*Note.* The numeric average of $\bar{s}_1$ and $\bar{s}_2$ is $(40 + 100)/2 = 70$ ms, but that is not the same as $\bar{s}$, the average value of $s$ for the mix of work under consideration.

### 16.1.4  QUEUEING TIME

While queueing theory enables the designer to predict several factors of a queue's behaviour, queueing time is perhaps the most significant prediction. The theory introduced later in this chapter first handles average values and the symbol used is $\bar{t}_q$. In this chapter, we will use $\bar{t}$ as an alternative form. Queueing theory predictions, as discussed in this chapter, are based on a definition of queueing time, $\bar{t}$, as 'the time in the queue up to the completion of service'.

In the airline example, if $\bar{s}$ is 1 minute and $\bar{t}$ is 3 minutes, the traveller waits in the queue on average for 2 minutes before the start of his check-in cycle.

The queueing theory and practice covered in this chapter are based on a despatch (selection) discipline of 'first in first out' 'FIFO'. Other despatch disciplines can exist. In real time systems, typical examples include the following:

- on priority but FIFO within priority class;
- last in first out LIFO.

Different selection criteria change the characteristic of a queue's performance, but $\bar{t}$ is not altered by the selection discipline if the discipline is independent of the service time.

Later sections of this chapter introduce further measures of a queue's behaviour, such as average length and distribution of time and length.

## 16.2  Average and Distributed Values

While queueing theory allows the designer to carry out calculations using average values only, the effect of the fluctuations needs to be understood.

Queueing theory relies on assumptions or knowledge of the *pattern* of fluctuations of $n$, the arrival rate, and $s$, the service time. Different patterns require different formulae or interpretations of results. Equally, the designer may wish to project both $\bar{t}$ and its pattern of fluctuation.

In discussing arrival rates the word random is often used, without precision, to describe fluctuations. In practical terms, the distribution of arrival rates can vary considerably, and in mathematical terms *random* applies to one specific distribution.

If we reconsider the airline check-in of section 16.1, and assume travellers arrive at the airport only by bus in batches, there is likely to be a very wide distribution of arrival rate at the check-in counter. On bus arrival, say 40 passengers arrive at the check-in in 2 minutes; $\bar{n} = 20/\text{min}$. Just before the next

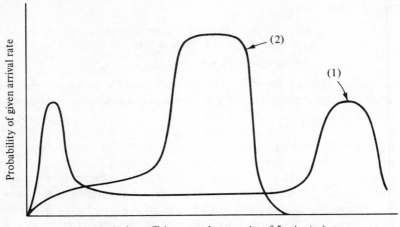

Arrival rate $\overline{n}$ (measured over units of 5 minutes)

**Fig. 16.4** Two distributions of $n$.

bus, say no-one arrives; $\overline{n} = 0$. If this is plotted on a histogram over the day, the wide distribution may appear as illustrated as curve 1 on Fig. 16.4.

Now assume there is a security check *before* check-in, and passengers travel to the airport by a variety of means. Passengers feed through security check at a fairly steady rate at busy periods (the maximum rate is limited by the speed and number of security checkers), and the distribution of arrival at the check-in counter may be as curve 2 in Fig. 16.4. The resulting queues at the check-in will be very different in the two cases considered. The two examples are rather extreme cases, but serve to illustrate the real variations in distribution of rates that can occur.

The illustration is of variation in average arrival rates arising from external effects. In queueing theory, one is concerned with the extent of instantaneous fluctuations in either arrival rates, $n$, or service times, $s$, and with predicting both the average queueing times, $\overline{t}$, and the fluctuations in $t$.

A convenient mathematical measure of the extent of dispersion of $n$, $s$, or $t$ is the standard deviation—symbol $\sigma$. The calculation of $\sigma$ is set out in section 16.2.1 below, and the special case of 'random' distribution is expanded further in section 16.2.2.

### 16.2.1   STANDARD DEVIATION, $\sigma$

The standard deviation of a series of measurements is a measure of the range of dispersions from the average value. Distributions can be represented pictorially as curves (e.g., Fig. 16.4) or histograms (see Fig. 16.6). The definition of a standard deviation is the root mean squared deviation of a set of values from their mean.

**288**

Given a set of values (50 plus if a sample is being taken) $\sigma$ for a variable $r$ can be calculated as

$$\sigma = \sqrt{\left(\frac{\sum_{i=1}^{N} (\bar{r} - r_i)^2}{N}\right)}$$

where $\sigma$ = standard deviation,
$r_i$ = value of $i$th sample,
$\bar{r}$ = average value of $r$,
$N$ = number of samples taken.

*Example*

**Table 16.1**   Standard Deviation

| Value, $(r_i)$ | Deviation from mean, $(\bar{r} - r_i)$ | Squared deviation $(\bar{r} - r_i)^2$ |
|---|---|---|
| 5 | −1 | 1 |
| 3 | −3 | 9 |
| 1 | −5 | 25 |
| 10 | 4 | 16 |
| 7 | 1 | 1 |
| 13 | 7 | 49 |
| 4 | −2 | 4 |
| 3 | −3 | 9 |
| 8 | +2 | 4 |
| 6 | 0 | 0 |
| 60 = R | | 118 = S |

Mean squared deviation $= \dfrac{118}{10} = 11\cdot8$

Standard deviation $= \sqrt{(11\cdot8)} = 3\cdot4$

In the selection of values given in the Table 16.1, $N = 10$, $\bar{r} = 6$, and the table shows how the calculation is carried out. Thus, the steps to determine a standard deviation are as follows:

— list values;
— determine how many ($N$);
— sum values, $\Sigma\, r = R$;
— calculate mean, $\bar{r} = R/N$;
— calculate deviations and square deviations $(\bar{r} - r_i)$ and $(\bar{r} - r_i)^2$;
— sum the square of the deviations $\Sigma\, (\bar{r} - r_i)^2 = S$;
— divide the sum of squares by $N$—mean squared deviation ($S/N$);
— take the square root of the mean squared deviation.

If a value is constant its standard deviation is 0.
If a value has a standard deviation equal to its mean value ($\bar{r} = \sigma$) the values may possibly be exponentially distributed, or random. For use of some of the following formulae, knowledge of the standard deviation $\sigma$ is required. The exact form of the distribution is immaterial.

## 16.2.2  RANDOM DISTRIBUTIONS

Random distributions are assumed in the main queueing formulae used in this chapter. The random distribution can be defined in several equally valid ways. Three are particularly common and have their own particular nomenclature: random, poisson, exponential. Each is expressed in terms of events. For arrival rates an event is the arrival of a demand for the service. For service times, the event is the completion of one service cycle.

### Random

A random distribution is one where 'the probability of an event occurring in a given period of time follows a uniform distribution'. See Fig. 16.5.

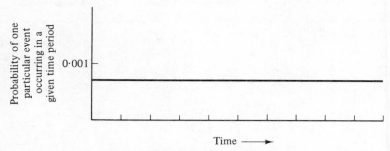

**Fig. 16.5**  Random arrival rate

### Poisson

A Poisson distribution is illustrated in Fig. 16.6. The distribution is based on 'the probability of $n$ events occurring in a given time period'. The mathematical formulation for this distribution is

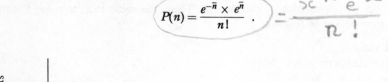

$$P(n) = \frac{e^{-\bar{n}} \times e^{\bar{n}}}{n!} \; . \qquad = \frac{x^{n} e^{-x}}{n!}$$

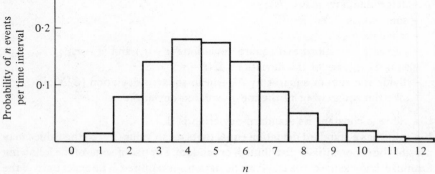

**Fig. 16.6**  Poisson distribution

290

*Exponential*

An exponential distribution is defined in terms of the probability that the time between events is less than a certain value. See Fig. 16.7. The mathematical formulation of this curve is

$$P(t \leqslant t^1) = 1 - e^{-t^1/t}.$$

Each of these three definitions has the particular property that the standard deviation equals the mean, i.e., $\sigma = \bar{r}$. Random and exponential are convenient ways of describing the same pattern of distribution in a continuous variable. In the exponential example, inter-arrival times are used as an alternative to arrival rate. Poisson also describes a similar pattern for a discrete variable.

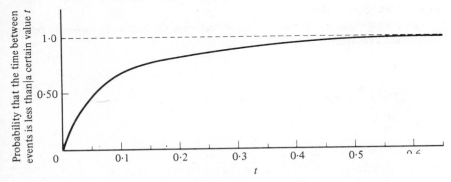

**Fig. 16.7** Exponential distribution

Where the distribution of a set of values equals the mean, it does not necessarily follow that the distribution is random. However, that is a reasonable assumption for the application of queueing practice to the level set out in this chapter.

Simple queueing calculations (see section 16.3) can be carried out on the assumptions that service times are exponential or constant. Most available queueing formulae assume exponential inter-arrival times (random). More complex formulae (see section 16.4) are available which take into account the observed standard deviation of service times. Thus, distributions that fall between exponential and constant can be more accurately handled. Many distributions in real time systems follow a distribution somewhere between random and constant.

When the precise distribution is not known and exponential distribution is assumed, the predictions are likely to be safe. The reader will see why later in the chapter.

## 16.3 Single-Server Queues

The single-server queue is the simplest case to which queueing theory can be applied. The queueing situation is represented diagrammatically in Fig. 16.1.

Queueing theory provides a method to project the characteristics of the queue, given:

$\bar{n}$ = average arrival rate,
$\bar{\sigma}_n$ = standard deviation of arrival rate,
$\bar{s}$ = average service time,
$\bar{\sigma}_s$ = standard deviation of service time.

The queueing characteristics can be projected in terms of $\bar{t}$, the average time in the queue, $\bar{q}$, the average queue length, and the distribution of $t$ and/or $q$.

It is a convenient first step in real time system design to quickly examine $s$ and decide whether it is constant. If not so (as is the most likely) the first evaluation can be on the conservative assumption that both $\bar{s}$ and $\bar{n}$ follow exponential distributions.

The average queue can then be calculated from the following formulae ($n$ and $s$ assumed exponential distributions):

$$- \rho = \bar{n}\bar{s};$$

$$- \bar{t} = \frac{\bar{s}}{1-\rho} = \frac{\bar{s}}{1-\bar{n}\bar{s}};$$

$$- \bar{q} \quad \frac{\rho}{1-\rho}.$$

## 16.3.1 APPLYING EXPONENTIAL DISTRIBUTION FORMULAE

The design steps in using these formulae are set out below. Sample values are included as illustrations, and are indicated by asterisks.

(1) Measure/predict general variations of $n$ with season and time of day. Select period for evaluation, remembering the definition of peak as discussed in section 16.1.3.
 *1300–1400 h daily.

(2) Measure/predict $\bar{n}$ over selected period.
 *$\bar{n}$ = 600 per minute with fluctuations.

(3) Measure or predict $\bar{s}$ over the same period, and decide whether $s$ is constant or variable.
 *$\bar{s}$ = 80 ms with fluctuations.

(4) Decide whether $\bar{s}$ is nearer constant or exponential.
 *exponential.

(5) Calculate $\rho = \bar{n}\bar{s}$, ensuring that units are adjusted to a common base of measurement (both units adjusted to seconds).

$$^*\rho = \frac{600}{60} \times \frac{80}{1000}$$
$$= 0.8$$

Check $\rho \leqslant 1$.

(6) Apply queueing formulae $t = \dfrac{\bar{s}}{1-\rho}$

$^*t = \dfrac{0 \cdot 080}{1 - 0 \cdot 8}$ s

$^*t = 0 \cdot 4$ s, i.e., average queueing time is $0 \cdot 4$ s.

At this stage, the designer will have forecast his average queue length (in seconds) but not yet know how sensitive is his design to minor changes in rates or service times, or how pessimistic is the use of the exponential formulae.

### 16.3.2 FACILITY UTILIZATION AND ITS EFFECT ON QUEUES

A quick inspection of the queueing formula $\bar{t} = \bar{s}/(1-\rho)$ shows how $t$ is dependent on $\rho$, particularly if the formula is rearranged as

$$\frac{\bar{t}}{\bar{s}} = \frac{1}{1-\rho}.$$

The re-arranged formula can be plotted in a service-time independent form as in Fig. 16.8.

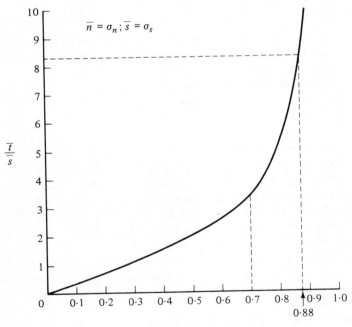

Facility utilization, $\rho$

**Fig. 16.8**  Single server queues

Inspection of the graph illustrates that the queueing time increases exponentially with $\rho$. For low $\rho$, the queue is relatively stable; that is to say, 10 per cent variation in $\rho$ has a minor effect on $\bar{t}$.

**293**

*Example*

$$\rho = 0 \cdot 1; \quad \frac{\bar{t}}{\bar{s}} = 1 \cdot 11,$$

$$\rho = 0 \cdot 11; \quad \frac{\bar{t}}{\bar{s}} = 1 \cdot 12 - \text{a 1 per cent increase in } \bar{t}/\bar{s}.$$

For high $\rho$, the queue is relatively unstable; that is, 10 per cent variation in $\rho$ can have a major effect on $\bar{t}$.

*Example*

$$\rho = 0 \cdot 80; \quad \frac{\bar{t}}{\bar{s}} = 5 \cdot 0,$$

$$\rho = 0 \cdot 88; \quad \frac{\bar{t}}{\bar{s}} = 8 \cdot 3 - \text{a 66 per cent increase in } \bar{t}/\bar{s}.$$

Those readers who wish can use the graph in Fig. 16.7 directly instead of using the formulae $\bar{t} = \bar{s}/(1 - \rho)$:

– calculate $\rho$;
– read $\bar{t}/\bar{s}$ from the curve for the appropriate value of $\rho$;
– multiply $\bar{t}/\bar{s}$ by $\bar{s}$ to determine $\bar{t}$.

At a simpler level, the designer can work, for initial design comparison, to a rule of thumb that '$\rho$ should be less than $0 \cdot 7$'. This rule of thumb directs the design to the more stable end of the curve.

The sensitivity of queue at high $\rho$ illustrates why the real time designers must resort to more detailed mathematical analysis, and/or simulation and/or more careful projections, of $\bar{n}$ and $\bar{s}$ if $\rho$ is high.

## 16.4 Non-exponential Distributions

While exponential distributions are a reasonable match for many of the practical real time distributions (message arrival rates, transmission time, etc.) and are reasonably safe assumptions, for other cases there are several occasions where the assumption is unnecessarily pessimistic, or occasionally optimistic. This is particularly the case when fluctuations, for some reason, are slight, i.e., the distribution is relatively constant, and at the same time the system or sub-system under study has a high facility utilization. Unnecessarily pessimistic predictions can lead to unnecessary design effort or hardware investment. (However, for many other reasons the more common error is underestimating, either in message arrival rates or in the service times.)

The single-server queueing formula $\bar{t} = \bar{s}/(1 - \rho)$ is derived from a more generalized formula, the theory for which was originally developed by Khintchine and Pollaczek. Their formulae for exponential inter-arrival times and any distribution of service times is

$$\bar{t}_q = \bar{s} + \frac{\rho \bar{s}}{2(1 - \rho)} \left[ 1 + \left( \frac{\sigma_s}{\bar{s}} \right)^2 \right],$$

where $\bar{t}_q(t)$ = average queueing time

$\bar{s}$ = average service time

$\rho$ = facility utilization

and $\sigma_s$ = the standard deviation of $s$.

In the case of exponential distribution of service time, i.e., where $\sigma_s = \bar{s}$, the formula can be seen to simplify to

$$\bar{t} = \bar{s}/(1 - \rho),$$

as already presented, and the corresponding formula for the average number in the queue, $\bar{q}$, simplifies, on putting $\sigma_s = \bar{s}$, to

$$\bar{q} = \rho/(1 - \rho).$$

In the case of constant service times, where $\sigma_s = 0$, the formulae simplify to

$$\bar{t} = \bar{s}\frac{(1 + \rho)}{2(1 - \rho)}$$

$$\bar{q} = \rho + \frac{\rho^2}{2(1 - \rho)}$$

In the more general case, where $\sigma_s \neq \bar{s}$ or $0$, the formula is complicated to use. However, its wide general usage has led to standard tables and graphs being produced, with $\bar{t}/\bar{s}$ plotted against $\rho$, as standard curves for various values of $\sigma_s/\bar{s}$. These curves are relatively simple to apply in practical situations, and are illustrated in Fig. 16.9.

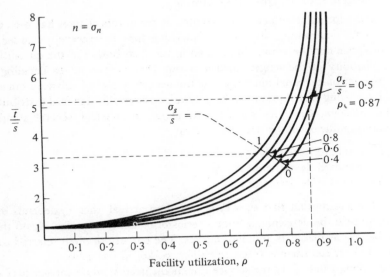

**Fig. 16.9**  Single server queueing

### 16.4.1 CALCULATION OF AVERAGE QUEUEING TIMES

The sequence of events to determine $\bar{t}$ is as follows:

 – determine $\bar{n}$, $\bar{s}$, $\rho$ and $\sigma_s$ and thus $\sigma_s/\bar{s}$;
 – select the curve (Fig. 16.10 or standard graphs) for $\sigma_s/\bar{s}$ nearest that determined above;
 – use the selected curve to read off $\bar{t}/\bar{s}$ for $\rho$;
 – multiply result by $\bar{s}$ to give $\bar{t}$.

*Example*

Consider a disk file sub-system.

$\bar{n}$ is 14 400 accesses per hour
$\bar{s}$ is 200 ms per file access
$\sigma_s$ is calculated to be 50 ms

Calculate $\sigma_s/\bar{s} = 0.25$.

$$\text{Calculate } \rho = \frac{14\ 000}{3600} \times \frac{200}{1000} = 0.8.$$

From graph, $\rho = 0.8$, $\sigma_s/\bar{s} = 0.25$, giving $\bar{t}/\bar{s} = 3.3$ (midpoint between two curves (0 and 0.4) selected).
Therefore $\bar{t} = 0.66$ s.

Had $\sigma_s$ been assumed to be equal to $\bar{s}$, then $\bar{t}$ would have been predicted as 1.0 s.

*Note.* the $\sigma_s/\bar{s} = 1$ curve is identical to the exponential server curve of Fig. 16.8.

## 16.5 Distribution of Queueing Times

Each of the formulae and curves presented so far in this chapter has been concerned with determining the average queueing time or average queue length. The designer may be equally interested in the distribution of the queue. It is the probability of the longer queues arising that is relevant to deciding on their impact on terminal operations or the necessary size of software queues.

The queueing distribution can be determined from the standard distribution of the queueing time. As we are now about to consider several standard deviations, suffices will be used as follows:

$\bar{\sigma}_s$ for standard deviation of $s$,
$\bar{\sigma}_n$ for standard deviation of $n$,
$\bar{\sigma}_t$ for standard deviation of $t$.

Given the assumption that $\sigma_n = \bar{n}$, i.e., random arrival, then $\bar{\sigma}_t$ depends on $\rho$ and $\bar{\sigma}_s$ and can be determined from a series of complex formulae. Again these formulae are available as standard curves. The curves are often referred to as Erlang 1, 2, 3, etc. (named often an earlier worker in the field).

The Erlang value, $E$, of the service time is the nearest whole integer to $(\bar{s}/\sigma_s)$. It takes the values 1 for exponentially distributed service times ($\bar{\sigma}_s = \bar{s}$), and $\infty$

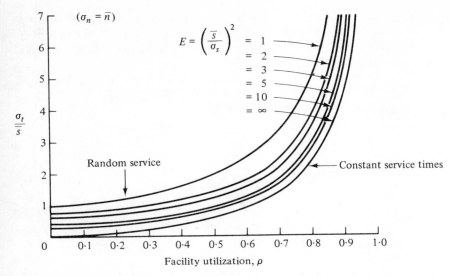

**Fig. 16.10**   Standard deviation of queueing times within single server queues

for constant service times ($\bar{\sigma}_s = 0$). Figure 16.10 illustrates typical Erlang curves.

### 16.5.1   CALCULATION OF $\bar{\sigma}_t$—STANDARD DEVIATION OF QUEUEING TIMES
The following steps are required to determine $\sigma_t$:

- determine $\bar{n}$, $\bar{s}$, $\rho, \lozenge_s$;
- calculate $\bar{s}/\sigma_s$ and select nearest integer;
- select appropriate Erlang curve and read off $\sigma_t/\bar{s}$ for the appropriate value of $\rho$;
- multiply result by $\bar{s}$ to give $\sigma_t$.

### 16.5.2   PREDICTING THE DISTRIBUTION OF QUEUEING TIME
Queueing theory predicts that the distribution of queueing times fits reasonably into a mathematically defined distribution called a gamma distribution. The exponential distribution defined earlier is a special case of the gamma function.

The objective of the designer is to determine what is the probability that the queueing time $t$ will be less than some target value, say $t'$. The Gamma distribution provides the answer from the formula

$$P(t \leqslant t') = \frac{\int_0^{t'} \left(\dfrac{Rt}{\bar{t}}\right)^{R-1} e^{-Rt/\bar{t}} \dfrac{R}{\bar{t}} d\bar{t}}{\int_0^{\infty} \left(\dfrac{Rt}{\bar{t}}\right)^{R-1} e^{-Rt/\bar{t}} \dfrac{R}{\bar{t}} d\bar{t}},$$

**297**

where $R = (\bar{t}/\sigma_t)^2$. Again, the formula is too complicated for convenient use in most real time design situations. Fortunately, it is also established as a series of standard curves that plot $P$ against $(t'/\bar{t})$ for various values of $R$. Figure 16.11 illustrates such a set of curves.

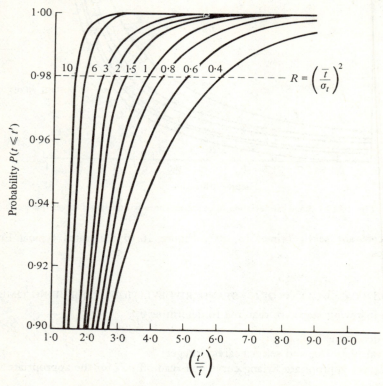

Fig. 16.11  Partial plot of the incomplete gamma function

### 16.5.3  APPLYING STANDARD DEVIATIONS

A real time designer will probably be carrying out his designs to meet target values for $t$ expressed as an average and a 'maximum' value. This 'maximum' is generally presented, as $P$ per cent of transactions should take less than $t'$ seconds (e.g., 95 per cent less than 10 s).

The steps to determine $P$ for a given queueing situation and given target $t'$ are therefore as follows:

– determine $\bar{n}$, $\bar{s}$, $\rho$, $\sigma_s$, $\bar{t}$, $\sigma_t$ (as described in section 16.5.1);
– calculate $R = (\bar{t}/\sigma_t)^2$;
– select gamma curve (e.g., Fig. 16.11) with nearest value to $R$;
– calculate $t'/\bar{t}$;
– use the selected curve to determine probability that $t$ is less than $t'$.

298

*Example*

$$\text{Let } \bar{t} = 2 \text{ s}, \quad t' = 6 \text{ s}, \quad \bar{\sigma}_t = 1 \text{ s}.$$

$$\text{Then } R = (2/1)^2 = 4, \quad \frac{t'}{\bar{t}} = \frac{6}{2} = 3.$$

From the incomplete gamma curve, $P = 0.995$. Therefore, 99.5 per cent of all demands on the server should be satisfied within 6 s.

As an example, let us consider the steps of sections 16.5.1 and 16.5.3 applied to an overall single-server real time system, e.g., central processor excluding line transmission and line queueing delays:

- $\bar{n}$ is given as 690 per minute;
- $\bar{s}$ and $\sigma_s$ are given as a sample of values of $s$;
- the target of $t'$ (central processor response) is 1.2 s;
- the values of $\bar{s}$ and calculation of $\sigma_s$ are as follows:

| $s$ (in ms) | $\bar{s} - s$ | $(\bar{s} - s)^2$ |
|---|---|---|
| 20 | −56 | 3136 |
| 40 | −36 | 1296 |
| 30 | −46 | 2116 |
| 80 | 4 | 16 |
| 150 | 74 | 5476 |
| 120 | 44 | 1936 |
| 90 | 14 | 196 |
| 110 | 34 | 1156 |
| 70 | −6 | 36 |
| 50 | −26 | 676 |
| 760 | | 16 040 |

$\bar{s} = 76$ s $\qquad \dfrac{(\bar{s} - s)^2}{N} = 1604;$

$\sigma_s = \sqrt{1604} = 40.05$—approximately 40;

$\rho = \bar{n}\bar{s} = \dfrac{690}{60} \times \dfrac{76}{1000} = 0.87$

$\left(\dfrac{s}{\sigma_s}\right) = \dfrac{76}{40} = 1.9 = 2$ to nearest integer;

Erlang 2, $\rho = 0.87$, therefore $(\sigma_t/\bar{s}) = 5.4$—(using Fig. 16.10);

$\sigma_t = 5.4 \times \bar{s} = 410$ ms;

using $\rho = 0.87$ and $(\sigma_s/\bar{s}) = $ approx 0.5;

$\dfrac{\bar{t}}{\bar{s}} = 5.2$—(using Fig. 16.9);

$\bar{t} = 5.2 \times \bar{s} = 395$ ms;

$R = \left(\dfrac{\bar{t}}{\sigma_t}\right) = 0.92;$

$\dfrac{t'}{\bar{t}} = \dfrac{1.2}{0.395} = 3;$

– The Gamma curve (Fig. 16.11) gives 95 per cent of transactions having a queueing time $t$ of $1 \cdot 2$ s or less, i.e., $\bar{t} = 0 \cdot 4$ s; 95 per cent are processed within $1 \cdot 2$ s.

## 16.6   Multi-server Single Queue Model

A multi-server single queue model is one where more than one independent identical server is available to serve any member of the queue. The front member of the queue is served by the first available server.

In the airline example at the beginning of this chapter, if 2 or more identical check-in desks were provided, a multi-server queueing model would apply. The model could be in question if check-in clerks shared a common reservation checking terminal.

Separate first class and tourist check-in desks do not correspond with this model, as all travellers cannot go to either counter. Rather, it is two parallel single servers if first and tourist classes are independent.

In real time systems, the multi-server single queue model may apply for terminal operators serving, say, telephone orders (callers queued at the switchboard and mutual interference from common real time system considered slight). A multi-server single queueing model will usually not apply with multi-disk drives. Any one file access can generally only be satisfied by one disk. This corresponds more to a parallel single-server situation, but if the disks share a control unit, the model is more complex (see chapter 15). The multi-server model is represented in Fig. 16.12.

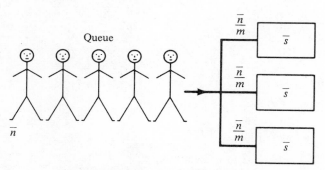

**Fig. 16.12**   Multi-server queueing

In the multi-server case, the following parameters apply:

$\bar{n}$ = average message rate,
$M$ = number of servers,
$\bar{s}$ = average service time.

If there is only 1 server, $\rho = \bar{n}\bar{s}$, but as there are $M$ servers each sharing the load equally on average,

$$\rho = \bar{n}\bar{s}/M.$$

**300**

The value for $\bar{t}$ in a multi-server situation can be determined by the solution of further complex equations or the further use of standard curves as in Fig. 16.13; $M = 1$ is the now familiar single-server curve.

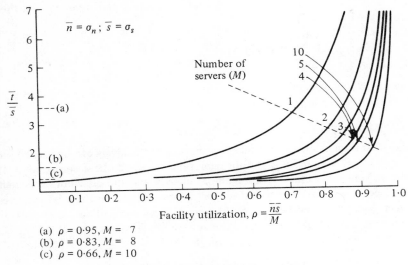

(a) $\rho = 0.95$, $M = 7$
(b) $\rho = 0.83$, $M = 8$
(c) $\rho = 0.66$, $M = 10$

**Fig. 16.13**   Multi-server queueing times

Figure 16.13 is based on exponential distribution of service times and arrival rates. Inspection of the curves will illustrate that multi-servers are less likely to have queues for a given individual load than a similar number of parallel single-servers.

### 16.6.1   APPLICATION OF MULTI-SERVER FORMULAE

Multi-server formulae are often applied in the context, 'given certain $\bar{n}$, $\bar{s}$, how many servers do I need?'
The procedure is as follows:

(1) determine $\bar{n}\bar{s}$ and target $\bar{t}$;
(2) calculate $\bar{n}\bar{s}$;
(3) select minimum $M$ so that $\bar{n}\bar{s}/M = \rho < 1$;
(4) select curve for $M$ and abstract $\bar{t}/\bar{s}$ for given $\rho$;
(5) multiply result by $\bar{s}$ to determine $\bar{t}$;
(6) if $\bar{t}$ is too high, increase $M$ by 1 and repeat from step 4.

*Example*
How many terminals are needed in the head office, given the following:

$\bar{n} = 200$ transactions per hour
$\bar{s} = 120$ seconds per transaction

$\bar{t}$ target is 3 minutes (1 minute waiting; 2 being served)?

$$\bar{n}\bar{s} = \frac{200}{60} \times 2 = 6 \cdot 66 \text{ (common time unit is minutes);}$$

If $M = 7$, $\rho = 0 \cdot 95$;

for $M = 7$, $\rho = 0 \cdot 95$, $(\bar{t}/\bar{s}) = 3 \cdot 6$ (taken from more detailed versions of the curves in Fig. 16.12);

$\bar{t} = 3 \cdot 6 \, \bar{s} = 7 \cdot 2$ min;

For $M = 8$, $\rho = 0 \cdot 83$, $(\bar{t}/\bar{s}) = 1 \cdot 5$;

$\bar{t} = 1 \cdot 5 \times \bar{s} = 3$ min.

Thus, for $M = 8$ servers, $\bar{t}$ is 3 min and
$\qquad M = 7$ servers, $\bar{t}$ is $7 \cdot 2$ min.

### 16.6.2 MULTI-SERVERS AND QUEUEING TIME

The distribution of queueing times for multi-server analysis can be carried out as for single-servers. As a first approximation, $\bar{t} = \sigma_t$ can be assumed ($R = 1$). In the example in section 16.6.1 while $\bar{t} = 3$ min and the distribution is such that 65 per cent can be expected within 3 min, 20 per cent can be expected between 3 and 6 min and 10 per cent between 6 and 9 min. Thus, if 95 per cent within, say, 7 min were the target, the system would not succeed.

In that case, the designer could work in reverse:

criterion 95 per cent within 7 min; $R = 1$ and 95 per cent give

$$\left(\frac{t'}{\bar{t}}\right) = 3 \quad \text{(gamma curves),}$$

Therefore
$$\bar{t} = t'/3 = 7/3 = 2 \cdot 3 \text{ min;}$$

$$\frac{\bar{t}}{\bar{s}} = \frac{2 \cdot 3}{2} = 1 \cdot 15;$$

If
$$M = 10, \rho = 0 \cdot 66, \text{ then } (\bar{t}/\bar{s}) = 1 \cdot 1;$$

thus, working forwards, $\bar{t} = 2 \cdot 2$ min, and as $R = 3$, the 95 per cent certainty is at $6 \cdot 6$ min. Thus, the designer choosing 10 servers would meet his criterion with average queueing time of $2 \cdot 2$ min and 95 per cent under 7 min. The reader may wish to check out the effect with 9 servers.

The notes below on 'limitations' particularly apply to this analysis.

## 16.7 Limitations of Queueing Theory

The predictions of queueing theory are based on a mathematical model, and the assumption that the message rates and service disciplines reasonably obey the rules of that model. Equally, the predictions depend on the accuracy of the input data on $\bar{s}$ and $\bar{n}$ and $\sigma_s$.

Regrettably, the more significant the projections (i.e., the more heavily loaded the system) and the more sensitive the results, the more prone the analysis is to be invalidated by actual real time systems performance.

Therefore, queueing theory and practice should be treated as follows:

(1) Apply queueing practice for first performance prediction and evaluation of designs.
(2) If the performance on selected designs is sensitive or marginally overloaded, then apply thorough mathematical analysis with good understanding of queueing theory. Standard curves still may be used if sufficiently detailed.
(3) Unless utilizations are light, check out the final design with suitable simulations or other modelling techniques.
(4) Even if easy to use, and sophisticated models are available, still use queueing theory including extension beyond that described in this chapter in preparation for modelling. Queueing analysis gives the designer an appreciation of the sensitivity of the potential changes in design, while *good* simulation is better at measuring the projected performance of the design as stated to the simulation model.
(5) Both good simulation models and good application of queueing theory models are subject to risk from:

– errors in input data;
– errors in defining the service mechanism and inter-queue relationships.

For readers interested in further study of queueing theory see Saaty, T. L. (1961), *Elements of Queuing Theory*, McGraw-Hill, New York and Lee, A. M. (1966), *Applied Queuing Theory*, MacMillan, London.

# 17. Data Transmission

In configuring terminal networks, as mentioned in chapter 10, the designer meets with a whole new set of jargon. This is the language of data transmission, and on first acquaintance it can be very confusing. Sometimes it is necessary to understand what this language is describing in order to achieve the right combination of hardware. At other times this understanding is not essential to pursue the job in hand, but it is difficult to decide that this is the case without some familiarity with the terms.

This chapter gives a simple introduction to the subject, so that a designer will be able to appreciate the technicalities of transmission techniques. A great deal of investigation at a very detailed level is required in getting the network configuration right; for example, in providing for attachment of terminals via the switched network following a dedicated line failure. In designing his system, the designer needs to know about two- and four-wire lines, synchronous and asynchronous transmission, line switching facilities, the characteristics of modems, and the standby provision and the way it is controlled by the terminals. Without a grounding in data transmission techniques, aspects of design like this are not possible.

In this chapter, the basics of data transmission are first considered. Following this, noise, and the means of dealing with consequent errors, are discussed. Lines and modems are then described; and the facilities offered by the British Post Office and several national common carriers are related to the techniques discussed in the chapter. Finally, a brief summary of line facilities in some other European countries is given.

## 17.1 Data Transmission Basics

As in the main computer, all transmitted data are represented by binary codes. This section looks at the codes used and the various techniques employed to transfer these codes across the lines.

### 17.1.1 CODES

There are several standard codes employed for transmission. The most commonly used are:

- ISO 7, Seven bit code (also known as CCITT Alphabet No. 5);

- ASCII, which is almost identical to the above;
- EBCDIC, eight bit code;
- CCITT Alphabet No. 2, five bit code (also known as Baudot code).

A seven level code, giving 128 combinations, is the minimum desirable for most commercial data transmission requirements, particularly since upper and lower case alphabetic characters are now commonly used.

In any of the codes, a sub-set of these characters is set aside for control purposes. These characters are given conventional mnemonics. Examples from the ISO 7 Code are,

STX – 'Start of text'.

ETX – 'End of text'.

ETB – 'End of a transmitted block' of text where the text is sub-divided into conveniently smaller sections for transmission purposes.

SOH – 'Start of heading' which contains routing or program control information for a following text.

EOT – 'End of transmission' which restores the connection to a quiescent state and may even cause actual termination in some simple systems.

ACK – 'Acknowledge' which is returned to inform that a text or a block of text has been correctly received, or a message is available for transmission.

NAK – 'Negative acknowledge' which is the opposite of ACK.

ENQ – 'Enquire' which is used to seek a response from the opposite end of the link before data flow commences. It can be prefixed by a number of address characters to define which station should answer in a multipoint system. This feature is referred to as 'polling'.

SYN – 'Synchronizing' character which can be inserted at any time prior to or during a transmission to fill idle periods, obtain synchronism or maintain synchronism. It is rarely transferred out of the receiving terminal.

DLE – 'Data link escape' which alters the meaning of characters which follow it and therefore offers an extension of the transmission control character set if required.

There are other control characters used for individual device control, such as HT, which causes horizontal tabulation.

More recent data link control systems (such as IBM, SDLC) replace the concept of control characters by bit settings. The control functions have predefined bit positions and combinations which each have a significance analogous to that of a single control character.

Most transmission links are only capable of transmitting one bit at a time, so the bits forming a character are sent serially. This contrasts to data transfers within the main computer, where sufficient paths are provided to transmit all the bits for a character at the same time from one part of the computer to another.

## 17.1.2 TIMING TECHNIQUES

The transmission of the bit train usually employs some timing method. This is not absolutely necessary (Fig. 17.1), since, if there were a rest condition between every bit, a receiver could decode reliably. However, the transmission would be slowed considerably because of the time taken in the rest condition. If this overhead is removed, some timing extraction is required to enable adjacent bits of the same value to be distinguished from each other. There are two common timing methods known as synchronous and asynchronous (see Fig. 17.1).

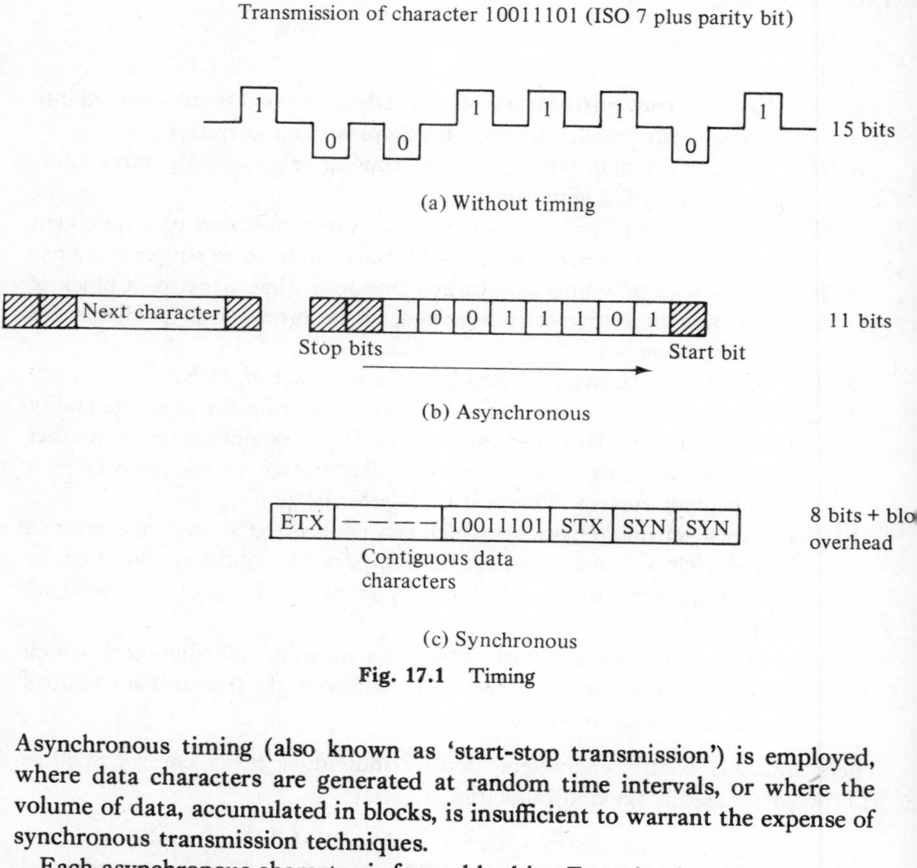

Transmission of character 10011101 (ISO 7 plus parity bit)

(a) Without timing

(b) Asynchronous

(c) Synchronous

**Fig. 17.1**  Timing

Asynchronous timing (also known as 'start-stop transmission') is employed, where data characters are generated at random time intervals, or where the volume of data, accumulated in blocks, is insufficient to warrant the expense of synchronous transmission techniques.

Each asynchronous character is framed by bits. For teleprinters there is one 'zero' bit preceding the character, which is followed by two 'one' bits. The start bit (0) triggers the timing mechanism, which then counts off the succeeding bits of the character, using a fixed time interval. The stop bits reset the line and receiver ready for the next character. Since a maximum of 8 bits are to be counted, the timing does not have to be extremely accurate. The bit framing overhead is reduced in some systems since only one stop bit is employed.

The synchronous method omits the bits framing individual characters, and

**306**

sends a contiguous stream of data characters as a block. Since a long stream of bits is sent, the timing circuits in the receiver which cause the line condition to be sensed after each bit interval need to be both accurate and capable of being dynamically adjusted for small changes in their performance or in actual transmission rate. The codes are often arranged so that there is at least one change of binary state within each transmitted character, or, at least, a change is caused within the time period during which the transmitter and receiver are designed to stay synchronous without adjustment. Since such a change of state is, by definition, an integral number of bit intervals since the last, the receivers can use this fact to calculate what the precise bit rate is at any time. The timing can thus be dynamically adjusted to allow for any drift in the transmitting rate. To enable bit synchronization to be established in this way, a message is preceded by a number of synchronization characters before the data are sent (Fig. 17.1). Thus bit synchronization is reliably established before data are read from the line. These synchronization characters (SYN in the ISO 7 code) are also used to establish character synchronization. The receiver by matching received bit sequences successfully against the fixed bit pattern expected for the synchronization characters, detects a match after all bits of one of these characters have been received. The next bit to be received is thus identified as the first bit of a valid character. After character synchronization is established in this way, character boundaries are identified thereafter by counting off bits according to the number per character appropriate for the system.

Synchronous transmission is more economic of line time than asynchronous for more than a few characters per block.

### 17.1.3  BIT REPRESENTATIONS ON LINES

The 'zero' and 'one' conditions are physically represented on lines in a variety of ways. The basic techniques are discussed below.

#### Unmodulated Transmission

In this technique, some physical condition on the line which may be set to two discrete levels is used to represent the binary conditions. Two possibilities are voltage and current. Figure 17.2 illustrates the transmission of a character using two voltage conditions. The appropriate voltage is applied to the line for the required number of bit intervals. In the example, if transmission were at 100 bits/second the +80 V level would be held for 0.03 s to represent the three consecutive zero bits. The same principle would apply for a system signalling by means of current. In this case, the binary conditions might be 0 and 20 mA.

#### Modulated Transmission

A basic carrier frequency, or tone, is switched between two states to represent the binary conditions. Two generic forms of modulation are used—analogue and pulse (digital).

Figure 17.2 illustrates the three basic analogue methods. In amplitude modulation the carrier frequency is either sent at full amplitude, or not at all, to represent the two conditions. In frequency modulation, the transmission is, in effect, switched between two frequencies, depending on the bit condition being sent. For phase modulation, the same frequency is sent throughout at constant amplitude, but where a transition from one state to the other occurs, a segment of the wave-form is in effect omitted. In the example in Fig. 17.2, it can be seen that $1\frac{1}{2}$ cycles of carrier have been sent for the one condition. At the time of the change to the zero condition, instead of completing the other half cycle, the positive-going part of the sine-wave is re-initiated.

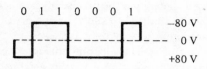

Unmodulated transmission

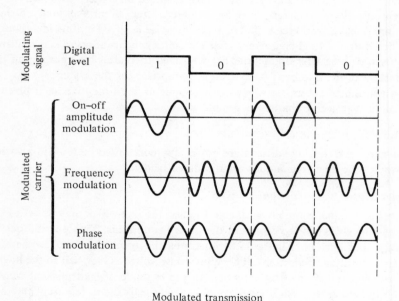

Modulated transmission

**Fig. 17.2** Physical bit representation

For the first two techniques, the appropriate modulation state is maintained for the time required to represent the number of bits of that state in sequence being sent. The phase modulation technique is different, in that only information relating to changes of state is sent. In between such changes, there is a common condition. Thus the number of like bits in sequence has to be inferred by the receiving equipment. In any of the systems, the remote end of the line

**308**

complementary equipment detects the modulations and converts back to a simple binary square wave-form.

There are several possible pulse modulation techniques available, but the one most relevant to data transmission discussion is pulse code modulation (PCM). Figure 17.3 illustrates this in outline. The first wave-form represents the original to be coded.

The signal is first quantized, i.e., reduced to a limited set of specific values (in the example this is restricted to range from one to six). When quantized, the signal is then sampled at a fixed rate. The sampling rate depends on the highest frequency to be transmitted. Communications theory shows that if the highest frequency to be transmitted is $X$ Hz, then a sampling rate of twice this frequency is sufficient to allow the signal to be reconstructed at the receiver. After sampling, the signal is coded. In the example shown, as no more than eight levels are in use, three

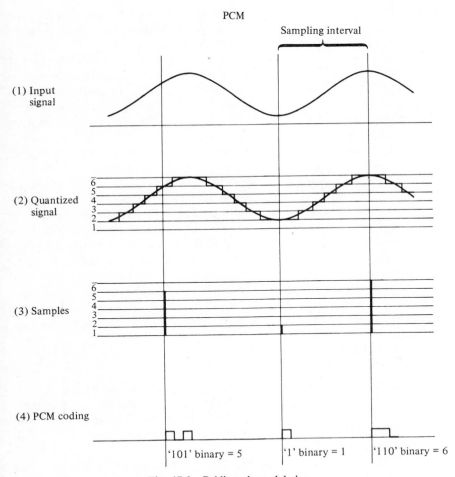

**Fig. 17.3** Public code modulation

bits are sufficient to code all possible values. The resulting stream of binary pulses is a pulse code modulated signal.

In conventional systems 128 or 256 quantized levels are used (128 gives quality comparable to a good analogue telephone line). PCM is discussed further in relation to multiplexing techniques.

### 17.1.4 MULTIPLEXING

Multiplexing describes any techniques which allows several logical channels to occupy one physical channel. Two major forms are used. These are frequency division multiplexing (FDM), and time division multiplexing (TDM), and are discussed in the following paragraphs.

*Frequency Division Multiplexing*

In the previous section, in discussing frequency modulation, it was implicit that only one data channel was provided. One pair of frequencies is used to represent the binary conditions of the data in this single channel.

However, equipment is available which will operate with multiple pairs of frequencies. One pair is used for each data channel to be sent. Since the pairs of frequencies are different in each channel, it is possible to send the separate streams of data in parallel. The equipment at the receiving end is able to filter out the modulation of a single pair of frequencies, for one data channel, from the signals being utilized for the other channels.

With multiple frequencies, it becomes more difficult to discriminate reliably between them the greater the number in use. To achieve reliability of decoding, the speed of each sub-channel must be limited to a fraction of the speed achievable in the physical channel (or line) used with simple frequency modulation. Thus, a telephone line capable of sending a single data stream at 1200 bits/second or above, when used to transmit 12 sub-channels, each with its own pair of frequencies, will be limited to 100 bits/second, per sub-channel.

In some equipment, this frequency division multiplexing is used to divide up the line into two channels, one for data, and the other for return supervisory signals. In this case, the main data channel rate is unaffected if the control sub-channel is slow by comparison. In one such system, data are transmitted at 1200 bits/second, and simultaneously supervisory signals at 75 bits/second are received.

*Time Division Multiplexing*

In this form, the available time is divided up into slots and each input signal is given a slot in a regular sequence. Each signal item occupies the channel completely for the duration of that slot. PCM techniques are normally used with TDM systems. Figure 17.4 shows two signals (similar to those in Fig. 17.3) being combined in a TDM system.

The input signals are first quantized and then sampled in sequence. The resulting samples are combined sequentially (signal 1, signal 2, signal 1, etc., in

310

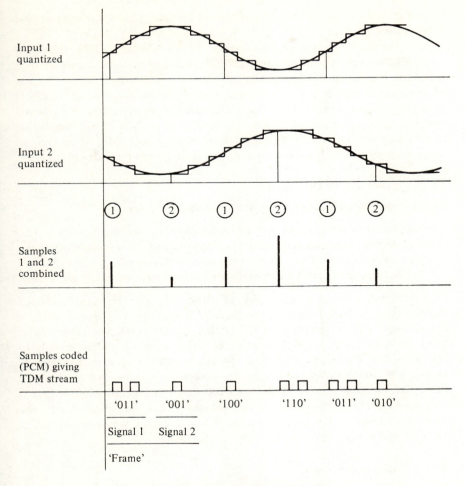

Input 1
quantized

Input 2
quantized

Samples
1 and 2
combined

① ② ① ② ① ②

Samples coded
(PCM) giving
TDM stream

'011'    '001'    '100'    '110'    '011'    '010'

Signal 1    Signal 2

'Frame'

**Fig. 17.4**   Time division multiplexing

the example shown). The resulting stream is then coded using PCM techniques
to give the pulse stream shown in the lower diagram. The result is a series of
'frames' each of 6 bits, which covers the complete cycle of samples (in this case
two). Systems currently in use are much more complex. The two most
widespread are Bell T1 and the CCITT System.

Bell T1 multiplexes 24 voice channels using 7 bit code (i.e., 128 levels). Each
frame consists of 193 bits, $24 \times 8$ (7 data + 1 supervisory) + 1 framing bit. As
the maximum frequency to be sent is 4000 Hz per channel this gives an overall
bit rate of $193 \times 8000 = 1\ 544\ 000$ bits/second. This system has also been used
by the UK PO, and other common carriers.

The CCITT system uses 30 voice channels and two supervisory channels.

**311**

Eight-bit code is used. This gives an overall bit rate of 2 048 000 bits/second (8000 × 32 × 8).

From the preceding, the obvious feature of both PCM and TDM techniques is their heavy use of band-width relative to analogue systems. However they are much less susceptible than analogue systems to interference, in that the use of repeaters at regular intervals to regenerate pulses reduces distortion effects to negligible proportions. Also, line termination costs are lower with digital systems. Although complex circuitry is needed, it is cheaper for comparable quality than in the case of analogue modulation. Finally, digital techniques make it easier to multiplex data, voice, vision, etc., over the same channel.

### 17.1.5 TYPES OF TRANSMISSION

Three basic types of transmission are possible. These are:

- simplex or one-way; data may be transmitted in only one direction;
- half duplex; data may be sent in one direction, and the transmitting facility then set to allow transmission in the reverse direction to take place;
- full duplex; data may be transmitted in both directions at the same time.

The possibility of achieving any of these depends on the combined characteristics of the terminal, modems (if required), and lines. Often, a transmission link is described as full duplex because it has the capability to transmit in both directions. However, the terminal connected might only be capable of half duplex operation. The operator is either sending data previously keyed, or receiving a response to a previous message—but not both at the same time. The significance of the full duplex transmission capability in this case is that since data in the two directions are actually sent down different paths, the time delay associated with turning round a half duplex transmission link is avoided, and a somewhat smaller delay is substituted.

## 17.2  Noise and Errors

Data transmitted over lines is subject to interference from various sources, and some means of detection and correction of resultant errors is necessary. This interference is normally referred to as noise.

### 17.2.1 NOISE

Noise on lines is of two types; background mush or 'white noise', and impulsive noise. The first is normally of a low level and, except for long intercontinental connections, is normally insignificant. The second arises from dialling pulses and switching in exchanges. Pulses on one circuit can induce noise pulses in adjacent circuits even if dedicated to data traffic.

The effect of impulsive noise on a data stream depends on the power level of the signal transmitting the data. The higher the power, the greater the signal-to-noise ratio, and the receiver can more readily separate the data pulses from noise. But, particularly on telephone lines, there is a relatively low limit to

312

signal power, since otherwise overloading of the line equipment would occur. Hence a significant number of errors do occur and must be dealt with.

Another source of interference is echoes of the data signal. Each time a line is connected into another, unless they are perfectly matched, an echo of the signal is reflected back. In an optical analogy, this boundary is like a partially reflecting window. Rays of light hitting it are transmitted through, but a small proportion of the energy of the beam is reflected back in the opposite direction. Echoes are dealt with by setting up the links in the first place to prevent these reflections from becoming serious in their effect. The number of connections between circuits is strictly limited. This is one reason why the star-network for multidrop lines (see chapter 10) is preferred to the alternative system, which has the main line connected to spur lines at many exchanges.

Exact figures for the incidence of noise are rarely quoted by common carrier services. One reason is that experience varies from circuit to circuit, and the equipment using it. Independent measurements on telephone lines have indicated that the range is very variable. Some examples are:

- a poor switched connection ; 1 bit in $10^3$;
- a typical leased line     ; 1 bit in $10^4/10^5$;
- a good leased line       ; 1 bit in $10^6$.

The noise pulses are not uniformly distributed, but come in bursts, since the sources of noise, such as dialling pulses, are themselves in groups. This means that the effect of noise on transmission is less than would be expected. With the worst example (1 in $10^3$), if blocks of $10^3$ bits were being transmitted, on average an error would be expected in each block. Hence, very few data would ever be successfully transmitted. In practice, however, a number of error free blocks might be successfully sent, followed by one which had a group of several errors within it.

Error rates are proportional to general traffic on the networks, and so, for instance, are higher in the mornings than afternoons.

## 17.2.2 DETECTION AND CORRECTION OF ERRORS

In many transmission systems, facilities are provided to detect, and correct, errors induced by line noise. No system is perfect in doing this, but those with tightest control reduce the undetected error rate to negligible proportions. For example, a line with an intrinsic error rate of 1 bit in $10^5$, with a good error detection system, causes an undetected error rate of the order of 1 bit in $10^9$. The detected errors typically give rise to a re-transmission, under hardware, software, or operator control, or any combination of these. The undetected errors are fed through to the terminal or computer, depending on the direction of data. If further data validation checks are carried out, many of the undetected errors are picked up. The proportion of communications-induced errors remaining undetected in a typical system would be negligible compared with human induced data errors, even if there were no data validation.

Various techniques are used for error detection. Examples are character parity, character plus block parity (two co-ordinate error checking), cyclic parity, and character return transmission (echo checking).

In character parity, an additional bit is added to the character before sending by the transmitter. The rule followed could be, for example, to make the total number of one bits even. On reception, the parity bit setting is predicted by the receiver, using the same rule on the data bits actually received, and compared to the received parity bit. This check detects some errors, but others, such as two bits having been corrupted to the opposite sense, is not discovered, since the predicted parity bit is the same as that sent. To further increase the success of error detection, a block check character can be added. This character appears at the end of the message, and each bit in this character is generated by a similar rule to the character parity system. The first bit in the check character is set according to the number of one bits in the first bit position of each character, and so on for the other bits. Figure 17.5 illustrates this technique. In this case, for instance, if a double bit transposition occurs within one character, which is therefore undetected by the character parity check, two other bits in corresponding positions in another character also have to be inverted to defeat the block parity check.

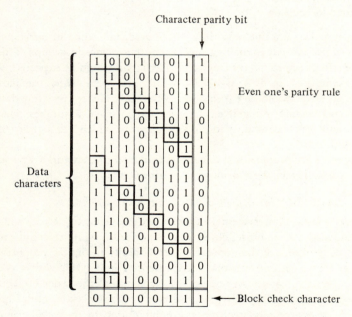

**Fig. 17.5**  Two coordinate parity checking

In cyclic parity checking no character parity bits are used, but one or more cyclic block checking characters are generated by accumulating the number of ones in a pattern traced diagonally down the block. In Fig. 17.4 the bit positions shown in hard outline could be used to create one parity bit in such a

**314**

cyclic block checking character. The adjacent diagonal would then be used to generate the second parity bit, and so on.

Character return transmission may be used for terminals having limited parity checking. The terminal is connected to a full duplex link, e.g., three-wire telegraph line. Characters keyed are transmitted up one path in the line and, as well as being taken into the computer, are reflected back to the terminal by the communications controller, where they are printed. Thus, if an operator sees a character printed as he intended, there is a very high probability that the same character was received at the computer.

## 17.3  Data Transmission Hardware

The physical facilities employed between the terminals and communication controllers are described in this section, and related to the techniques so far considered. These facilities are the lines, and, if necessary, modems.

### 17.3.1  LINES

There are three types of line available. These are:

- telegraph lines;
- telephone lines;
- wideband lines.

Although they appear in the appropriate physical form at the user's premises, the PTT often multiplexes the slower lines together in a higher speed channel. Thus, if a telephone line is being used, it may, over much of its route, actually be using part of a wide-band line.

### Telegraph Lines

Telegraph lines use unmodulated signalling, and thus modems are not required. Data bits are transmitted as voltage or current square waves, as described in section 17.1.3. The lines have a narrow bandwidth (i.e., low capacity for information transmission; bandwidth is approximately 170 Hz). This limitation means that the high frequency elements required to produce the sharp corners of these square waves are rapidly degraded (attenuated and distorted) as the signal passes down the line. To prevent this degradation reaching serious proportions, which would make it impossible to decode the bit information at the receiver reliably, two courses of action are necessary. First, the signal is regenerated by equipment provided by the PTT at regular intervals down the line and second, the speed is limited so that the degradation affects only a small proportion of the duration of the signal levels transmitted—the rounded corners, so to speak, do not meet. For example, in the UK, the speed is limited to 110 bits/second maximum.

Telegraph lines, if leased, may be connected into the user's premises as a three-wire line—one common, and the other two available for independent data traffic. This provides the capability for full duplex transmission, and is used, for example, to achieve character return transmission error checking (see section 17.2.2).

Many PTTs do not provide multi-drop telegraph lines (e.g., in UK). In these cases, line sharing is best achieved by using channelizers (see section 10.4.3). This technique uses a telephone line, which has a much greater bandwidth than a telegraph line, the former being divided into a number of sub-channels using frequency division multiplexing (see section 17.1.4). For normal quality telephone lines, and telegraph transmission at 110 bits/second, a maximum of 12 sub-channels can be provided down one telephone line in this way. Multi-drop telegraph lines (narrow band) are used in the USA, for example, where the timing disadvantage arising from use of unbuffered terminals is outweighed by cost saving. The delays caused by a terminal requiring the line for the time of keying a complete message can be reduced by using buffer storage, electronic or via paper tape, local to each terminal.

On telephone lines, modulated signalling is used. For a simple transmission link, a pair of modems, one at each end of the line, is required. Data bits are represented as modulations of frequency, amplitude, or phase, as described in section 17.1.3. The bandwidth of a typical good quality telephone line is of the order of 4000 Hz. As a result of this, the signal degradation is much less severe than for telegraph lines, and much higher rates of transmission can be achieved. Up to 9600 bits/second is achievable, but the limitation arises from the effect of both line and modem characteristics acting together.

A telephone line is normally connected from exchange to user's premises as a two-wire line (this part of the line is known as an exchange line). A two-wire line with simple binary modulation allows only one way or half duplex transmission. However, telephone lines normally have four wires between exchanges, so, for a moderate extra cost, four-wire presentation at the user's premises can be provided. This gives the facility for full duplex transmission, since there are then two independent two wire systems. Although occasionally used for simultaneous transmission of data to and from a terminal, this facility is more frequently used to reduce the modem turn-round time required in the case of half duplex transmission—data only being sent in one direction at a time.

Frequency division multiplexing, and other forms of line sharing, can be used to provide more than one channel of data transmission even within a two-wire line. If four pairs of frequencies are used, for example, then a full duplex capability is obtained (as for the Datel 200 Service of the UK Post Office).

Multi-dropping of telephone lines is possible in many countries. A single line connected between exchanges is provided with spur connections from the exchanges to a modem at each terminal location. The configuration considerations for such lines are dealt with in chapter 10.

For speeds up to 1200 bits/second, a normal voice grade telephone line is adequate in most countries. For higher speeds, some upgrading of the standard lines is normally required, although increasingly in the more technically advanced countries speeds of 2400 bits/second are possible. The attenuation of frequencies at the high and low ends of the spectrum is reduced. The loss of

**316**

signal at any frequency caused by its passage down the line is improved, and the tendency for different frequencies to travel at differing speeds down the line is also reduced. These changes make transmission at higher speeds much more reliable.

Switched connections are usually more error prone due to the number of temporary connections required in the link. As a consequence, speeds are limited to 1200 bits/second, although on certain routes, reliable operation at 2400 bits/second is possible. A further limitation of switched connections is that certain parts of the otherwise available frequency spectrum are dedicated for trunk signalling purposes. This means that some equipment that is satisfactory on a leased line, cannot be used on switched lines, even for stand-by purposes. The channelizers already discussed suffer from this limitation.

*Wideband Lines*

These circuits are accomplished by the PTT either by micro-wave transmission between transmission towers, or by special coaxial cables. The data rates achievable are 48 000 bits/second, or greater, depending on the bandwidth and modems used. These links are normally used for fast transmission of large bulks of data, although in principle they could be used for channels of data from 12 normal telephone lines in an analogous manner to telegraph channelizing. In the UK PO, facilities limit use to transmission of a single data stream at the rate of 48 000 bits/second. Because of the use of special coaxial cables, installation costs are very high; consequently such links are outside the scope of the typical commercial installation.

17.3.2 MODEMS

Modems are used on telephone lines:

- to modulate a carrier to transmit a digital signal at the transmitting end;
- to demodulate the transmitted signal at the receiving end, and pass it on to the equipment connected, represented again as a simple binary voltage pattern.

Hence the name arises from *MO*dulator and *DEM*odulator. Usually modems are designed to transmit data both ways, although modems are available which only transmit in a single direction.

A modem designed for use at speeds up to 1200 bits/second uses simple two-state frequency modulation. The Datel Modem 1 from the UK PO uses frequencies as follows. At 600 bits/second: 1300 Hz (1), and 1700 Hz (0). At 1200 bits/second the zero condition is represented by 2100 Hz.

At speeds of 2400 bits/second, typically phase modulation is used, as for example in the PO Datel Modem No. 7. In this case, the transmission link is actually capable of representing four states. These states are represented by phase changes of 0°, 90°, 180°, and 270°. In other words, a jump in the wave-form of $0, \frac{1}{4}, \frac{1}{2}$, and $\frac{3}{4}$ of a cycle occurs, respectively. The change can occur at the rate of

**317**

1200 times per second. However, since there are now four possible line conditions, each may be used to represent two bits of data. Data are divided up, as they are received by the modem, into groups of two bits. The four possible combinations (dibits) are:

- 00    0°;
- 01   -90°;
- 11  -180°;
- 10  -270°;

and the phase change used to represent them is given alongside. The receiving modem interprets the phase changes, and recreates a normal bit stream for delivery to the attached equipment. Because of this doubling up of bits, the effective data rate is 2400 bits/second (twice the transition rate on the line—the transition rate is 1200 per second, or 1200 baud. Sometimes, erroneously, baud is used synonymously with bit/second). Although initially provided only for working on leased lines, the full rate of 2400 bits/second is achievable over some routes using the normal switched network.

The modems at each end of a link have to be synchronized for this type of transmission. Timing information may be transmitted over a separate channel, or derived from the transitions in the incoming data stream. This synchronization is necessary for the operation of the modem, and is distinct from the timing techniques described in section 17.1.2. Using UK PO equipment as an example, a Datel Modem No. 1 is an asynchronous modem (i.e., it has no timing circuits built into the modem), but it is still capable of sending a synchronous data stream. The latter use of the word synchronous refers to the fact that the receiver requires to carry out the form of timing extraction which identifies character boundaries.

Modems working at speeds of greater than 2400 bits/second often use techniques which are more complex than four level phase modulation, to increase the rate of data transmission.

Modems provided by many PTTs (e.g., the UK PO), whether or not used on leased lines, are required to have a telephone hand-set connected to them. The handset is connected, via the modem, to a normal exchange line, and may be used for voice communication. A button on the hand-set enables this exchange line to be switched to send data from the device attached to the modem. When normal connection is via a leased line, this facility provides for a fall-back data path if the line fails. At rates of 2400 bits/second in normal use, transmission via this stand-by path may be designed for a maximum of 1200 bits/second, and so the data rate must also be switched to conform. The availability of the hand-set also enables the modem to be tested. In this case, connection to a remote testing centre is made, and test signals are transmitted from the suspect modem, to the centre, enabling diagnosis to take place. Many modem faults can be detected in this way.

For transmission at 48 000 bits/second, a pair of modems is required at each end of the link. One modem is provided in the user's premises at each end, and one at the exchanges at the other end of the wide-band link. This is because the signals received from the user via the co-axial cable must be converted to occupy the appropriate frequency band in the micro-wave link.

## 17.4 Data Transmission Services

### 17.4.1 SERVICES IN THE UK

Table 17.1 summarizes the main services provided by the UK PO. The principle telephone services are under the generic title 'Datel'. The associated

**Table 17.1**  UK Data Transmission Service

| Service | Type of circuit | System tariff | Modem required | Two- or four-wire | Transmission mode | Maximum rate (bits/ second) |
|---|---|---|---|---|---|---|
| Datel 100 | Telegraph | Telex | — | — | $\frac{1}{2}$ duplex | 50 |
| | | Leased 'H' | — | — | $\frac{1}{2}$ or full duplex | 50 |
| | | Leased 'J' | — | — | $\frac{1}{2}$ or full duplex | 100 |
| Datel 200 | Telephone | Switched or Leased 'S' | Datel Mod No. 2 | 2 | $\frac{1}{2}$ or full duplex | 300 |
| Datel 600 | Telephone | Switched | Datel Mod No. 1 | 2 | $\frac{1}{2}$ duplex | 600 (possibly 1200) |
| | Telephone | Leased 'S' | | 2 | $\frac{1}{2}$ duplex | 600 or 1200 |
| | Telephone | Leased 'S' | | 4 | $\frac{1}{2}$ or full duplex | 600 or 1200 |
| Datel 2400 | Telephone | Switched Leased 'S' | Datel Mod No. 7 | 2 | $\frac{1}{2}$ duplex $\frac{1}{2}$ or full duplex | 2400 or 600/1200 2400 or 600/1200 |
| Wideband (micro-wave) | X 12 Telephone circuits equivalent | Coaxial lines/micro- wave link | Modem No. 8 & 9 | 4 (equi- valent) | $\frac{1}{2}$ or full duplex | 48,000 |
| Midnight line | Special Switched line | 12–6 a.m. | No. 1 | 2 | $\frac{1}{2}$ duplex | 1200 |

number, e.g., Datel 600, represents the speed in bits/second for which the service was originally planned, although in the latter case the maximum speed is actually double. The table gives the modems required if PO facilities are to be used throughout, and relates the Services to some of the techniques discussed in this chapter, and to the PO Tariffs of line charges.

Datel 200 uses frequency modulation with four frequencies, giving the capability of full duplex transmission. This is not often used for actual simultaneous transmission of two streams of data, but sometimes for character reverse transmission (echo checking).

Speeds greater than 2400 bits/second, commonly up to 4800, and in some places, 7200, or 9600, are available using privately supplied modems which are approved by the PO. A modem supplied by the UK PO for 4800 bits/second is planned for 1977.

## 17.4.2 SERVICES IN EUROPE

European services are broadly similar to those described for the UK. Some differences are noted below.

Telex in France has been used at up to 200 bits/second with private terminals. Leased telegraph circuits, particularly in Germany, operate at speeds up to 200 bits/second. Telephone circuits generally provide for speeds of 1200 bits/second, although in some areas there are restrictions to 600 where equipment is older. Italy, in common with the UK, now provides for 2400 bits/second on the switched telephone network. On leased lines, similar capabilities to those in the UK are available throughout the major industrial countries.

## 17.4.3 SERVICES IN THE USA

These are broadly similar to those offered in the UK and Europe. However, the nature of US utilities is different (they are public companies regulated by a government agency), and this has facilitated the emergence of 'specialized common carriers' in recent years. These companies offer more sophisticated facilities (high speed, low error rates, digital transmission, etc.) over high volume routes (e.g., between major cities). Some supply their own transmission equipment, others 'build' on that supplied by the common carriers. (The actual techniques used are mentioned in the following section.) These have acted as an incentive to the utilities to upgrade their own services, while in the meantime providing sophisticated services for a limited user population. The structure of European PTTs makes this development impossible in Europe (it is illegal). However, the various techniques exploited by the special carriers in the USA are being investigated by the PTTs.

## 17.5   Future Developments

The expected pattern for the future can be characterized as increased capacity, lower errors and increasing use of digital technology. However, a fully digital data transmission system is unlikely before the end of the century.

Systems currently in use or being investigated are summarized below.

### Packet Switching

This is a development of message switching using high speed links and short fixed-length messages ('packets'). Longer messages are composed of several packets. The message breakdown into, and reassembly from, packets can be performed either by the user or by the network supplier. Packet switching can be used either with existing analogue systems or any of the proposed digital systems. Currently, packet switched services are being offered by the specialized common carriers in the USA and are being examined by European common carriers (e.g., UK PO Experimental Packet Switching Services, EPSS). Various national and international networks used for scientific research use this approach.

320

## Leased Digital Lines

This involves provision of digital links in parallel with existing services. Thus, a user's network could have both digital and analogue elements. It represents the first step towards a fully digital service and can, for example, be expected in the UK before the end of the 'seventies. The specialist carriers offer this service in the US. Also, packet switched networks can be implemented over these links.

## Public Switched Digital Network

Again, this is in parallel with and separate from existing analogue equipment. It provides the same facilities as analogue systems, but using digital technology. Possible implementation dates for the UK and parts of Europe are the end of the 'seventies or early 'eighties.

The major present argument is whether packet switching or line switching is best for data. There is no clear answer—both have advantages and this makes it most likely that the two will continue to co-exist.

# 18. Reliability Calculations

This chapter is provided for reference purposes for those carrying out fail-soft design and associated reliability calculations. Readers should read this chapter in conjunction with chapter 12.

The calculations and formulae are developed against examples of hardware units. The reader is reminded that the analysis can also be applied to software or systems, e.g., 'The operating system', 'The disk file including data'.

## 18.1 Mean Time Between Faults

MTBF is defined as the mean time between faults for a piece of equipment.

$\dfrac{1}{\text{MTBF}}$ is a measure of frequency of failure.

## 18.2 Combined MTBFs

When a configuration is made up of several items whose individual MTBFs are known, the overall MTBF can be calculated as

$$\frac{1}{M} = \frac{1}{M_1} + \frac{1}{M_2} + \frac{1}{M_3} + \cdots + \frac{1}{M_n}$$

where $M$ is the overall MTBF and $M_1$, $M_2$, etc., are the MTBFs of individual *essential* components.

*Example*

If the MTBFs in hours are

$$M_1 = 500, \ M_2 = 3000, \ M_3 = 3000, \ M_4 = 6000 \ (2 \text{ units needed})$$

where $M_1$–$M_4$ are essential units, then

$$\frac{1}{M} = \frac{1}{500} + \frac{1}{3000} + \frac{1}{3000} + \frac{1}{6000} + \frac{1}{6000}$$

$$= \frac{12 + 2 + 2 + 1 + 1}{6000};$$

hence $M = 333$ hours. Hence, one failure of the set $M_1$–$M_4$ ($2 \times M_4$) every 333 hours is predicted.

## 18.3  Mean Time to Repair

MTTR is defined as the mean time to repair. For final calculations, MTTR includes all time from point of failure to repair. This includes diagnosis and communication delays before repair and reinstatement.

*Example*

Consider the event of a system malfunction which makes the system unavailable to a terminal. It may take the users, say the terminal operators, 2 minutes to establish that there is a system malfunction, and when contact is made to the operations staff a further 2 minutes may have elapsed. The operations staff fail to re-establish the system and contact the duty on-line programmer, who will instruct that certain diagnostics are taken. By the time this is done a further 10 minutes have elapsed. The duty on-line programmer studies the diagnostics, arrives at a solution to the problem, and prepares a patch to enable the problem to be overcome—let us say that this takes another 30 minutes. A patch is then made to the system and the operations staff have to run certain recovery programs which involve a further 10 minutes elapsed time. Finally the system is on the air again. The MTTR in this case is 54 minutes, and not 40 minutes as might be seen by the duty programmer.

MTTR may alternatively be defined as the period from unit failure to return to availability for use.

## 18.4  Availability

'Availability' reflects the percentage time available for useful work, and has the characteristic of 'probability' of availability. The availability of a unit or system can be defined as

$$\text{Availability, } A = \frac{\text{MTBF}}{\text{MTBF} + \text{MTTR}}.$$

Thus, if a given CPU has

$$\text{MTBF} = 500 \text{ hr}$$
$$\text{MTTR} = \phantom{0}4 \text{ hr}$$
$$A = \frac{500}{500 + 4} = 0.99.$$

## 18.5  Combined Availability

There are two possible basic configurations, referred to as 'serial' and 'parallel'. Serial refers to the case where all units are required. 'Parallel' is used to reflect a choice.

The availability of a configuration can be calculated from components as with MTBF. The calculation is easier than in the MTBF case and the formula to apply for serial availability is:

$$A = A_1 \times A_2 \times A_3 \times \cdots ,$$

where $A$ is overall availability and $A_1$, $A_2$, $A_3$, etc., are the availabilities of the essential components.

To assist in the evaluation of availability, configurations are drawn to a convention such that each *essential* unit is drawn as a box in a *serial* chain. Thus

$$A = A_1 \times A_2 \times A_3 \times \ldots \times A_n$$

is sometimes called the serial configuration formulae. Two examples are given below.

*Example 1 (see Fig. 18.1)*

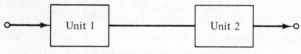

**Fig. 18.1**  Two units

Unit 1 has an availability of $0 \cdot 992 = A_1$
Unit 2 has an availability of $0 \cdot 973 = A_2$
The overall availability is calculated thus:

$$A = A_1 \times A_2 = 0 \cdot 992 \times 0 \cdot 973 = 0 \cdot 965.$$

*Example 2 (see Fig. 18.2)*

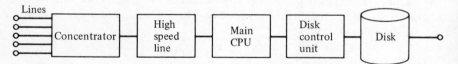

**Fig. 18.2**  Multiple units

The system components have the following availabilities:

- Concentrator  $0 \cdot 971 = A_1$
- High speed line  $0 \cdot 982 = A_2$
- Main CPU  $0 \cdot 997 = A_3$
- Disk file unit  $0 \cdot 925 = A_4$
- Disk control unit  $0 \cdot 969 = A_5.$

The overall availability $A$ is calculated

$$A = A_1 \times A_2 \times A_3 \times A_4 \times A_5$$
$$= 0 \cdot 971 \times 0 \cdot 982 \times 0 \cdot 997 \times 0 \cdot 925 \times 0 \cdot 969 = 0 \cdot 852$$
$A = 0 \cdot 852$ is the availability of the central hardware as seen by each line.

324

## 18.6  Multiple Serial Availability

In Example 2, in section 18.5, the availability of the central site only was calculated. A terminal operator sees a wider picture as per Fig. 18.3.

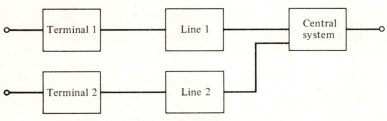

**Fig. 18.3**  Mixed paths

In this case, both terminals and lines are assessed to be independent, and therefore their availability diagram is as Fig. 18.4, and their relevent

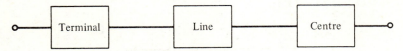

**Fig. 18.4**  Terminal view

availabilities are

$$\text{Terminal 1, } A = T_1 \times L_1 \times A_c$$
$$\text{Terminal 2, } A = T_2 \times L_2 \times A_c,$$

where $A_c$ is availability for the whole computer centre and could be substituted
  by $0.852$ as calculated in section 18.5,
  $L_1$ is availability for line 1
  $L_2$ is availability for line 2
  $T_1$ is availability for terminal 1
  $T_2$ is availability for terminal 2

## 18.7  Parallel Availability

In the parallel, or alternative, case, the system under study can operate if either one of a choice of devices is available. In the diagrammatic convention, *parallel* boxes are drawn on the availability diagram and the overall availability is calculated as:

$$A = 1 - (1 - A_1)(1 - A_2).$$

*Example 3 (see Fig. 18.5)*

The system availability where one only of the CPUs must always be available is calculated as follows:

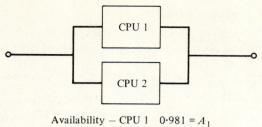

Availability – CPU 1   $0.981 = A_1$
             CPU 2   $0.981 = A_2$

**Fig. 18.5**   Alternative paths

The system availability, $A = 1 - (1 - A_1)(1 - A_2)$
$$= 1 - (1 - 0.981)(1 - 0.981)$$
$$= 1 - (0.019)^2 = 1 - 0.000361 = 0.999639$$
$$= 0.999.$$

This approach can be extended for any 1 of $n$ as indicated in Example 4.

*Example 4 (see Fig. 18.6)*

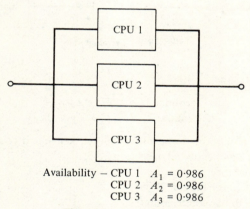

Availability – CPU 1   $A_1 = 0.986$
             CPU 2   $A_2 = 0.986$
             CPU 3   $A_3 = 0.986$

**Fig. 18.6**   Multiple choice

The system availability where any and only one of the CPUs must always be available is calculated as follows:

The system availability $= 1 - (1 - A_1)(1 - A_2)(1 - A_3)$
$$= 1 - (0.014)(0.014)(0.014)$$
$$= 1 - (0.014)^3 = 1 - 0.000\,002\,744$$
$$= 0.999\,997\,256 = 0.999.$$

In the general case, the formula for 1 out of any $n$ identical units is $A = 1 - (1 - A_1)^n$.

With careful study, the availability calculations can be adjusted for wider options such as any 2 or 3 units to be available, or in the more general case $(n - 1)$ out of $n$ units.

326

In this situation, the following applies:

– availability of a single unit is $A$
– availability of $n$ components is $A^n$
– availability of $n-1$ of $n$ is $A^{n-1}(1-A)$.

But there are $n$ ways the $n$th can be unavailable.

– availability of any $(n-1)$ only of $n$ is $n\,A^{n-1}(1-A)$;
– availability of at least $(n-1)$ (i.e., $n$ or $n-1$ available) is $A^n + nA^{n-1}(1-A)$
  $n$
– thus availability of $(n-1)$ of $n$ is:
$$-n\,A^{n-1}-(n-1)An.$$
By further application of this approach (based on probability theory), further situations can be covered, e.g., for $n-2$ out of $n$, the form is built from

$$A^n + nA^{n-1}(1-A) + n(n-1)A^{n-2}(1-A^2).$$

## 18.8   Mixed Systems

Most practical configurations, with redundancy, have elements of serial and parallel availability. The simplest approach is to draw availability diagrams and then group into sets whose availability you can calculate. For simplicity of presentation, the following convention is used:

*Serial*   $A = A_1 \times A_2$ presented directly as $A_1 \times A_2$
*Parallel*   $A = 1 - (1 - A_1)(1 - A_2)$ presented as $\overline{A_1 A_2}$
or $n\overline{A_1 A_2 A_3}$ for any $n$ of a set in parallel.

### Example 5 Serial within Parallel

The problem is to calculate the availability of the system (sub-system) illustrated in Fig. 18.7. The calculation is handled in two steps.

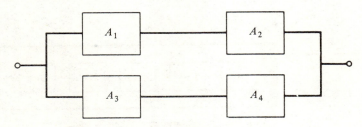

Fig. 18.7   Serial/parallel

*Step 1* Determine sets as reflected in the availability diagram in Fig. 18.8

Combined sub-unit's availabilities are

$$C_1 = A_1 \times A_2, \quad C_2 = A_3 \times A_4.$$

**327**

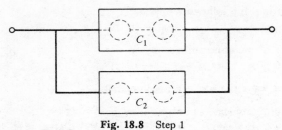

**Fig. 18.8**  Step 1

*Step 2*  From Fig. 18.8 we can see

$$A = \overline{C_1 \, C_2} = 1 - (1 - C_1)(1 - C_2) = C_1 + C_2 - C_1 \times C_2$$
$$= (A_1 \times A_2) + (A_3 \times A_4) - (A_1 \times A_2 \times A_3 \times A_4).$$

### Example 6 Resolving Complex Availability

An example configuration under study may be represented as Fig. 18.9.

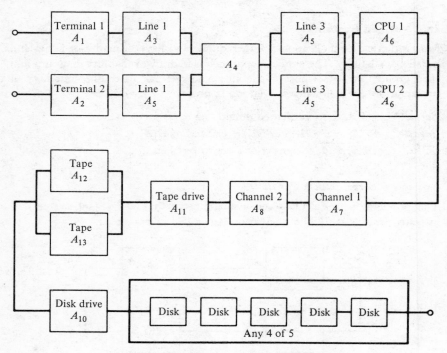

**Fig. 18.9**  Configuration availability

Redundant equipment is being considered for the

| CPU/communication processor channel | – link |
| Central processor | – CPU |
| Disk drives | – Disk |
| Tape decks (2 different types) | – Tape. |

328

In preparing to calculate availability, the first step is to determine the availability of sets where alternative paths apply. In this case, alternatives apply for such sub-systems as:

| Sub-system | Combined availability |
|---|---|
| Link | $C_1 = \overline{A_5 A_5}$ |
| CPU | $C_2 = \overline{A_6 A_6}$ |
| Disk | $X_3 = 4\,\overline{A_9\,A_9\,A_9\,A_9\,A_9}$ |
| | $= 5A_9^4 - 4A_9^5$ |
| Tape | $C_\eta = \overline{A_{12} A_{13}}$ |

and the availability diagram can be re-drawn as in Fig. 18.10 for all terminals of type 1. A similar diagram can be drawn for all terminals of type 2.

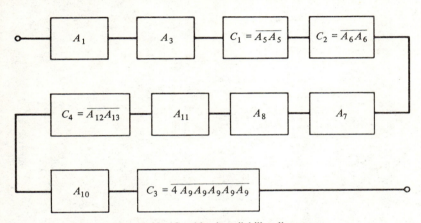

**Fig. 18.10**   Combined availability diagram

Once $C_1 - C_4$ are evaluated, $A$ (overall) can also be determined. Inspection of Fig. 18.10 will show

$$A = A_1 \times A_3 \times A_4 \times C_1 \times C_2 \times A_7 \times A_8 \times C_3 \times A_{10} \times A_{11} \times C_4.$$

## 18.9   Rounding and Accuracy

Designers are advised not to round calculations too simply or to stop calculations too early.

0.99 may look like reasonable rounding on 0.994,

but notice the effect during the parallel calculation, where $1 - 0.99$, i.e., 0.01, may be compared with $1 - 0.994$, i.e., 0.006.

Thus the moral is perhaps to go for too many places of decimals to start the calculations and round at the end.

If complex or extended availability calculations become an important issue, then the designer is advised to:

- remember the inaccuracy of data used for MTBFs MTTRs, etc.;
- ask a mathematician fluent in probability theory to check the calculations (unless one himself).

# 19. File Techniques

File design for real time (see chapter 11) is concerned with the selection of appropriate file structures, many of which are equally applicable to batch processing.

This chapter summarizes, from a real time viewpoint, a number of the more basic techniques that may be familiar to many readers. However, while in batch processing analysts and designers can afford to take a general view, in real time a more detailed understanding of the physical characteristics of storage devices and file handling mechanisms is probably required. (See also chapter 5.)

This chapter outlines the important characteristics of file devices and the more common basic file structures. Some of the basic structures will not have been used by many readers whose experience is limited to batch processing.

## 19.1  Direct Access Devices

Direct access devices have reflected a history of continued development in performance specifications, a process unlikely to cease. Many technical innovations have solved yesterday's problems, yet today's designers have continued to have good reason to seek better performance.

Tape files play their role in real time systems—statistics, batch input, logs, etc., and are therefore included in this chapter. Special purpose slow access devices such as magnetic cards, strip or tape cartridge retrieval systems are not covered.

The faster direct access devices (say access time less than 250 ms) can be classified in 7 general types:

— drum, one fixed head for each track;
– drum, set of movable heads;
– fixed disk, fixed head for each track;
– fixed disk, set of movable heads;
– exchangeable disk, set of moveable heads;
– exchangeable disk, heads included in disk unit (fixed and movable);
– mass main storage.

For the purpose of general comparison, however, these (excluding mass core) may be amalgamated into three groups:

- drum or fixed disk, one head for track;
- drum or fixed disk, moving heads;
- exchangeable disks, moving heads.

| Type | Drum/disk one head per track | Drum/disk moving heads | Exchangeable disk units |
|---|---|---|---|
| Typical devices (limited sample) | IBM 2301 B 9375 IBM 2305 | Univac fastrand II  Univac 8460 | IBM 3340 DSS 190 ICL EDS60 |
| Characters/unit (millions) | 1–15 | 120–500 | 30–200 |
| Average seek (ms) | 0 | 55–95 | 25–60 |
| Average latency (ms) | 2–20 | 25–35 | 8–13 |
| Transfer rate (kch/s) | 230–3000 | 150–500 | 300–1000 |
| Average time to read 1000 characters (ms) | 3–12 | 85–125 | 35–80 |
| Cost/character (p) | 1·2–3·2 | 0·01–0·08 | 0·02–0·04 |

Fig. 19.1  General characteristics of fast access devices

Figure 19.1 compares the general characteristics of these groups (with a restricted sample of devices). The one-head-per-track devices are very fast, high cost, low capacity devices. The moving-head fixed devices are low cost, high capacity, but are relatively slow. Exchangeable disk units are more average in most respects. However, they are reasonably fast, and not only have a high capacity per device, but a much more even cost/character against characters-stored profile than the fixed devices, due to the way in which disk capacity can be increased by attaching more spindles to a single control unit. There are, of course, exceptions to the general classifications, e.g., fixed head per track disks, are slower than similar size moving head disks.

One-head-per-track devices tend to be reliable, due to the simple mechanical arrangement. Modern exchangeable disk units are also reliable owing to the sophisticated error checking, track reposition and re-try, and diagnostic procedures, built into the unit/controller. The exchangeable disks with the heads built into the disk pack carry this reliability improvement still further.

Hardware development continues with specifications continually improving. However, history suggests that the capacity provided by faster devices is taken up by more demanding systems requirements and the design problems remain similar.

## 19.1.1  DEVICE OPERATIONS

To retrieve a record directly, the first operation is to move a read/write head so that it is over the requisite track. This operation is not needed for one-head-per-track devices. On drums, the head (or heads) is moved along the drum. On disks, the set of heads, one for each surface, is moved radially to the right cylinder, and the relevant head is then electronically selected. Moving the heads in this way is a relatively slow mechanical operation, known as a *SEEK*. A cylinder is not a physical entity, but merely a set of tracks, all of which are accessible by the set of read heads at one time without further head movement.

The head is now positioned over the track, which is revolving rapidly beneath it. The next operation is to wait for the record to reach the head. This delay is called the *Latency*. Frequently it averages half the rotation time of the device. However, some access methods demand that the track's home address (a start-point) be found before the record can be searched for, which increases the latency.

The final step is to read the record through the head and into main storage via the channel. The actual unit of data transferred is the *block*. Some software access methods allow the block to be composed of several physical records, in which case the access method software will present to the application program only the requested physical record on that read. Nevertheless, the whole block is transferred and must be accommodated in the buffer. The transfer rate is governed by the rotation speed and data density of the device.

Track formats vary according to the manufacturer. One method is to have the track as the smallest hardware-addressed unit of storage. Blocks, which can vary in length, are stored on the track with gaps and count (serial number within track, often also logical key) areas separating them. Blocks are then recognized either by being the $n$th on the track or by using the hardware search key command. An alternative approach is to divide the track into fixed-length sectors, which thus form a more specific hardware addressed unit. During all these steps, the seek, the latency and the data transfer, the device is satisfying only the one read request. Only one read/write head at the same time is operational.

Where a number of devices are connected to a single control unit, itself connected to the computer by a channel, multiple requests can be simultaneously satisfied on different devices, if their usage of the channel time is less than their usage of the device, and if these channel usages by different requests can be interleaved. Many devices are capable of off-line seeking (as this technique is often called), by which several units may be simultaneously seeking, under control unit control, while another unit may be transferring data using the channel. A single request therefore ties up the channel during the latency and data transfer operations only. For such devices, a request to read a 1000 character block utilizes the channel for 15—35 per cent of the time for which it utilizes the device. Devices, such as the IBM 3330, only use the channel for a very small proportion of the latency time. This feature, known as rotational position sensing, may only be used with certain software access methods. When it can be used, the above request would give a 4 per cent channel/device utilization ratio instead of 15—35 per cent.

Thus, when timing file access mechanisms, each basic access is made up from a series of *SEEK—LATENCY—READ (WRITE)*; each loads the channel and device dependent on the particular devices and the software used. On one-head-per-track devices—fixed heads (or within that part of a device with fixed heads)—the *SEEK* does not apply.

## 19.2 Basic File Organization

This section considers files in terms of the transfer of data in/out of the processor and secondly in terms of basic file structures.

The appropriate file design for real time is often other than simple use of the manufacturer's standard file packages, and therefore the real time designer needs to acquire an understanding of the general technique, as well as specific package implementations. The standard index sequential manufacturer package may not meet the project needs, but a tailored index sequential access method, or a modification of the standard package may.

### 19.2.1 DATA TRANSFER

When a read request is carried out, the unit transferred into main storage is the block, which may consist of several records. In sequential processing, records are blocked to reduce the number of physical accesses needed to scan the whole file, and multiple buffers are often used so that the processing of one buffer can be overlapped with the re-filling of another. In real time, such considerations do not apply, as the sequence of records required is generally not predictable. Records may still be blocked, either to save backing storage space or because a set of records is required, but multiple buffers are not used in the same way as in batch.

A buffer pool may be used, however. This is an area of main storage capable of holding multiple file blocks, from the same or different files. Before any read request is issued to the disk, the buffer pool is scanned for the record wanted. If it is not there, the block is read into the pool from disk, where it overwrites the record least likely to be wanted again. Various algorithms can be used to determine which block should be over-written; one such criterion is the block which has not been accessed for the longest time.

A block in the pool which has been modified is marked as such, and is written to disk before being overwritten in the pool. The relevant logic for the use of a buffer pool may be in the manufacturer's software; more likely it will have to be written as part of the real time control program. With this look-aside technique, common records, particularly index records, may often be read without a physical access. The size of the buffer pool is a readily tunable parameter which frequently has a considerable effect upon central processor message throughput.

### 19.2.2 BASIC STRUCTURES

As stated above, it is important for the real time designer to consider tailored structures as valid alternatives to standard packages. For example, the use of a direct access method to read records whose position is determined by means of an index in main storage may be required from a timing point of view, where straightforward use of index sequential would solve the problem logically. The final design trade-off will be risk and cost of the tailored development versus improved run time performance. Experience in real time shows the decision falls on both sides in practical cases. Sometimes the straightforward access method works from all points of view, and is thus the right choice.

It is also useful for the newcomer to tailored file structures to recognize the subtle difference between the method of storage and method of access. Packages tend to merge the two in one's thinking, e.g., 'index sequential access method'. However, index sequential files in their simplest form decide where to place a record using a serial or sequential insertion logic, but the access uses an indexed logic. The index access concept is basically independent from the sequential storage logic, except where it handles overflows on insertion.

### 19.2.3 SEQUENTIAL FILES

Such files may be sequenced according to a key or 'time of addition'. If a file is not sequenced by key, a record may be found only by reading through the file; records may be added on the end of the file. A key sequenced file may be accessed by serial search or by binary chop; records can be inserted only by rewriting the file or by writing them to a subsidiary suspense file which on access is always searched first. The two files are then merged at intervals. Binary chop requires approximately $\log_2 N$ accesses to locate a particular record from a file of $N$ records, so is usually too slow for real time use.

Sequential files are rarely used as real time main files due to their slowness; their main uses are for log files and queue files in main storage.

### 19.2.4 DIRECT FILES

The simplest file organization is obtained when each possible logical record key corresponds directly to the address of one record slot on the disk. For this to be possible, each record slot must be the same size (i.e., the size of the biggest record type to be stored) or record overflow must be provided. This enables the access method to convert a relative slot number into a disk, cylinder, track and slot address.

The logical record keys may actually be 1, 2, 3, ... $N$, where $N$ is either equal to or not much greater than $n$, the number of records in the file. They may be a series such as 5, 10, 15, ... $N$, where $N/5 = n$, or the relationship may be more complex. As an example, consider a firm with, say, 12 000 employees working at three different sites, each site issuing its own employee numbers from the ranges shown in Fig. 19.2.

| Site | 1 | 2 | 3 |
|---|---|---|---|
| Number of employees | 1–4000 | 1–1000 | 1–8000 |

**Fig. 19.2**  Distribution of employee numbers by site

Figure 19.3 represents a possible direct algorithm for finding a given employee's record; on exit, the EMP-NO is a relative record slot number in the

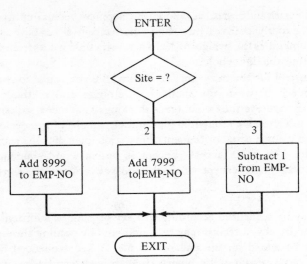

**Fig. 19.3** Employee number direct algorithm

range 0–12999. As an example, employee 3254 at site 1 yields a relative slot number of 12253. The disk has 400 cylinders, 20 tracks per cylinder, 5 employee record slots per track. The algorithm passes the slot number, 12253, to the access method routine, which, knowing that the employee record file is contiguous, beginning at cylinder 205, track 0, slot 0, calculates that the slot is at disk address cylinder 327, track 10, slot 3.

The direct access method is ideal. The record is always obtained on the first access; rotational position sensing can be used if available on the hardware, because the access method can calculate the position of the record on the track; and the records are actually held in key sequence, so the file can be used for sequential processing. If possible, then, this method should be used. Often this can be achieved by using the computer to generate the keys. Thus, seat reservations or product orders can be input without a reservation or order number; the relevant record created and stored in a direct file, and the address where the record was stored, possibly modified in format, is output to the terminal operator and subsequently used as the record key. Unfortunately, however, the keys often do not form a dense sequence, nor can they be computer-generated. For example, if a firm uses 10 000 different parts, and each part number is 9 digits, it is unlikely that a reasonable direct algorithm exists. If the part number was taken as the slot number directly, only 0·001 per cent of the record slots would be occupied. Files like this need a different approach.

Another frequent example of a simple direct file in real time systems is a terminal slot file, with 1 record per terminal (section 12.4.1): Terminal No = Record No.

### 19.2.5 RANDOMIZED FILES

A common technique with files, such as the parts file just described, which have

**336**

a sparse key series, is randomizing. As for the above direct file, the file consists of a number of slots, but now sufficient to hold 10–40 per cent more records than are actually present in the file. Unlike the direct file, the slots may be big enough to hold more than one record, when the term 'bucket' seems particularly appropriate. Sometimes each track is a bucket.

If there are many more logical keys than bucket numbers, the algorithm is many to one, i.e., many possible keys are converted to the same bucket number. Such keys are known as synonyms. The objective of the algorithm is therefore to achieve as even a spread of records over buckets as possible, and it does this by randomizing the key. A fully randomizing algorithm distributes $n$ records across $N$ buckets according to a Poisson distribution with a mean of $n/N$. Overflows, i.e., records that cannot be fitted into the predicted bucket because it is full of synonyms, therefore always occur.

In practice, algorithms cannot produce fully randomized distributions of addresses from non-randomly distributed keysets; they may produce either more, or less, overflows than Poisson would predict. In particular, the division-taking-remainder method (Fig. 19.4) often produces less overflows because runs of consecutive keys are transformed into runs of consecutive addresses.

Plainly, the number of overflows decreases if the available record space is increased. Since overflows mean extra accesses to store or retrieve records, a balance must be sought between an excessive file size and an excessive average number of accesses for retrieved record. Typical randomized files require an average $1·1$–$1·4$ accesses to retrieve a record, having prime packing densities (ratio of record space occupied to the record space available) of 70–90 per cent. Having fewer, larger buckets, at a given packing density, decreases the incidence of overflows, but increases bucket search time for all accesses.

The average number of accesses per record is determined not only by the efficiency of the algorithm in minimizing the number of overflows, but also by the efficiency of the overflow retrieval technique. A common technique is to put overflows into the next bucket (in sequence) that will accept them. If the record is not found in the expected bucket, the file is searched sequentially. While simple, this technique may cause further, unnecessary, overflows. Another method is to assign certain tracks on each cylinder as overflow tracks, which are searched sequentially. Alternatively, each bucket may have within it the address of an overflow bucket; overflowed records are thus searched for via a chain of overflow buckets. Whether overflows are stored in the prime area or a separate overflow area, space must be allowed, thus reducing the overall packing density to 60–80 per cent.

The design problem here is that the file access timing is dependent both on the algorithm, the overflow structure and the actual data finally operationally stored. Thus, the performance is not known unless real data are test loaded during design or performance tests carried out on near 'life size' files (see chapter 5).

There are several randomizing algorithm techniques, which are often used in combination. Figure 19.4 shows a number of examples. No method can be

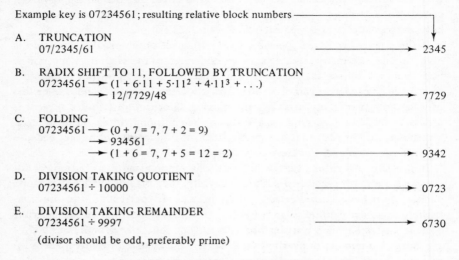

Keys are in range     00000000–99999999,
File has 10000 buckets; all algorithms generate relative bucket numbers
in range 0–9999 (9996 in example E).

Example key is 07234561; resulting relative block numbers

A.  TRUNCATION
    07/2345/61                                                          2345

B.  RADIX SHIFT TO 11, FOLLOWED BY TRUNCATION
    $07234561 \longrightarrow (1 + 6 \cdot 11 + 5 \cdot 11^2 + 4 \cdot 11^3 + \ldots)$
    $\longrightarrow 12/7729/48$                                        7729

C.  FOLDING
    $07234561 \longrightarrow (0 + 7 = 7, 7 + 2 = 9)$
    $\longrightarrow 934561$
    $\longrightarrow (1 + 6 = 7, 7 + 5 = 12 = 2)$                       9342

D.  DIVISION TAKING QUOTIENT
    $07234561 \div 10000$                                               0723

E.  DIVISION TAKING REMAINDER
    $07234561 \div 9997$                                                6730

    (divisor should be odd, preferably prime)

**Fig. 19.4**  Randomizing algorithms

described as optimum; only optimum for a particular key set. However, division taking the remainder is simple and powerful, and folding is convenient for key sets containing alphabetics.

Finding an effective algorithm for a particular key set can only be a matter of trial and error. One approach is to use an analysis program that reads the key set, converts each key and calculates the number of overflows and average retrieval accesses. From this, a particular disadvantage of randomized files is obvious; as time passes, the key set in a file changes as records are inserted and deleted, and the algorithm efficiency deteriorates. Additionally, the sequence of the records is random, making the file unsuitable for sequential processing, unless input data are sorted to physical address sequence after applying the algorithm to the keys. Files using some overflow techniques, particularly the push-into-the-next-bucket one, need occasional re-organization. With some algorithms acting on long keys, the CPU time can be appreciable; and overall packing densities of only 60–80 per cent imply considerable wastage of disk space. Nevertheless, the technique is common in real time systems due to the fast access (typically around 1·2 accesses per retrieval).

Perhaps one of the greatest credits to randomized files is the wide application (1000+) of Cincom's Total system, where main files rely on the randomizing of keys and address generation.

### 19.2.6  UNORDERED FILES

The file organization described in section 19.2.4, namely a set of addressable,

**338**

equal-sized record slots, is of considerable general applicability. With the direct and randomized organization, which are special cases of this type of organization, the logical key can be converted directly into the slot address, and this solves two problems: which slot to store a new record in, and from which slot a record with a known key can be retrieved. And in both cases only one access is needed (except with overflow).

An unordered file has the same organization, but the records are assigned into record slots in a random fashion (not randomized). In effect a record is stored in any available slot. To retrieve such a record, its slot address must be known, and this can be achieved in a number of ways. One way has already been described; to make the slot address the external logic key of the record. The address may also be obtainable from an index, or it may be stored, as a pointer, in another record elsewhere in the data base. Exceptionally, the whole file can be searched.

An unordered file also needs a mechanism to determine where a new record can be inserted. A common technique is the free space chain. Each empty slot contains a dummy record, which holds the address of another empty slot. The file's free space is thus chained together; the first record of the file contains the first chain pointer. On starting up the real time system, this first pointer is read into core, where it remains till close-down. Figures 19.5–19.7 show how such a

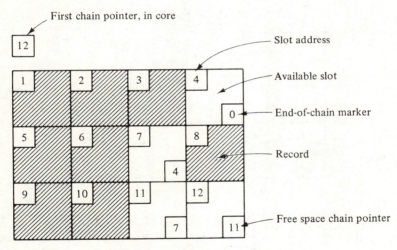

**Fig. 19.5**  Unordered file before activity

free space chain is used when records are inserted and deleted. It should be noted that no extra accesses are needed. The chain is LIFO, i.e., empty slots created by deletions are added to the start of the chain, and empty slots needed for insertions are taken from the start of the chain.

An alternative method is the free-space bit map. At the start of the real time day, a bit map is read into core. There is one bit for each slot; the bit is set 'on' if the slot is empty. To find an empty slot, the bit map is sequentially scanned.

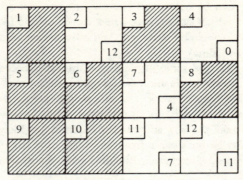

**Fig. 19.6** Unordered file after deletion

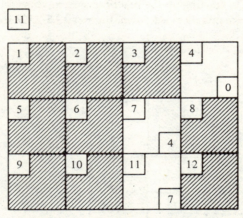

**Fig. 19.7** Unordered file after insertion

If the first 'on' bit is bit 181, then slot 181 is used, and bit 181 turned off. If a record is deleted, the appropriate bit is turned on. If the file is large, core is saved if the map is split into pages, and only one page at a time is held in core. When all the bits on the page are off (i.e., the corresponding section of the file is full), a new page is read in. Deletions cause a problem, since it is unlikely that the right page will be in core; but it is not essential to turn the bits on in real time; this can be done, a page at a time, as a background task or at regular intervals.

### 19.2.7 INDEXES

The file structures described in sections 19.2.3–6 all provide a clear logic for

340

deciding where to store a record, e.g.,

| | |
|---|---|
| Sequential | – by sequence |
| Direct | – by key |
| Randomized | – by key and algorithm |
| Unordered | – by free space. |

However, the first and last do not provide convenient methods of accessing records. One solution is to build an index structure on the relevant files in order to obtain the address of a record. Indexes have wider application but are here first considered as being built on a single file.

An index is a file (or a list) in which each record consists essentially of a logical key and an address—a *Basic Index*—see Fig. 19.8.

When the key range of the index is fairly full, i.e., most values are present, the index can be compressed by dropping the index entry from a basic index and implying the value from its position—*Implicit Index* (key implied)—see Fig. 19.8.

In other circumstances, when the file space is fairly full, it may be advantageous to imply the address (see also Fig. 19.8). In both implicit indices, the index includes space for non-existent keys/records in the relevant range.

Indexes to key-sequenced files may also be nested in multiple levels. An example is shown in Fig. 19.8, where the higher level index is a limit index, since each key in the index represents the upper limit of a range of keys. The corresponding address is that of a lower-level basic index covering only that key range.

Since an index is a file in its own right, it requires a search mechanism. This is often a serial scan, but if the index is sequenced on key, binary chop can be used.

If the index is sequenced on key, it can be compressed by removing or modifying characters redundant to the sequential search. The compressed index is considerably smaller and therefore faster to search on the disk, but may require more CPU time to interpret.

### 19.2.8  INDEX SEQUENTIAL

Index sequential is offered by most manufacturers as standard software. In principle, the file is sequenced on key and also has a multi-level index; it thus can be used for sequential and direct access; the latter is illustrated in Fig. 19.9. Even when newly created, the file is slower for direct access than direct or randomizing algorithm files, due to the index accesses required. Records inserted into the file after initial creation are chained into overflow areas; these overflow records slow down the average access time for both sequential and direct access. Index sequential files therefore need periodic reorganization. This consists of dumping and reloading the file; in the process the overflow records are merged into the prime area of the file.

Since the file is sequenced, it is unneccessary for the lowest level of index to contain an entry for each record. Instead, the file is divided into buckets, usual-

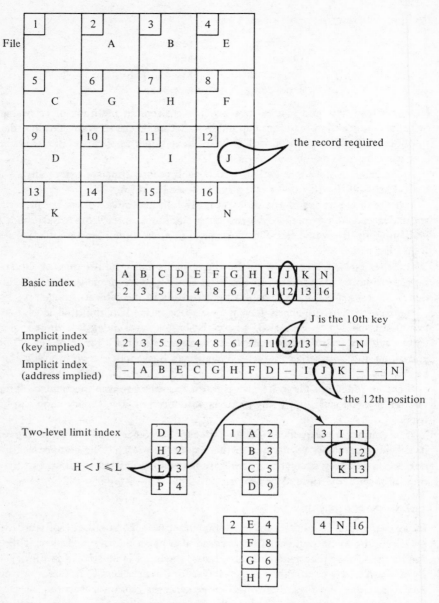

**Fig. 19.8** Basic, implicit, and multi-level indexes

ly tracks. The lowest-level index is a limit index, with one entry per bucket, the key being the highest key in the bucket. The bucket is searched sequentially to find the requested record. Since the access method cannot predict the location of the record in the bucket, rotational position sensing cannot be used.

342

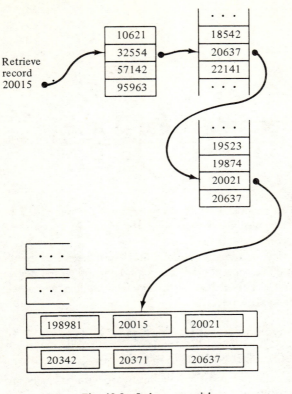

**Fig. 19.9** Index sequential

While index sequential is available as a package, variations on index sequential files are equally valid structures, as are indexed unordered files. Both these alternatives require user file handling routines to be written.

A third alternative to be considered with care is modification of the standard index sequential package.

# 20. Defining Real Time

As identified in chapter 1, an understanding of the use of the term 'real time' can best be achieved by a review of the range of types of terminal based systems that commonly exist.

To place such systems in context it is first useful to review quickly the history of computers, identifying the main steps up to the development of real time applications. This review of history is simplified, but serves to place real time in the general perspective.

## 20.1  The Development of Computers

*Basic (Card) Computer Systems*

The earliest machines having simple hardware with basically serial operations, i.e., limited hardware simultaneity.

*Systems Providing for Concurrent Operation*

Hardware operations could now proceed in parallel, but the programmer needed to plan carefully to gain such advantages.

*Multi-programming Systems*

The above development in hardware was soon followed by multi-programming software for which most manufacturers claim a first. Multi-programming operating systems provided a standard way of optimizing simultaneity and reflected the imbalance between the speeds of peripherals and processors.

*Terminal Based Systems*

The connection of terminals to computers (other than operator's consoles) not only opened the possibilities for greater user interaction with the computer, but also extended the potential of the concept of simultaneity used in multi-programming. In the case of terminal systems, each individual user could potentially consider the whole system belonged to him, while at the same time the same impression could be gained at the other terminals.

Having reached this fourth step, the development of computer systems using terminals has followed several distinct paths in government and private commercial data processing installations, as well as being developed for other uses elsewhere. These include:

- program development and bulk data transfer systems (remote job entry);
- program development systems (multi-access);
- data processing application systems (the subject of this book);
- process control;
- time sharing and on-line bureau.

To clarify the use of the expression 'real time' in this book, each of the areas is examined in more detail below.

## 20.2 Remote Job Entry

Early developments in the use of terminals for program development were concerned with enabling the terminal to be used as an alternative to the computer room card reader and operator's console, leading to remote job entry (RJE) systems and simple program development aids. The ability to load programs and data at a remote location has provided considerable scope both for program development and live operation of commercial systems. However, this use of terminals is not the prime concern of this book. Nevertheless, any analyst or designer starting the study or development of a communication based system must consider the relevance of using a remote batch terminal as a valid alternative to more interactive systems. Those concerned with such systems will consequently find a number of the chapters in this book relevant to their needs.

## 20.3 Multi-access

University and scientific users of computers were early developers of multi-access systems, with perhaps Massachussetts Institute of Technology's Project Mac being a classic example. Such systems are typified by the use of the interactive terminal as an aid to the rapid development of programs and the running of short jobs, often of a scientific or technical nature. Those concerned with developing such multi-access systems face similar challenges to those developing commercial systems.

Most major computer manufacturers now include a multi-access system among their products, and many include support to such facets as terminal conversations, program development with real time syntax checking, and job initiation aids, library facilities and access to most operating system features.

Much of the software provided by manufacturers for multi-access systems also provides a framework that can handle data processing application data. However, software can seldom be all things to all men, and multi-access systems are generally relatively inefficient for general real time operations, unless very specific situations exist—usually low volume work built on existing hardware/software features. The systems team planning a user application with real time needs should not reject multi-access, but for this purpose should treat its more optimistic supporters' evidence with suspicion.

## 20.4  Real Time for Commerce, Government and Industry

These real time systems are concerned with user applications where terminal conversations involve the communication of data (including formatted enquiries) between the computer system and the user's staff. Most such real time systems involve dedicated application programs linked by the development team with the supplier's network handling and operating software.

Real time systems cover a wide range of complexity and scale, and this range may be considered as a continuous spectrum. However, there is an important step in the range that is worth emphasizing by considering real time systems to fall into two broad levels of complexity—'simple' and 'complex'.

### 20.4.1  'SIMPLE' SYSTEMS

Simple real time systems—often called on-line systems (by those who wish to differentiate them from real time complex)—are those where the *prime* flow of data is one way, i.e., they include data capture systems, data enquiry systems and independent combinations of these.

The label 'simple' reflects a lack of requirement for real time access, to data recently input to the system, i.e., no on-line updating. Simple systems can involve data files, but each file is either for reference only, such as for data validation, or for enquiry access by the user (updated in batch mode), or for sequential storage of input transactions.

### 20.4.2  'COMPLEX' SYSTEMS

Complex real time systems (often called 'real time' as opposed to 'on-line') are those where the logic of the processing requires files to be updated and referenced during the real time operation. This simple advance in definition generally implies a major step in the complexity of the system's design and development. It is certainly good design practice to try to reduce a complex real time system to a simple real time system by suitable change to performance specification or design without ignoring the user's real need. The main benefits are achieved more quickly and more economically if the system can be kept 'simple'.

Unfortunately, this definition appears to be the most common, and initial thoughts of systems teams working on feasibility studies for terminal based systems are often restricted to 'complex' even if not strictly justified by the application.

Factors that contribute to the level of complexity and thus to the more complex real time systems include:

Large volumes   – terminals;
                   – transaction rates;
                   – large file sizes.

Systems scope   – wider range of applications logic;
                   – number of transaction types;
                   – number of terminal types;

| Complexity | — file complexity; |
| | — application logic complexity; |
| | — transaction interaction and use of common logic and files. |
| Speed | — the requirement for regular fast response, say three seconds or less. |
| Reliability | — low level of acceptable failure rate, and high speed and completeness of recovery from failure. |

The extremes of complexity in real time systems are found in those with tight specifications on reliability and time, and a work load that potentially leads to heavily loaded hardware.

---

- Only 20 per cent of current hardware required for real time job (other *low* priority work is available to fill (through multi-programming);
- Ten second responses are acceptable if not too frequent;
- Energetic recovery without loss of data is the key reliability criteria.

---

**Fig. 20.1**   Features of a real time system of normal complexity

Developing a real time system that may have the features set out in Fig. 20.1 is a very different problem from developing a real time system that has the same application logic but has the features set out in Fig. 20.2. Many of the recommendations developed in this book become all important at the 'more extreme' end of the spectrum reflected in Fig. 20.2. Experience has shown that most recommendations are equally applicable to the less complex systems, as in Fig. 20.1, and for simple systems. *The difference of approach between the most complex and the simplest systems is in the emphasis put on different aspects of the good practice, not in its rejection where the job is simple.*

---

- Minimize hardware required, no suitable background work;
- Two second average response needed with 98 per cent of all responses under 5 seconds;
- Only minor disruptions permitted after any unit failure.

---

**Fig. 20.2**   Features of a complex real time system under pressure

## 20.5   Process Control

Process control systems are those in which a number of the terminals are mechanical/electronic devices rather than human operated, i.e., such devices as sensors, transducers, measuring instruments, valve controls and activators.

In their early development, computer based process control systems were very different from their commercial counterparts, especially where time was concerned and programming involved eliminating fractions of a millisecond in a program loop.

However, as both commercial and process control disciplines became more established, the good practices became more common to both. In fact, the similarity was further increased due to the shift in process control systems towards more human operators on line and more reference data, and the increase in commercial systems to link mechanical/electrical devices into the network.

Many systems have in fact bridged the gap, and are impossible to assign to either (commercial) real time or process control. One system on which the authors worked provided a continuous real time control in both aspects. In response to transaction data the system:

- accepted and processed orders via terminals;
- received requests and monitored progress reports on delivery vehicles;
- physically monitored quantity and safety factors in the despatch of various grades of petroleum product;
- monitored physical stock as real time process recording;
- produced despatch documentation in real time;
- produced various batch reports.

As can be seen from this brief description, not only were commercial terminals operating in complex real time mode, but the process control elements were both passive (measurement) and active (control). This system used one computer with common files across both the commercial and process control elements.

## 20.6  Time Sharing

Many bureau services have been developed using terminals on a multi-access or a remote job entry basis. This book is not written primarily for users of these services, who in the main are not designers. However, such services can be used to achieve real time systems, and if so used, some of the subjects dealt with in this book are relevant.

## 20.7  Other Developments

While this book is written for those who are evaluating or developing real time systems on their own machine or their client's installation, those working on early phases of a project (systems surveys, feasibility studies, etc.) must also consider the other options open, which include the following:

(1) developing a system on a central computer (existing, new);
(2) choosing a dedicated computer (mini?) for the application;
(3) using a central computer, building on a packaged environment for real time access (a time sharing package; packaged data base/enquiry system);
(4) using a commercial bureau with terminal services for dedicated applications;
(5) using a time sharing service.

Even if these options involve the use of an existing service, a knowledge of real time design is important to evaluate that service to the depth required, in order to judge its practical ability to provide the application system at an acceptable running cost.

The biggest development job is the do-it-yourself approach (options (1) or

(2)), usually with the advantage of the lowest running cost if the system is reasonably well designed and implemented. However, there are likely to be many persuasive salesmen advocating the benefits of easier development arising from one of the last three options. Although the claims of easier development may be true, the extra running costs ((3)–(5) versus (1) or (2)) are not always slight. The judgement of the right balance remains with the project team and can only result from careful study coupled with a good understanding of the options.

Real time was illustrated as the fourth step in computer development earlier in the chapter, but it is certainly not the last. For example, data base systems have also moved from the 'pioneer' stage to at least 'common place' in the products available. Very often data base require terminal access, and many are developed as combined RT/DB systems. The authors' experience is that the approach to the real time element is similar whether the file system uses conventional files, dedicated special real time files, or data base software, and therefore those readers who are working on combined RT/DB systems need to use the contents of this book as well as works more specific to data base.

A further development, that is becoming increasingly practical, is the application of small local computers as part of an overall on-line network. Distributed intelligence systems bring their own advantages, disadvantages and good practices. However, a good understanding of real time is an important background to a full appreciation of the communications elements of a distributed intelligence system. Often each of the distributed processing modes is a small real time system in its own right, and as such its design requires the application of similar techniques to those covered in this book.

## 20.8 Real Time Is?

The following is a summary of the answer to the question posed by this chapter. What is a real time system?

A real time system is one where a service is being provided to a user through the use of terminals directly linked to the computer. Data are input and received at the terminals by the user without him having to apply programming or job control skills. The time of computer response relates to the user's time cycle, be it measured as 1 second, 5 seconds, or 2 minutes.

The system consists of applications code handling the logic of the application and interfacing to file and terminal software as necessary. To develop the system, the development team (data processing personnel and users as appropriate) specify user requirements, design the system with an understanding of the interaction of terminals, lines, central hardware, software and application code; and program and test the system. A live operational system is established under the detailed operational control of the user through his terminals and under the general operation control of the computer centre operations department.

# Index

Acceptance testing, 108–9
Accidents, 223
Accuracy, 24, 26–27, 69, 104, 158–62, 329
Activity measuring routines, 236
Analysis (*see* Systems analysis)
Application code, 91
  programming, 92–93
Application routines:
  integration of, 97–100
  testing, 95–97
Availability, 323
  calculation, 323–30
  combined, 323, 329
  configuration, 328
  definition, 323
  evaluation, 324
  mixed systems, 327–29
  multiple serial, 325
  overall, 324, 325
  parallel, 323, 325–27
  serial, 323
  system, 325–26

Back end processors, 211
Batch systems:
  comparison with, 7, 16, 23, 32, 70, 79, 114, 172,
     174, 175, 232
  interface to, 85
  testing, 106
Block flags, 213
Block header, 212
Blocks, 333
Buffer areas, 241
Buffer pool, 334
Buffered terminals, 152, 163, 168

Centralization versus decentralization, 29
Channelizers, 148, 167
Character multiplexor, 254
Charting technique, 85
Chief analyst, 41
Chief designer, 40, 83
Chief programmer, 41, 46

Codes, 304–5
Coding rates, 91
Communications commissioning testing, 103
Communications controllers, 136–38
  multi-line, 254–55
  multi-line hardware, 137
  multi-line software, 138
  single-line, 136–37
  timing, 254
Communications handler, 98, 100, 101, 241, 242–43
Communications interface task, 246
Communications justified systems, 23, 26
Communications network, fail-soft, 199
Communications processors, 211
Communications software, 138–45, 230
  environment of, 139
  generation of, 144–45
  important facilities, 140
  in mainframe, timing, 255–56
  problems, 145
  relationships to system, 139
  requirements, 140–45
Communications timing, 254–56
Complex systems, 5, 346–47
Computer department, 39
Computer response time, 173
Computer room, fail-soft, 198
Computer system design, 35, 45, 69, 79–89
  and project phases, 79–81
  cost of hardware, 80
  detailed, 86–89
  document content, 87
  documentation, 81
  objective, 80, 83
  overall, 84–86
  phase of, 82
  plan for, 83
  planning task, 83
  presentation, 89
  subsequent activities, 88–89
  tasks involved, 83
  testing, 106
Computer turn-round time, 152, 153, 167

Computers, development of, 344
Configuration planning and control (CPC), 51, 60
Control task, 246, 249
Corruption:
  by clerical error, 226
  detecting, 227–28
  from chance coincidences, 224
  protection against accidental, 229
Costs, 22, 24, 27–29
  data capture and dissemination, 28
  of hardware, computer system design, 80
  systems analysis, 69
  technical design control, 60
  terminal, 155
  training programmes, 125
Customer contact, 21
Cut-over, 112

Damage, 223
Data base systems, 181–83, 349
Data capture and dissemination, costs, 28
Data compression techniques, 185–86
Data files, 84
Data link control systems, 305
Data transmission, 304–21
  asynchronous timing, 306
  basic principles, 304–12
  bit representations on lines, 307
  codes, 304–5
  error detection and correction, 313–15
  future developments, 320–21
  hardware, 315–19
  modulated, 307
  noise, 312–13
  synchronous timing, 306
  timing, 306–7
  types of, 312
  unmodulated, 307
Data transmission components, 145–50
Data transmission services, 319–20
  datel, 319
  Europe, 320
  UK, 319
  USA, 320
Delayed response, 19
Delays, 14, 16, 30, 52–53, 333
Design (see Computer systems design)
Design control (see Technical design
  control)
Designer, use of term, 65
Digital lines, leased, 321
Digital network, public switched, 321
Disk failure, 38
Disk space criterion, 190
Disk utilization, 186
Documentation of information flow, 72
Documentation technique, 71
Double buffering, 233
Duplex transmission, 312

Education requirements, 4–5
Erlang value, 296
Error correction, 158, 229
Error effects, 52, 93
Error messages, 72, 78
Error reports, 27
Errors:
  acceptance testing, 103
  application routines, 98
  clerical, 226
  detection, 142, 227
  , file, 212
  noise, 312
  on-line testing, 104
  operator, 223
  prevention, 203, 204
Expansibility, 236
Exponential distribution, 291, 292, 295

Fail-soft, 84, 194–219
  calculations, 196
  check list, 200
  communications network, 199
  computer room, 198
  design, 322
  design approach, 208–9
  hardware, 194–200
  hardware configuration, 198
  overview, 214–15
  planning and design decisions, 202
  preparation, 202
  prevention, 201
  requirements, 219
  techniques, 209–14
  24 hr systems, 200–1
Failures, 30
  chance coincidences, 225
  detection, 202
  diagnosis, 196, 203–4
  disk, 38
  hardware, 198
  integration, 196, 197
  isolation, 196, 197, 204
  live running, 46
  mean time between (MTBF), 196, 198, 200, 322
  reaction, 203
  real time, 94, 194
  terminal, 218
Feasibility studies, 23, 67–69, 70, 81
  activities, 68
  objectives, 67, 80
  planning, 31
  project cycle, 45
  project phases, 33
  recovery targets, 30
  report contents, 68
  user involvement, 67
Field compression, 185
File access, 92
  mechanisms, 269

patterns, 190
performance optimization, 184
security, 222–23
software, 187
File allocation, 38
File data requirements, 189
File design, 172–93
approach to, 188–89
assessment, 190
control, 192–93
criteria, 172, 191
objectives, 172, 173
overall, 191–92
resource usage criteria, 189–90
secondary objectives, 174
File dumping, 211–12
File handler, 243
File information, 112
File levels, 222
File organization, 334
File performance factors, 192
File recovery, 213
File re-creation, 212–13
File response time, 190
File size reduction techniques, 184–86
File structures, 331–43
basic, 174–75, 334
chain, 177–79
combination, 175–76
device operations, 332–34
direct, 335
direct access devices, 331–34
index sequential, 341–43
indexed random, 176
indexed unordered, 175–76
indexes, 340–41
inverted, 179
linked, 176–83
overflow techniques, 337–38
packaged software, 182–83
personnel, 179
pointer list, 179
random-index unordered, 176
randomized, 336
sequential, 335
unordered, 338–40
File timing, 256, 257–69
fixed head disks, 268
head movement optimization, 264
multiple disk drive analysis, 261–65
multiple moving head disk drives, 259–61
rotational position sensing, 264
single moving head disk drive and control unit, 258
Files:
integrity and recoverability, 174
tape, 331
Fraud, protection against, 220, 221
Frequency division multiplexing, 310
Front end processors, 211, 254

Gamma distribution, 297

Hostility, 214

Images, before and after, 213–17
Implementation, 49
Index sequential, 341–43
Indexes, 340–41
Information flow, documentation of, 72
Input/output handler, 98, 101
Input time, 158
Installation, 49
Integration, 36, 85, 197
Integrity, 223–28
design approach, 229

Justification of project, 22–31

Key to disk systems, 27
Keyboard, 130

Latency, 333
Limited service, 214
Line calculations, 167–69
Line control, 140
Line delay, 169
Line sharing, 148, 152, 153
Line transmission time, 168
Live running, 46
Load testing, 107–8
Loading problems, 13–16
Lock lists, 225
Lock out, 214
Locking processes, 225–26
Logging, 210–11

Maintenance, 207
Manual procedures, 77
Mean time between failures (MTBF), 196, 198, 200, 322
Mean time to repair (MTTR), 196, 198, 200, 323
Message accuracy, 104
Message arrival, 7
pattern of, 8
random pattern, 10
rate of, 8, 76
Message block, 95, 97, 101, 240–49, 277
Message buffer, 130, 140
Message pair, 17, 18
Message processing, simultaneous, 233
Message processing pattern, 256
Message storage requirements reduction, 255
Message structure, 72
Messages, 241
path of, 241
terminology, 17
Modems, 147–48, 169, 317–19
Modulation forms, 307–10
Module testing, 36

MONITOR structure, 237, 238–45, 252, 270, 273
  advantages, 245
  programming, 91
  software, 97
  testing, 95, 97, 100–1
  transaction tasking with, 249
Monitoring, 48–62, 87
Multi-access systems, 345
Multi-drop line, 149, 168, 169, 316
Multi-key retrievals, 180
Multi-line controllers, 137, 138
Multiplexing, 310
Multi-programming, 214, 232, 233, 237, 344
Multi-server (*see* Queueing)
Multi-serving disks, 186–87
Multi-terminal controller, 149
Multi-threading, 234, 235, 237, 245, 246, 248
  timing, 275–78

Network controllers, 37
Network-structure data base, 181
Noise, 312–13
Non-exponential distributions, 294

Office organization, 77
Office physical design, 78
Office system design, 77–78
On-line systems, 346
Operating system, 244
Operational problems, 37
Operational training (*see* User involvement)
Operations department, 36, 37
Operations liaison, 43, 45
Operator control, facilities, 37
Operator guidance, 159
Order processing, 9, 24, 25, 30, 170
Overlaying:
  planned, 232
  technique, 85, 273
  virtual operating system, 233
Overloads, 14, 20, 21

Packet switching, 320
Passwords, 222
Pereto 80:20 principle, 184
Performance measurement, 61–62
PERT planning systems, 48
Phase/task planning methods, 48
Phasing-in, 112–13
Planning and control techniques, 48–51
Pointers, 177, 179
Poisson distribution, 290, 337
Policy training, 120
Priority systems, 16
Process control systems, 347
Processing routines, 84
Processing sequence, 17
Program faults, 223
Program language, 93
Program library control, 43

Program load testing, 101–3
Program organization, 230–52
  service routines, 235
  transaction orientation, 232
Program specification, 36, 46
Program structure, 85, 230
  design approaches, 236–38
  software selection, 249
Program testing, 95–104, 106
  live, 103–4
Programming, 36, 39, 46, 91
  application code, 92–93
  real time framework (MONITOR), 91
  structured, 39, 252
Project control, 41, 51, 84
Project cycle, 43
Project justification, 22–31
Project management, 32
Project manager, 40
**Project phases, 33**
Project structures, 32–47
  and scale, 32
  basic, 39
  developing, 39–43
  extending, 41
  large complex, 43
  summary of, 46–47
Pseudo batch data capture, 23
Pseudo batch environment, 12
Pulse code modulation, 309–10

Quality control, 42, 46
Queueing formulae
  multi-server, 301
  single-server, 292, 293, 294, 295
Queueing theory, 12, 20, 52–53, 168, 283–303
  arrival rate, 284
  average and distributed values, 287
  basic parameters, 284
  despatch (selection) disciplines, 287
  facility utilization $\rho$, 258, 259, 261, 262, 274, 275, 277, 285, 293
  limitations, 302–3
  multi-server parameters, 300
  multi-server single queue model, 300–2
  service time, 284
  single-server, 284, 291, 293, 294
  use of techniques, 283
Queueing times:
  calculation, 296
  distribution, 296
  distribution prediction, 297
  multi-server, 302
  prediction, 287
  single-server, 293
  standard deviation of, 297
  standard distribution of, 296

Random distributions, 290

Randomizing algorithm techniques, 337
Read locks, 225
Real time, 344–49
    definition of, 5
    use of term, 344
Real time systems, 3–6
    characteristics, 231
    comparison system with batch, 7, 16, 23, 32, 70,
        79, 114, 172, 174, 175, 232
    definition, 349
    development, 349
    for commerce, government and industry, 346
    normal complexity, 347
    other options open, 348
    program structure, 231
    project justification, 22–31
    requirements, 7–21
    study of techniques and methods, 4
    summary of requirements, 21
    (see also Complex systems; Simple systems)
Reconfiguration, 204
Recovery, 30, 195, 197, 200, 204
    program, 217
    routine testing, 98
    user involvement, 214
Re-institute, 207
Release control, 109–12
Reliability, 21, 30, 195
    calculations, 322–30
    performance, 31
Remote job entry, 345
Repair, 206, 207
Repair time, 195
Replacement, 195
Re-process, 206
Request Monitor, 97, 239, 240, 242, 244
Rescheduling, 205
Reserve equipment, 195, 196, 200
Response speed, 22, 23
Response time, 17, 18, 20
    perceived, 152–53
    requirements, 76
    target, 18, 23
Re-start, 206, 218
Re-step, 206
Risks, 4, 22

Sales and costs, 29
Scale and project structure, 32
Security, 30, 77, 85, 124, 174, 189, 220–23
    design approach, 228
    file access, 222–23
    location identity, 222
    on-line, 221
    physical, 220
    run-time, 221
    user identity, 222
Security codes, 221
Security matrix, 223

Selection projects, 151
Sequence Monitor, 97, 239–45
Serial configuration formulae, 324
Service monitor, 242, 244
Simple systems, 5, 7, 346
Simplex transmission, 312
Simulation, 123, 278
Single-line controllers, 136
Single-thread timing, 273–75
Single-threading, 225
Snap shot, 212
Software selection:
    in-house system, 249–50
    package evaluation check list, 250–52
Speed justified systems, 23
Speed requirements, 24–26
Staff skills, 33, 36, 39, 45, 83
Staff structure, 39
Standard deviation, 288–89
    application, 298
    calculation, 289
    of queueing times, 297
Standard distribution of queueing time, 296
Structured programming, 39, 252
System definition, 35
System flow, 215
System test data, 105–6
System testing, 38, 105–8
    load testing, 107–8
    planning, 105
    via terminals, 106–7
Systems analysis, 34, 45, 65–78
    costs, 69
    deficiencies, 69
    distribution of variants, 75–76
    objectives, 80–81
    phase of, 69–70, 81
    purpose of, 81
    statistics of importance, 75
Systems analyst:
    activities of, 65
    relationship of responsibilities, 65–66
    use of term, 65
Systems design (see Computer systems design)
Systems development, 48, 49
Systems specification, 35, 71–77, 82
    outline examples, 72
    re-challenging, 117
    response time requirements, 76
    user agreement, 116
    user refinement, 116–17

Task list, 51
Task structure, 247
Tasking, 237–38, 246–49
    functional, 246
    transaction, 248
Tasking structure, advantages of, 249

Technical design control (TDC), 51–62, 107
    application, 54, 60
    as design aid, 53, 60
    benefits, 60
    costs, 60
    dependence dimension, 55
    detail dimension, 54
    essential elements, 58–59
    forms, 59
    impact of minor changes, 52–53
    performance measurement, 61–62
    recognizing the implications, 53
    time dimension, 56
    when is it needed?, 60
Telegraph lines, 147, 167, 315
Telephone lines, 146–47, 149, 167, 316
Telephone services, 319
Telex, 147, 320
Terminal based systems, 344
Terminal control coversation, 140
Terminal controllers, 169
Terminal failure, 218
Terminal network configuration, 129–71
    choice of hardware and software, 150–51
    costing, 155
    design approach, 151–71
    design process, 152–54
    design uncertainties, 170–71
    separation of design activity, 152
Terminal numbers, 152–53, 156
    calculation of, 164–67, 170
Terminal reconfiguration, 143
Terminals, 130–36
    buffered, 152, 163, 168
    cash dispensers, 134
    choice of, 154–56
    compatibility, 135–36, 154
    connecting to lines, 169
    costs, 155
    general considerations, 136
    general purpose, 130–34
    hard copy, 130, 155
    intelligent, 133
    intelligent hard copy, 131
    intelligent video, 132–33
    method of connection, 154
    monitoring, 150
    multi-terminal controller, 145–50
    optional mark or character readers, 135
    point of sale, 134
    remote batch, 133
    remote clusters of basic types, 133
    shop floor, 134
    simultaneous display, 135
    special types, 134
    stock control, 134
    telegraph, 167
    touch-tone/voice response, 135
    using switched telephone lines, 167
    video, 130, 132, 155

Testing, 36, 46, 85
    acceptance, 108–9
    application routines, 95–97
    batch system, 106
    communications commissioning, 103
    computer design system, 106
    creating the right environment, 94
    integration of application routines, 97–100
    levels of, 94, 95
    MONITOR, 100–1
    on-line, 103
        user involvement, 118
    program load, 101–3
    programs (see Program testing)
    recovery routines, 98
    system (see System testing)
    technical design control, 93
    transactions, 98
    user involvement, 94–95
Time division multiplexing, 310
    Bell T1 system, 311
    CCITT system, 311–12
Time sharing, 348
Timing, 85, 170, 253–80
    basic information, 270
    central system, 256–57
    communications, 254–56
    communications controllers, 254
    communications software in mainframe, 255–56
    data transmission, 306–7
    files (see File timing)
    multi-thread, 275–78
    single-thread, 273–75
    summary of approach, 278–80
    transactions, 162–64
    whole processor, 257, 269–78
Training (see Education requirements; User
        involvement)
Transaction code, 222
Transaction elements, 162
Transaction layouts and sequences, 160
Transaction oriented program, 232
Transaction tasking, 248
Transaction times, 158
Transactions, 16, 17, 76, 78
    arrival pattern of, 8
    categories of, 162
    design, 157–62
    end of cycle, 216–17
    example, 159
    handling, 84
    identification, 17
    main path through, 78
    psuedo batch, 162, 164, 168
    random, 162, 165, 168
    response time criteria, 30
    terminology, 17
    testing, 98
    timing, 162–64
    types of, 15

**356**

unit of user activity, 17
volumes, 170–71
Tuning, 236

Units of work, 16
Updating, 5, 19, 213, 226, 229, 346
User involvement, 114–26
  agree specification, 116
  development training, 121
  familiarization, 118
  in development, 114–17
  in going live, 117–19
  live operation training, 124
  on-line testing, 118
  operational management training, 122
  operational responsibility, 118
  operational training, 122
  operator guidance, 159
  operator training, 122–25
    case study, 126
  policy training, 120
  pre-live operation training, 124
  recovery systems, 214
  refine specification, 116
  requirements communication, 115
  scope of training, 126
  supervisory/middle management training, 122

systems guidance, 125
task list in going live, 119
training, 118, 120–25
training courses, 123–25, 125–26
training overview, 125–26

Validation routines, 203
VDU, 215
Version control, 42, 109–12

Wideband lines, 317
Work:
  range of, 15
  units of, 16
Work area, 241
Work area control, 243–44
Work load, 8
  analysis, 16
  daily pattern, 9
  increasing, 20
  overload, 14
  peak, 14
  peak delaying, 16
  **peak load and capacity levels, 11**
  peak removal, 15
  seasonal loading, 9
  variations in, 9